JON BUCKLIN
1514 MAXFIELD RD.
HARTLAND, MI 48029
(313) 632-7526
1-800-821-6681

The Dow Jones-Irwin
Guide to Using
The Wall Street Journal

About the author . . .

MICHAEL B. LEHMANN, Ph.D., is
professor of Economics at the University of
San Francisco. He recently completed
twelve years of research and writing on the
business cycle and current economic
conditions.

Professor Lehmann received his Ph.D. from
Cornell University. He is a member of the
American Economic Association.

The Dow Jones-Irwin Guide to Using The Wall Street Journal

Second Edition

Michael B. Lehmann

DOW JONES-IRWIN
Homewood, Illinois 60430

This publication is designed to provide accurate and
authoritative information in regard to the subject matter
covered. It is sold with the understanding that the
publisher is not engaged in rendering legal, accounting, or
other professional service. If legal advice or other expert
assistance is required, the services of a competent
professional person should be sought.

*From a Declaration of Principles jointly adopted by a Committee
of the American Bar Association and a Committee of Publishers.*

Library of Congress Catalog Card No. 86-71441
Printed in the United States of America
1 2 3 4 5 6 7 8 9 0 K 4 3 2 1 0 9 8 7

To My Father
Dr. Frederick Lehmann

Preface

*W*hen I first proposed this book to Dow Jones-Irwin, they asked me if its purpose was to show the reader "how to be your own economist." Not exactly, I said. The objective was to show the reader "how to use *The Wall Street Journal* to be your own economist."

After all, the *Journal* is the authoritative source for business news in America; it is published coast to coast; and it has the largest daily circulation of any newspaper in the country. By focusing on a handful of key statistical reports in the *Journal,* you can acquire a surprisingly quick and firm comprehension of the ups and downs of the American business economy. This book will facilitate that comprehension, clearly and accurately—but, I hope, in a pleasing and nontechnical manner.

A word of caution. This is not a get-rich-quick manual; it is *not* designed to offer investment advice. You should always seek competent professional counsel before placing business or personal capital at risk.

This book *is* designed to help you develop a sound overview of our economy so that your grasp of economic events as well as your business and investment decisions will be more informed and more confident.

Michael B. Lehmann

Acknowledgments

I would like to express my gratitude to the people who assisted me in developing, writing, and producing this work. First, I wish to thank my good friend and colleague Alan Heineman, professor of English at the University of San Francisco, and my principal editor. To the extent that the book reads well, it is in large measure due to his efforts; any stylistic defects remain only because there was not time to further refine the book. I also want to express gratitude to my wife, Millianne, for her patient assistance in sorting through draft after draft, weeding out the unimportant material, identifying topics that demanded inclusion, and revising the text with grace and wisdom.

Jonathan Miller, a free-lance writer in Los Angeles and an old friend, helped me focus on the central facets of the Federal Reserve System; Chapters 4 and 5 are much better because of his contribution. Peter Lindert, whom I've known since student days, now professor of economics at the University of California at Davis, made valuable comments on the international transactions chapter. Tom Soden, vice president of Davis, Skaggs and Company in San Francisco and a former student of mine, provided significant commentary on the financial markets.

Betty Blecha, Yuan-Li Wu, Martin Brown, and Fr. Richard Mulcahy, S. J., my colleagues in the Economics Department at USF, also read the text and provided helpful comments. Further appreciation goes to the University of San Francisco for providing the opportunity to develop the course that launched this entire project. I am grateful to all my students who sat through it from beginning to end while it was being developed, and whose responses have reinforced my sense of what most needed to be said on these topics.

Associate Dean John Dwyer was very cooperative in providing secretarial support; Lou Martin, Emily White, and Monica Roskos heroically typed rough drafts of the text, and Terry Harned had the monumental job of putting the final drafts on the university's computer and doing the word processing necessary to produce the text. Kathy Woo, USF's periodicals librarian, helped me find several elusive *Wall Street Journal* articles. I wish also to express my appreciation to the entire university computer center staff, especially Chuck Wilcher, who gave up his nights and weekends to help me meet the deadline.

Let me record, finally, my acknowledgments to the staffs of *The Wall Street Journal* and Dow Jones-Irwin who assisted me along the way. Without their help, there would be no book, let alone a book that came out on time.

ACKNOWLEDGMENTS FOR THE SECOND EDITION

Chapters 6 (Interest Rates) and 13 (Profits and the Stock Market) were revised and expanded in the second edition to include all the statistical series and reports on these matters appearing regularly in *The Wall Street Journal*. Jeffrey Silk served as my research assistant in preparing these chapters. He maintained a file of clippings on these series and reports on interest rates, profits, and the stock market, and worked up a general description and explanation of each one, which was then woven into the text. As a result, Chapters 6 and 13 are now vastly improved over the first edition. I wish to express my gratitude and appreciation for his hard work and effort.

Finally, and once again, if the text reads well and smoothly, it is thanks to Alan Heineman, professor of English at the University of San Francisco, and my principal editor and collaborator.

M. B. L.

Contents

chapter 1   *Introduction*   *1*

chapter 2   *The Business Cycle*   *5*

chapter 3   *The Transformation of the Postwar Economy*   *11*

chapter 4   *The Federal Reserve System*   *17*

chapter 5   *The Money Supply*   *29*

chapter 6   *Interest Rates*   *39*

chapter 7   *The Business Cycle Phase One: From Trough to Recovery*   *73*

chapter 8   *The Business Cycle Phase Two: From Recovery to Expansion*   *109*

chapter 9   *The Business Cycle Phase Three: From Expansion to Peak*   *145*

chapter 10   *The Business Cycle Phase Four: From Peak to Contraction*   *153*

chapter 11   *Inventories*   *161*

chapter 12   *Business Capital Expenditures*   *169*

chapter 13   *Profits and the Stock Market*   *181*

chapter 14   *U.S. International Transactions*   *227*

chapter 15   *Leading Economic Indicators*   *249*

chapter 16   *Federal Fiscal Policy*   *255*

chapter 17   *Summary and Prospect*   *265*

appendix A   *Alphabetical Listing of Statistical Series*
                  Published in The Wall Street Journal   *269*

appendix B   *Statistical Series Published in* The Wall
                  Street Journal *in Chapter Order*   *271*

appendix C   *Listing of Statistical Series According to*
                  The Wall Street Journal *Publication*
                  Schedule   *273*

index   *277*

Introduction

G NP, consumer price index, Treasury bills, housing starts, labor pro- ductivity, the money supply. . . .

Can you effectively analyze these statistical series and reports? Can you use them to gain an understanding of developing economic and business trends? Or are your judgments and opinions based on popular analyses and secondary sources?

Perhaps you would like to deal with the data on your own but don't know how. It's worth some time and effort to learn, because until you come to grips with the data you can't honestly say that you have formed your own opinion about current economic and business events, let alone about what the future holds in store. The news media now serve as intermediaries between you and the data. Furthermore, no matter how many experts are quoted, you still aren't dealing with the facts, only with someone else's interpretation of them. And these interpretations are often contradictory—and therefore confusing. At some point you have to wonder, do the "experts" know what they're talking about?

Your desire to master the data may stem from your own business needs. Will demand for your product be weak or strong two quarters from now or two years from now? Is this the time to lay in additional inventory, hire key personnel, and build more plant? Or, despite the current level of orders, would it be more prudent to cancel those plans? Can you beat the competition to the punch, one way or another? Are interest rates likely to rise or to fall? Is disinflation (as deflation is some- times called) merely a buzzword, or has inflation really been licked? That's just a hint of the issues you can begin to analyze on your own: all it takes is learning to come to grips with a small number of regularly released statistical reports.

You may wish to conduct your own analysis of current economic events because they are the foundation for so many other social and political developments. Were President Reagan's tax cut and supply-side economics responsible for the decline in inflation and today's healthy economic environment, or should the Federal Reserve System take the credit? And how serious are the problems of the federal government's budget deficit and the balance-of-trade deficit? Do your answers to these questions reflect your analysis of the data, your political point of view, or the opinions of your favorite commentator? Maybe they should reflect all three, but they can reflect only the last two until you learn to deal with the numbers on your own. Once you do that, your own judgment will be of greater importance to yourself and others.

Don't misunderstand: dispensing with expert advice is not the objective. Even the world's leading authority on a subject must consult other experts as a continual check on his or her understanding. This challenges the authority and helps prevent sloppy thinking. The point is: become the expert by handling the data on your own, and you will know whether or not the other experts make sense. Otherwise, you'll never be certain whether you're being given sound or flimsy advice.

If you want to be your own economist, if you wish to master the daily data, you need two things: (1) a readily available, reliable, and comprehensive statistical source and (2) a guide to organizing and interpreting the information you receive.

As to the first requirement, *The Wall Street Journal* is your best source of business and economic information; you really don't need anything else. It contains all of the reports necessary to conduct your own analysis.

With respect to the second requirement, this book can be your guide. In it, the nature of the statistics will be explained so that what they measure and how they are computed will be clear. GNP, the money supply, the consumer price index, and the Dow Jones Industrial Average cannot remain vague and indefinite terms if you are going to be in control of the information.

For example, when the *Journal* reports that the money supply has increased, it is important to know that this fact has virtually nothing to do with the availability of paper money. The money supply is composed largely of checking accounts; currency is the petty cash of the economy.

Understanding the nature of the various statistical series is, of course, not enough. You must be able to place them in both historical and contemporary contexts. These essential skills will develop and gain strength with each chapter. Your historical perspective will deepen, providing the background or benchmark for evaluating contemporary events. When a *Journal* article states that the trade deficit or the budget deficit is the largest ever, or that the Dow Jones Industrial Average has hit a new high, the comparison can provide perspective only if you grasp the frame of reference, for knowledge of the past aids evaluation of the present by providing a standard against which recent developments are measured. Auto sales and housing starts may be slightly higher or lower than they were a year ago, but if you know that current levels of activity are substantially lower than the peaks reached in the 1970s, your perspective provides evidence that today's economy has not yet approached boom conditions.

As you read on, you will become aware that none of the statistical reports stands alone. Understanding the relationships among them provides insight into the economy's operation, for each is a piece of the puzzle, and together they compose the picture. For instance, mortgage interest rates and home construction have been featured in the *Journal* lately, and there is a simple, vital link between them: as mortgage interest rates fall, home construction increases.

Consider another example. In 1985 we asked our major trading partners to intervene in the foreign exchange markets in order to depress the value of the dollar. The hope was that cheaper dollars—and hence cheaper prices for American goods in world markets—would boost our exports and reduce our balance-of-trade deficit. Thus, the statistical reports on the value of the dollar and on our ability to export are inextricably linked, as you will see in more detail in Chapter 14.

All of the statistics analyzed in this book can be interrelated in this fashion, so they need not be a series of isolated events, released piecemeal on a day-to-day basis. Instead, they will form an unfolding pattern that clearly reveals the direction of economic and business activity.

Finally, you need a framework, a device to give a coherent shape to these historical insights and contemporary interrelationships. The business cycle, that wavelike rise and fall of economic activity, provides the necessary framework. You are already familiar with the cycle in your own business or personal situation, and the news media have provided increased coverage of the ups and downs of the economy in recent years. Economic expansion and contraction, easy or tight credit conditions, inflation, and unemployment are recurring facts of life. Who escapes them?

The business cycle is the best vehicle for illuminating the *Journal's* regularly appearing statistical series. Its phases bring life and meaning to the statistical reports. They establish the perspective through which the illustrations and examples in the book are interwoven into a unified exposition.

Each chapter will introduce one or more statistical series, and each will be devoted to a theme (such as the money and credit markets) that is used to describe and explain the statistical series introduced in the chapter, beginning with the simplest and most basic elements of the business cycle and proceeding to additional topics that will complete your understanding. This step-by-step progression of topics will not, however, prevent you from breaking into any chapter, out of order, if you wish to examine a particular statistical series or group of series. Indeed, you may already have a firm grasp of some of these topics and need only to fill in the missing elements to round out your comprehension of the essential workings of American business. A complete listing of all the statistical series discussed in this guide can be found in the appendixes following Chapter 17.

Each chapter will describe the statistical series under discussion in the context of the business cycle and explain the relationship of the new series to the overall picture. Analysis will be based on charts drawn from official publications so that you can visualize the data and put the current information in perspective. Recent *Wall Street Journal* articles containing the statistical series will be reproduced and discussed so that you can interpret the data in light of the visual presentation made by the charts. Finally, you will be alerted to what future developments can be expected.

You will enjoy putting the puzzle together yourself. Anyone can do it, with a little help. The ebb and flow of the business cycle will channel the stream of data that now floods you in seemingly random fashion, and you will experience a genuine sense of accomplishment in creating order out of something that has appeared chaotic.

A word of caution before you begin. This will be neither an economics or business cycle course or text nor a precise forecasting device. There will be no formula or model. The business cycle is used strictly as a vehicle to make the statistical information usable in as easy a manner as possible. The objective is not to make a professional economist out of you but to enable you to conduct your own analysis of the data just as soon as you are able. You will dive into the data and "get your hands dirty" by taking apart the cycle, analyzing it, and reassembling it. When you have finished this book, you will feel confident that you can deal with the data on your own.

Finally, please realize that this work is designed to help you understand *The Wall Street Journal* in the context of the business cycle. It is not an investment guide. To understand, for example, how the stock market fits into our economy, which this book tries to help you do, is a very different matter from knowing which stock to invest in at any particular moment. Seek competent professional counsel before you invest your money.

Now, before exploring the business cycle in detail, take time for a leisurely overview.

2-

The Business Cycle

*T*he business cycle is nothing new. It's been a characteristic of every capitalist economy in the modern era. Nations have endured boom followed by bust, prosperity and then depression, a period of growth and confidence trailing off into a decade of despair.

It is all so familiar to us that images of its human effects are scattered among our popular stereotypes. Men in top hats peer at ticker tape emerging from a little glass dome. They wheel and deal, corner wheat markets, play with railroads, and organize steel companies. Fortunes are quickly won and just as quickly lost. Former tycoons are seen selling apples on street corners. Factory gates shut and signs go up saying, "No help wanted." Soup kitchens appear, and desperate families flee the dust bowl in Model A pickup trucks.

These caricatures—based on real history, actual power, blows of ill fortune, human suffering—persist in our collective consciousness, permanently etched by the Great Depression. Although the stock market collapse of 1929 is the most notorious such event in our history, it is by no means unique. Cycles in the American economy can be traced and analyzed going back to the beginning of the 19th century.

The settlement of the West is an example. The frontier assumes such importance in our history and folklore that we tend to think of the westward migration as a smooth, if hazardous, inevitable flow, driven by the doctrine of Manifest Destiny. It didn't happen that way. The settlement of the West proceeded in a cyclical pattern.

Farmers and ranchers were (and are) businesspeople. The sod house and subsistence farming of the 1800s were temporary inconveniences, converted as quickly as possible to growing cash crops and raising livestock for the market. The settlers wanted to know the bottom line, the difference between revenue and expense. They wanted the best price for their cotton, corn, cattle, wheat, and hogs. They wanted to maximize production and minimize cost by using modern cultivation techniques and the latest equipment. Railroads and banks concerned them because transportation and interest rates affected the cost of doing business and thus their profit margin. Finally, and most important, farmers wanted their capital to grow. They expected their net worth to increase as their farms appreciated in value and their mortgages were paid.

This experience was not confined to the United States; European settlers in Canada, Australia, and Argentina produced the same commodities under similar conditions. All were part of the growing world economy. Every farmer and rancher counted on industrialization and urbanization at home and in Europe to build demand for his or her commodities.

And worldwide demand for food and fiber did increase rapidly. Farmers responded by boosting production as best they could on existing holdings. Eventually, however, their output reached its limit even though demand continued to grow. As a result, prices began to creep, and then race, upward. The venturesome dreamed of moving west and doubling or tripling their acreage. Record crop and livestock prices made the costs of moving and financing a new spread seem manageable, and existing farms could always be sold to the less intrepid. Thousands upon thousands of families streamed across the frontier, claiming millions of acres offered by generous government policies or buying from speculators who held raw land.

Nobody planned the westward migration; nobody coordinated it; nobody governed it. Everyone made his or her own calculation of the market. Farmers borrowed in order to purchase land and building materials and to buy livestock, seed, and equipment. Newly opened banks faced an insatiable demand for credit. Towns sprang up at railroad sidings where grain elevators and livestock yards were constructed. Merchants and Main Street followed. High prices brought a land boom, and the land boom brought settlement and opened the West.

It took a while for the newly converted prairie to produce a cash crop. But when it did, thousands of new farms began dumping their output on the market. The supply of agricultural commodities increased dramatically. Shortage changed to surplus, and prices dropped. Time after time during the 19th century, commodity prices fell to record lows after a period of inflation and the subsequent land rush.

Many farmers were wiped out. They could not pay their debts while commodity prices scraped bottom, and banks foreclosed on farm property. If a bank made too many loans that went bad, then it was dragged down too. Merchants saw their customers disappear and had to close up shop. Settlers abandoned their land, and boomtowns became ghost towns.

Prices inevitably remained low for years, and most farmers barely made it, living on returns far below expectations. In every instance, it took a while before the steady growth in world demand absorbed the excess agricultural commodities.

But as time passed, the cycle would repeat itself. After the inflation that accompanied the Civil War, western settlement continued to occur in waves until the end of the century, despite 30 years of deflation. The process happened at least half a dozen times until the frontier closed in the last years of the 19th century.

By the turn of this century, progress had been spectacular. Untold thousands of acres of prairies had been transformed into productive field and pasture. Commodities worth billions of dollars were produced annually for the domestic and world markets. Billions of dollars of wealth had been created in the form of improved farmland. But the discipline of the business cycle governed the advance. For every two steps forward, there had been one step backward, as those who borrowed or lent the least wisely, settled the poorest land, or had the worst luck went broke.

Things haven't changed. Agriculture's fortunes are still guided by the cycle. Remember the boom of the early 70s? Consumption of beef was up; President Nixon negotiated the wheat deal with Russia; the Peruvian anchovy harvest had failed, and soy beans were used to fill the gap (as a protein extender). Agricultural commodity prices doubled, even tripled, and therefore, of course, farm income shot up. As a result, farmers spent the rest of the decade investing heavily in land and equipment. Ultimately, supply outstripped demand at current prices, and farm prices deteriorated throughout the early 80s.

We've seen the result. It's nothing that hasn't happened before: foreclosures, bankruptcies, falling land values, broken families, and ruined lives. Eventually, of course, prices will stabilize—until the next cycle comes along to start the process all over again.

What was true for farming was equally true for the nation's railroads: they developed in the same cyclical pattern. On the eve of World War I, America's railway system was complete, representing a total capital investment second only to that of agriculture. It was a remarkable feat of creative engineering and equally creative financing.

We marvel at the colorful exploits of the Goulds, Fisks, Drews, Vanderbilts, Stanfords, Hills, et al. History refers to some of them as "robber barons"; they seemed to skim off one dollar for every two invested, and it's a wonder that the railway system was ever completed or operated safely. Yet there it was, the largest in the world, a quarter of a million miles of track moving the nation's freight and passenger traffic with unparalleled efficiency.

Promoters speculatively pushed the railroads westward in anticipation of the freight and passenger traffic that settlement would bring. Federal, state, and local governments, vying for the routes that would generate progress and development, gave the railroad companies 10 percent of the nation's land. Improving rights-of-way, laying track, building trestles, stations, and marshaling yards, and purchasing locomotives and rolling stock required the railway company to raise more capital than had ever been mobilized for any other single business venture. The companies floated billions of dollars in stocks and bonds, and investors eagerly ventured their capital to take advantage of prospective success. Flush with funds, the railroads raced toward the Pacific Coast, hoping that revenue would grow quickly enough to justify their huge investment. Periodically, however, the generous rate of expansion exceeded the growth in traffic. Prospects for profits, which had seemed so bright, grew dim. Investors stopped providing funds, and railroad track construction came to a halt. Since operating revenues could not recover costs, many railroads were forced into receivership and were reorganized. Stock and bond prices plunged, wiping out investors long after the promoters had made off with their killings.

Eventually, traffic grew sufficiently to justify existing lines and raise hopes that construction could profitably resume. Investors were once again lured into advancing their funds, and a new cycle of railway expansion began. It, too, was followed by a bust, and then by another wave of construction, until the nation's railway system was complete.

The tracks spanned a continent, from New York, Philadelphia, and Baltimore to Chicago, and from there to New Orleans, Los Angeles, San Francisco, Portland, and Seattle. Profit had motivated the enterprise, and enormous tangible wealth had been created. Losses had periodically and temporarily halted the undertaking and impoverished those who had speculated unwisely or who had been duped. Construction had proceeded in waves. It was an unplanned and often disorganized adventure, but given the institutions of the time, no other method could have built the system as rapidly.

In this century, we have seen the business cycle not only in the heroic proportions of the Roaring Twenties and the Great Depression but also during every succeeding business expansion or recession. We're in the cycle now, and we will be tomorrow and next year.

Business activity always expands and then contracts. There are periods when production, employment, and profits surge ahead, each followed by a period when profits and output fall and unemployment increases, and then the entire cycle repeats itself once again. During the expansion, demand and production, income and wealth grow. Homes and factories are constructed, and machinery and equipment are put in place. The value of these assets grows too, as home prices and common stock prices increase. But then comes the inevitable contraction, and all the forces that mark the expansion shift into reverse. Demand, production, and income fall. The level of construction and the production of machinery and equipment are drastically curtailed. Assets lose their value as home prices and common stock prices fall.

No doubt you realize that business cycles occur and repeat themselves in this way. But why? No completely satisfactory theory has yet been created. No one can accurately predict the length and course of each cycle. Economics, unlike physics, cannot be reduced to experiments and repeated over and over again under ideal conditions. There is no economic equivalent to Galileo on the tower of Pisa, proving that objects of unequal weight fall with equal speed, because the economic "tower" is never quite the same height; the "objects" keep changing in number, size, and even nature; and the "laws of gravity" apply unequally to each object. Yet one thing is certain: the business cycle is generated by forces within the economic system, not by outside forces. These internal forces create the alternating periods of economic expansion and contraction. And you should recognize that certain crucial features of the cycle endure.

First, the forces of supply and demand condition every cycle. Our ability to enjoy increasing income depends on our ability to supply or create increased production or output; we must produce more to earn more. But the level of demand, and the expenditures made in purchasing this output, must justify the level of production. That is, we must sell what we produce in order to earn. With sufficient demand, the level of production will be sustained and will grow, and income will increase; if demand is insufficient, the reverse will occur. During the expansionary phase of the cycle, demand and supply forces are in a relationship that permits the growth of production and income; during the contractionary phase, their relationship compels a decrease in production and income.

Second, neither consumers nor businesses are constrained to rely solely on the income they have generated in the process of production. They have recourse to the credit market; they can borrow money and spend more than they earn. Spending borrowed funds permits demand to take on a life of its own and bid up a constantly and rapidly growing level of production. This gives rise to the expansionary phase of the cycle. Eventually, the growth in production becomes dependent on the continued availability of credit, which sustains the growth in demand. But once buyers can no longer rely on borrowed funds (because of market saturation, the exhaustion of profitable investment opportunities, or tight credit), demand falls, and with it, the bloated level of production and income. The contractionary phase has begun.

Third, every expansion carries with it the inevitability of "overexpansion" and the subsequent contraction. Overexpansion may be impelled by businesses that invest too heavily in new plant and equipment in order to take advantage of a seemingly profitable opportunity, or by consumers who borrow too heavily in order to buy homes, autos, or other goods. But when businesses realize that the expected level of sales will not support additional plant and equipment, and when consumers realize that they will have difficulty paying for that new home or car, then businesses and consumers will curtail their borrowing and expenditure. Since production and income have spurted ahead to meet the growth in demand, they fall when the inevitable contraction in demand takes place.

Fourth, during contractions, production and income recede to a sustainable level, that is, to a level not reliant on a continuous growth in credit. The contraction returns the economy to a more efficient level of operation.

Fifth, every contraction sows the seeds of the subsequent recovery. Income earned in the productive process, rather than bloated levels of borrowing, maintains the level of demand. Consumers and businesses repay their debts. Eventually, lower debt burdens and interest rates encourage consumer and business borrowing and demand. The economy begins expanding once more.

Yet there is progress over the course of the cycle. Overall growth takes place because some, or even most, of the increase in output remains intact. Nor is all the created wealth subsequently destroyed. The tools and dies needed to make the Edsel will be scrapped, but the plant and equipment used to make Mustangs will remain on-stream. Subdivisions developed in 1976, when interest rates were low, will turn a profit for their developers, while those completed in 1980, when interest rates rose, may be liquidated at a loss after standing empty for a year. And so on. The tree grows, but the rings in its trunk mark the cycles of seasons that were often lush but on occasion were beset by drought.

The Transformation of the Postwar Economy

*U*p to now we have discussed the business cycle as if it were independent and autonomous. In fact, in modern history, the American business cycle has been influenced by a variety of attempts to guide and direct it. The economic events of the 15 years from 1965 to 1980 provide a vivid example of well-intentioned economic meddling gone awry.

During these years the federal government and the Federal Reserve System attempted to stimulate demand for goods and services with liberal spending, tax, and credit policies. Their objective was to boost the economy higher and faster, thereby generating increased employment opportunities. They thought that as supply rose to meet demand, increased production would accomplish their objectives. Unfortunately, as demand grew more rapidly than supply at current prices, prices spiraled upward. And as inflation became more severe, the only solution appeared to be a periodic reversal of those liberal spending, tax, and credit policies—which invariably plunged the economy into recession. These policy reversals exacerbated the cycle so that inflation escalated during boom and unemployment rose during bust.

These policies had their origin in the 30s, when economists were attempting to cope with the ravages of the Great Depression. At that time it was obvious that the economy was stagnating due to insufficient demand for the goods and services business could produce. The factories were there; the machines were there; the labor was there; only the customers were missing. The great question of the day was, How can we generate effective demand for goods and services?

Traditional economists had no solution to the problem. They viewed the Depression as a trough in a particularly severe cycle that would correct itself with time. Therefore, they prescribed laissez-faire (leave it alone) as the best possible course of action. Why not? It had always worked in the past.

A new generation of economists surveyed the scene and came up with a different answer. They saw the Great Depression as inaugurating an era in which demand was (and could remain) chronically depressed. To deal with the problem they recommended a two-pronged solution.

First, stimulate demand directly. Clearly consumers were not going to spend more, for many were unemployed, and those who were working were afraid to spend because they might lose their jobs. Business was not going to buy new factories and machinery since even existing facilities were underutilized. Only the government was in a position to spend more. Such government spending would involve deficit financing as the level of expenditures exceeded tax revenues, but the New Dealers were prepared to run the risk. If the government had to borrow now, it could pay back later. In this way the government would be the employer of last resort, hiring people to build dams, bridges, roads, and parks.

Second, the Federal Reserve System (the nation's central bank, known as *the Fed*) could push interest rates down and thereby depress the cost of borrowing money. This would motivate businesses (to the extent that they could be motivated) to borrow funds in order to buy equipment and machinery and to build additional factories and other establishments. Making credit easy was a way of stimulating economic activity.

These policies, applied in the late 30s, were interrupted by World War II when there was no need to stimulate the economy. But when the war came to an end, people feared that the economy would slip back into a chronic state of depression. That anxiety was unfounded, but so strongly felt that the ideological revolution of the 1930s survived. The new school of economists believed it was the government's duty to stimulate demand until the economy reached its maximum potential of full employment. This attitude meshed with other liberal and progressive views regarding government's responsibility for the social welfare of all.

Conservatives, on the other hand, continued to feel that laissez-faire was the best policy. Thus, throughout the Eisenhower years, the conservative administration drew fire from progressive economists for not implementing the lessons that had been learned in the 30s. They wanted additional federal spending and easy money in order to spur the economy.

When John F. Kennedy ran for office in 1960 he charged that the Eisenhower administration's conservative policies had reduced the rate of economic growth, and he promised to get the economy moving again. After he took office in 1961, he made good on that pledge by inviting the new school of economists into his administration, urging them to apply the progressive policies that had been developed under Roosevelt.

They did prescribe those policies, but with a new wrinkle. Rather than stimulate demand directly with increased government spending, they proposed putting more purchasing power in the pockets of consumers by cutting taxes. The government would still have to borrow to meet the deficit, except that this time it would do so to pay for a shortfall of revenue rather than a growth in expenditure. One way or the other, demand would grow. Increased consumer spending was just as good as government spending—and, as a rule, politically more advantageous. The extra spending would stimulate economic growth and create jobs as production expanded to meet the surge in consumer demand. At the same time President Kennedy's new wave of economists urged the Federal Reserve to maintain an easy policy so that liberal credit would be available at low rates of interest for consumer and business needs.

The views of President Kennedy's economists remained in fashion for two decades. A generation of students was trained to believe that an inadequate level of demand was the paramount problem facing the economy and that economics should be studied in order to determine how the federal government and the Federal Reserve could best stimulate the level of economic activity to provide full employment. They all recognized that excessive stimulation of demand could lead to inflation, but they felt that inflation would not be a problem until the economy attained full employment.

In each recession the Federal Reserve depressed interest rates, and the government stimulated spending directly with tax cuts for consumers and business. Demand roared ahead in short order, and when it exceeded supply at current prices, prices surged upward. At this point the federal government and the Federal Reserve reversed course and employed policies designed to dampen inflation. They slammed on the brakes, raising taxes and interest rates, depressing demand temporarily, and causing recession. But as soon as the inflation rate dropped, they reverted to their old ways and helped bring on the next round of expanding demand and inflation.

No one—not the economists, not the government, not the Federal Reserve—realized that World War II had profoundly changed the underlying circumstances and that policies appropriate for the 30s were not suited for the 60s and 70s. The Great Depression, which preceded the war, was a time of inadequate demand. But government borrowing from banks during the war, and the expenditures of those funds, had placed a wealth of liquid assets at the consumer's disposal. When the war ended, consumers were prepared to spend those funds, and were also increasingly prepared to borrow in order to supplement their expenditures. In the postwar world, demand, buttressed by borrowing, would chronically exceed supply at current prices, bidding prices upward. Excessive demand, not inadequate demand, would be the problem.

Thus began the first American peacetime period with significant and continuing inflation. In all other eras inflation had been the product of wartime government spending financed by borrowing, while peacetime had been a period of stable prices or even deflation. Consequently, government spending financed by borrowing, whether in time of war or peace, was viewed by almost everyone as the single source of inflation, and this mindset spilled over into the postwar world. No one realized that we now faced a whole new era in which inflation would be generated by private (consumer and business) borrowing and spending. Ever greater waves of borrowing by the private sector (not government) would drive the inflationary cycle.

The new generation of economists and their students, whose intellectual mold had been cast during the New Deal, were like generals who conduct a war by fighting the previous campaign. How to keep demand under control, how to restrain it and prevent it from generating inflation, was the real issue facing the postwar world. The Eisenhower years, when demand did seem to stall, confused economists into thinking that the chronically depressed conditions of the 1930s were a real possibility in the postwar world.

This was a major miscalculation. In fact, the escalating inflation of the 70s showed us that the potential runaway horse of the economy was champing at the bit—and all the while economists and policymakers were deciding how vigorously to apply the spurs.

By 1980, after two decades of inappropriate policies, the Federal Reserve determined to come to grips with the problem. The policies of the new generation of economists had to be discarded. The spurs had to be removed, the reins taken in hand, the runaway horse restrained. So the Fed tightened up, interest rates reached the stratosphere, borrowing and spending dried up, and the economy came closer to collapsing in 1981–82 than at any time since the war. After the recession of 1981–82 contained demand and eliminated inflation, the Fed slowly began to ease up. But the Fed was determined not to return to the errors of the past; it would not let credit become easy, nor demand grow too rapidly, nor inflation get out of control again.

At present, even though the "new" generation of economists has aged and their policy prescriptions have been largely discredited, the contrasting wisdom of the Federal Reserve's restraint has also increasingly been challenged. The Fed is under pressure to loosen the reins and permit the horse to gallop forward once again. If the Fed relents, and those who wish to abandon restraint win the day, you can expect renewed inflation and a return of the bad old days. As the philosopher Santayana said, those who do not understand the past are condemned to repeat it.

Now that you have had a brief overview of the Federal Reserve's pivotal role in these events, it is time to examine the Federal Reserve System in greater detail.

The Federal Reserve System

*T*he United States was the last major industrial nation to establish a central bank. The modern German state commissioned a central bank in 1875; the Bank of France was founded in 1800; and the Bank of England had entered its third century of operation when the Federal Reserve System was created in 1913.

America's tardiness was due to our traditional suspicion of centralized financial power and authority. Historically, we have felt more comfortable with small banks serving a single community. For instance, some states limit branch banking to this day, requiring that most of a bank's business be conducted under one roof. Ironically, the Continental Illinois Bank in Chicago is one of the nation's biggest, even though Illinois law severely constrains its branch facilities. California's liberal branch banking laws once helped Bank of America build its position as the nation's largest bank, while the big New York City banks (until recently) were hampered by legislation that confined them to the city and its suburbs and kept their branches out of upstate New York.

Alexander Hamilton proposed a central bank shortly after the country's founding. The two early attempts to create one both failed when confronted with the nation's suspicion of the Eastern financial community. Consequently, our economy grew until the eve of World War I without benefit of coordination or control of its banking activity. Banking, like the sale of alcohol following the repeal of Prohibition, was largely a matter of local option.

Under these circumstances, the banks had to fend for themselves, and the business cycle created perils for them as well as opportunities for profit. During periods of recession, when business income was down (usually following periods of speculative excess), banks found it difficult to collect on loans.

At the same time, nervous businesspersons and investors made large withdrawals, sometimes demanding payment in gold or silver specie. These precious metal coins composed the ultimate reserve for deposits; however, no bank possessed enough of them to secure every depositor, and the banking system functioned on the assumption that only a minority of depositors would demand their funds on any one day. When panic set in and a queue formed out the door and around the block, a bank could be wiped out in a matter of hours. As rumor spread, one bank after another would fail, until only the most substantial institutions, with the greatest specie reserve, were left standing. The chain reaction damaged many people, not the least of whom were innocent depositors who could not reach their funds in time.

Congress took up the issue after the panic of 1907. In that crisis—as the story goes—J. P. Morgan kept New York's most important bankers locked up in his home overnight until they agreed to contribute a pool of specie to be lent to the weakest banks until the run subsided. But the near-disaster had made it clear that the time had come to establish an American central bank with the capability of lending to all banks in time of panic; the nation's financial system could no longer rely on the private arrangements of J. P. Morgan. Thus, the Federal Reserve System was established by Congress in 1913. All member banks were required to make deposits to the system, creating a pool of reserves from which financially strapped banks could borrow during a crisis.

The system was originally conceived as a lender of last resort. In times of severe economic stress, it would use the pooled reserves of the banking system to make loans to banks under stress. When conditions improved, the loans were to be repaid. As time went by, however, the Fed discovered two things: first, that the reserve requirement could be used to control banking activity; and second, that control over the banking system provided a means of influencing the business cycle.

The reasoning was straightforward; it will be outlined for you here and developed more fully later. Bank lending is a key ingredient in the business cycle, driving the cyclic expansion of demand. It cannot, however, grow beyond the limits set by bank reserves, so when the Fed wants to give the economy a boost by encouraging banks to lend more, it increases reserves. On the other hand, by decreasing reserves and thereby shrinking available credit, the Fed exerts a restraining effect on the economy.

The mechanism used by the Fed to manipulate the banking system's reserves is astonishingly simple: it buys or sells securities on the open market. Briefly put, when the Fed buys securities, the sellers deposit the proceeds of the sale in their banks, and the banking system's reserves grow. On the other hand, when the Fed sells securities, buyers withdraw funds from their banks in order to make the purchases, and bank reserves fall.

The Fed exercised increasing power over the economy as the years passed, which led to conflict with the president and Congress. On occasion, politicians took the Fed to task for being too restrictive, for not permitting the economy to grow rapidly enough. At other times, the Fed was criticized for being too lenient and permitting demand to grow so rapidly that inflation threatened.

Why the conflict? Shouldn't the Fed's policy reflect the wishes of Congress and the president? Maybe, but it need not, for—as many do not realize—the Fed is *not* an agency of the U.S. government, but a corporation owned by banks that have purchased shares of stock. Federally chartered banks are required to purchase this stock and be members of the Federal Reserve System; state-chartered banks may be members if they wish. All banks, however, are subject to the Fed's control.

True, the Fed does have a quasi-public character because its affairs are managed by a Board of Governors appointed by the president of the United States with the approval of Congress. Nonetheless, once appointed, the Board of Governors is independent of the federal government and is free to pursue policies of its own choosing. New laws could, of course, change its status. That's why the chairman of the board is so frequently called upon to defend the policies of the Fed before Congress, and why Congress often reminds the Fed that it is a creature of Congress, which can enact legislation to reduce, alter, or eliminate the Fed's powers. Indeed, legislators and others do suggest from time to time that the Fed be made an agency of the U.S. government in order to remove its autonomy. So far, however, Congress has kept it independent, and it is likely to remain so, exercising its best judgment in guiding the nation's banking activity.

In some ways, the Fed's control over the banking system's reserves is the most important relationship between any two institutions in the American economy. The Fed can increase or reduce bank reserves at will, making it easier or more difficult for the banks to lend, and thus stimulating or restricting business and economic activity. This chapter will show you how to use the weekly report of the Fed's operations to understand the impact of its actions on the banks. The report appears each Friday in *The Wall Street Journal* under the caption "Federal Reserve Data" and is usually printed in the *Journal's* second section.

FEDERAL RESERVE DATA

"Federal Reserve Data" contains Wednesday figures that are released on Thursday for publication the following day. Thus, statistics for Wednesday, April 9, 1986, appeared on Friday, April 11, 1986 (see next page).

Look at **Free Reserves,** the next-to-last line under the heading **Reserve Aggregates.** It reveals the impact of the Fed's actions on the banking system. This section will explain its derivation and how to use it.

In examining free reserves, keep in mind that the discussion refers to all banks collectively, not to individual banks. This distinction is important, because banks can competitively drain one another of reserves to augment their ability to lend, but this activity does not increase the entire system's reserves. That explains the fierce rivalry among banks for deposits. When deposits are moved from one bank to another, the reserves of the first bank fall and those of the second bank increase. The first bank must restrain its lending, while the second bank can lend more. This competitive reshuffling of reserves, however, has not altered the overall level of reserves, and so the lending ability of the banking system remains the same.

Consequently, the reserves of the entire banking system depend on the Fed's open-market operations. The banks cannot augment their reserves independently through their own actions. The Fed supplies the banking system with reserves by buying securities, and it deprives the system of reserves by selling securities. When the Fed buys securities, the seller deposits the proceeds of the sale in his or her bank, thus increasing bank reserves. When it sells them, the buyer pays with funds withdrawn from his bank, thus decreasing bank reserves. More reserves make it easier for the banks to lend, stimulating economic activity; less reserves make it difficult for the banks to lend, restraining economic activity.

That sounds very hard on the banks. Suppose the Fed's policy becomes restrictive in the midst of an economic expansion; it sells securities, and so deprives the banks of reserves. If the banks are making loans while the Fed is reducing the level of bank reserves, the banking system will be short of reserves. Do the banks have a cushion to protect them in such an event?

Yes, the banks may borrow reserves from the Fed at a rate of interest called *the discount rate.* And to avoid a penalty for falling short, banks initiate such borrowing before their reserves are completely exhausted, thus maintaining a margin of *excess reserves.*

FEDERAL RESERVE DATA

MONETARY AGGREGATES
(daily average in billions)

	One week ended:
	Mar. 31, Mar. 24,
Money supply (M1) sa	640.1 639.2
Money supply (M1) nsa	630.1 624.7
	Four weeks ended:
	Mar. 31, Mar. 3,
Money supply (M1) sa	638.9 632.1
Money supply (M1) nsa	630.2 620.0
	Month
	Mar. Feb.
Money supply (M1) sa	638.2 631.0
Money supply (M2) sa	2589.9 2576.3
Money supply (M3) sa	3258.6 3240.6

nsa-Not seasonally adjusted. sa-Seasonally adjusted.

KEY ASSETS AND LIABILITIES
OF THE 10 LEADING NEW YORK BANKS
(in millions of dollars)

ASSETS:	April 2, 1986	Change from March 26, 1986
Total loans, leases and investments, adjusted	185,650	+ 129
Commercial and industrial loans	58,513	+ 1,373
Loans to depository and financial institutions	13,533	+ 153
Loans to individuals	17,904	+ 32
Real estate loans	31,063	+ 139
U.S. government securities	10,228	+ 57
Other securities including municipal issues	15,228	− 339
Municipal securities	13,141	− 241
LIABILITIES:		
Demand deposits	56,887	+ 3,040
Other transaction deposits including NOW accounts	4,946	+ 323
Savings and other nontransaction deposits	83,250	+ 388
Includes large time deposits of $100,000 or more	35,043	− 724

COMMERCIAL PAPER OUTSTANDING
(in millions of dollars)

All issuers	300,411	+ 309
Financial companies	219,343	+ 1,138
Nonfinancial companies	81,068	− 829

MEMBER BANK RESERVE CHANGES
Changes in weekly averages of reserves and related items during the week and year ended April 9, 1986 were as follows (in millions of dollars)

	Apr. 9, 1986	Chg fm Apr. 2, 1986	wk end Apr. 10, 1985
Reserve bank credit:			
U.S. Gov't securities:			
Bought outright	176,160 +	111	+ 14,619
Held under repurch agreemt	....	....	....
Federal agency issues:			
Bought outright	8,187	.... −	185
Held under repurch agreemt	....	....	....
Acceptances – bought outright			
Held under repurch agreemt	....	....	....
Borrowings from Fed	952 +	157 −	911
Seasonal borrowings	70 −	12 −	47
Extended credit	579 +	6 −	709
Float	691 −	375 −	122
Other Federal Reserve Assets	15,439 −	201 +	3,407
Total Reserve Bank Credit	201,429 +	309 +	16,808
Gold Stock	11,090	....	-3
SDR certificates	4,718	.... +	100
Treasury currency outstanding	17,232 +	14 +	615
Total	234,469 +	295 +	17,520
Currency in circulation	194,389 +	1,138 +	13,055
Treasury cash holdings	613	.... +	44
Treasury dpts with F.R. Bnks	3,365 +	439 −	824
Foreign dpts with F.R. Bnks	231 −	13 +	40
Other dpts with F.R. Bnks	469 +	15 +	105
Service related balances, adj	1,760 −	303 +	105
Other F.R. liabilities & capital	6,092 −	82 −	422
Total	206,921 +	1,195 +	12,192

RESERVE AGGREGATES
(daily average in millions)

	Two weeks ended:	
	Apr. 9,	Mar. 26,
Total Reserves (sa)	46,695	46,578
Nonborrowed Reserves (sa)	45,821	45,809
Required Reserves (sa)	46,073	45,583
Excess Reserves (nsa)	621	995
Borrowings from Fed (nsa)-a	298	234
Free Reserves (nsa)	323	761
Monetary Base (sa)	222,301	221,375

a-Excluding extended credit. nsa-Not seasonally adjusted. sa-Seasonally adjusted.

Reserve Aggregates

Free Reserves Positive (+) $323 million for two weeks ending April 9, 1986

The Wall Street Journal, *April 11, 1986*

Now you can calculate the *free reserve* figure for the entire banking system, which appears in the **Reserve Aggregates** section of "Federal Reserve Data."

When bank lending grows rapidly and the Fed is not supplying the banks with sufficient reserves, the banks will be obliged to borrow heavily from the Fed. If borrowing exceeds excess reserves, free reserves is a negative (−) figure. This is a signal that bank lending is expanding at a rapid pace and that the Fed is trying to restrain the banks and the expansion of economic activity.

On the other hand, during a period of slack economic activity, bank lending (and hence required reserves) will decline. Banks will not have to borrow reserves from the Fed. When excess reserves are large and bank borrowing is negligible, free reserves will be positive (+). A high level of free reserves shows that the Fed is not restraining the banks.

In returning to the April 11, 1986, "Federal Reserve Data," you can see that free reserves averaged $323 million in the 2 weeks ending April 9, 1986. The Fed had provided banks with sufficient reserves. Excess

Acceptances—bought outright				
Held under repurch agreemt	....		....	....
Borrowings from Fed	952 +		157 −	911
Seasonal borrowings	70 −		12 −	47
Extended credit	579 +		6 −	709
Float	691 −		375 −	122
Other Federal Reserve Assets	15,439 −		201 +	3,407
Total Reserve Bank Credit ...	201,429 −		309 +	16,808
Gold Stock	11,090		....	-3
SDR certificates	4,718		.... +	100
Treasury currency				
outstanding	17,232 +		14 +	615
Total	234,469 +		295 +	17,520
Currency in circulation	194,389 +		1,138 +	13,055
Treasury cash holdings	613		.... +	44
Treasury dpts with F.R. Bnks	3,365 +		439 −	824
Foreign dpts with F.R. Bnks	231 −		13 +	40
Other dpts with F.R. Bnks ...	469 +		15 +	105
Service related balances, adj	1,760 −		303 +	105
Other F.R. liabilities				
& capital	6,092 −		82 −	422
Total	206,921 +		1,195 +	12,192

Reserve Aggregates

Total reserves $46,695 million

Less: Required
reserves   46,073

Excess reserves   621*

Less: Borrowed
reserves   298

Free reserves $ 323 million

*Components do not add up to total because of rounding.

RESERVE AGGREGATES
(daily average in millions)

	Two weeks ended:	
	Apr. 9,	Mar. 26,
Total Reserves (sa)	46,695	46,578
Nonborrowed Reserves (sa)	45,821	45,809
Required Reserves (sa)	46,073	45,583
Excess Reserves (nsa)	621	995
Borrowings from Fed (nsa)-a	298	234
Free Reserves (nsa)	323	761
Monetary Base (sa)	222,301	221,375

a-Excluding extended credit. nsa-Not seasonally adjusted. sa-Seasonally adjusted.

reserves exceeded the banks' borrowing from the Fed, so free reserves were positive (+).

In summary, free reserves will be positive (+) when the Fed is supplying the banks with enough reserves through its open-market operations that the banks need not borrow. Free reserves are negative (−) when the Fed is restricting bank reserves. When, in the course of the business cycle, the former is true, the Fed's actions are referred to as an *easy money* policy or an *expansionary* monetary policy. When the latter is true, and free reserves are negative by a large amount, the Fed's actions are referred to as a *tight money* policy or a *contractionary* monetary policy.

What are the Fed's objectives in implementing these policies?

Expansionary policy: If the Fed buys securities, thus increasing member bank reserves, the banks will be able to lend more, stimulating demand. Such an expansionary policy has traditionally been pursued during a period of recession when the economy is at the bottom of the business cycle.

Contractionary policy: If the Fed sells securities, and bank reserves are reduced, the banks will not be able to lend as much, which will curtail the share of demand that depends on borrowing and hence will reduce the total level of demand. This policy has been followed at the peak of the cycle to restrain the growth of demand and inflationary increases in prices.

These relationships can be easily summarized in the following manner. Read ↑ as "up," ↓ as "down," and → as "leads to."

Expansionary policy: Fed buys securities → Bank reserves ↑ → Bank lending ↑ → Demand ↑.

Contractionary policy: Fed sells securities → Bank reserves ↓ → Bank lending ↓ → Demand ↓.

Thus, free reserves are positive (+) when the Fed pursues an expansionary policy, because open-market operations (Fed buys securities) have provided banks with such a large volume of reserves that excess reserves exceed bank borrowing from the Fed. Free reserves are negative (−) when Fed policy turns contractionary and open-market sales of securities deprive banks of reserves, obliging them to borrow more than their excess reserves from the Fed.

With these principles in mind, you can examine the Fed's record of expansionary (free reserves positive) and contractionary (free reserves negative) monetary policies since World War II. (See Chart 4–1 on page 24.) Negative free reserves are called *net borrowed reserves.*

Remember that the Fed's objective had always been to counteract the natural swing of the cycle, stimulating demand at the trough by making

Chart 4–1
Bank Borrowings of Reserves from Fed, Excess Reserves, Free Reserves, and Net Borrowed Reserves

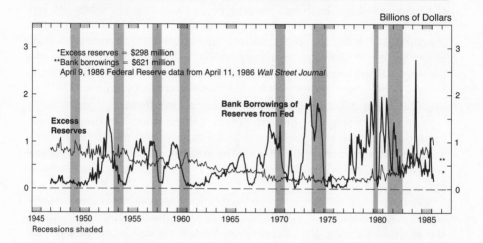

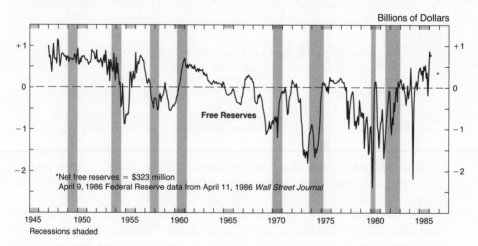

Source: U.S. Department of Commerce, *Business Conditions Digest* and *Handbook of Cyclical Indicators,* series 93 and 94; *Federal Reserve Bulletin.*

it easy for the banks to lend and curbing inflation at the peak by making it difficult for the banks to lend. The peaks and valleys of the cycle are reflected in the bank borrowings of reserves. Recessions are shaded in gray, and data quoted from *The Wall Street Journal* is indicated with an asterisk.

The economic events that began in the early 70s clearly illustrate these ideas. Do you recall the feverish inflationary boom of 1973, when demand for autos and housing was so insistent that the United Auto Workers Union was complaining of compulsory overtime and there were shortages of lumber? The demand for borrowed funds was very strong; bank lending was heavy; and required reserves grew apace. Accordingly, the Fed instituted a tight money policy, compelling banks to borrow heavily from the Fed (see top chart for years 1973–74) in order to maintain adequate reserves. You can see the consequences in the (mirror image) bottom chart: net borrowed reserves reached a record $3 billion in 1974. As the Fed applied the brakes, the boom came to a halt.

More than 2 million people were thrown out of work when the full force of recession hit in late 1974 and early 1975. The Fed switched to an easy money policy to stimulate the economy. As a result, bank borrowings of reserves from the Fed dropped sharply, so that for most of the period from 1975 through 1977 the banks had free reserves (excess reserves exceeding borrowing from the Fed).

By 1977 economic expansion was in progress. In response, the Fed reversed itself again, adopting a tight money policy, and the banks' position swung back into net borrowed reserves. First, bank lending to business increased steadily, and with it the level of required reserves. Second, the Fed began to exercise a policy of restraint in order to prevent too rapid an expansion of the economy. As the Fed pursued a restrictive policy, bank reserves became less adequate, which forced the banks to borrow reserves from the Fed.

Net borrowed reserves grew from 1977 onward, averaging almost $2 billion monthly by early 1980; it was 1974 all over again, except that inflation was even more severe. While the Fed pursued its traditional tight money policy, President Carter instituted voluntary wage and price controls. By the week of March 12, 1980, net borrowed reserves exceeded $3 billion. The cyclical peak had arrived, and a downturn was inevitable. When the recession struck, net borrowed reserves plummeted as the Fed's stance eased, until free reserves appeared briefly on July 9, 1980.

In summary, then, the overall aim of the Fed since World War II had been to curb and ultimately reverse the extremes of the cycle: to dampen inflation and to stimulate a depressed economy.

However another look at the chart of net borrowed and free reserves on page 24 reveals that the Fed's policies contributed to the cycle's severity. Like an inexperienced driver with one foot on the gas and the other on the brake, attempting to achieve a steady speed only to surge forward after screeching to a halt, the Fed alternately stimulated and restrained the economy. Record levels of net borrowed reserves at the cyclical peaks of the late 60s and the middle and late 70s provide evidence of the Fed's desperate attempts to bring inflationary expansion under control. Yet these sudden stops were partly the result of previous attempts, such as those made in 1972 and 1976, to stimulate rapid expansion by providing banks with plentiful free reserves. As the economy accelerated and inflation began to go out of control, the Fed slammed on the brakes.

Meanwhile, the business cycle of the 70s rose higher and higher, with inflation becoming more severe with each boom and unemployment becoming more severe with each bust. The Fed's policies had failed.

Now, although the Fed was unable to control the cycle or inflation in the 70s, it was not solely responsible for the course of events. You can see tidal waves of consumer and business borrowing in Chart 4–2 on page 27, doubling every five years: $100 billion in 1969, $200 billion in 1974, $400 billion in 1979. This borrowing drove demand forward during the expansionary phase of the cycle, creating the inflationary conditions that provoked the Fed's tight money policy and the subsequent crash into recession. The downturn would have occurred in the Fed's absence; the Fed's policies just made it more severe. Unfortunately, after recession took hold, the quick shift to an easy money policy fostered the next giant wave of borrowing, spending, and inflation, and this inevitably produced (once the wave's internal energy was spent and the Fed tightened up) a major collapse.

The Fed realized that a new approach was necessary after the 1980 recession. In earlier recessions, the Fed had always permitted a substantial period during which the banks could maintain free reserves or benefit from a decline in net borrowed reserves. During this slump, however, the Fed decided to prevent rapid recovery and expansion by maintaining a very tight money policy during the early phases of recovery. The Fed was convinced that inflation had become so severe that the usual easy-money-aided recovery could not be tolerated. The rate of inflation had risen over each successive cycle and had barely declined during the 1980 recession. Rapid stimulation and recovery of demand would quickly bid prices up once again. This time, tight money was called for, even if it stunted the recovery. (See Chart 4–1 on page 24.)

In consequence, the Fed's 1981 tight money policies caused the worst recession since World War II. For the first time, the Fed had stopped a recovery in its tracks and watched the economy slide off into back-to-back recessions. The Fed had made up its mind that restraining demand in order to control inflation was worth the price of economic contraction.

The Fed relaxed its grip in the summer of 1982, first, because inflation had been wrung out of the economy and unemployment had reached

Chart 4–2
Total Private Borrowing

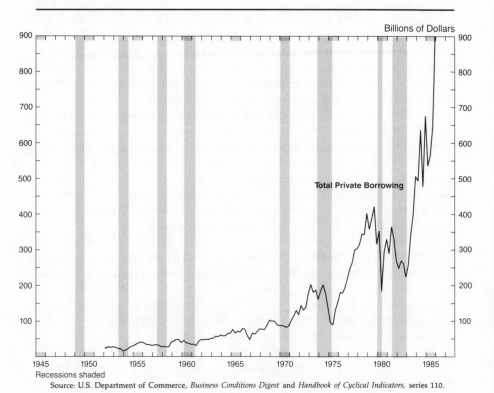

Billions of Dollars

Recessions shaded

Source: U.S. Department of Commerce, *Business Conditions Digest* and *Handbook of Cyclical Indicators*, series 110.

an intolerable level; and second, because there were strong signs that Congress was losing patience with the Fed's restrictive policies. The Fed had accomplished its objective, so there was no need to further antagonize those who had the power to terminate the Fed's independent status. But you should realize that the Fed's 1981 policies marked a major shift in strategy and had significant and far-reaching consequences for our economy. If severe inflation has been eliminated for the foreseeable future, it is no exaggeration to say that the Fed beat it back single-handedly.

Events since 1982 have nonetheless required the Fed's constant vigilance. When the Fed permitted easier conditions in late 1982, the economy roared ahead, as you can see from Chart 4–2. Business and consumer borrowing grew rapidly in 1983, reaching $500 billion (a record high at the time) by early 1984. Was this to be a repeat of earlier inflationary cycles, where demand, financed by easy credit, would be permitted to leap upward, bidding the rate of inflation to a new record? Would the bitter and wrenching experience of 1981–82, which had brought inflation under control, have been suffered in vain?

Immediate action was required if just such a painful reaction was to be avoided. So the Fed fine-tuned a minislowdown, restricting bank reserves sufficiently through open-market operations to compel banks to borrow reserves from the Fed. Chart 4–1 shows net borrowed reserves growing quickly in spring 1984, as banks were obliged to dip into the Fed in order to maintain their required reserves. That solved the problem: the growth in demand was stymied, and the economy cooled off.

The Fed's policies in the early 80s were a radical departure from those of the 60s and 70s. The 1981–82 recession and the minislowdown of 1984 signaled a new era, a major turning point in postwar economic history. The Fed had abandoned its old game plan: spurring the economy onward during slack conditions only to apply a chokehold when boom and inflation got out of hand, and then dealing with a repeat performance in the next cycle but on a new, ratcheted, higher plateau. General restraint over the course of the cycle was the new game plan.

Paul Volcker knew that those easy conditions and pro-growth attitude contributed to the disaster of the 70s. He knew that he was on a tightrope, and that the cautious attitude described above could not lapse into complacency. But by the mid-80s, new appointees to the Board of Governors who favored an easy money policy had undermined Mr. Volcker's go-slow approach. You will notice (page 24) that free reserves became positive once again, signalling dramatically easier conditions.

That's why you should be so concerned with the composition of the Board of Governors and the tendency to appoint new members to the board who are predisposed to easier conditions. Mr. Volcker wanted to leave behind a board that would maintain restraint because it understood the errors of the past. If the new appointees frustrate this policy, the economy will once again grow too quickly, and a new round of damaging inflation will inevitably result.

5

The Money Supply

*O*ne reason so much controversy surrounds the money supply is that many people misunderstand its nature. Currency and coins in circulation together make up only about one quarter of the money supply. Checking accounts (or *demand deposits,* as they are formally called) constitute the remaining three quarters. The one quarter of the money supply that exists as cash comes from two different sources: the U.S. Treasury mints coins and prints paper money for the Fed, and the Fed distributes all our currency and coin.

These arrangements have an interesting and important history. Before the Civil War, with the exception of the two short-lived attempts at a central bank that were mentioned in Chapter 4, all paper money was put out by private banks and called *bank notes.* These bank notes resembled modern paper currency and entered circulation when banks lent them to customers.

The banks' incentive to issue bank notes to borrowers, instead of gold and silver coins, came from the limited supply of gold and silver coins (specie). Each bank kept a specie reserve that was no more than a fraction of its outstanding bank notes. This reserve was used to satisfy those who demanded that a bank redeem its notes with specie; as long as the bank could do so, its notes were accepted at face value and were "good as gold." Bank notes and minted coins circulated together.

After the Civil War, checking accounts replaced bank notes. They were safer and more convenient because the customer (borrower) had to sign them and could write in their exact amount. In modern times, all customers, whether depositors or borrowers, began to make use of checking accounts. The private bank note passed into history.

The U.S. Treasury first issued paper money during the Civil War, and it continued to do so until some time after World War II. During the 20th century, however, most of our paper money has been issued by the Federal Reserve System, and today the Fed has that exclusive responsibility; if you examine a piece of currency, you will see that it is a "Federal Reserve Note." Thus, ironically, bank notes constitute all of our currency today, just as they did before the Civil War. But today the notes are issued by the central bank rather than a host of private banks.

Since the Treasury prints currency at the Fed's request to meet the public's needs, the common notion that the federal government cranks out more paper money to finance its deficits *has no factual basis*. The amount of paper money in circulation has nothing to do with the deficits of the federal government. When the federal government runs a deficit (expenditures exceed revenue), the Treasury borrows by issuing bonds that are bought by investors: the government gets the money, and the investors get the bonds. If a bond is sold to a bank (and banks are major purchasers of U.S. Treasury securities), the bank pays for it by crediting the checking account of the U.S. Treasury, thus increasing the total volume of all checking accounts. This is called *monetizing the debt;* it enlarges the money supply but does not affect currency in circulation. (If the bond is purchased by the Fed, the transaction is also referred to as monetizing the debt, and the effect is similar to an expansionary monetary policy in which the Fed buys U.S. Treasury securities through open-market operations.)

By contrast, the Fed issues paper money not in response to the budget deficits of the *federal government* but to the *public's* requirements for cash. It supplies banks with cash, and the banks pay for it with a check written on their reserve account. Checks written to "cash" by bank customers then determine the amount of currency circulating outside banks. This demand for cash has no impact on the money supply because checking accounts decrease by the amount currency increases when the check is "cashed."

Then how does the money supply grow? In the same fashion that bank notes outstanding grew in the 19th century. When banks lend, they create demand deposits (checking accounts) or credit an existing demand deposit. The more that banks lend, the more that the money supply (which is mostly demand deposits) increases. Today, as 100 years ago, bank reserves set the only limit on bank lending and, therefore, on the money supply. The difference is that instead of keeping specie as reserves, the banks must maintain reserves with the Fed.

Keep this in mind: *Bank loans create deposits,* not the other way around. As long as the banking system has sufficient reserves, it can make loans in the form of demand deposits (money). You must abandon the notion that depositors' funds provide the wherewithal for bank lending. That may be true for the traditional mortgage lending activity of a savings and loan association, but it is not true for commercial banks. After all, where would depositors get the funds if not by withdrawing them from another checking account? But this actually does not increase deposits for the entire system; it only reshuffles deposits among banks. The total is unchanged.

Thus, demand deposits, and with them the money supply, grow when banks lend, and it makes no difference who the borrower is. When a business borrows from its bank in order to stock goods for the Christmas season, the bank creates a deposit (money) on which the business writes checks to pay for merchandise. If you borrow from your bank to buy a car, the loan creates a demand deposit that increases the money supply. Therefore, as you can see, it is not just the federal government that "monetizes debt" when it borrows from the banking system; businesses and consumers "monetize" their debt too.

One last point must be made about the nature of bank reserves. A hundred years ago they consisted of gold and silver specie. Today they are deposits that banks maintain with the Federal Reserve System. Of what do these reserves consist, if not specie? They are merely checking accounts that the banks have on deposit with the Fed, very much like the checking account you have at your own bank. Recall, from Chapter 4, that the banks' checking accounts (reserves) increase when the Fed buys securities with a check written on itself (akin to a cashier's check) and the purchaser deposits the Fed's check with his or her bank. The banking system gains reserves when the bank deposits the Fed's check in its reserve account at the Fed.

If it sounds like a house of cards, or like bookkeeping entries in a computer's memory, that's because it is. Nothing "backs up" the money supply except our faith in it, expressed every time we accept or write a check. And those checking accounts, and hence the money supply, built on borrowing, *must keep growing* if the economy is to grow over the business cycle. The forward surge of the cycle, when demand grows rapidly and pulls the economy's output with it, is founded on spenders' ability and willingness to borrow, to go into debt.

This, then, is the critical significance of the money supply: it measures the increase in demand made possible by bank lending. With that in mind, turn once again to *The Wall Street Journal's* "Federal Reserve Data."

One-Week Money Supply Figure
MI averaged $640.1 billion
during week ending March 31, 1986

Four-Week Money Supply Figure
MI averaged $638.9 billion
during four weeks ending March 31, 1986

Monthly Money Supply Figure
MI averaged $638.2 billion
in March 1986

FEDERAL RESERVE DATA

MONETARY AGGREGATES
(daily average in billions)

	One week ended:	
	Mar. 31,	Mar. 24,
Money supply (M1) sa	640.1	639.2
Money supply (M1) nsa	630.1	624.7
	Four weeks ended:	
	Mar. 31,	Mar. 3,
Money supply (M1) sa	638.9	632.1
Money supply (M1) nsa	630.2	620.0
	Month	
	Mar.	Feb.
Money supply (M1) sa	638.2	631.0
Money supply (M2) sa	2589.9	2576.3
Money supply (M3) sa	3258.6	3240.6

nsa-Not seasonally adjusted. sa-Seasonally adjusted.

KEY ASSETS AND LIABILITIES
OF THE 10 LEADING NEW YORK BANKS
(in millions of dollars)

		Change from
ASSETS:	April 2, 1986	March 26, 1986
Total loans, leases and		
investments, adjusted	185,650	+ 129
Commercial and industrial loans	58,513	+ 1,373
Loans to depository and		
financial institutions	13,533	+ 153
Loans to individuals	17,904	+ 32
Real estate loans	31,063	+ 139
U.S. government securities	10,228	+ 57
Other securities including		
municipal issues	15,228	− 339
Municipal securities	13,141	− 241
LIABILITIES:		
Demand deposits	56,887	+ 3,040
Other transaction deposits		
including NOW accounts	4,946	+ 323
Savings and other		
nontransaction deposits	83,250	+ 388
Includes large time deposits		
of $100,000 or more	35,043	− 724

COMMERCIAL PAPER OUTSTANDING
(in millions of dollars)

All issuers	300,411	+ 309
Financial companies	219,343	+ 1,138
Nonfinancial companies	81,068	− 829

MEMBER BANK RESERVE CHANGES

Changes in weekly averages of reserves and related items during the week and year ended April 9, 1986 were as follows (in millions of dollars)

		Chg fm	wk end
	Apr. 9,	Apr. 2,	Apr. 10,
	1986	1986	1985
Reserve bank credit:			
U.S. Gov't securities:			
Bought outright	176,160 +	111	+14,619
Held under repurch agreemt	....	....	....
Federal agency issues:			
Bought outright	8,187	....	− 185
Held under repurch agreemt	....	....	....
Acceptances—bought outright			
Held under repurch agreemt	....	....	....
Borrowings from Fed	952 +	157	− 911
Seasonal borrowings	70 −	12	− 47
Extended credit	579 +	6	− 709
Float	691 −	375	− 122
Other Federal Reserve Assets	15,439 −	201	+ 3,407
Total Reserve Bank Credit	201,429 −	309	+16,808
Gold Stock	11,090	....	−3
SDR certificates	4,718	....	+ 100
Treasury currency			
outstanding	17,232 +	14	+ 615
Total	234,469 +	295	+17,520
Currency in circulation	194,389 +	1,138	+13,055
Treasury cash holdings	613	....	+ 44
Treasury dpts with F.R. Bnks	3,365 +	439	− 824
Foreign dpts with F.R. Bnks	231 −	13	+ 40
Other dpts with F.R. Bnks	469 +	15	+ 105
Service related balances, adj	1,760 −	303	+ 105
Other F.R. liabilities			
& capital	6,092 −	82	− 422
Total	206,921 +	1,195	+12,192

RESERVE AGGREGATES
(daily average in millions)

	Two weeks ended:	
	Apr. 9,	Mar. 26,
Total Reserves (sa)	46,695	46,578
Nonborrowed Reserves (sa)	45,821	45,809
Required Reserves (sa)	46,073	45,583
Excess Reserves (nsa)	621	995
Borrowings from Fed (nsa)-a	298	234
Free Reserves (nsa)	323	761
Monetary Base (sa)	222,301	221,375

a-Excluding extended credit. nsa-Not seasonally adjusted. sa-Seasonally adjusted.

THE MONEY SUPPLY (M1)

M1 is demand deposits (checking accounts) and currency in circulation. In the report that appeared on Friday, April 11, 1986, M1 averaged $640.1 billion for the week ending March 31, 1986, $638.9 billion for the four

Money Growth vs. the Fed's Targets
Monthly averages, seasonally adjusted

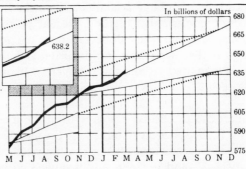

M1 Private checking deposits and cash. The Fed is seeking 3%-to-8% growth this year, as shown by the upper cone and, more flexibly, by the dotted lines. In the second half of 1985 the goal also was for a 3%-to-8% growth rate. The inset shows the latest period.

In billions of dollars

638.2

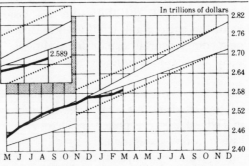

M2 Adds to M1 most types of personal savings including money market funds and money market deposit accounts. The 1986 target, depicted by the large cone and dotted lines, is 6%-to-9% growth, unchanged from last year.

In trillions of dollars

2.589

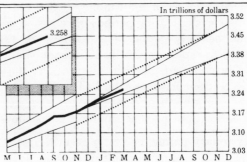

M3 Includes M2 plus some investments such as large certificates of deposit and money market funds sold to institutions. The Fed is seeking 6%-to-9% growth this year, compared with 6%-to-9.5% last year.

In trillions of dollars

3.258

The Wall Street Journal, *April 11, 1986*

weeks ending March 31, and $638.2 billion in March of 1986. (See excerpt on page 32.)

The annotation "sa" means seasonally adjusted. All seasonal fluctuations, such as the large increase and subsequent decline in the money supply associated with the Christmas shopping season, have been removed from the data.

You'll see references now and then to a variety of "Ms," and the *Journal* tracks them on Fridays together with the Fed's targets for their growth. See the excerpt from the April 11, 1986, issue on page 33. *M2* is M1 plus savings accounts and money market fund shares, and *M3* is M2 plus certain other large accounts at financial institutions. All of these have become increasingly volatile in recent years due to the revolution in consumer banking. The public can now use interest-bearing savings accounts as if they were demand deposits, and the distinction between savings and loan associations and commercial banks is rapidly disappearing. As a result, it's difficult to maintain the dividing lines among the "Ms."

Use Chart 5–1 to observe the growth in the money supply (M1) since World War II. (See page 35.) You can see the money supply's rapid increase in the 70s. It was quickest during the business cycle expansions of the late 60s, 1972–73, and 1977–78, and it slowed with the subsequent recessions. This is consistent with the earlier discussion of bank lending over the course of the cycle. Bank lending increased with cyclical expansions, generating a commensurate rise in demand deposits (money supply), and it decreased in the subsequent recessions, restricting money supply growth.

The money supply's headlong advance and the cyclical fluctuation in its rate of growth fueled a sharp debate, which led to an announced change in Federal Reserve policy in October 1979. That debate can be summed up in a few paragraphs.

As you recall from Chapter 4, the Fed was traditionally activist, alternately pursuing easy or tight money policies, depending on the state of the business cycle. During periods of recession and through the recovery stage and the early period of expansion, the Fed's easy money policy contributed to rapid growth in the money supply as banks lent money freely in response to plentiful reserves. As the expansionary phase of the cycle reached its peak, the Fed switched to a tight money policy, restricting the growth of bank reserves and, hence, the money supply.

The Fed's actions may be summarized as shown:

Expansionary policy: Fed buys securities → Bank reserves ↑ → Bank lending ↑ → Money supply ↑ → Demand ↑.

Contractionary policy: Fed sells securities → Bank reserves ↓ → Bank lending ↓ → Money supply ↓ → Demand ↓.

Chart 5–1
The Money Supply (M1)

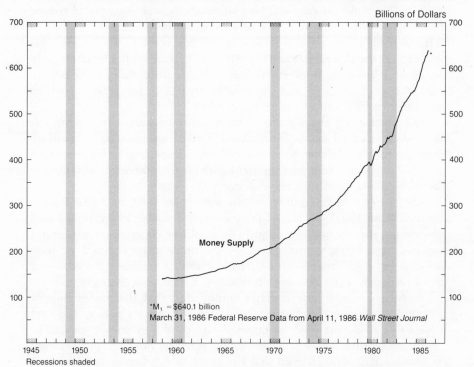

Billions of Dollars

*M₁ = \$640.1 billion
March 31, 1986 Federal Reserve Data from April 11, 1986 *Wall Street Journal*

Money Supply

Recessions shaded

Source U.S. Department of Commerce. *Business Statistics* and *Survey of Current Business,* various issues, and Federal Reserve Board.

In the 70s, a growing group of economists began to criticize the Fed's policy, accusing the Fed of contributing to the severity of the business cycle instead of reducing cyclical fluctuations. In their view, the Fed's contractionary policy, applied at the peak of the cycle, only added to the severity of the impending recession, while expansionary policy, during the early stages of recovery, only set the stage for the subsequent inflations.

These economists, known as the *monetarist* school, believe that the rate of increase in the money supply is the single most important determinant of business cycle conditions. If the money supply grows rapidly, the economy expands; if the money supply does not grow rapidly, or even contracts, economic activity also contracts. The monetarists also believe that because other forces intrinsic to the economy will lead to normal cyclical activity and fluctuation in the rate of growth in the money supply, the Fed's best course of action is to attempt to keep the money supply's growth on an even keel, preferably at a low rate, reflecting the economy's long-range ability to increase output. According to the monetarists' view, anything beyond that rate will lead to inflation, and attempts to reduce the swings of the cycle will instead only exacerbate them.

It's as if the monetarists were saying, "If you want a comfortable temperature, set the thermostat and leave it. Don't fiddle with it by alternately raising and lowering it every time you feel a little chilly or a bit too warm, because this will just cause wide swings in temperature, which only heighten discomfort rather than reduce it."

In October 1979, shortly after Paul Volcker began his term of office, the Fed announced an accommodation with the monetarist position. Henceforth, Mr. Volcker said, the Fed would set targets for monetary growth that it believed were consistent with an acceptable rate of inflation. The monetarists claimed a big victory.

Then, when the Fed tightened the screws in 1981, as the economy emerged from the 1980 recession, pursuing a tight money policy and announcing that money supply growth would be constrained until inflation had been brought under control, the monetarists cheered. At long last, the Fed had broken out of its old habit of reflating the economy to aid recovery. After decades of mischief, it had seen the light.

Recently, however, the Fed has emphasized that the money supply is only one of several indicators on which it bases its policy, and that it feels free to depart from its targeted rate of money supply growth as conditions require. These remarks were greeted by howls of protest from the monetarists, who claimed that the Fed was chickening out just as it was about to drive the stake into inflation's heart.

Whose side should you take? Beware, because much of this theoretical "economics" debate is a veneer that thinly disguises ideological differences not always susceptible to common sense. The monetarists are conservatives who believe that government governs best when it governs least. And that includes the Fed. Hence, the monetarists argue that the Fed should not play an active, intervening role. The monetarists' liberal opponents advocate an activist, interventionist government, and so they believe that the Fed should intercede to control the vicissitudes of the cycle. Thus, the controversy has as much to do with what is politically "correct" as with what is economically effective. The emotion each side brings to the debate is your clue that more than objective analysis is at stake.

In any case, you need not take sides, nor need you permit debate over the money supply's importance to distract your attention from the Fed's policy reversal in 1981. The Fed used its familiar, old-fashioned tight money policy to fight inflation; it was the *timing* of that policy that was not traditional and thus represented a concession to the monetarists. The Fed conceded that its activities during the 70s had contributed to the cycle's severity and to inflation. Therefore, following the 1980 recession, it took the unprecedented action of flattening the recovery, and the cycle, in order to stop the inflation that the monetarists considered the economy's number one problem. In mid-1982, as inflation subsided and unemployment became severe, the Fed moved to an easy money policy in a pragmatic adjustment to the prevailing economic and political realities.

As you can see from this example, the Fed has refused to join the monetarist camp completely; and this won't change unless there's a sudden and radical shift in the composition of the Board of Governors, and monetarists achieve a majority position on the board.

The Fed has fought hard to maintain its independence from Congress, the president, and all other outside influences. Why should it abandon its cherished independence by slavishly following the dictates of the monetarists? Limiting the Fed's policies to monitoring the growth of the money supply and attempting to restrict that rate of growth to the pace at which the economy increases its output of goods and services, as the monetarists suggest, would tie the Fed's hands far more severely than if it were an agency of the federal government. No, Mr. Volcker's vision, and that of the Fed, was and is far broader than the monetarists' policy prescriptions.

You can therefore expect the Fed to pay lip service to the broadest interpretation of monetarist goals because they are still somewhat in fashion and fit the Fed's eclectic approach. Consequently, the Fed will announce that it intends, through its policies, to restrict the money supply's growth to a specific range. But don't anticipate any drastic moves on the Fed's part if the goals are not met and the money supply grows either more or less rapidly than the target range.

Interest Rates

*E*very commodity has a price; the *interest rate* is the price of money. As with any commodity, that price fluctuates according to the laws of supply and demand.

The demand for money increases and interest rates rise during economic expansion as consumers and businesses finance increased spending by drawing upon three sources of funds: current savings, liquidation of financial assets, and borrowing.

During recessions, as the economy moves from trough to recovery, cash becomes plentiful once again. Savings are ample; financial assets accumulate; and debt is repaid. Interest rates fall as the supply of funds exceeds the demand for funds at current rates.

This cycle occurs with or without the Federal Reserve System. Yet you can weave the cyclical fluctuation of interest rates into Chapters 4 and 5's description of Federal Reserve policy. The Fed traditionally pursued an easy money policy to hold interest rates down and promote relaxed credit conditions during the recovery phase of the cycle. Eventually, when the expansion was fully under way, the peak of the cycle not far off, and credit availability constricting, the Fed switched to a tight money policy, which reduced the supply of credit even further and drove up interest rates.

The Fed's actions can be summarized as follows:

Easy money policy: Fed buys securities → Bank reserves ↑ → Bank lending ↑ → Money supply ↑ → Interest rates ↓ → Demand ↑.

Tight money policy: Fed sells securities → Bank reserves ↓ → Bank lending ↓ → Money supply ↓ → Interest rates ↑ → Demand ↓.

The Fed reversed course in 1981 when it clamped its tight money policy on the recovery from the 1980 recession, sending interest rates to record highs. The Fed relaxed its grip in 1982, allowing interest rates to fall, but only after it was sure that inflation had been throttled. It remains to be seen whether the Fed will hold the reins firmly to prevent inflation's resurrection and not fall back into the trap of the 70s.

Thus, whether you observe historical or recent events, interest rates are an important gauge of both Federal Reserve policy and the cycle.

So far, interest rates have been treated collectively, as if they were a single entity. A closer examination of the credit markets, however, reveals a complex scene.

There is a great variety of credit instruments: U.S. Treasury securities, corporate bonds, residential mortgages, and so forth, each with its own market. The market conditions for a particular form of credit determine its rate of interest, and the markets for all forms of credit are interrelated. For instance, the federal government can borrow by selling U.S. Treasury securities. In order to attract lenders and dispose of all securities, the Treasury may offer an increased interest return. This will draw investors away from corporate bonds, requiring business to increase the return on its debt. Thus, the federal deficit may have an impact throughout the credit markets.

The Wall Street Journal publishes the most important interest rates on a daily basis.

SHORT–TERM INTEREST RATES

In every Tuesday's *Journal,* you will find a summary of the U.S. Treasury's Monday auction of *Treasury bills;* look for the "Credit Markets" article in the front-page index. Pages 41 and 43 provide an example drawn from the Tuesday, April 8, 1986, edition of the *Journal.*

Our national debt made the news when it passed $2 trillion, and it continues to mushroom. Treasury bills (T-bills) constitute about a quarter of the total, and this huge dollar volume makes them the most important short-term investment instrument and establishes their return as the interest rate to watch.

The U.S. Treasury borrows by selling bills (and *notes* and *bonds,* as the longer-term debt instruments are called) at *auction* (primary market) every Monday in New York. They are sold on a discount basis, which means that buyers pay less than the $10,000 face value they will receive when the bill matures in 90 days (actually, 13 weeks). If bidding is strong,

Bonds Slump Amid Investor Concern About Another Increase in Oil Prices

CREDIT MARKETS ·

By EDWARD P. FOLDESSY
And TOM HERMAN
Staff Reporters of THE WALL STREET JOURNAL

NEW YORK—Bond prices slumped yesterday amid investor concern about another rise in oil prices.

Some actively traded U.S. Treasury bonds wound up the session with declines of about a half point, or around $5 for each $1,000 face amount of securities. Prices swung widely during the session, although trading was relatively light.

The volatility mainly reflected confusion about the Reagan administration's stance on oil prices. Vice President George Bush, meeting with Saudi Arabian officials over the weekend, hinted that the U.S. may abandon its free-market approach to oil policy in an effort to help the depressed U.S. oil industry.

The White House reiterated yesterday that the administration wants market forces to determine world oil prices, but some private economists remain skeptical in light of Mr. Bush's remarks. Yesterday's increase in oil prices came largely in response to a strike that has closed down Norway's North Sea oil production. Crude oil futures rose on the New York M.... tile Exchange for the fifth con~ ...in the sion.   ..at, he said,

Investors "are ..spects for a dis-
news," said P ... ine U.S. Federal Re-
preside~'
cu~' ... government is scheduled to release
...s preliminary estimate of first-quarter economic growth April 17. Private economists generally have been lowering their estimates recently because of a stream of government reports showing unexpectedly lethargic business activity.

Mr. Platt estimates that the gross national product, adjusted for inflation, grew at an annual rate of 2% to 3% in the first quarter. GNP is the total value of the nation's output of goods and services. He predicted that the second quarter won't be "any stronger." He also predicted that figures to be released Friday will show retail sales fell 1.2% last month after declining 0.1% in February.

Mr. Platt contends that the Federal Reserve already is easing its credit reins

The Wall Street Journal, *April 8, 1986*

Key Interest Rates

Annualized interest rates on certain investments as reported by the Federal Reserve Board on a weekly-average basis:

	Week Ended:	
	Apr. 4,	Mar. 28,
	1986	1986
Treasury bills (90 day)-a	6.31	6.39
Commrcl paper (Dealer, 90 day)-a	7.02	7.13
Certfs of Deposit (Resale, 90 day)	7.02	7.16
Federal funds (Overnight)-b	7.39	7.25
Eurodollars (90 day)-b	7.23	7.43
Treasury bills (one year)-c	6.67	6.89
Treasury notes (three year)-c	7.03	7.19
Treasury notes (five year)-c	7.22	7.36
Treasury notes (ten year)-c	7.39	7.63
Treasury bonds (20 year)-c	7.54	7.93
Treasury bonds (30 year)-c	7.47	7.81

a-Discounted rates. b-Week ended Wednesday, April 2, 1986 and Wednesday, March 26, 1986. c-Yields, adjusted for constant maturity.

slightly in an effort to bolster the economy. He argued that the Fed is trying to keep federal funds trading in a range of 7% to 7¼%. That would compare with ab~ ...ıı ıs-7¼%-to-7⅜% range in recent we~ ...ısylvania eral funds are reserves that ' ıo investors another overnight.   ..ıl by Morgan Stan-

The Fed yes~ ...year issue, carrying an from the ba~' ...rate, was priced after auc-ties to ~ ...ıt par. The debentures are rated dou-ri~ ...A-1 by Moody's Investors Service Inc. and double-A-plus by Standard & Poor's Corp.

In the municipal market, a two-part offering of about $166 million of revenue refunding bonds by the Cape May County, N.J., Municipal Utilities Authority was tentatively priced by underwriters. Under the proposed scale, yields range from 5.7% in 1991 to 7.29% in 2016, according to a spokesman for Prudential-Bache Securities Inc.

Here are the details of yesterday's U.S. Treasury bill auction:

Rates are determined by the difference between the purchase price and face value. Thus, higher bidding narrows the investor's return while lower bidding widens it. The percentage rates are calculated on a 360-day year, while the coupon equivalent yield is based on a 365-day year.

	13-Week	26-Week
Applications	$25,310,330,000	$21,721,415,000
Accepted bids	$7,014,920,000	$7,016,005,000
Accepted at low price	56%	49%
Accepted noncompet'ly	$1,205,815,000	$957,115,000
Average price (Rate)	98.435(6.19%)	96.881(6.17%)
High price (Rate)	98.443(6.16%)	96.891(6.15%)
Low price (Rate)	98.443(6.20%)	96.876(6.18%)
Coupon equivalent	6.38%	6.46%

Both issues are dated April 10. The 13-week bills mature July10,1986, and the 26-week bills mature Oct.10, 1986.

and the price high, the effective rate of interest will be low, and vice versa.

Place yourself in the role of buyer. If you pay $9,750 for a bill maturing in 90 days (about a quarter of a year), your effective annual rate of return is approximately 10 percent. Remember, $250 in a quarter-year is the equivalent of $1,000 in a year, or 10 percent of a $10,000 base. (Use $10,000 as the base for calculating the rate of return, rather than $9,750, because Treasury bills' yields are usually quoted on a discount basis. That is, the discount—$250—is measured against face value—$10,000.) If strong bidding drives the price to $9,875, your return falls to 5 percent. If weak bidding permits the price to fall to $9,500, the effective return rises to 20 percent; the more you pay for the Treasury bill, the lower your rate of return, and vice versa. The examples are summarized below.

Face (redemption) value	$10,000	$10,000	$10,000
Selling price	$9,875	$9,750	$9,500
(note: prices falling)			
Discount (difference)	$125	$250	$500
Rate of return	5%	10%	20%
(note: interest rate rising)			

Your motivation for buying Treasury bills is probably quite simple: you have idle cash on which you wish to earn an interest return. Therefore, the key question is, "How much will you pay now in order to receive $10,000 in 90 days' time?" If you and all other bidders for Treasury bills have ample funds and are eager to buy, you will drive the price close to $10,000 and earn a low rate of return. If you and all other bidders do not have ample funds, you can be enticed only by a very low price for the right to receive $10,000 in 90 days, and you will receive a high rate of interest. The Treasury, which is the seller of the bills, must pay the rate of interest determined by the bidding.

Look at the blowup from the article on page 43. You can see that 6.19 percent was the average discount rate yield on 90-day bills purchased at the Treasury's April 7, 1986, auction as reported in Tuesday's April 8, 1986, *Journal*. That is, on the average, the U.S. Treasury received $9,843.50 (98.435 percent of face value) for each $10,000 bill auctioned. The difference between $9,843.50 and $10,000 over 13 weeks ($156.50), calculated over a "year" of 360 days, yields a discount rate of 6.19 percent. The excerpt also informs you that the true (coupon equivalent) yield over 365 days on a base of $9,483.50 ($10,000 less $156.50) is 6.38 percent.

Now, this discussion has been presented as if you could participate in the bidding for Treasury bills. Well, you can't. The auction is conducted in New York by the Fed, acting as the Treasury's agent, and is reserved for a closed list of large firms that deal in, and make a market for, Treasury bills. They bid for the bills at the weekly Monday auction (primary market) so they can resell them at a markup on any business day (secondary

Here are the details of yesterday's U.S. Treasury bill auction:

Treasury Bill Auction

On Monday, April 7, 1986, the Treasury auctioned bills in the primary ➤ market which had a yield of 6.19 percent.

Rates are determined by the difference between the purchase price and face value. Thus, higher bidding narrows the investor's return while lower bidding widens it. The percentage rates are calculated on a 360-day year, while the coupon equivalent yield is based on a 365-day year.

	13-Week	26-Week
Applications	$25,310,330,000	$21,721,415,000
Accepted bids	$7,014,920,000	$7,016,005,000
Accepted at low price	56%	49%
Accepted noncompet'ly	$1,205,815,000	$957,115,000
Average price (Rate)	98.435(6.19%)	96.881(6.17%)
High price (Rate)	98.443(6.16%)	96.891(6.15%)
Low price (Rate)	98.443(6.20%)	96.876(6.18%)
Coupon equivalent	6.38%	6.46%

Both issues are dated April 10. The 13-week bills mature July 10, 1986, and the 26-week bills mature Oct. 10, 1986.

The Wall Street Journal, *April 8, 1986*

market). You *can* go to your regional Federal Reserve Bank and buy Treasury bills, but you'll have to do so noncompetitively at the average rate (discount) established at the New York auction.

Once you have purchased a Treasury bill, however, you need not wait 90 days to have it redeemed. You can sell it on the open market (secondary market) at any time. Chances are you will have a broker act as your agent, because the daily trading takes place in New York and is reserved for large financial institutions dealing in millions of dollars at a time. The daily trading is called the *money market,* a term that suggests the fact that Treasury bills are the safest, most convenient, and most liquid (marketable) interest-earning alternative to cash. (The term also lets you know where the "money market funds" took their name, though they deal in markets for other financial instruments, too.)

The huge volume of outstanding Treasury bills offers a readily available investment vehicle. The Federal Reserve, treasurers of large corporations, state and local governments, pension funds, and banks and other financial institutions can get into and out of the money market on a daily basis as their requirements for cash and their desire for an interest-earning alternative may dictate. This demand for Treasury bills fluctuates with the cycle.

As a general rule, cash holdings accumulate during and immediately after recession as demand and expenditures fall. Businesses, for instance, look for alternative uses for their funds as they curtail investment in new factories and machinery. As they enter the money market, seeking a return on idle funds, their demand for Treasury bills drives prices upward, and interest rates fall.

At the same time, bank lending falls and loans are repaid because neither consumers nor businesses have growing levels of expenditures that need financing. Free reserves accumulate, representing the banks' lost opportunity to generate earnings, so the banks invest in Treasury bills, and their purchases also push prices up and interest rates down. And if the Fed pursues an easy money policy at the same time in order to spur the economy, its purchase of bills (securities) will contribute to the interest rate decline. Hence, the general improvement in liquidity brought by the recession generates a growing demand for Treasury bills and a drop in their interest rate. Finally, a decline in Treasury bill rates will prompt investors to switch to other instruments, pushing their prices up and their rate of return down.

As the cycle develops from recovery to expansion, the demand for cash increases apace. The process is reversed: expenditures climb; Treasury bills are liquidated to obtain cash; and so interest rates climb, too. As bank lending recovers, free reserves disappear and banks are obliged to sell Treasury bills to generate reserves. If the Fed begins to pursue a tight money policy in order to restrain the growth in demand, its sale of securities (bills) will also contribute to the rise in interest rates. Market forces pull other interest rates along the same cyclical path. Investors are free to sell other instruments and buy Treasury bills when Treasury bill rates rise, thereby depressing the price and raising the return on the other instruments, too.

Thus the daily, secondary market in Treasury bills is the key market to follow in order to track short-term interest rates. *The Wall Street Journal* reports activity in this market each day, under the heading "Treasury Bonds, Notes & Bills." Find this table listed as "Treasury Issues," by using the index on the front page.

Look at the excerpt for April 8, 1986, on pages 45 and 46, keeping in mind that these bills are auctioned on Mondays, issued on Thursdays, and mature 13 weeks later (also on a Thursday). Thus, using the report for Monday, April 7, 1986, you know that the latest 90-day bill included in the report was auctioned on Monday, March 31, and issued on Thursday, April 3. It will mature 13 weeks later, on July 3 (7–3). On April 7 that bill carried an interest rate (bid) of 6.24 percent. This figure is located in the row opposite 7–3 under the column headed "Bid." That is, buyers (bidders) paid a price (less than $10,000) that would yield 6.24 percent if the Treasury bill were held to maturity and cashed in for $10,000. Sellers on May 20 were asking a higher price (lower interest rate) equivalent to 6.22 percent. The last column gives the interest rate on a 365-day (rather than a 360-day) basis. (The maturity dates other than 7–3 are for older bills and for bills with maturities of more than 90 days.)

TREASURY BONDS, NOTES & BILLS

Monday, April 7, 1986
Representative mid-afternoon Over-the-Counter quotations supplied by the Federal Reserve Bank of New York City, based on transactions of $1 million or more.
Decimals in bid-and-asked and bid changes represent 32nds; 101.1 means 101 1/32. a-Plus 1/64. b-Yield to call date. d-Minus 1/64. k-Nonresident aliens exempt from withholding taxes. n-Treasury notes. p-Treasury note: nonresident aliens exempt from withholding taxes.

Treasury Bonds and Notes

Rate	Mat. Date	Bid	Asked	Bid Chg.	Yld.
11¾s,	1986	Apr n	100.8	100.12 − .1	5.01
7⅞s,	1986	May n	100.2	100.6	5.80
9¼s,	1986	May n	100.7	100.11	5.69
12⅝s,	1986	May n	100.24	100.28	6.17
13¾s,	1986	May n	100.21	100.25 − .1	5.55
13s,	1986	Jun n	101.12	101.16	6.07
14⅞s,	1986	Jun n	101.25	101.29 − .1	6.10
12⅜s,	1986	Jul p	101.25	101.29	6.25
8s,	1986	Aug n	100.14	100.18	6.30
11⅜s,	1986	Aug n	101.18	101.22 − .1	6.39
12⅜s,	1986	Aug p	102.3	102.7	6.47
11⅞s,	1986	Sep n	102.12	102.16 − .1	6.44
12¼s,	1986	Sep n	102.18	102.22 − .1	6.41
11⅜s,	1986	Oct p	102.20	102.24	
6⅛s,	1986	Nov	99.21	100.21	7.96
10¾s,	1986	Nov p	102.7	10r 01.22	7.85
11s,	1986	Nov n	10c y.8 100		7.87
13⅞s,	1986	Nov n			
16⅛s,	1986	Nov n			
9⅞s,	1986	Dec n	.96		
10s,	1986	... .o.30	8.03		
9¾s,	10r-	...e.14 108.26	7.88		
9	...r6	109.20 109.24	7.90		
...10 12-97		94.20 95.8	7.72		
12.35 12-13		123.22 124.22	9.75		
12.65 3-14		126.14 127.14	9.77		
10.35 12-15		125.2 125.18	8.07		
8.20 3-16		102.6 102.18	7.97		

Federal Farm Credit

Rate	Mat	Bid	Asked	Yld
10.85	4-86	100.4	100.7	4.55

U.S. Treasury Bills

Rate of 90-Day Bills, 6.24%

		Bid	Asked	Yld
13.35	9-86	102.12	102.18	6.68
14.50	9-86	102.31	103.4	6.39
7.70	9-86	100.8	100.9	7.01
7.10	10-86	100.3	100.4	7.10
9.95	10-86	101.13	101.19	6.85
10.75	10-86	101.27	102	6.86
12.00	10-86	102.16	102.22	6.80
10.00	12-86	101.25	101.31	6.81
9.90	1-87	102.1	102.7	6.91
13.20	1-87	104.19	104.25	6.79
14.63	1-87	105.22	105.27	6.80
11.45	3-87	103.22	103.28	6.92
12.40	3-87	104.17	104.25	6.81
14.38	4-87	107.1	107.7	7.00
14.40	4-87	107.4	107.9	6.97
9.13	6-87	102.2	102.8	7.03
10.55	6-87	103.16	103.28	6.96
10.63	7-87	103.30	104.10	7.03
10.13	9-87	103.26	104.2	7.01
10.45	10-87	104.16	104.28	7.04
10.55	10-87	104.20	105	7.05
10.30	12-87	104.18	104.26	7.14
10.65	12-87	105.4	105.12	7.12
9.45	1-88	103.16	103.22	7.20
8.20	1-88	101.18	101.20	7.21
10.90	3-88	106.2	106.14	7.20
11.35	3-88	106.27	107.7	7.20
10.25	4-88	105.9	105.19	7.24
12.65	4-88	109.20	110	7.27
11.50	7-88	108.7	108.23	7.27
11.70	7-88	108.20	109.4	7.28
12.88	9-88	111.14	111.26	7.40
11.50	10-88	108.30	109.10	7.40
8.75	1-89	103.12	103.16	7.33
11.65	1-89	109.28	110.8	7.30
13.05	1-89	113.6	113.18	7.56
12.50	4-89	112.24	113.4	7.57
13.70	7-89	116.22	117.6	7.67
7.75	9-89	100.8	100.24	7.49
10.60	10-89	108.8	108.24	7.73
15.65	10-89	123.14	123.30	7.78
12.45	10-89	113.24	114.8	7.77
10.95	1-90	109.26	110.10	7.75

World Bank Bonds

Rate	Mat	Bid	Asked	Yld
8.38	7-86	99.21	100.1	8.05
12.76	9-86	101.4	101.16	8.10
16.38	11-86	103.20	104	8.10
7.80	12-86	99.16	99.28	8.05
14.63	12-86	103.8	103.20	8.10
7.65	5-87	99.4	99.16	8.10
10.38	3-87	101.13	101.25	8.10
7.75	8-87	99.9	99.21	8.00
9.23	9-87	101	101.12	8.10
13.45	9-87	106.27	107.7	8.20
10.38	3-88	104.18	104.30	7.6c
10.00	5-88	103.18	103.30	8.5c
13.00	12-88	115.6	115.18	8.50
11.00	10-89	107.28	108.8	8.30
4.50	2-90	89.5	89.17	7.65
5.38	7-91	87.1	87.13	8.35
16.63	11-91	136.10	136.22	8.35
15.13	12-91	128.18	128.30	8.65
5.38	4-92	84.13	84.25	8.65
14.75	6-92	129.21	130.1	8.45
13.63	9-92	125.12	125.24	8.40
10.90	3-93	113.6	113.20	8.30
10.38	5-93	110.13	110.25	8.25
5.88	9-93	83.26	84.6	8.80
6.50	3-94	86.10	86.22	8.80
6.38	10-94	84.5	84.17	9.00
11.63	12-94	118.21	119.1	8.50
8.63	8-95	97.18	97.30	8.95
8.13	8-96	94.3	94.15	8.95
9.35	12-00	103.8	103.20	8.90
8.85	7-01	101.9	101.21	8.65
8.38	12-01	97.8	97.20	8.65
8.25	5-02	96.5	96.17	8.65
8.35	8-02	97	97.12	8.65
12.38	10-02	129.31	130.11	8.85

Federal Land Bank

Rate	Mat	Bid	Asked	Yld
7.60	4-87	100.9	100.21	6.93
7.25	7-87	100.2	100.14	6.88
7.85	1-88	100.25	101.5	7.14
8.20	1-90	101.14	101.30	7.60
7.95	4-91	100.20	101.4	7.68
7.95	10-96	99.10	100.2	7.94
7.35	1-97	94.27	95.19	7.96

Inter-Amer. Devel. Bk.

Rate	Mat	Bid	Asked	Yld
14.00	12-86	103.23	104.3	8.15
10.75	8-87	102.21	103.1	8.15
15.00	4-89	116.17	116.29	8.62
5.20	1-92	85.13	85.25	8.40
14.63	8-92	129.13	129.25	8.50
6.50	11-92	90.8	90.20	8.40
12.13	10-93	116.28	117.8	8.10
6.63	11-93	89.13	89.25	8.50
13.25	8-94	126.25	127.5	8.65
11.63	12-94	118.8	118.20	8.55
11.38	5-95	117.9	117.21	8.55
8.63	10-95	99.26	100.6	8.60
9.00	2-01	101.21	102.1	8.75
8.75	7-01	99.20	100	8.75
8.75	3-88	94.12	94.24	8.75

Rate	Mat. Date	Bid	Asked	Bid Chg.	Yld.
10⅞s,	1987	Feb n	103.9	103.13 + .1	6.71
12¼s,	1987	Feb n	104.28	105 + .1	6.64
10¼s,	1987	Mar n	103.7	103.11 + .1	6.65
10¾s,	1987	Mar p	103.23	103.27 + .2	6.62
9¾s,	1987	Apr p	102.31	103.3 + .2	6.68
9⅛s,	1987	May p	102.14	102.18 + .2	6.76
12s,	1987	May n	105.12	105.16 + .2	6.73
12½s,	1987	May n	105.29	106.1 + .2	6.72
14s,	1987	May n	107.14	107.18 + .1	6.76
8½s,	1987	Jun p	101.28	102 + .1	6.78
10½s,	1987	Jun n	104.5	104.9 + .1	6.81
8⅞s,	1987	Jul p	102.14	102.18 + .2	6.80
8⅞s,	1987	Aug p	102.19	102.23 + .3	6.8c
12¾s,	1987	Aug p	106.28	107 + .2	
13¾s,	1987	Aug p	108.20	108 ..	7.92
9s,	1987	Sep p	10? .. − 1.6		7.93
11⅛s,	1987	Sep n	..v5.7 − .10		7.64
8⅞s,	1987	Oct n	.y.27 140.3 − .5		7.90
7⅜s,	1987	Nov n	127.29 128.5 − 1.6		7.89
8½s,	1987	Nor...	116.30 117.6 − .9		7.65
11s,	1987		99.7 99.23 − .4		7.65
12¾s,		Nov...	101.22 102.6 − .9		7.64
	...u3-08	Aug	106.3 106.11 − .19		7.71
..4s,	2003-08	Nov	109.3 109.11 − .26		7.77
9⅛s,	2004-09	May	112.15 112.23 − .29		7.80
10¾s,	2004-09	Nov	124.19 124.27 − .14		7.82
11¾s,	2005-10	Feb	137.8 137.16 − .13		7.89
10s,	2005-10	Nov	120.29 121.5 − .7		7.84
12¾s,	2005-10	Nov	147.13 147.21 − .14		7.92
13⅞s,	2006-11	Nov	161.1 161.9 − .20		7.92
14s,	2006-11	Nov	161.3 161.9 − .18		7.91
10⅜s,	2007-12	Nov	125.11 125.19 − .14		7.89
12s,	2008-13	Aug	142.17 142.25 − .2		7.91
13¼s,	2009-14	May	156.14 156.22 ...		7.88
12½s,	2009-14	Aug k	148.4 148.12 − .16		7.92
11¾s,	2009-14	Nov k	140.18 140.26 − .18		7.91
11¼s,	2015	Feb k	138.17 138.21 − .13		7.85
10⅝s,	2015	Aug k	131.30 132.2 − .26		7.82
9⅞s,	2015	Nov	124.10 124.14 − .7		7.83
9¼s,	2016	Feb k	120.4 120.8 − .8		7.54

U.S. Treas. Bills

Mat. date	Bid	Asked	Yield	Mat. date	Bid	Asked	Yield
-1986-	Discount			-1986-	Discount		
4-10	6.33	6.25	6.34	8- 7	6.19	6.15	6.37
4-17	7.13	7.09	7.20	8-14	6.19	6.15	6.38
4-24	6.49	6.43	6.54	8-21	6.23	6.19	6.43
5- 1	6.20	6.16	6.27	8-28	6.18	6.14	6.38
5- 8	6.20	6.16	6.28	9- 4	6.09	6.05	6.29
5-15	6.29	6.23	6.36	9-11	6.14	6.10	6.35
5-22	6.28	6.24	6.37	9-18	6.18	6.14	6.40
5-29	6.28	6.24	6.38	9-86	6.10	6.06	6.32
6- 5	6.25	6.21	6.36	10- 2	6.22	6.20	6.48
6-12	6.26	6.22	6.38	10-30	6.20	6.16	6.45
6-19	6.24	6.20	6.36	11-28	6.21	6.17	6.47
6-26	6.19	6.15	6.32	12-26	6.18	6.14	6.45
7- 3	6.24	6.22	6.40				
7-10	6.20	6.18	6.37	-1987-			
7-17	6.20	6.16	6.35	1-22	6.22	6.18	6.51
7-24	6.20	6.16	6.36	2-19	6.22	6.18	6.54
7-31	6.18	6.14	6.35	3-19	6.17	6.17	6.57

U.S. Treas. Bills Mat. date -1986-	Bid	Asked Discount	Yield	Mat. date -1986-	Bid	Asked Discount	Yield
4-10	6.33	6.25	6.34	8- 7	6.19	6.15	6.37
4-17	7.13	7.09	7.20	8-14	6.19	6.15	6.38
4-24	6.49	6.43	6.54	8-21	6.23	6.19	6.43
5- 1	6.20	6.16	6.27	8-28	6.18	6.14	6.38
5- 8	6.20	6.16	6.28	9- 4	6.09	6.05	6.29
5-15	6.29	6.23	6.36	9-11	6.14	6.10	6.35
5-22	6.28	6.24	6.37	9-18	6.18	6.14	6.40
5-29	6.28	6.24	6.38	9-86	6.10	6.06	6.32
6- 5	6.25	6.21	6.36	10- 2	6.22	6.20	6.48
6-12	6.26	6.22	6.38	10-30	6.20	6.16	6.45
6-19	6.24	6.20	6.36	11-28	6.21	6.17	6.47
6-26	6.19	6.15	6.32	12-26	6.18	6.14	6.45
7- 3	6.24	6.22	6.40	-1987-			
7-10	6.20	6.18	6.37	1-22	6.22	6.18	6.51
7-17	6.20	6.16	6.35	2-19	6.22	6.18	6.54
7-24	6.20	6.16	6.36	3-19	6.17	6.15	6.52
7-31	6.18	6.14	6.35				

On Monday, April 7, 1986, the 90-day Treasury bill rate on the open (secondary) market was 6.24 percent for bills auctioned on March 31 (Monday), issued on April 3 (Thursday), and maturing 13 weeks later on July 3 (Thursday).

The Wall Street Journal, *April 8, 1986*

You know from Chapter 4 that banks pay an interest rate, called the *discount rate,* when they borrow reserves from the Fed. Banks can borrow reserves from one another, too; the interest rate on such loans is called the *federal funds rate.*

Banks outside the main commercial centers of the nation often have more reserves than they need. They are therefore in a postition to lend reserves (called *federal funds*) on a day-to-day basis to large banks in the major commercial centers. This practice is profitable for lenders because they earn interest on funds that would otherwise be idle, and it is profitable for the large city banks because they acquire reserves that enable them to attract and hold borrowers, whose loyalty is important. Arrangements for the transfer of funds are made on the telephone by the banks.

The federal funds rate is published daily in the *Journal* under the heading "Money Rates"; check the front-page index for the page reference. Take the excerpt from the April 11, 1986, edition (see page 47) as a representative example.

Notice under **Federal Funds** in the "Money Rates" column on page 48 that four different percentages are listed: 7⅛ percent high, 7 percent low, 7 percent near closing bid, and 7⅟₁₆ percent offered. These numbers show that during trading on April 10, 1986, 7⅛ percent was the highest interest rate proposed by a potential lender bank, and 7 percent was the lowest interest rate bid by a prospective borrower. The last two percentages describe the state of trading near the end of the day: lender banks were offering 7⅟₁₆ percent, and borrower banks were still bidding 7 percent. Use the closing bid (7 percent) when following this interest rate. But beware: sharp fluctuations occur from day to day.

Federal Funds, 7%

Commercial Paper, 6.55%

Certificates of Deposit, 6.47%

MONEY RATES

Thursday, April 10, 1986
The key U.S. and foreign annual interest rates below are a guide to general levels but don't always represent actual transactions.

PRIME RATE: 9%. The base rate on corporate loans at large U.S. money center commercial banks.

FEDERAL FUNDS: 7⅛% high, 7% low, 7% near closing bid, 7 7/16% offered. Reserves traded among commercial banks for overnight use in amounts of $1 million or more. Source: Prebon Money Brokers Inc., N.Y.

DISCOUNT RATE: 7%. The charge on loans to depository institutions by the New York Federal Reserve Bank.

CALL MONEY: 8% to 8½%. The charge on loans to brokers on stock exchange collateral.

COMMERCIAL PAPER placed directly by General Motors Acceptance Corp.: 6.70% 30 to 59 days; 6.65% 60 to 89 days;6.55% 90 to 119 days; 6.45% 120 to 179 days; 6.40% 180 to 209 days; 6.35% 210 to 270 days.

COMMERCIAL PAPER: High-grade unsecured notes sold through dealers by major corporations in multiples of $1,000: 6.75% 30 days; 6.65% 60 days; 6.55% 90 days.

CERTIFICATES OF DEPOSIT: 6.47% one month; 6.47% two months; 6.47% three months; 6.41% six months; 6.47% one year. Typical rates paid by major banks on new issues of negotiable C.D.s, usually on amounts of $1 million and more. The minimum unit is $100,000.

BANKERS ACCEPTANCES: 6.67% 30 days; 6.47% 60 days; 6.42% 90 days; 6.39% 120 days; 6.37% 150 days; 6.34% 180 days. Negotiable, bank-backed business credit instruments typically financing an import order.

LONDON LATE EURODOLLARS: 7% to 6⅞% one month; 7% to 6⅞% two months; 6 15/16% to 6 13/16% three months; 6 15/16% to 6 13/16% four months; 6 15/16% to 6 13/16% five months; 6 15/16% to 6 13/16% six months.

LONDON INTERBANK OFFERED RATES (LIBOR): 6⅞% three months; 6⅞% six months; 6 15/16% one year. The average of interbank offered rates for dollar deposits in the London market based on quotations at five major banks.

FOREIGN PRIME RATES: Canada 12%; Germany 7.25%; Japan 5.69%; Switzerland 6%; Britain 11½%. These rate indications aren't directly comparable; lending practices vary widely by location. Source: Morgan Guaranty Trust Co.

TREASURY BILLS: Results of the Monday, April 7, 1986, auction of short-term U.S. government bills, sold at a discount from face value in units of $10,000 to $1 million: 6.19% 13 weeks; 6.17% 26 weeks.

FEDERAL HOME LOAN MORTGAGE CORP. (Freddie Mac): Posted yields on 30-year mortgage commitments for delivery within 30 days. 9.66%, standard conventional fixed-rate mortgages; 8.375%, 5/2 rate capped one-year adjustable rate mortgages.

FEDERAL NATIONAL MORTGAGE ASSOCIATION (Fannie Mae): Posted yields on 30 year mortgage commitments for delivery within 30 days (priced at par). 9.375%, standard conventional fixed rate-mortgages; 8.35%, 5/2 rate capped one-year adjustable rate mortgages.

MERRILL LYNCH READY ASSETS TRUST: 7.71%. Annualized average rate of return after expenses for the past 30 days; not a forecast of future returns.

The Wall Street Journal, *April 11, 1986*

The rates on **Commercial Paper** and **Certificates of Deposit** are important also, and you can track them under "Money Rates" as well. Note in the excerpt on page 48 that 6.55 percent was the going rate on 90-day commercial paper on April 10, 1986. Commercial paper is unsecured debt issued by the very largest corporations. These giant companies are able to go to investors for short-term funds in much the same manner as the U.S. Treasury. Commercial paper is the private equivalent of the Treasury bill, so in order to attract investors, its rate of interest has to be higher. Corporations issue commercial paper to avoid the higher interest rate (prime rate) levied by banks on business borrowers.

Certificates of deposit (CDs) are issued by large commercial banks in denominations of $100,000. They are like savings accounts for which the investor receives a "certificate of deposit" from the bank. The investor,

Excerpt from Page 47 ⟶ **FEDERAL FUNDS:** 7⅛% high, 7% low, 7% near closing bid, 7 1/16% offered. Reserves traded among commercial banks for overnight use in amounts of $1 million or more. Source: Prebon Money Brokers Inc., N.Y.

Excerpt from Page 47 ⟶ **COMMERCIAL PAPER** placed directly by General Motors Acceptance Corp.: 6.70% 30 to 59 days; 6.65% 60 to 89 days;6.55% 90 to 119 days; 6.45% 120 to 179 days; 6.40% 180 to 209 days; 6.35% 210 to 270 days.
COMMERCIAL PAPER: High-grade unsecured notes sold through dealers by major corporations in multiples of $1,000: 6.75% 30 days; 6.65% 60 days; 6.55% 90 days.

however, may sell the certificate of deposit to another investor before the 90-day term of maturity is over, and the rate of interest will reflect current market conditions. Banks issue certificates of deposit to compete with Treasury bills and commercial paper for the investor's dollar.

In the example below, the reported percentages reflect the interest rates offered by banks on April 10, 1986, for different terms of deposit. Notice that the 90-day CD carried with it an interest rate of 6.47 percent, and that this rate is usually very close to the 90-day commercial paper rate.

Excerpt from Page 47 ⟶ **CERTIFICATES OF DEPOSIT:** 6.47% one month; 6.47% two months; 6.47% three months; 6.41% six months; 6.47% one year. Typical rates paid by major banks on new issues of negotiable C.D.s, usually on amounts of $1 million and more. The minimum unit is $100,000.

On Tuesdays, under the heading "Key Interest Rates," the *Journal* will report the weekly average of these interest rates. See the example on pages 41 and 49 from the April 8, 1986, edition of the *Journal*. In the week ended April 4, 1986, Treasury bills averaged 6.31 percent; commercial paper, 7.02 percent; CDs, 7.02 percent; and federal funds, 7.39 percent.

But this discussion of short-term interst rates would be incomplete if it did not include a description of how you can compare the yield on your own interest-earning investments with market rates.

On Thursday or Friday of each week, the *Journal* publishes the "Banxquote Deposit Index" together with "High Yield Savings" and "High

Key Interest Rates

Annualized interest rates on certain investments as reported by the Federal Reserve Board on a weekly-average basis:

	Week Ended: Apr. 4, 1986	Mar. 28, 1986
Treasury bills (90 day)-a	6.31	6.39
Commrcl paper (Dealer, 90 day)-a	7.02	7.13
Certfs of Deposit (Resale, 90 day)	7.02	7.16
Federal funds (Overnight)-b	7.39	7.25
Eurodollars (90 day)-b	7.23	7.43
Treasury bills (one year)-c	6.67	6.89
Treasury notes (three year)-c	7.03	7.19
Treasury notes (five year)-c	7.22	7.36
Treasury notes (ten year)-c	7.39	7.63
Treasury bonds (20 year)-c	7.54	7.93
Treasury bonds (30 year)-c	7.47	7.81

a-Discounted rates. b-Week ended Wednesday, April 2, 1986 and Wednesday, March 26, 1986. c-Yields, adjusted for constant maturity.

The Wall Street Journal, *April 8, 1986*

Yield Jumbos." The excerpt from the April 11, 1986, *Journal,* on pages 50 and 51, provides an example. The deposit index lets you compare the yield you can earn on a variety of accounts at different maturities with the average earned nationally and in six key states. The savings figures make the comparison with specific insitutions for accounts requiring a small minimum balance, while the jumbos cover minimum balances of $100,000. On April 9, 1986, the national average for bank money market and 30-day accounts was 6.54 percent.

A separate listing, "Consumer Savings Rates," prepared by the Bank Rate Monitor, appears on Thursdays. See the example from the April 10, 1986, *Journal* on pages 52 and 53. It compares the average rate paid by 100 banks on the previous day for a variety of accounts. According to this report, money market deposits were paying 6.45 percent on April 9, 1986.

In the early 80s, when the federal government applied its chokehold on the economy and interest rates climbed to the sky, money market mutual funds became extremely popular among investors and savers. These funds pooled the capital of small savers by offering shares for small minimum amounts, and investing the capital in T-bills, CDs, commercial paper, and other liquid assets usually denominated in large amounts and not available to the small saver. Since, at the time, banks

BANXQUOTE® DEPOSIT INDEX

Wednesday, April 9, 1986

Savings yields of major banks in key states

	MMA*	30 days	60 days	90 days	Six Months	One Year	2½ Years	5 Years
NEW YORK								
Avg.	6.72%	6.72%	6.72%	6.89%	7.14%	7.25%	7.54%	7.93%
CALIFORNIA								
Avg.	6.24%	6.00%	6.00%	6.55%	6.85%	7.13%	7.32%	7.75%
PENNSYLVANIA								
Avg.	6.35%	6.25%	6.25%	6.64%	6.78%	6.80%	6.99%	7.50%
ILLINOIS								
Avg.	6.86%	6.55%	6.55%	6.62%	7.13%	7.24%	7.47%	7.73%
TEXAS								
Avg.	6.55%	6.98%	6.92%	6.90%	6.88%	7.00%	7.25%	7.68%
FLORIDA								
Avg.	6.53%	6.45%	6.60%	6.88%	7.22%	7.56%	8.02%	8.17%
National								
Avg.	6.54%	6.54%	6.55%	6.76%	7.00%	7.16%	7.42%	7.78%
Wkly Chng	−0.04	−0.07	−0.08	−0.08	−0.13	−0.12	−0.13	−0.09

*Money Market Accounts.   z-Unavailable.

Each depositor is insured by the Federal Deposit Insurance Corp. (FDIC) or Federal Savings and Loan Insurance Corp. (FSLIC) up to $100,000 per institution.

Methods of compounding (continuously, daily, weekly, monthly, quarterly, semiannually, annually or simple interest), minimum balance requirements, number of days in one year (360 or 365), interest payment schedule and other conditions vary among institutions. Effective annual yield can be influenced by these factors, which should be carefully evaluated to obtain a valid rate comparison.

The information included in this table has been obtained directly from the participating institutions, but the accuracy and validity cannot be guaranteed. Rates are subject to change. Yields, terms and creditworthiness should be verified before investing.

HIGH YIELD SAVINGS

Small minimum balance, generally $500 to $2,500

		...eid
		9.55%
ο./5%	9.14%
......	8.75%	9.14%
...un Texas	8.75%	9.14%
	8.75%	9.04%

Savings Money Market Accounts	Rate	Yield
Citisavings, San Antonio Texas	8.38%	8.74%
Meridiain Svgs, Arlington Texas	8.00%	8.45%
OBA Federal, WWashington DC	8.00%	8.??
Vista Federal, Reston Va	8.00%	..ɔ%
Colonial Nat'l Bank,Wilmington De ..	? ˮ	8.00%

Six M...	Rate	Yield
M... ..avings CDs		
...dian Fed, Bridgeport Ct	9.25%	9.69%
Killeen Svgs, Killeen Texas	9.25%	9.69%
Laurel Svgs, Laurel Md	9.15%	9.58%
Peoples Svgs, Llano Texas	9.00%	9.55%
Ramona Svgs, Orange Ca	9.00%	9.55%

30-Day Savings CDs		
Skyline Savings, Dalla˟		
Benjamin Frankl˟		
Pacific Co˟˟˟		
Char˟˟	.ɿ0%	8.00%

HIGH YIELD JUMBOS

Large minimum balance, generally $100,000.

Jumbo Money Market Accounts	Rate	Yield
Citisavings, San Antonio Texas	8.38%	8.74%
Vista Federal, Reston Va	8.25%	8.57%
Meridian Svgs, Arlington Texas	8.00%	8.45%
OBA Federal, Washington DC	8.00%	8.33%
Alice Svgs, Alice Texas	8.00%	8.30%

Six Months Jumbo CDs	Rate	Yield
Western Svgs, Phoenix Az	8.10%	8.35%
Ben Milam Svgs, Cameron Texas	8.35%	8.35%
Home Svgs, Midland Texas	8.25%	8.25%
Vista Svgs, Odessa Texas	8.25%	8.25%
Bayou Fed, New Orleans La	8.25%	8.25%

30-Day Jumbo CDs	Rate	Yield
Benjamin Franklin, Houston	7.70%	7.98%
Western Svgs, Phoenix Az	7.65%	7.87%
Plaza Bank, Del Rio Texas	7.75%	7.75%
Vista Svgs, Odessa Texas	7.75%	7.75%
Universal Svgs, Chickasha Ok	7.75%	7.75%

One Year Jumbo CDs	Rate	Yield
Benjamin Franklin, Houston	8.20%	8.60%
Home Svgs, Midland Texas	8.50%	8.50%
Meridian Svgs, Arlington Texas	8.50%	8.50%
Vista Svgs, Odessa Texas	8.50%	8.50%
Pan American Svgs,San Francisco	8.50%	8.50%

60-Day Jumbo CDs	Rate	Yield
Benjamin Franklin, Houston	7.70%	7.98%
Creditbanc Svgs, Austin Texas	7.75%	7.75%
Plaza Bank, Del Rio Texas	7.75%	7.75%
Vista Svgs, Odessa Texas	7.75%	7.75%
University Svgs, Houston	7.75%	7.75%

2½ Years Jumbo CDs	Rate	Yield
Guardian Fed, Bridgeport Ct	8.50%	8.87%
Home Svgs, Midland Texas	8.75%	8.75%
Great American, Corinth Ms	8.63%	8.63%
Provident Bank, Boston	8.30%	8.62%
Benjamin Franklin, Houston	8.20%	8.60%

90-Day Jumbo CDs	Rate	Yield
Ben Milam Svgs, Cameron Texas	8.25%	8.25%
Benjamin Franklin, Houston	8.00%	8.24%
Western Svgs, Phoenix Az	7.85%	8.08%
Victoria Svgs, Victoria Texas	8.00%	8.00%
Vista Svgs, Odessa Texas	8.00%	8.00%

5 Years Jumbo CDs	Rate	Yield
Guardian Fed, Bridgeport Ct	9.25%	9.69%
Guaranty First Trust,Waltham Ma ...	9.00%	9.31%
Home Svgs, Midland Texas	9.25%	9.25%
Killeen Svgs, Killeen Texas	9.25%	9.25%
Great American, Corinth Ms	9.15%	9.15%

Source: BANXQUOTE ONLINE, New York.
BANXQUOTE is a registered trademark and service mark of MASTERFUND INC.

The Wall Street Journal, *April 11, 1986*

| | National Avg. | 6.54% | 6.54% | 6.55% | 6.76% | 7.00% | 7.16% | 7.42% | 7.78% |
| Excerpt from Page 50 ──▶ | Wkly Chng | −0.04 | −0.07 | −0.08 | −0.08 | −0.13 | −0.12 | −0.13 | −0.09 |

The Wall Street Journal, *April 9, 1986*

and savings and loan companies were prohibited from offering above-passbook rates to small depositors, huge sums poured into the money market funds as interest rates climbed. As the interest rate ceilings were removed from small denomination accounts at banks and savings and loan companies, and these accounts began to offer rates that moved with market conditions, some investors deserted the money market funds.

You can see, however, from the excerpt from the April 11, 1986, *Journal,* on pages 53 and 54, that the money market funds still have over $200 billion in assets. Each week, usually on Friday, the *Journal* presents a chart depicting the funds' assets together with an article reporting their yield in the latest week.

In the week ending Tuesday, April 8, 1986, the seven-day yield averaged 6.76 percent and the 30-day yield averaged 6.87 percent, while the average maturity of the investments in the funds (T-bills, CDs, commercial paper, etc.) was 47 days. Money market funds paid slightly more than banks. (Compare excerpts at the top of this page and the top of page 54.)

You can track the performance of your money market mutual fund and most others with a report that appears in the *Journal* on Thursday or Friday and covers the average maturity, yield, and value of assets as of the previous Wednesday. (See excerpts on pages 54 and 55.)

Thus, the April 11, 1986, *Journal* reported that Value Line Cash Management funds had an average maturity of 69 days, an effective yield of 7.14 percent, and assets of $443.6 million. That beat the average for banks and money market funds.

Finally, each Monday the *Journal* reports a variety of interest rates under "Buying and Borrowing," including two bank money market deposit accounts. In the April 7, 1986, excerpt on pages 56 and 57 you can see a report on corporate bond and mortgage interest rate yields, too.

Chart 6–1 on page 58 presents the relationship among Treasury bills, federal funds, and prime interest rates since World War II. Compare the record with Chart 4–1 on page 24. In the earlier chart you saw the impact of the business cycle and Federal Reserve policy on net free reserves and net borrowed reserves. As business activity expanded (and the Fed tightened up), banks borrowed reserves from the Fed. When recession brought easier credit conditions (and the Fed provided the banking system

Interest Rates Drop as Optimism Grows
Fed Will Soon Reduce Its Discount Rate

CREDIT
MARKETS

By Edward P. Foldessy
And Tom Herman
Staff Reporters of The Wall Street Journal.

NEW YORK—Interest rates continued to fall yesterday, reflecting increased optimism among investors that the Federal Reserve System will soon cut its discount rate.

Evidence is mounting that the central bank already has eased its credit policy to pave the way for another reduction in the discount rate, many analysts contend. They say the Fed wants to drive down interest rates further in an attempt to keep the economic expansion from fizzling.

The discount rate, which is the fee the Fed charges on loans to banks and savings institutions, was reduced to 7% from 7½% March 7. The move was part of a carefully orchestrated global effort to lower interest rates.

Another round of international interest rate cuts may be in the offing. Economic officials from leading industrial nations, in a series of Washington meetings this week, generally agreed that a further drop in interest rates would be benefici... ..pared stopped short of a form... ..sday. As resing rates down. S... ...ed April 2, the funds several n... ..39%. bef...

...ute Evidence'

Analysts have been especially encouraged by the fact that the Fed hasn't taken any overt action to prevent the slide in the funds rate. This offers "definite evidence" that the Fed eased its credit stance at the April 1 meeting of the Federal Open Market Committee, the central bank's policy-making arm, said William V. Sullivan ... a senior vice president of Dean ... ...ent's nolds Inc.

Only the "tim... ...er, compared with discount ... ...nnual rate of increase of ti... ...e first quarter. As a result, bond ...elds are likely to fall, he said, predicting the yield on the Treasury's 30-year bonds, currently about 7.30%, will go below 7% "within a month."

Yesterday, prices of some actively traded Treasury bonds rose more than a half point, or over $5 for each $1,000 face amount of securities. That followed a three-point jump Tuesday.

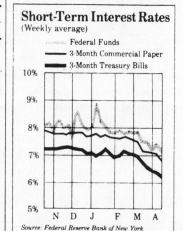

Short-Term Interest Rates
(Weekly average)

Source: *Federal Reserve Bank of New York*

March. That would leave M2 we... the Fed's target range whe... ...ne weekly depicted in the tra... ...s implied by the ion. An incre... ...he middle column con- is gen... ...es already reported, in billions ... ...ollars:

Week Ended	Lower	Actual	Upper
Feb.24	$625.2	$634.1	$633.6
March3	625.6	631.9	634.5
March10	625.9	637.5	635.5
March17	626.3	638.3	636.4
March24	626.6	639.3	637.4
March31	627.0	....	638.3
April7	627.4	....	639.3
April14	627.7	....	640.2

The M1 measure consists of checki... deposits and cash held by the n... ... includes everything in M... ... types of savings, s... ...iterest rates this deposit acc... ...ed many companies to lower ... ...ie bond market to pay off older, ...e expensive financing.

Consumer Savings Rates

Money Market Deposits-a	6.45%
Super-NOW Accounts-a	5.83%
Six-month Certificates-a	7.04%
One-year Certificates-a	7.27%
Thirty-month Accounts-a	7.54%
Five-Year Certificates-a	7.92%
U.S. Savings Bonds-b	8.36%

a-Average rate paid yesterday by 100 large banks and thrifts in the 10 largest metropolitan areas as compiled by Bank Rate Monitor
b-Current annual yield. Guaranteed minimum 7.5%.

Consumer Savings Rates

Money Market Deposits-a	6.45%
Super-NOW Accounts-a	5.83%
Six-month Certificates-a	7.04%
One-year Certificates-a	7.27%
Thirty-month Accounts-a	7.54%
Five-Year Certificates-a	7.92%
U.S. Savings Bonds-b	8.36%

a-Average rate paid yesterday by 100 large banks and thrifts in the 10 largest metropolitan areas as compiled by Bank Rate Monitor.
b-Current annual yield. Guaranteed minimum 7.5%.

The Wall Street Journal, *April 10, 1986*

Money Fund Assets Post Biggest Rise Since January '85

By CHARLES W. STEVENS
Staff Reporter of THE WALL STREET JOURNAL

NEW YORK—Money market fund assets posted their biggest jump since January 1985, reflecting profit-taking in the stock market.

The assets of the nation's 360 money funds grew $4.83 billion to $221.99 billion in the week ended Wednesday, according to the Investment Company Institute, a Washington-based trade association.

Alfred Johnson, vice president and chief economist of the group, cited last week's sell-off in equities for the large jump in money fund assets. "With stock prices retreating from their high level last week, some investors may have taken profits and channeled them into broker-dealer and general purpose money market funds," he said.

Meanwhile, according to Mr. Johnson, "continued declines in interest rates on short-term securities available in the market increased the attractiveness" of money funds to institutions. Money funds are attractive when interest rates are falling since they provide longer maturities than

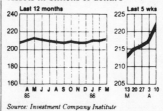

Money Market Funds
Assets in billions of dollars

Source: Investment Company Institute

some short-term securities.

Last week's bulge in money fund assets was the sixth consecutive week in which assets rose, and the second consecutive week that the assets of all categories of funds showed gains, the association said.

Assets of the 188 general purpose funds climbed $315.6 million to $60.17 billion; assets of the 87 broker-dealer funds increased $1.54 billion to $101.14 billion; and assets of the 85 institutional funds leaped $2.97 billion to $60.68 billion, the institute said.

The average seven-day yield for funds in the week ended Tuesday fell to 6.76% from 6.88% a week earlier, according to Donoghue's Money Fund Report, a Hollis-ton, Mass.-based newsletter. The average 30-day yield for funds dropped to 6.87% from 6.94%, and the average maturity of funds slipped to 47 days from 48 days.

Money Market Funds Yield

The Wall Street Journal, *April 11, 1986*

Excerpt from Page 53 ⟶

The average seven-day yield for funds in the week ended Tuesday fell to 6.76% from 6.88% a week earlier, according to Donoghue's Money Fund Report, a Holliston, Mass.-based newsletter. The average 30-day yield for funds dropped to 6.87% from 6.94%, and the average maturity of funds slipped to 47 days from 48 days.

The Wall Street Journal, *April 11, 1986*

MONEY MARKET MUTUAL FUNDS

The following quotations, collected by the National Association of Securities Dealers Inc., represent the average of annualized yields and dollar-weighted portfolio maturities ending Wednesday, April 9, 1986. Yields are based on actual dividends to shareholders.

Fund	Avg. Mat.	7Day YLD.	7Day EFF.	Assets
AARP Money	(z)	(z)		
ActvAsst GovSc	62	6.63	6.85	194.3
ActvAsst Money	63	7.09	7.34	2313.6
ActvAsst TxFr	25	4.36	4.33	1029.6
AlexBCash Gvt	34	6.82	7.06	169.4
AlexBCash Prm	33	6.95	7.19	688.2
Alliance Capital	41	6.57	6.79	919.6
AllianceGvt Res	35	6.17	6.36	224.4
Alliance TaxEx	90	4.50	4.60	636.0
AmCap Resrv a	16	6.23	6.43	216.4
Am Genl MM a	(z)	(z)		
Amer Natl MM	16	6.81	7.04	14.3
AMEV Money	27	6.71	6.94	75.3
AT Ohio Tax Fr	79	4.22	4.31	145.4
AutomCash Mgt	46	7.10	7.35	788.8
AutomGvt MTr	47	6.74	6.97	1407.8
Babson Prime	25	6.62	6.84	56.0
BenhamCal TF	27	3.98	3.98	149.0
BenhamNatl TF	31	4.53	4.57	38.8
BirrWilson MFd	27	6.14		
BLC Cash Mgt	17	6.53	6.74	41.6
Boston Co Cash	39	6.89	7.13	241.9
BostonCo Gvt	45	6.42	6.63	22.9
BostonCo Mass	75	4.29	4.38	117.2
Bull&Bear DRs	58	6.89	7.13	77.0
CalvrtSocInv af	34	6.67	6.89	54.9
CalvertTF Rsrv	106	4.76	4.87	450.3
CAM Fund	23	6.33	6.54	44.2
CapCash MgtTr	17	6.86	7.10	95.3
Cap Preservtn	61	6.74	7.00	1828.0
Cap Preservtn 2	2	6.61	6.64	439.7
Capital T MM	44	6.75	6.98	192.4
Cap T ins MM	32	6.34	6.54	50.1
Capitl T TxFr	52	4.00	4.08	42.4
CardGovt SecTr	4	6.81	7.04	435.2
Cardinal TEMT	34	4.19	4.28	60.5
CarngieGov Sec	40	6.67	6.89	148.0
CarnegieTax Fr	34	4.45	4.55	291.5
Cash&Plus Fed	30	6.96	7.21	93.6
Cash&Plus MM	40	7.31	7.58	334.7
CashAssett Tr	29	6.79	7.02	81.5
Cash Equiv MM	36	7.00	7.25	5437.3
CashEq GovSec	19	6.91	7.15	604.4
CshMgt TrAm a	17	6.83	7.07	613.6
Cash Rsv Mgt a	41	7.21	7.47	4031.0
CBA Money Fd	83	7.63	7.93	90.9
Centenl GovtTr	40	6.49	6.70	75.5
CentennlMM Tr	35	6.70	6.93	174.8
Centennial Tax	46	4.24	4.33	436.6
Churchill Cash	12	6.71	6.94	77.8
Cigna Cash Fd	48	6.83	7.06	
CignaMM Fd b	55	6.93	7.17	
Cigna TxEx	68	4.55	4.65	
CimcoMM Trst	43	6.98	7.22	20.3
CMA GovtSec a	71	7.56	7.85	1956.6
CMA MnyFd a	68	7.23	7.50	18484.0
CMA Tax Ex	69	4.35	4.45	7351.1
Col Daily Inc af	28	6.77	7.00	423.6
Colonial MnyM	18	6.46	6.67	9.9
CommMnyF a	47	7.08	7.33	1207.6
Comp Cash M a	24	6.46	6.67	132.6
ConnDaily TF	56	4.09	4.15	124.5
Cortland GnMM	38	6.63	6.85	162.0
Cortland TxFr c	48	3.87	3.95	29.9
Cortland USGv	36	6.15	6.35	31.9
CountryCp MM	22	6.43	6.63	22.4
Current Interest	38	6.62	6.84	924.3
CurrentIn TxFr	51	4.26	4.35	111.6
CurrentInt USG	37	6.41	6.62	84.4
Daily cash Fd1	40	6.80	7.03	2452.8
DailyDollar Rs	43	6.93	6.97	217.1
Daily Incm Fd	57	6.90	7.01	497.7
DailyTaxFree c	52	4.43	4.51	1170.7
DBL GvtSc Prtf	65	6.79	7.02	244.1
DBL MM Portf	55	7.04	7.29	1500.8
DBL Tax Free	46	4.61	4.71	582.9
[illegible]WS Liqd Asset	64	7.09	7.34	6721.4

Fund	Avg. Mat.	7Day YLD.	7Day EFF.	Assets
DWS TF Daily	27	4.40	4.49	974.4
DWS USGvtMM	65	6.51	6.72	440.3
DelaCashRsrv f	61	6.89	7.13	1281.6
DelaTaxFr MF	73	4.40	4.50	72.3
DelaTreas Rsrv	67	6.43	6.64	51.5
DreyfsInst Govt	75	6.99	7.24	965.2
DreyfsInst MM	38	7.16	7.42	630.6
DreyfsLiq Asst	44	7.10	7.35	7716.9
DryfusGvt Sers	83	6.77	7.00	989.5
DryfMnyMk Ser	44	7.00	7.25	665.0
DryTaxEx MM	47	4.49	4.59	2697.2
EatonVan Cash	33	6.83	6.96	208.9
EatonV TF Res	48	4.54	4.68	48.7
EGT MMTrust f	48	6.52	6.73	65.5
Empire TxFr	85	4.07	4.13	150.3
Equit MMkt Ac	52	6.71	6.97	203.8
Fahnestock Dly	3	6.62	6.86	144.3
FBL MnMkFd b	19	6.02	6.20	25.8
FedMaster Trst	48	7.14		2908.6
FedrtTaxFree c	42	4.47		3986.7
FidelCal TaxFr	51	4.12	4.21	103.2
FidelCash Resv	39	6.89	7.13	4230.5
FidelDlyIncm b	39	6.89	7.13	2465.0
FidUS Govt Res	51	6.72	6.95	483.3
FidMM USTrea	46	6.91	7.15	264.0
FidMM Domstc	35	7.20	7.46	1284.5
FidMM Govmnt	41	7.11	7.37	733.1
FidMass TaxFr	38	4.23	4.36	276.5
FidNYTxF MM	83	4.08	4.16	151.0
FidTaxExmpt c	55	4.84	4.96	3525.2
FnclDlyInc Shr	17	6.65	6.87	186.2
FnclPlanFed Sc	35	1.80	2.56	2.5
FstAm Money	33	7.39	7.66	54.3
FirstInstTax Ex	60	4.43	4.52	38949.7
FstInvCshMgt f	22	6.56	6.76	283930.3
First Variable	53	6.72	6.95	526.6
Flex Fund MM	20	7.07	7.32	34.9
Founders MMk	13	6.54	6.75	20.0
Frnk CATEMF	51	4.27		
Franklin FedMF	1	6.26		
FrnklnMnyFd a	30	6.64		
Frnkln TaxEx c	62	4.64		
Fund For TxFr	73	4.40	4.50	30.8
FundGov Invst	49	6.51	6.61	724.9
GenlGovt Secur	78	6.53	6.74	140.8
GenlMoney Mkt	44	6.81	7.04	565.8
GenlTxEx MM	64	4.54	4.64	584.2
GovtInvstTrst a	30	6.67	6.90	229.7
GovtSecur Cash	5	5.81	5.98	9.7
Gradison Cash	52	6.69	6.82	436.3
GradisonUS Gv	26	6.21	6.32	26.8
GuardCsh Mgt	22	6.53	6.74	22.3
Guard CashFd	24	6.87	7.11	65.2
Heritg Cash Tr	(z)	(z)		
Hilliard Gov't	4	6.39	9.06	99.8
Hutton AMA Fd	41	7.22	7.48	2073.0
Hutton Govt Fd	42	6.84	7.08	1070.0
IDS Cash Mngt	38	6.95	7.19	843.2
IDS Stratgy Fd	39	5.88	6.05	8.1
IDS TxFrMny c	79	4.08	4.16	92.0
IntegrtMM Sec	31	6.66	6.89	176.8
Inv Csh Resv	50	6.60	6.85	43.7
JohnHanc Cash	45	6.56	6.78	330.0
JonesDly Pssp f	47	6.67	6.89	661.6
Kempr Gvt MM	17	6.66	6.88	86.9
Kemper MnyM	37	7.24	7.50	4680.2
Keystone LiqTr	45	6.54	6.75	200.3
KidderP GovtM	40	6.59	6.83	221.0
KidderP PrmAc	37	6.97	7.22	586.0
KidderP TaxEx	78	4.59	4.71	806.7
Lndmrk Cash	52	6.79	7.02	146.3
LndmrkTF Rsv	54	4.28	4.37	128.9
Lndmrk NYTF	90	4.13	4.21	150.0
LeggMasn Csh f	39	6.69	6.91	267.1
Lazard CashM	24	7.02	7.27	714.2
Lazard Govt	7	6.92	7.16	474.8
Lazard TxFree	60	4.56	4.66	479.7
LehmnM CshRs	39	7.11	7.36	278.1
LehmnM GvSec	34	6.68	6.90	44.6
LehmM TF Rsv	72	4.49	4.59	142.9
LexGvtScMM a	6	6.35	6.56	15.7
LexMoneyMkt a	26	6.79	7.02	224.3
LexTaxFrDly c	103	4.64	4.74	90.5

Fund	Avg. Mat.	7Day YLD.	7Day EFF.	Assets
LFRoth EarnLq	16	6.78	7.01	446.3
LF Roth Exmpt	21	4.29	4.38	124.5
LibrtyCash Mgt	27	6.23	6.43	37.2
LibertyUS Govt	48	6.35	6.55	2051.5
LiquidCapitl Tr	20	6.69	6.91	1252.4
LiquidCAshTR f	2	7.17		913.6
LiquidGrn TxFr	79	4.39	4.49	30.4
LiquidGreen Tr	37	6.73	6.95	190.0
LordAbbet Cash	29	6.62	6.85	181.5
LuthBrMon Mkt	45	6.56	6.77	389.2
MAP GovtFund	48	6.95	7.19	21.5
Mariner Cash	29	7.02	7.27	622.1
Mariner Govt	16	6.85	7.09	365.5
Mariner TxFree	46	4.22	4.31	89.9
MarinerUS Trs	24	6.71	6.94	109.8
MassCashMgt a	52	6.88	7.12	599.4
MasaCshM Trst	38	6.48	6.71	38.1
MassMtl Liquid	31	6.86	7.09	40.5
McDonald MM	29	6.42	6.63	149.4
McDonald TxE	61	4.31	4.40	102.8
MerrLGovtFd a	49	6.63	6.85	1496.5
MerrLInstFd af	45	7.18	7.44	1520.7
MerlInst TxEx	38	4.43	4.53	523.3
MerrLRdyAst a	66	7.19	7.45	12238.2
MerrLRetRsv a	69	7.27	7.54	2442.3
Merrl USA Gr	72	7.33	7.60	237.5
Met NYTF	24	4.51	4.61	100.0
MidwstGrp TF	67	4.61	4.72	131.4
Midwst Incm Tr	48	6.25	6.45	135.0
Midwst IT Cash	22	6.41	6.62	44.0
MnyMgtP Govt	36	6.52	6.73	6.6
MnyMgtP Pr	45	6.70	6.93	21.5
MnyMgtPl TxF	103	4.56	4.67	77.7
MoneyMrkt Fd	15	6.71	6.84	24.7
MoneyMktMgt f	48	6.84	7.07	236.7
Money Mkt Trst	42	7.11		193.6
MorganKeegn f	44	6.53	6.74	85.1
MuniCashRsv c	66	4.73	4.85	1998.0
MuniFundInv c	42	4.55	4.65	1950.9
MtlOmCash Res	35	6.51		
MtlOmMny Mkt	40	6.68		
Natl Cash Resv	31	6.10	6.29	25.9
NEL Cash Mngt	54	6.89	7.13	748.0
NEL TxEx MM	61	4.50	4.60	48.0
NEL US Govt	81	6.72	6.95	43.0
ThMcK NtlGovt	27	6.50	6.72	47.3
ThMcK Ntl MM	29	6.86	7.10	1888.7
ThMcK Ntl TxE	69	4.49	4.59	286.6
Nationwide MM	(z)	(z)		
NeubrgBer Gov	50	6.35	6.54	94.5
Neuberger TxF	59	4.34	4.44	122.9
Newton Money	46	7.15	7.41	30.1
NLR Cash Port	34	6.95	7.19	1320.0
NLR Govt Prt	36	6.67	6.89	97.0
NuveenTaxEx c	45	4.64	4.75	2307.1
Nuveen TaxFr	40	4.39	4.49	220.5
NuveenTF Acct	28	4.39	4.48	269.9
Oppn Mny Mrkt	40	6.78	7.02	725.1
Oxford CshMgt	16	6.91	7.15	149.0
PacHrzGov MM	79	6.86	7.10	896.7
PacHrzMM Prt	19	7.01	7.26	515.9
PacHrz TaxEx	40	4.07	4.15	57.8
PW Cash	36	6.92	7.16	4211.2
[illegible]	[illegible]	3.71	3.78	266.9
[illegible]	[illegible]	6.69	6.91	132.8
[illegible]	[illegible]	6.79	[illegible]	[illegible]
[illegible]	[illegible]	6.95	7.19	169.6
[illegible]	[illegible]	6.51	6.61	280.1
[illegible]	47	7.05	7.18	3741.0
PrudB TaxFr c	82	4.69	4.70	603.4
PutnamDly Div	46	6.95		
Renaisnc GvFd	1	6.87	6.94	76.9
Renaissnc MM	24	7.07	7.19	193.1
ReservConn TE	55	4.20	4.29	188.6
Reserv GOV'T	2	6.50	6.71	341.4
Reserv PRIMR	26	6.72	6.95	1678.8
Reserv INTRST	68	4.35	4.45	241.9
Reserv NY TxE	77	4.07	4.16	88.9
PW RMA Mony	40	6.72	6.95	1689.3
PW RMA TaxF	42	4.11	4.20	865.9
PW RMA USGv	50	6.49	6.70	198.2
RowePrPrRes f	39	6.89	7.13	2818.0

Value Line Cash ⟶

Fund	Avg. Mat.	7Day YLD.	7Day EFF.	Assets
RowePTxEx cf	85	4.79	4.90	1039.0
RowePUSTrea f	31	6.04	6.22	152.0
Safeco MnyMk f	30	6.90	7.12	41.0
StClair Prime	29	6.75	6.97	63.0
StClair TxFr	41	4.62	4.73	77.6
ScuddCashInv f	42	6.82	7.05	1065.1
ScuddrGvt Mny	41	6.23	6.42	152.8
ScuddrTaxFr cf	32	4.15	4.24	318.8
Secur Cash Fd	16	6.80	7.14	43.4
Select Mny Mkt	35	6.40	6.56	22.5
Selig CalTE	14	4.00	4.09	34.2
SelgmnCM Prm	28	6.65	6.87	315.2
SeligmnGov Prt	4	6.42	6.63	25.5
Sentinel Cash	45	6.67	6.89	41.9
SentryCash Mgt	(z)	(z)		
Shrsn Cal Dly	53	4.15	4.24	85.8
ShrsnDailyDiv f	39	6.75	6.98	3807.9
ShrsnDaily TxF	55	4.28	4.37	699.2
ShrsnFMA Cash	35	6.89	7.13	1448.9
ShrsnFMA Govt	86	6.78	7.01	372.4
ShrsnFMA Mun	45	4.33	4.42	940.0
ShrsnGovt Agen	91	6.83	7.06	1567.6
Shrsn NY Dly	66	4.07	4.15	-98.6
ShrtTmIncm Fd	59	6.44	6.54	214.0
ShortTm Asset	36	6.96	7.20	155.8
ShortTerm Govt	50	6.75	6.89	456.7
ShortTermYld a	17	5.86	5.97	9.9
Sigma MnyMkt	9	6.60	6.82	8.1
SthFrmBur Csh	(z)	(z)		
Standby Reserv	38	6.99	7.24	330.8
SteinRoeCsh Rs	34	6.83	7.07	755.2
SteinRoe Govt	33	6.06	6.23	33.4
SteinRoe Tax	29	4.25	4.34	212.9
StrongMM Fnd	20	6.60	6.82	4.9
Summit Cash	71	7.26	7.53	622.9
TaxExmpMM c	56	4.58	4.69	1272.1
TF CshRsv Gen	30	4.49	4.59	225.6
TaxFrInst Tr	43	4.32		1341.9
TaxFree Mny c	38	4.33	4.42	910.0
TempInvest Fd	36	7.29	7.56	7031.3
Trnsam CashRs	35	6.97	7.21	218.9
Trinity LiqdAst	36	7.05	7.30	358.8
Trust CashRes f	42	6.69	6.91	178.3
Trustfd East	68	4.54	4.65	575.6
Trustfd West	47	4.52	4.62	217.3
TrFdTreas Prtf	44	6.96	7.21	1927.7
TrFdUS Agency	33	7.06	7.32	253.1
TrFd Commercl	28	7.24	7.51	112.6
TrFd Obligation	43	7.17	7.43	1449.8
TrShtTr FedFd	33	7.09	7.34	1854.4
TrShtTFed TFd	35	7.11	7.36	1521.6
TrShTer US Gvt	48	6.86		5884.1
TrstUSTrea Obl	53	6.82		3937.3
TuckerA CashM	38	6.75	6.98	515.0
TuckerA GvtSc	42	6.47	6.57	172.5
TuckerA TxEx	64	4.50	4.59	165.8
20thCent Cash	47	7.07	7.39	49.9
UMB Federal	31	6.55	6.76	98.0
UMB Prime	27	6.87	7.11	61.0
UnitedCshMgt a	74	7.18	7.14	
USAA FedSMM	78	6.38	6.58	19.4
USAA MutlMM	52	6.80	7.03	267.1
USAA TxExMM	64	4.85	4.97	170.1
UST MSTR Gvt	26	6.99	7.24	69.2
USTMSTR Mny	63	7.22	7.48	177.8
UST MSTR TxE	44	4.84	4.96	329.8
US Treas SecFd	54	6.20	6.35	80.8
ValueLine Cash	69	6.97	7.14	443.6
ValLineMM Prt	91	4.42	4.45	27.5
VangdMMFed f	43	6.78	7.01	502.8
VangrdMM Pr f	34	7.09	7.38	1808.5
Vangrd Insure f	21	6.38	6.54	55.0
VangMunMM cf	79	4.68	4.87	927.9
VantageCsh Prt	33	6.89	7.13	370.0
VantageGvt Prt	47	6.64	6.86	63.0
Viking MM Fnd	24	7.23	7.49	27.6
WayneHum MM	21	6.53	6.74	78.9
WebstrCash Rs	38	6.92	7.18	1426.0
Working Assets	36	6.63	6.85	81.9

a-Yield may include capital gains and losses. b-Account size varies yield due to fixed charges. c-Primarily federally tax exempt securities. e-Effective 7-day yield. f As of previous day. z-Unavailable.

The Wall Street Journal, *April 10, 1986*

Excerpt from Page 54 ──────►

UST MSTR TxE	44	4.84 4.96	329.8
US Treas SecFd	54	6.20 6.35	80.8
ValueLine Cash	69	6.97 7.14	443.6
ValLineMM Prf	91	4.42 4.45	27.5
VangdMMFed f	43	6.78 7.01	502.8

with ample reserves), the banks' net borrowed reserves dropped steeply, and on occasion they had net free reserves. You can observe the same forces at work on interest rates. The upswing of the cycle and its inevitable tight money policy pulled interest rates higher. Recession and easy money let interest rates fall.

Be sure to notice as well that interest rates rose over time due to the ever-escalating demand for funds. You saw this in Chart 4–2 on page 27, when consumer and business borrowing doubled every five years in the 1970s. As the demand for funds continuously exceeded the supply of funds at current prices, interest rates (the price of borrowed money) climbed in the long run.

Finally, the Fed's 1981–82 tight money policy drove interest rates to record levels. You can see this in Chart 6–1 on page 58, as well as the Fed's easier grip since then and the interest rate bulge that produced the minislowdown of mid-1984.

That carries the story to the present date and raises the issue of "fine-tuning," which was introduced in Chapters 4 and 5. How did the Fed manage to bring about an effective minislowdown in 1984, when it seemed limited only to stop-or-go policies in the 70s? The answer is partly that the Fed had a relatively small and easy task before it in 1984. But that's not all. In the 70s and earlier, interest rate regulations constrained the Fed to operating a switch that was either "off" or "on." But deregulation permitted a metamorphosis, the switch became a valve, and the flow of credit could be more finely calibrated.

The history of this transition deserves some explanation. Until the end of the 70s, banks and savings and loan companies were not permitted to pay more than a statutory maximum of slightly over 5 percent on consumer savings accounts. During the rapid expansions of 1968–69 and 1973–74, Treasury bill interest rates climbed to well above 5 percent, providing an incentive for large depositors to withdraw their funds from these financial intermediaries and invest them in Treasury bills in order to earn the higher market return.

This process was called *disintermediation* because savers bypassed the financial intermediaries to invest their funds directly in Treasury bills; savings and loan companies suffered especially severely because of their dependence on consumer savings accounts.

Many Analysts See Lower Prime Rate, But Some Contend Fed Must Act First

CREDIT MARKETS

By EDWARD P. FOLDESSY
And TOM HERMAN
Staff Reporters of THE WALL STREET JOURNAL

NEW YORK—Almost all the ingredients are in place for a reduction in the banking industry's prime rate to 8½% from 9%, according to many economists and analysts.

Weak demand for business loans and declines in banks' own cost of funds offer bankers plenty of leeway to cut the prime rate, these analysts say. But many argue that banks will hold off, preferring to fatten their profit margins rather than compete for new loan business.

Some analysts contend it will take another reduction in the Federal Reserve System's discount rate to prod bankers into cutting their prime, or base, rate on corporate loans. The Fed lowered the discount rate, the fee it charges on loans to banks and savings institutions, to 7% from 7½% March 7. Banks reacted quickly to that move by lowering the prime rate to 9% from 9½, putting it at the lowest level since August 1978.

Pressures on Fed

The odds of another discount rate cut by the Fed have increased recently becau~~ of growing evidence that the ecor~~ mains sluggish, according `      ` ~~s on the Sullivan Jr., a sen'   ~~anks increased Dean Witter ⌐   ~~nual rate in the first build~~ ~~n from a 5.2% clip in the ~~   ~~t quarter, according to David M. Jones, an economist at Aubrey G. Lanston & Co. The Fed reported Friday that such loans plunged $1.72 billion in the week ended March 26 to a total of $256.69 billion.

Loan demand is likely to weaken further, Mr. Jones predicted. He noted that the recent steep decline in bond yields is prompting many companies to borrow in the bond market, using the funds to pay off short-term loans. Still, banks aren't eager to cut the prime rate because they want "to keep profit margins as wide as possible in order to have a cushion" against potential loan losses stemming from the woes in the energy industries, he said.

Little to Lose

Analysts say banks have little to lose by keeping the prime rate unchanged, at least for now. Banks often lend to big corporations at rates well below the prime rate in an effort to keep those companies from turning to alternative sources of credit, such as commercial paper.

The Wall Street Journal, *April 7, 1986.*

Bond Yields

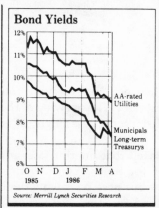

Source: *Merrill Lynch Securities Research*

But many medium-sized and smaller businesses, whose loans are tied to the prime rate, don't have access to other, cheaper sources of funds. Many consumer loans, such as those backed by mortgages, also are tied ` ` ~~s rate.

"The prim~~   ~~e 2.1% annual clip in the 8½%" ~~ ~~er, after adjusting for inflation.

~~ ~~ary Shilling, who heads a consulting firm bearing his name, contends that first-quarter growth was only about 1%, and that it could be "even weaker" this quarter. He expects the Fed to push short-term interest rates lower soon.

Frederick H. Schultz, a former vice chairman of the Federal Reserve Board, said there are increasing signs that the economy "isn't strong." But he contended the Fed is likely to wait for more economic statistics before moving to drive down interest rates further. "I think another move (by the Fed to ease credit conditions) is coming but not imminently," he said.

Jay N. Woodworth, a vice president and economist at Bankers Trust Co., says further declines in short-term interest rates appear likely over the next few weeks. With the economy looking "fairly soft," he said the Fed probably will ease credit conditions "around the middle of this month." Such a move, he said, would likely be made "in concert with West Germany and Japan." Shortly after those two countries lowered their rates last month, the Fed cut its discount rate.

But Mr. Woodworth contends that long-term bond yields aren't likely to decline. "Inflation expectations are unrealistically low," he argues. "I think it is just dead wrong to assume that there isn't any continuing inflation problem in the American economy." He predicted that pressures for higher inflation and increased in+~ ~~, rates will intensify in the secon~~ ~~ ~~ 1.42%. year because of risin~~ ` ~~ell. The latest "major difficul+'~ ~~ closed at 6.22% bid, slashing '' ~~ 6.35% Thursday. The bid on cit~ ~~est 26-week bill dropped to 6.23% ~~rom 6.36%. In addition, the interest rate on federal funds—reserves that banks lend one another overnight—hovered between 6⅝% and 7¼% most of the day. That was down from an average of 7.44% Thursday.

KEY ASSETS AND LIABILITIES
OF THE NATION'S LARGE COMMERCIAL BANKS
(in millions of dollars)

ASSETS:	Mar. 26, 1986	Change from Mar. 19, 1986
Total loans, leases and investments, gross adjusted	894,326	− 5,518
Commercial and industrial loans	256,688	− 1,718
Loans to depository and financial institutions	42,384	− 211
Loans to individuals	132,772	− 45
Real estate loans	185,250	+ 82
U.S. Government securities	90,187	+ 383
Other securities including municipal issues	68,830	− 34
Municipal securities	57,485	− 277
LIABILITIES:		
Demand deposits	200,490	− 4,630
Other transaction deposits including NOW accounts	43,203	− 267
Savings and other nontransaction deposits	494,362	+ 917
Includes large time deposits of $100,000 or more	162,062	− 94

Buying & Borrowing

Here are some recent figures on financial trends affecting consumers and individual investors.

—DOW JONES INDUSTRIALS—
Closing: 1739.22. Year earlier: 1259.05.

—MOODY'S CORPORATE YIELDS—
Average for Aa-rated bonds:
9.24. Year earlier: 12.93.

—FEDERAL HOME LOAN BANK—
Average effective rate for conventional
fixed-rate mortgage on new homes:
10.93%. Year earlier: 13.77%.
Average price on new homes:
$109,200. Year earlier: $91,300.

—BANK MONEY MARKET DEPOSITS—
Rates for accounts with minimum bal-
ance of $2,500:
At one major commercial bank: 6.60%.
At one major savings & loan association:
6.25%.

The Wall Street Journal, *April 7, 1986*

The upshot was that as soon as boom conditions developed and the
Fed began exercising a tight money policy, driving interest rates up, an
ocean of deposits drained out of the banks and especially out of the
savings and loan companies. The savings and loans literally ran out of
money. They couldn't make mortgage loans, even if borrowers were willing to pay exorbitant rates of interest.

You can understand, then, why the Fed's tight money policies did
not gradually restrict credit as interest rates climbed during these earlier
periods. Instead, the availability of credit suddenly dried up for certain
key areas of the economy. (For instance, residential construction almost
shut down.)

Then, when the boom peaked and the economy slipped off into recession, the Fed switched to an easy money policy. As soon as Treasury
bill interest rates fell below the statutory maximum that banks and savings
and loan companies were able to pay, depositors sold their Treasury bills
and redeposited the funds, propelling a tidal wave of deposits back into
the financial intermediaries. As a result, savings and loan companies practi-
cally gave money away to finance home building.

Chart 6–1
Short-Term Interest Rates: The Prime Rate, the Federal Funds Rate, and the Treasury Bills Rate

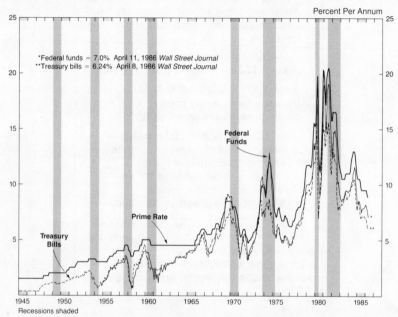

Source: U.S. Department of Commerce. *Business Conditions Digest* and *Handbook of Cyclical Indicators,* series 109, 114, and 119.

These fund flows out of and then back into the banks and savings and loan companies exacerbated the business cycle. In 1969 and 1974, analysts didn't talk about tight conditions; they talked about the "credit crunch" and how it had stopped the economy in its tracks. Then, as deposits came flooding back into the system in 1970–72 and 1975–77, demand fueled by cheap credit took off like a rocket.

By 1980, deregulation had begun to remove interest rate ceilings from consumer savings accounts. The new, flexible-rate accounts were even called "T-bill accounts" because they were pegged to the Treasury bill rate and were designed to prevent consumers from defecting to the savings account's chief competitor, the Treasury bill.

When the Fed made its desperate stand against inflation in 1981–82, deregulation had been partially accomplished: the T-bill accounts prevented a run on the savings and loan companies' deposits. Yet these accounts required a minimum amount of $10,000. Many savers were attracted by recently created money market funds, which had much smaller minimum deposit requirements and invested in commercial paper and other short-term instruments, thus providing yields slightly higher than those of Treasury bills. Consequently, banks and savings and loan companies faced only a partial drain on their deposits.

Deregulation had begun to work. The savings and loan companies did not run out of money in 1981–82, but they were obliged to raise mortgage rates to prohibitive levels as T-bill account interest rates went up with the yield on Treasury bills. Residential construction was at last constrained by the *price* borrowers had to pay for funds rather than by the *availability* of those funds.

After the Fed eased up in mid-1982, and as the economy rebounded strongly in 1983, banks and savings and loan companies received permission to offer "money market accounts," which competed directly with the money market funds. Although deregulation was not 100 percent complete, there was little reason now for depositors to keep their funds elsewhere, and so a large volume of funds returned to the banks and savings and loan companies from the money market mutual funds.

Now that the Fed had a finely honed scalpel, it could maintain interest rates at sufficiently low levels to encourage demand but could easily nudge them upward whenever inflationary conditions threatened. And it would not have to fear the destructive flows of funds out of and into banks and savings and loan companies.

Early 1984 provided the first test; to confirm the results, review the recent interest rate record in Chart 6–1 on page 58 once again. Interest rates collapsed in late 1982, but the Fed didn't wait long before it began to tighten up again. Demand had roared ahead throughout 1983; and, by the end of the year, there were many alarming signs that inflation was about to be rekindled. The Fed had allowed interest rates to drift upward throughout 1983, but by early 1984 decisive, positive action was required.

Recall from Chart 4–1 on page 24 that the Fed's tight money policy in the spring of 1984 had forced the banks to borrow reserves from the Fed. You can see in Chart 6–1 that interest rates quickly shot upward in response. By mid-1984, Treasury bill rates were two percentage points higher than they had been in early 1983.

That induced the minislowdown first mentioned in Chapter 4; and, by the summer of 1984, there was talk of recession. But the Fed had carefully fine-tuned the slowdown and would not let it develop further. It permitted interest rates to drop sharply in late 1984 (recall the decline in net borrowed reserves in Chapter 4), and demand began to grow once again.

For a while after the minislowdown of 1984, the Fed carefully fine-tuned credit conditions, keeping interest rates low enough to permit demand's continued growth but high enough to prevent its reckless advance. Look once again at the record in Chart 6–1. The Fed cannot let interest rates fall to their 1971–72 or 1976–77 levels, or else demand will explode. Credit restraint is the Fed's challenge for the late 80s.

The *Journal* provides a **Short-Term Interest Rates** chart each Thursday in the "Credit Markets" report (see the front page index). The April 10, 1986, article on page 52 (excerpt below) provides an example.

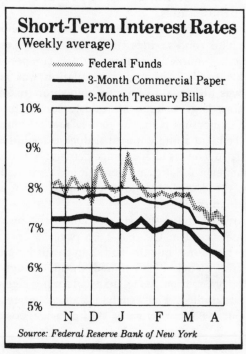

Short-Term Interest Rates
(Weekly average)

Federal Funds
3-Month Commercial Paper
3-Month Treasury Bills

Source: Federal Reserve Bank of New York

The Wall Street Journal, *April 10, 1986*

LONG–TERM INTEREST RATES

Bonds and mortgages are the two principal instruments of long-term credit. Interest rates on the former are reported on Monday by *The Wall Street Journal* in a chart labeled **Bond Yields,** which accompanies the "Credit Markets" article. The April 7, 1986, chart is reproduced on pages 56 and 61.

The **Bond Yields** chart on page 61 depicts three series. The top line describes the interest rate that financially healthy public utilities must pay on debt instruments maturing in 10 years or more, the second line

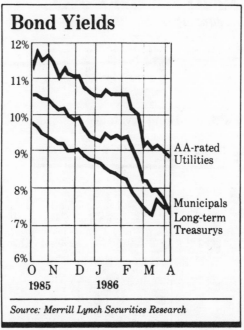

Bond Yields

AA-rated
Utilities

Municipals
Long-term
Treasurys

O N D J F M A
1985 1986

Source: Merrill Lynch Securities Research

The Wall Street Journal, *April 7, 1986*

describes the interest rate that the federal government must pay on debts that mature in 15 years or more, and the bottom line portrays the rate paid by state and local governments. Public utilities, such as electric, gas, and telephone companies, issue substantial amounts of long-term debt to finance their continual capital expansion. Mere profits cannot cover the cost of new generating and switching stations, satellites, and transmission lines, so the difference has to be made up by borrowing. Since the projects of public utility companies are long term and generate income for these companies over the extensive life of productive assets, it's appropriate that the financing be long term too. The stretch-out in earnings on these assets will provide for the steady, eventual payment of interest and principal. The federal government and state and local governments sell bonds on a long-term basis, too.

Investors who buy the utility and government bonds want a secure interest return over several years. The interest earned is usually higher than on short-term instruments because the borrower is asking the lender to take an extended risk. And whereas the short-term market offers investment vehicles that are fairly uniform, and by definition relatively easy

NEW YORK EXCHANGE BONDS

Thursday, April 10, 1986

Total Volume $42,640,000

SALES SINCE JANUARY 1

1986	1985	1984
$3,379,394,000	$2,366,115,000	$1,868,801,000

	Domestic Thu.	Domestic Wed.	All Issues Thu.	All Issues Wed.
Issues traded	1036	1007	1040	1017
Advances	499	498	502	502
Declines	293	283	293	284
Unchanged	244	226	245	231
New highs	170	157	171	160
New lows	4	4	4	4

Dow Jones Bond Averages

1984 High	1984 Low	1985 High	1985 Low	1986 High	1986 Low		Thursday 1986		Thursday 1985		Thursday 1984	
72.92	64.81	83.73	72.27	91.26	83.73	20 Bonds	91.26	+0.12	74.27	+0.50	68.18	+0.02
70.31	59.43	82.88	68.62	92.22	81.85	10 Utilities	92.22	+0.04	70.75	+0.40	63.15	+0.25
76.22	69.61	84.58	75.61	90.30	84.82	10 Industrial	90.30	+0.23	77.80	+0.60	73.21	−0.22

Bonds	Cur Yld	Vol	High	Low	Close	Net Chg.
FrdC 4½96	cv	2	195	195	195	+2
FrdC 8.7s99	9.1	1	96	96	96	−1⅛
FrdC 8¼88	8.3	10	100	100	100	.....
FrdC 8⅜01	8.9	4	94½	94½	94½	+ ¾
FrdC 7⅞89	7.9	50	100	99⅞	100	+ ¼
FrdC 7.85s88	7.9	17	100	99⅝	100	+1
FrdC 8½88	8.5	10	100	100	100	− ½
FrdC 8⅞90	8.8	122	100½	100½	100½	− ⅜
FrdC 9.55s89	9.4	119	101⅛	100¾	101⅛	+ ⅜
FreptM 10½14	cv	1	101	101	101	− ¾
Frmnt 12⅞90	13.	1	100¾	100¾	100¾	+ ¾
Fruf 5½94	cv	26	125	122	123½	+1½
FrufF 8s87	8.0	232	100	99⅞	100	+ ¼
Fuqua 9½98	10.	49	93	91	93	+1½
Fuqua 9⅞97	10.	12	95⅜	95⅛	95⅜	+ ⅛
GTE 10½07	cv	87	120	119	119½	+ ¼
Gelco 14⅝99	14.	11	106¾	106⅛	106⅛	.....
Gelco 14s01	cv	128	108½	108	108	− ½
GCinem 10s08	5.4	35	185	178	185	+7
GCinem 10s09	6.6	25	151	151	151	+1
GnDev 12⅝05	12.	1	101½	101½	101½	.....
GnEl 7½96	7.8	2	95⅝	95⅝	95⅝	−1⅛
GnEl 8½04	8.5	47	100	99⅞	99⅞	....
GElCr 7⅝88	7.6	25	100	100	100	−1¾
GElCr 8¼97	8.2	6	100¾	100¾	100¾	+ ½
GElCr 11½90	11.	85	104⅜	103⅛	103⅛	− ⅞
GElCr 14s90	13.	25	107¼	107	107	+ ½
GElCr 13⅝91	12.	10	110½	110½	110½	.....
GFood 14⅜89	14.	3	105	105	105	− ½
GnHme 15½95	14.	40	111	111	111	+1½
GnInst 5s92	cv	20	107	106¼	106¼	+ ¼
GMills zr88s	..	110	86⅜	86⅜	86⅜	.....
GMA 4⅞87	5.1	120	96¾	96	96	− ¾
GMA 6¼88	6.4	8	97½	97⅛	97⅛	+ ⅜
GMA 7⅛90	7.3	23	98¼	97⅝	98⅛	+1
GMA 8s93	8.0	101	100	99¾	100	− ¼
GMA 7¾94	7.8	32	98¾	98¾	98¾	− ¼
GMA 7¼95	7.7	10	94¼	94¼	94¼	+ ¼
GMA 7⅛92	7.3	15	97	97	97	− ⅜
GMA 8⅞99	8.8	35	100⅞	100¼	100⅞	+ ⅝
GMA 8¾s01	8.8	42	99	98½	99	.....
GMA 8⅛96	8.2	34	99⅞	99⅝	99⅝	− ¼
GMA 7.35s87	7.4	31	99 31-32	99 27-32	99 27-32	
GMA 8s02	8.5	10	94	94	94	.....
GMA 8s07	8.4	1	94⅞	94⅞	94⅞	+2⅞
GMA 8.2s88	8.2	23	100⅜	100⅜	100⅜	− ½
GMA 8⅝88	8.6	15	100⅝	100⅝	100⅝	+ ⅛
GMA 9⅝89	9.5	11	102½	101½	101½	−1⅜
GMA 9¾03	9.4	37	103⅝	100¾	103⅝	+ ¾
GMA 9¼89	9.2	40	100¼	100¼	100¼	− ⅛
GMA 9.4s04	9.2	28	102¾	102⅝	102⅝	.....
GMA 12s05fb	11.	10	110¾	110¾	110¾	.....
GMA 11⅝90	11.	140	103¼	103	103¼	+ ¼
GMA 12s05	11.	37	112¼	112	112¼	+1⅛
GMA 11¾00	11.	163	110½	110	110½	−1¼
GMA 14⅜91	13.	125	111¾	111½	111¾	− ¼
GMA d6s11	7.8	177	77¼	77⅛	77¼	+ ¼
GMA 14⅝89	14.	52	107¾	107½	107¾	+1½
GMA 11¾89	11.	25	106¼	105½	106	+ ½
GMA 11s88	10.	5	107	107	107	+4
GMA 10¼90	9.7	2	105¼	105¼	105¼	+ ¼
GMA 10s90	9.5	135	105½	105½	105½	+ ¾
GTE 4s90	cv	4	115½	115½	115½	− ½
GTE 4s90r	cv	3	115	115	115	.....
GTE 6⅝91	7.2	5	92⅛	92⅛	92⅛	....
GTE 5s92	cv	11	116½	116½	116½	− 1⅞
GTE 9⅜99	9.3	31	101	99	101	+2
Gene 15¼94	16.	21	94	93¼	93¼	− ¾
GaPac 5¼96	cv	43	113⅝	113	113⅝	+ 1⅝
GaPw 8⅞00	9.4	34	95	94⅜	94⅜	− ⅛

Bonds	Cur Y'ld	Vol	High	Low	Close	Net Chg	
GranC 4⅝94	cv	30	68	68	68	.....	
GWstFn 8½10	cv	5	132	132	132	+1	
Greyh 9⅜01	9.8	5	96	96	96	− ⅞	
GreyF 16⅛92	14.	18	116¼	116¼	116¼	−1	
GreyF zr94	..	40	48⅛	46½	46½	+ ¼	
Groler 13s02	13.	12	101½	101½	101½	+1	
Grolr 13⅝03	13.	5	103	103	103	.....	
GrowGp 8½06	cv	50	102¼	102¼	102¼	+1	
Grumn 9¼09	cv	30	110	110	110	.....	
GlfWn 7s03A	9.0	37	79¼	78⅛	78⅛	+ ⅛	
GlfWn 7s03B	8.9	133	79½	78⅞	79	+1	
GlfOil 8½95	8.4	20	100⅝	100⅛	100⅝	+ ⅝	
Harns 15s94	13.	4	112	112	112	+1	
Harnis d12s04	12.	10	101½	101	101½	.....	
Hawn 9s2000	9.0	75	99¾	99¾	99¾	+2¾	
HltUSA 8¼03	cv	5	71½	71½	71½	+ ½	
Heilm zr03	..	31	31	30⅛	30½	.....	
Hellr 7¾93	8.4	5	92	92	92	+ ⅞	
Hellr 8.1s87	8.1	5	100	100	100	+ ¼	
Hercul 6½99	cv	125	131	129	131	+ ¾	
Hercul 8s10	cv	220	121	120½	120½	+ ½	
HerCm 7s11	cv	65	119	118⅝	119	.....	
HmeDp 8½09	cv	87	94½	94	94	.....	
HoCp 10¾90	10.	20	104	103	103	−1	
HoCp 8½08	cv	183	106¼	105½	106	+ ½	
HoCp 9s98	cv	91	103⅞	103	103	−1	
HouF 7.85s86	7.9	78	100	100	100	.....	
HousF 8⅜03	9.0	5	93	93	93	+10½	
HouF 8.45s97	8.6	20	98	98	98	+3	
HugheT 9½06	cv	50	94½	93¾	94¼	+ ½	
Humn d13½02	13.	18	104¾	104¾	104¾	+ ¼	
Humn 8½09	cv	107	112½	112	112	+ ½	
vjHuntIR 9⅞04f	..	2	8¼	8¼	8¼	.....	
Hutton 12s05	11.	26	105⅞	105½	105⅞	− ⅜	
IBM Cr 9⅜90	9.2	16	105	105	105	+ ⅛	
IdelB 9¼00	17.	62	57	54	55	−2½	
IllBel 7⅝06	8.5	10	90⅛	88⅞	90⅛	+ ⅜	
IllBel 8s04	8.5	9	94⅞	93½	93¾	+ ¼	
IllBel 8¼16	8.8	25	94	94	94	+ ¼	
IllBel 12¼17	11.	62	110⅞	110⅞	110⅞	.....	
IlCnt 11¼99	11.	7	102	102	102	+ ¼	
IllPw 10½04	10.	12	104	104	104	.....	
IllPw 8⅝06	9.4	27	92	91¾	91¾	−1⅞	
InMic 10¼87	10.	22	100¼	100¼	100¼	.....	
IndBel 8⅛11	8.7	2	93¼	93¼	93¼	.....	
IndBel 10s14	9.5	10	105	105	105	+1⅜	
IndBel 8⅛17	8.8	35	92½	92½	92½	.....	
Inexc 8½00	cv	504	39½	38½	39½	+1	
IngR 12⅜90	12.	10	103½	103⅜	103½	+1	
InldStl 11¼90	11.	10	101	101	101	− ½	
Insilco 9s10	cv	127	121	118½	121	+3½	
ItgRs d8⅝97	11.	14	78¾	78¼	78¼	+1⅛	
Intrfst 7¾05	cv	82	68½	68	68⅛	− ⅜	
IBM 9⅜04	9.2	22	103	102⅛	102⅛	− ⅝	
IBM 7⅞04	cv	839	124	122¼	123¾	+ ¾	
IBM 10¼95	9.4	10	109⅝	109⅝	109⅝	−1⅞	← IBM
IntTT 10s00	9.8	5	102	102	102	+1½	
Intnr 10½08	...	15	110¼	110	110¼	+1¼	
IntrBk 5½87	cv	10	99½	99½	99½	− ½	
Jamswy 8s05	cv	32	104	104	104	.....	
JCP 9⅝06	9.8	5	97⅞	97⅞	97⅞	+ ¾	
JCP 9¾06	9.9	10	98⅝	98¼	98¼	−2⅛	
JCP 9s08	9.7	20	92½	92½	92½	+4½	
vjJnM 9.7s85mf	..	26	88	87½	88	.....	
JonsLI 6¾94	11.	10	59⅝	59⅝	59⅝	−1⅞	← Jones & Laughlin
JoneL 9⅞95	13.	20	76	75½	75½	− ½	
JoneL 8s98	12.	11	66½	66½	66½	− ½	
K mart 6s99	cv	183	127¾	126	127¾	+ ¾	
Kaisr 9s05	cv	8	87	87	87	−1	
Kenn 7⅞01	8.8	3	89⅝	89⅝	89⅝	.....	
Keycrp 7¾02	8.9	30	87	86¾	87	+ ⅝	

The Wall Street Journal, *April 11, 1986*

to get into and out of, the long-term markets offer a far greater diversity
of investment opportunities.

For instance, you may wish to purchase or keep track of a particular
corporate bond. If this bond is traded on the New York Stock Exchange,
you will find it listed in *The Wall Street Journal* under "New York Exchange
Bonds." Consult the front-page index for the daily listing.

Consider the following example from the April 11, 1986, edition, as
shown on page 62.

Excerpt from Page 62 ⟶

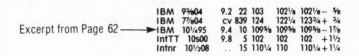

Bonds	Cur Yld	Vol	High	Low	Close	Net Chg
IBM 10¼ 95	9.4	10	109⅝	109⅝	109⅝	−1⅞

With the IBM bond shown above, the interest rate at issue (10¼ percent) and the year of maturity (1995—the year when the bond is due
for redemption) follow the company's name. (You'll find an *s* after the
interest rate when a fraction is absent.)

Corporate bonds are issued in denominations of $1,000, and this partic-
ular IBM bond originally paid an annual fixed-dollar interest return of
$102.50 (10¼ percent of $1,000 = $102.50). That is, IBM promised to
pay the bearer $102.50 a year until the bond matured in the year 1995,
at which time Dow would redeem the bond for $1,000.

You can see from the next column that the current yield is 9.4 percent.
How can that be true if the bonds were issued at 10¼ percent? Because
IBM promised to pay a fixed-dollar return of $102.50 a year until maturity
based on an initial value, and a redemption value, of $1,000. If the bond's
price varies from $1,000 between issuance and maturity, the current yield
will vary from 10¼ percent, because the fixed annual return of $102.50
would be more than 10¼ percent if the bond's value dropped below
$1,000 and less than 10¼ percent if it rose above $1,000. As the bond's
price rises, the yield (interest rate) falls, and vice versa.

To understand this better, look at the columns following the Volume
column. (Volume is reported in thousands of dollars—10 bonds with a
face value of $1,000 were traded on April 10, 1986.) You can see the
high, low, and closing prices for the day. Since bonds are issued in denominations of $1,000, the reported prices are a percentage of the face value of

$1,000. Thus, 109⅝ means a price of $1,096.25 (109⅝ percent of $1,000 = $1,096.25). This bond was bought and sold for $1,096.25 throughout the trading day on April 10, 1986, so the high, low, and closing prices are all the same. The last column informs you that the April 10 closing price was 1⅞ points ($18.75) lower than the previous close. Now, if you bought this bond on April 10, your yield would be 9.4 percent, not 10¼ percent, because on April 10 the bond had a value of $1,096.25, not $1,000. An annual return of $102.50 on an investment of $1,096.25 is the equivalent of 9.4 percent, not 10¼ percent.

When commentators speak of the bond market rising and falling, they mean the *price* of the bond, not the interest rate. Bondholders want interest rates to fall so that the value of their bonds will rise. That's why the IBM bond went from $1,000 to $1,096.25 as its yield fell from 10¼ percent to 9.4 percent.

Not only interest rates, but also the relative strength of a company, will affect the price of its bonds. IBM was investment quality because of its healthy financial condition and secure earnings potential. Jones & Laughlin Industries was speculative because it was a much weaker company in a weak industry (steel). Hence, Jones & Laughlin had to pay a higher return to attract investors' funds.

JCP	9s08	9.7	20	92½	92½	92½+4½
vjJnM	9.7s85mf	..	26 88	87½	88	.....
JonsLI	6¾s94	11.	10	59⅝	59⅝	59⅝−1⅞
JoneL	9⅞s95	13.	20	76	75½	75½− ½
JoneL	8s98	12.	11	66½	66½	66½− ½

Excerpt from Page 62 ──────▶

On April 10, 1986, you could have bought this bond for $596.25, held it for eight years (during which you would have received an 11 percent annual interest return), and then cashed it in for $1,000, at a gain of $403.75 per bond (assuming the company survived). Substantial capital gains can be made in the bond market for an equivalent risk.

Compare the two bonds one last time. They matured a year apart for $1,000 each. Yet you would have had to pay $1,096.25 for the IBM bond and received a 9.4 percent return, while the Jones and Laughlin bond would have cost you $596.25 for an 11 percent return. A wide range of investment opportunities awaits you in the bond market.

Yet you probably would prefer to make your investment decision without being surprised by the riskiness of the bonds you select. Each day the *Journal* publishes a "Credit Ratings" report summarizing the actions of Standard & Poor's and Moody's, the nation's major bond-rating services. These services rate bonds according to the likelihood of payment of principal and interest. The rating services arrive at their decision by investigating the profitability and strength of the companies issuing the bonds. You will notice that different companies pay varying rates of interest on their debt according to the ratings they have received. The excerpt from the April 11, 1986, *Journal* serves as an example (see page 66).

Finally, you may wish to purchase municipal (state and local government) or tax-exempt bonds, as they are sometimes called, because earnings from these bonds are not subject to federal income tax and may not be subject to income tax in your state. These bonds were granted tax exemption in order to reduce the borrowing cost of states, cities, and local districts that issue them. Wealthy investors purchase them knowing their return is not taxable and will therefore be satisfied with an interest return substantially below that of comparable federal or corporate bonds. State and local governments save billions of dollars in interest costs because of this indirect subsidy.

But it won't pay you to purchase them unless you're in a high tax bracket. That is, your tax saving must be substantial in order to justify the lower yield. You can check the yield on municipals in the chart accompanying the "Credit Markets" article in the *Journal* (see page 61). Also, the *Journal* publishes a daily listing of actively traded municipal bonds under the heading "Tax-Exempt Bonds." (See the excerpt from the April 11, 1986, *Journal* on page 67.) Finally, a "Municipal Bond Index" prepared by Merrill Lynch is published each Friday. The excerpt from the April 11, 1986, *Journal* serves as an example (see page 68). In addition to an overall index, this report presents the latest yield on a variety of municipal bond categories.

Each Monday the *Journal* lists the federal, municipal, and corporate bonds to be offered for sale during the week, together with the common stock offerings to be made by corporations. An excerpt on page 69 from the April 7, 1986, *Journal* serves as an example. You can contact your broker if you wish to purchase a security issued in the week.

Mortgage rates are watched intensely by everyone involved in buying, selling, and constructing homes and other buildings. The *Journal* devotes a long article, usually appearing toward the beginning of each month, to these rates. The sample reprinted here was published on April 4, 1986. (See page 70.)

The same forces operate on the mortgage funds market as on the other credit markets. If short-term rates are high, for example, then banks and savings and loan associations must pay their depositors a high rate of return. Otherwise, funds will drain out of these financial intermediaries as depositors buy higher-yielding investments. In order to bear the additional interest expense, the banks and savings and loan associations must charge their mortgage customers more.

CREDIT RATINGS

BAUSCH & LOMB INC.—Standard & Poor's Corp. raised its rating on Bausch & Lomb's $4.1 million of industrial revenue bonds to single-A-plus from single-A. The rating concern also rated the company's offering of $100 million of senior notes, due 1996, single-A-plus. S&P said Bausch & Lomb, based in Rochester, N.Y., "can rely on its contact lens solutions, optical products and breeding of laboratory animals for the majority of its earnings" as competition for its contact lens business increases. S&P also said that the recent divestiture of Bausch & Lomb's less profitable businesses has increased its return on capital and added to the company's cash.

* * *

FREMONT GENERAL CORP. — S&P said it lowered its rating on the subordinated debt of the Los Angeles-based insurance and financial services concern to double-B-minus from double-B-plus. Fremont said it has $47 million of subordinated debt currently outstanding. A Fremont spokesman declined to comment on the S&P action. S&P said it believes Fremont won't be able to return its property and casualty insurance lines to "normal profitability within S&P's previous expectations."

* * *

HUGHES TOOL CO.—Moody's Investors Service Inc. lowered the company's senior debt rating to Baa-2 from single-A-3 and its subordinated debt rating to Baa-3 from Baa-1. About $291 million of debt of the Houston-based oil field tools and services concern is affected by the downgrading. The rating agency said depressed conditions in the oil industry has forced the company "to accelerate its consolidations and cost-cutting programs and future asset write-downs are a possibility." A spokesman at Hughes Tool declined to immediately comment.

* * *

ZALE CORP.—S&P, citing the jewelry retailer's deteriorating profits and poor capital returns, lowered the rating on Zale's $100 million of senior notes to triple-B-minus from triple-B-plus. The rating concern said a recently reported plan to write down inventories and sell some units should help the Irving, Calif.-based company, but said, "The success of Zale's new merchandising strategies will have to be demonstrated." S&P also said a hostile takeover bid from Peoples Jewellers Ltd. was a factor in the decision. Zale declined to comment.

Tax-Exempt Bonds

Thursday, April 10, 1986

Here are current prices of several active tax-exempt revenue bonds issued by toll roads and other public authorities.

Agency	Coupon	Mat	Bid	Asked	Chg.
Alabama G.O.	8⅜s	'01	107	110	....
Bat Park City Auth NY	6⅜s	'14	86	91	....
Chelan Cnty PU Dist	5s	'13	81	84	....
Clark Cnty Arpt Rev	10½s	'07	113½	116½	....
Columbia St Pwr Exch	3⅞s	'03	92	94	....
Dela River Port Auth	6½s	'11	94	97	....
Douglas Cnty PU Dist	4s	'18	61	64	....
Ga Mun El Auth Pwr Rev	8s	'15	98	101	....
Intermountain Pwr	7½s	'18	96	100	....
Intermountain Pwr	10½s	'18	122	126	....
Intermountain Pwr	14s	'21	136	140	....
Jacksonville Elec Rev	9¼s	'13	107	111	....
Loop	6½s	'08	74	77	....
MAC	7½s	'92	101½	105½	+ ½
MAC	7½s	'95	103	107	+ ½
MAC	8s	'86	100	104	....
MAC	8s	'91	101	103	....
MAC	9.7s	'08	112	116	− ½
MAC	9¾s	'92	102½	106½	− ½
MAC	10¼s	'93	107	111	....
Mass Port Auth Rev	6s	'11	89	93	....
Massachusetts G.O.	6½s	'00	97	100	....
Mass Wholesale	6⅜s	'15	73	76	....
Mass Wholesale	13⅜s	'17	122	125	....
Metro Transit Auth	9¼s	'15	107½	111½	....
Michigan Public Pwr	10⅝s	'18	121	125	....
Nebraska Pub Pwr Dist	7.1s	'17	94	98	....
NJ Turnpike Auth	4¾s	'06	79	82	....
NJ Turnpike Auth	5.7s	'13	87	90	....
NJ Turnpike Auth	6s	'14	89	92	....
NY Mtge Agency Rev	9½s	'13	106	110	....
NY State Pwr Escr	5½s	'10	85	90	....
NY State Pwr	6⅝s	'10	92	97	....
NY State Pwr Escr	9½s	'01	111	117	....
NY State Pwr	9⅞s	'20	111	116	....
NY State Thruway Rev	3.1s	'94	80	84	....
NY State Urban Dev Corp	6s	'13	79	84	....
NY State Urban Dev Corp	7s	'14	90	95	....
NC East Mun Pwr Agcy	11¼s	'18	120	124	....
Okla Tpke Auth Rev	4.7s	'06	78	81	....
Port of NY & NJ	4¾s	'03	77	82	....
Port of NY & NJ	6s	'06	88	92	....
Port of NY & NJ	7s	'11	99	104	....
Port of NY-Delta	10½s	'08	115	119	....
Salt River-Arizona	9¼s	'20	107	110	....
SC Pub Svc Auth	10¼s	'20	116	119	....
Texas Munic Pwr Agcy	9½s	'12	107	111	....
Valdez (Exxon)	5½s	'07	80	83	....
Valdez (Sohio)	6s	'07	81	84	....
Wshngtn PPSS #4-5	f6s	'15	9	12	....
Wshngtn PPSS #4-5	f7¾s	'18	9½	12½	....
Wshngtn PPSS #4-5	f9⅞s	'12	10	13	....
Wshngtn PPSS #4-5	f12½s	'10	11	13½	....
Wshngtn PPSS #2	6s	'12	69	72	....
Wshngtn PPSS #1	7¾s	'17	83½	86½	....
Wshngtn PPSS #2	9¼s	'11	98	102	....
Wshngtn PPSS #3	13⅞s	'18	122	125	....
Wshngtn PPSS #2	14¾s	'12	126½	129½	....
Wshngtn PPSS #1	15s	'17	136½	140½	....

f-Trades flat without payment of current interest.

The Wall Street Journal, *April 11, 1986*

Also, many mortgage loans are "passed through" to insurance companies and other investors to whom corporate bonds offer an alternative investment vehicle. If mortgages don't offer an attractive yield, investors will buy corporate bonds. These market pressures keep bond and mortgage yields on a parallel course.

Compare Chart 6–2 on page 71 with Chart 6–1 on page 58, and you will find, not surprisingly, that long-term interest rates parallel short-term rates, although at a slightly higher level. Borrowers must pay more if they wish to hold lenders' funds for a longer time. And long-term Treasury bonds and corporate bonds are bought and sold on primary and secondary markets just like Treasury bills and commercial paper. If

Municipal Bond Index
Merrill Lynch 500
Week ended Wednesday, April 9, 1986

The following index is based on yields that about 500 major issuers, mainly of investment grade, would pay on new long-term tax-exempt securities. The securities are presumed to be issued at par; general obligation bonds have a 20-year maturity and revenue bonds a 30-year maturity. The index is prepared by Merrill Lynch, Pierce, Fenner & Smith Inc., based on data supplied by Kenny Information Systems, a unit of J.J. Kenny & Co.

—OVERALL INDEX—
7.53   +0.17

—REVENUE BONDS—
Sub-Index   7.67   +0.11

	4-9-86	Change In Week
AAA-Guaranteed	7.38	. . . .
Airport	7.66	+ 0.03
Electric-Retail	7.48	− 0.02
Electric-Wholesale	7.79	+ 0.11
Hospital	7.82	+ 0.24
Housing	7.73	+ 0.08
Miscellaneous	7.63	+ 0.28
Pollution Control/ Ind. Dev.	7.57	− 0.03
Transportation	7.68	+ 0.09
Utility	7.61	+ 0.16

—GENERAL OBLIGATIONS—
Sub-Index   7.17   +0.37

	4-9-86	Change In Week
Cities	7.32	+ 0.45
Counties	7.25	+ 0.43
States	6.91	+ 0.31
Other Districts	7.33	+ 0.32

The transportation category excludes airports; utility excludes electrics. Other districts include school and special districts.

The Wall Street Journal, *April 11, 1986*

short-term rates surge upward, closing in on long-term rates, why should lenders keep their funds in long-term instruments? They would desert long-term instruments for short-term ones, and then long-term borrowers would have to pay higher rates to keep lenders' funds, in which case long-term rates would move up with short-term rates. Conversely, if short-term rates fell sufficiently to cause a wide gap between the two, lenders would desert the short-term market and move into long-term. The increased availability of funds would also depress long-term rates.

One way or the other, over the long run there will be a hierarchy of rates from short (the lowest) to long (the highest), and they will move together. Occasionally, market forces or special circumstances warp the

Securities Offering Calendar

The following U.S. Treasury, corporate and municipal securities tentatively are scheduled for offering this week, according to Dow Jones Capital Markets Report:

U.S. TREASURY
Today
$14 billion of 13-week and 26-week bills.
Thursday
$9.25 billion of 52-week bills.
CORPORATE
Today
Bell Telephone Co. of Pennsylvania – $275 million of debentures due 2026, via competitive bidding.
General Telephone Co. of the Northwest – $125 million of first mortgage bonds due 2016, via competitive bidding.
Tomorrow
One Day This Week
H.F. Ahmanson & Co. – Four million common shares, via Merrill Lynch Capital Markets.
Ashton-Tate – 1.3 million common shares, via L.F Rothschild, Unterberg, Towbin.
Bausch & Lomb Inc. – $100 million of notes due 1996, via Kidder, Peabody & Co.
BCI Holdings Corp. – $1.2 billion of senior subordinated debentures due 1998, $650 million of senior notes due 1996, $500 million of subordinated debentures due 2001 and $150 million of floating-rate junior subordinated debentures, via Drexel Burnham Lambert Inc.
Cannon Group Inc. – $75 million senior debentures due 2001 and a separate offering of $25 million convertible debentures due 2001, via Drexel Burnham.
Ducommun Inc. – $35 million of convertible debentures, via Donaldson Lufkin Jenrette Securities Corp.
Far West Financial Corp. – 650,000 common shares, via Bear, Stearns & Co.
Federal Home Loan Mortgage Corp. – $475 million of collateralized mortgage obligations to be offered in five classes in the U.S. and overseas, via First Boston Corp. in the U.S. and Nomura Securities International Inc. overseas.
Fremont General Corp. – $75 million of convertible debentures due 2011, via Smith Barney, Harris Upham & Co.
John Hanson Savings & Loan Association – Initial three million common shares, via Prudential-Bache Securities Inc.
Holiday Inns Inc. – $150 million of notes due 1996, via Smith Barney.
Integrated Resources Inc. – $100 million of senior debentures due 1996, and $60 million of convertible exchangeable preferred stock, via Drexel Burnham.
Knoll International Inc. – $50 million of senior debentures due 2001, via Drexel Burnham.
Lucky Stores Inc. – $100 million of sinking fund debentures due 2016, via Goldman, Sachs & Co.
MCI Communications Corp. – $500 million of debentures due 2011, via Drexel Burnham.
VLSI Technology Inc. – 2.5 million common shares, via Goldman Sachs.

The Wall Street Journal, April 7, 1986

Prices of Recent Issues

Current quotations are indicated below for recent issues of corporate senior securities that aren't listed on a principal exchange

Issue	Moody's Rating	Bid	Asked	Chg.	Yield %
UTILITIES					
NE Tel	9s '26	Aa1	100⅛	100½	¾ 8 4₂
N J BellTel	9¾s '26	Aa1	104⅜	104¾	¾ 8 4₄
PacBell	9¼s '26	A1	101	101½	– ¾ 9.1₆
PacG&E	9.4s '19	A1	101	101½	⅝ 9 25
SoCalEd	9¼s '16	Aa2	101	101½	– ½ 9 1₆
INDUSTRIALS					
Arco	9¼s '11	A2	98⅝	99⅛	½ 9 2₆
GMAC	8⅞ '96	Aa1	103	103½	¼ 8.35
McDonalds	8⅞s '16	Aa2	103	103½	½ 8.5₂
FOREIGN					
ExpDvCorp	8¾s '91	Aaa	104¼	104¾	⅜ 7.5₃
Ontario	12½s '94	Aaa	124¼	124¾	⅜ 8.2₁
QuebHydro	11¾s '12	A1	132⅜	133⅜	¼ 8 5₃

Source: PaineWebber Inc. (Quotes are for round lots)

MUNICIPALS
Tomorrow
Gwinnett County School District, Ga. – $44 million of school unlimited tax bonds, due 1989-2008, via competitive bidding.
Colorado Springs, Colo. – $70 million of utilities system revenue bonds, via competitive bidding.
Lafayette, La. – $30 million of Series 1986 public improvement sales tax bonds, via competitive bidding.
Wednesday
Alabama Public School and College Authority – $310 million of capital improvement revenue bonds, via competitive bidding.
Thursday
Rutherford County, Tenn. – $34,495,000 of school unlimited tax bonds, via competitive bidding.
One Day This Week
New York State – $3.5 billion of tax and revenue anticipation notes consisting of $300 million due Sept. 30, 1986, $650 million due Dec. 31, 1986, and $2.55 billion due March 31, 1987, via a Merrill Lynch group.
Grand River Dam Authority, Okla. – $275 million of refunding revenue bonds, via a Smith Barney group.
Metropolitan Water District of Southern California $160 million of waterworks refunding revenue bonds, via a Merrill Lynch group.
Cape May County Municipal Utility Authority, N.J. – $156 million of sewer revenue refunding bonds, via a Prudential-Bache group.
Alief Independent School District, Texas – $76.6 million of unlimited tax schoolhouse and refunding bonds, via a Rauscher Pierce Refsnes Inc group.
Massachusetts State College – $60 million of building authority project and refunding revenue bonds, via a Kidder Peabody group.
University of Houston Board of Regents – $30 million of general tuition revenue refunding bonds, via an Underwood, Neuhaus & Co group.

---

relationship among the rates, but these are usuallly temporary phenomena. A major realignment, such as corporate bonds made in the late 60s (see Chart 6–2 on page 71), is rare.

During the craziness of the late 70s, when rampant recourse to credit was pumping up the inflationary balloon, many observers suggested credit rationing as a solution. That was the only way, they argued, to provide funds for productive business investment in new technology and capital goods, while curtailing unproductive consumer expenditures financed by installment plans, credit cards, and so forth. Otherwise, industry had to compete with consumers in the capital markets for scarce funds. Consumers, the argument continued, were notoriously insensitive to interest rates;

Mortgage Rates Declined Again During March

Drop Was Sixth in a Row, And Several Economists See Lower Levels Soon

By JOANN S. LUBLIN
Staff Reporter of THE WALL STREET JOURNAL

WASHINGTON – Mortgage rates declined during March for the sixth consecutive month, and several economists predicted that even lower rates are coming soon.

Lenders last week were asking an average interest rate of 10.1% on 30-year conventional fixed-rate mortgages, the Federal Home Loan Mortgage Corp. reported. That compares with 10.51% a month earlier and 13.29% the year before. Except for one other week last month when rates were slightly lower, the latest figure represents the lowest point for mortgage rates since November 1978.

A separate survey conducted in early March by the Federal Home Loan Bank Board also showed decreasing rates on both adjustable-rate mortgages and fixed-rate loans. But fixed-rate mortgages dropped the most.

Bank Board's Figures

The Bank Board said lenders early last month were quoting a 9.93% average effective interest rate for the most popular type of adjustable loans, those that restrict rate increases. This compares with a revised 10.05% in early February. The Bank Board figures apply to loans maturing in 25 years or more for single-family homes.

For adjustable mortgages without rate limits, the average rate in early March was 9.73%, down from a revised 9.83% a month earlier. The Bank Board poll also found that lenders in early March were asking a 10.93% average effective interest rate for fixed-rate conventional mortgages, down from a revised 11.36% in early February. It was the biggest monthly decline since December.

Meanwhile, as adjustable-rate mortgages are losing popularity with borrowers, lenders are changing tactics in an effort to make adjustable rates more appealing (see story on page 21).

Mortgage rates have been falling since October, after holding generally steady last summer. But the sizable decrease—nearly a full percentage point this year alone—has failed to boost sales and starts of new homes much lately. Sales dropped 3.8% and starts were off 3.5% in February.

Some Disagreement

Many analysts expect mortgage rates to drop another half percentage point over the next several months. And then, they predict, fixed-rate loans tracked by the Federal Home Loan Mortgage Corp.—called Freddie Mac—will remain in the single-digit range at least through year-end. But there is disagreement over whether the lower rates will last beyond 1986, because of uncertainty over the impact of falling oil prices on overall economic growth.

One optimist is Allen Sinai, senior vice president and chief economist for Shearson Lehman Brothers Inc. "Interest rates are in or headed for the single digits and should stay there for the rest of the decade," Mr. Sinai asserted. "For housing, home sales, home building and construction in general, the rate outlook is very positive."

Freddie Mac's basic weekly figures refer to conventional loans for 80% of the purchase price of a new single-family home. The figures don't include certain initial fees amortized over a decade. Primarily by charging higher fees, lenders in a number of cities in recent weeks have started to offer fixed-rate mortgages as low as 9.5%.

"Right now, I don't see anything that's around to push them (mortgage rates) back up a lot" any time soon, observed David Andrukonis, a Freddie Mac economist. "But ultimately, the economy will pick up steam and put a floor under rates," and any subsequent pickup in rates isn't likely to be very big, he said.

The average term for all conventional mortgages closed in early March was 25.3 years, up a bit from 25.2 years in early February, the Bank Board said. Loans averaged 74.9% of the purchase price, up from a revised 74.1% in the previous month.

The Wall Street Journal, *April 4, 1986*

Chart 6–2

Long-Term Interest Rates: Secondary Market Yields on FHA Mortgages, Yield on New Issues of High-Grade Corporate Bonds, and Yield on Long-Term Treasury Bonds

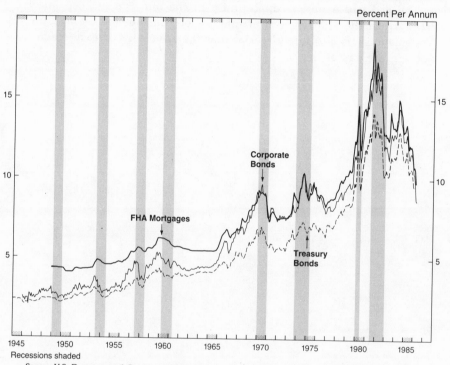

Recessions shaded

Source: U.S. Department of Commerce, *Business Conditions Digest* and *Handbook of Cyclical Indicators*, series 115, 116, and 118.

all they cared about was the size of the monthly payment, and this could be held down by stretching out the length of payment. Consequently, as consumers borrowed more and more for second homes, boats, the latest electronic gadget, or whatever, business was forced to pay ever-higher interest rates as it competed for scarce funds. This not only limited industry's ability to modernize and improve our nation's capital stock, it also added *business* debt-financed demand on top of *consumer* debt-financed demand. Too many dollars chased too few goods as supply could not keep pace with demand at current prices, and therefore prices inevitably rose too quickly. Or so the credit rationers believed.

You don't hear many suggestions for credit rationing today. Deregulation and the Fed's determination to bring inflation under control drove interest rates up to the point where consumer expenditures *were* sensitive to the cost of borrowing. Now the Fed could fine-tune the level of residential building and auto manufacturing, permitting sufficient ease to maintain a healthy level of activity yet sufficient restraint to prevent runaway expansion. The same was true for business borrowing.

The Fed had a unique opportunity in the mid-80s to keep interest rates at just the right level to maintain good (but not too rapid) growth in demand. It is absolutely crucial that the advocates of easy credit do not win the day at the Fed.

7

The Business Cycle Phase One: from Trough to Recovery

Chapter 2 asserted that you cannot scientifically test hypotheses in economics as you can in physics. Yet one law of physics does apply to economics: Whatever goes up must come down. Fortunately for us, in economics the reverse is also true. Although boom inevitably goes bust, each recession is also self-correcting and carries with it the seeds of economic recovery.

But *why* does the business cycle always rebound and return, never falling into permanent depression, never achieving continuous expansion?

Well, to begin with, every expansion ends inevitably in recession because every expansion is fueled by credit. Consumers and businesses can borrow to buy new homes, cars, factories, and machinery. The more they borrow and spend, the faster demand grows, and production is pushed into high gear in order to keep pace with demand. But sooner or later, the upward spiral of borrowing and spending comes to an end. Consumers find that their incomes cannot support the burden of additional debt repayment. Businesses, having accomplished their targeted growth in plant and equipment, see that demand will not greatly increase in the near future and cut back or cease their expenditures in this area. Once business and consumer borrowing and spending start to decline, the slump begins and production and income fall.

The recession hits bottom when the components of demand that were financed by credit stop shrinking. Remember that these components are a limited, though highly volatile, share of total demand. (The demand for many items that are not financed by credit, such as food and medical care, will hardly decline at all.) As consumers and businesses cease borrowing and turn their attention to liquidating their expansion-generated debts, the price of credit, namely interest rates, falls, until a point is finally established where debt burden and interest rates are low enough that consumers can again borrow and spend. At this juncture, auto production, home construction, and business investment in new plant and equipment stop falling, the slide ends, and economic recovery is in sight.

Generally speaking, expansion ceases when consumers are no longer willing to borrow and spend; contraction ends when their confidence returns. In the 1970s, these cyclical changes in consumer confidence were closely tied to the rate of inflation. Rapid economic expansion brought swiftly rising prices with an attendant and sobering drop in real income and consumer confidence. Recession cooled the pace of inflation, encouraging a resurgence of confidence.

In the 1980s, the normal course of the cycle was interrupted by the Fed's tight money policy of 1981–82 and strongly influenced by the Fed's new posture toward inflation. Yet, although the cycle won't have the same clothing as in the 70s, it will still be recognizable.

Chapters 4, 5, and 6, which examined the Federal Reserve System and the money and credit markets, described the 70's cycle, and the new climate of the 80s, in financial terms. Look at the cycle now from a different perspective, weaving in the elements of production, income, and consumer demand.

Consumers borrowed heavily in 1972 and 1973 to make record purchases of new homes and automobiles. Business responded by adding plant and equipment to meet the demand and by stockpiling inventory to satisfy customer orders. The sharp growth in consumer and business demand boosted prices rapidly, and the rate of inflation increased from 4 percent in 1972 to 12 percent in 1974. Interest rates moved in parallel fashion. Soon consumers became discouraged as their incomes failed to keep pace, so their expenditures on homes, autos, and other goods plunged.

This led to a general decline in production, and by early 1975 unemployment was at a postwar record. The cycle was complete.

The drop in demand reduced both inflation and interest rates. By 1976 consumers were regaining confidence, and the revival of their willingness to spend brought recovery and expansion. Boom conditions and rising inflation and interest rates returned in 1978, eroding consumer confidence once again. Consumer demand fell, and the 1980 recession began; another cycle had come full circle.

Recovery from the 1980 recession had barely begun when the Fed strangled the credit markets in 1981–82. But the ensuing recession, designed to curb inflation, had the standard impact on consumer confidence—dramatic improvement—and as soon as the Fed relaxed its grip, consumer expenditures surged forward. Certainly, if the cycle follows its normal pattern, renewed inflation will bring on the next recession. But the 80s are not a repeat of the 70s; the minislowdown of 1984 proved that the Fed can fine-tune a reduction in demand. Will the Fed maintain its vigilant attitude toward inflation? That's the question of the late 80s.

So far, the business cycle has been painted with fairly broad strokes. The time has come to take up a finer brush so that essential details and connections can be clearly drawn. This chapter introduces the statistical series that are particularly useful in charting output, efficiency, and inflation and the relationships among them. Gross national product, industrial production, and capacity utilization measure the economy's output; productivity measures its efficiency. As output increases, efficiency decreases, and inflation—as reported by the producer price index—inevitably becomes a problem. The initial connections between output, efficiency, and inflation form this chapter's central theme.

At the peak of the cycle, when output is at its maximum, production facilities are strained to the point where production costs rise sharply. Overburdened equipment fails, accelerating the expense of maintenance and repair. The quantities of labor added to the productive process are relatively greater than the increase in output. Inevitable inefficiencies force up costs, and consequently prices, even though the product itself has not changed. The obvious result: inflation increases rapidly.

With the recession's drop in production, the strain on facilities and labor eases. Costs fall, inflation declines, and the stage is set for a new round of expansion and growth.

This chapter focuses on the earliest phase of the business cycle, the passage from trough to recovery. Subsequent chapters will examine the remaining three phases of the cycle. Turn now to an examination of the statistical releases that will be of particular importance in charting the course of production and the interaction of efficiency and inflation as the economy moves from trough to recovery.

GROSS NATIONAL PRODUCT (GNP)

GNP is a good place to start. It is the broadest available measure of economic activity and provides the official scale with which fluctuations in the economy are measured.

The Wall Street Journal publishes the U.S. Department of Commerce's quarterly release on the GNP about three weeks after the close of each quarter. Then, around the 20th of the two subsequent months of the next quarter, it reports revisions of the data. The first revision of fourth quarter 1985 figures appeared in the February 21, 1986, *Journal.* (See page 77.)

Look for the following features: *constant-dollar (real) GNP, current-dollar (nominal) GNP,* the *rate of inflation,* and the *statistical summary.*

Constant-Dollar (Real) GNP—Paragraph 1 and Paragraph 6.

WASHINGTON — The economy expanded at a meager 1.2% annual rate in the fourth quarter, the Commerce Department said, half the pace estimated by the agency last month.

Because there's so much focus on the rate of growth, the GNP revision appears unusually large. The actual fourth-quarter GNP figure, however, was only 0.2% less than the one originally reported. The agency's latest figure was $3.595 trillion at an annual rate, adjusted for both inflation and seasonal changes.

Current-Dollar (Nominal) GNP—Last Paragraph.

Before adjustment for inflation but after seasonal adjustment, the nation's total output in the fourth quarter was estimated at an annual rate of $4.062 trillion, up from $4.017 trillion in the third quarter.

GNP Expands At Half the Rate Thought Earlier

Revision in Growth Data For 4th Quarter Is Tied To Trade and Inventories

By Rose Gutfeld

Staff Reporter of The Wall Street Journal

Constant-Dollar (real) GNP

WASHINGTON — The economy expanded at a meager 1.2% annual rate in the fourth quarter, the Commerce Department said, half the pace estimated by the agency last month.

For the full year, the real gross national product, the inflation-adjusted value of the nation's output of goods and services, rose 2.3%, unchanged from last month's report, after rounding. That follows 6.6% growth in 1984 and represents the worst peformance since the recession year of 1982.

The fourth-quarter revision refle^· .. sharper deterioration in the ᵖ·⁺ ...ink the deficit and lower iⁿ·· .. than previousⁱʸ· ..ᵤnists suggested that mists. ᵗ .,entories will contribute to ᵉᵇ .., nigher growth in the current quarter.

"There's a silver lining here," said Robert Wescott, senior economist at Wharton Econometric Forecasting Associates, in a telephone interview. "Two big categories are likely to turn around." At the same time, he noted that the sharp revision suggests "we ended 1985 on a softer note than people had thought."

Because there's so much focus on the rate of growth, the GNP revision appears unusually large. The actual fourth-quarter GNP figure, however, was only 0.2% less than the one originally reported. The agency's latest figure was $3.595 trillion at an annual rate, adjusted for both inflation and seasonal changes.

Constant-Dollar (real) GNP

Robert Ortner, the Commerce Department's chief economist, said the revision wasn't out of line with earlier changes between the preliminary and revised estimates. He said the primary factor in the revision was a sharp increase in imports. As reported last month, the merchandise trade deficit in December swelled to a record $17.37 billion. The original GNP estimate was made before that figure came

out. Mr. Ortner noted that changes in the department's schedule of reporting import and export figures may also have contributed to the change.

The revision in inventory data reflected December figures that weren't available previously.

The 1.2% fourth-quarter rate followed increases at a 3% pace in the third quarter and 1.1% in the second.

Economists generally expect it will be midyear before the decline of the dollar on foreign-exchange markets in the past year begins to narrow the trade deficit. A weaker dollar makes imports more expensive and exports more competitive. But many analysts contend that the deficit has stopped worsening significantly.

The trade deficit represents money going to buy foreign goods. Any increase in the deficit is subtracted from national output in the GNP statistics. If the deficit narrows or stops widening, that adds to GNP growth. Robert Gay, senior economist at Morgan Stanley & Co., said he expects ᵗ˙ trade deficit to "flatten out" iⁿ ..edicts half. ..ᵤse 4% this

Concerning iⁿ·· suggested ᵗ˙ . revision, the department foᵘʳᵗ ..ᵤed its estimate of personal con- ..ᵤmption expenditures. The latest report said this spending grew at an annual rate of 0.1% in the fourth quarter; previously, the agency said it declined at an annual rate of 0.2%.

Rate of Inflation

According to a GNP-based measure known as the deflator, prices rose at an annual rate of 3.3% in the fourth quarter, following an increase at a 2.9% rate in the third quarter. Those figures are unchanged from last month's report.

Inflation is likely to be far more subdued in the current quarter, largely as a result of the sharp drop in oil prices. The Labor Department reported last month that producer prices for finished goods fell 0.7% in January, or 7.8% at a compounded annual rate.

Current-Dollar (nominal) GNP

Before adjustment for inflation but after seasonal adjustment, the nation's total output in the fourth quarter was estimated at an annual rate of $4.062 trillion, up from $4.017 trillion in the third quarter.

Statistical Summary

Here are some of the major components of the gross national product expressed in seasonally adjusted annual rates in billions of constant (1982) dollars:

	4th. Qtr. 1985	3rd. Qtr. 1985
GNP	3594.8	3584.1
less: inventory change	−6.7	−1.8
equals: final sales	3601.5	3585.8
Components of Final Sales		
Personal Consumption	2330.	2329.6
Nonresidential invest.	485.	473.7
Residential invest.	175.	173.1
Net Exports	−134.0	−119.8
Gov't Purchases	744.3	729.2

In the fourth quarter, the implicit price deflator rose to 113.0% of the 1982 average, from 112.1% in the previous quarter.

The Wall Street Journal, *February 21, 1986*

Rate of Inflation—Third Paragraph from End of Article.

According to a GNP-based measure
known as the deflator, prices rose at an annual rate of 3.3% in the fourth quarter, following an increase at a 2.9% rate in the
third quarter. Those figures are unchanged
from last month's report.

Statistical Summary—End of Article.

Here are some of the major components of the gross
national product expressed in seasonally adjusted annual
rates in billions of constant (1982) dollars:

	4th. Qtr. 1985	3rd. Qtr. 1985
GNP	3594.8	3584.1
less: inventory change	−6.7	−1.8
equals: final sales	3601.5	3585.8
Components of Final Sales		
Personal Consumption	2330.3	2329.6
Nonresidential Invest.	485.1	473.7
Residential Invest.	175.8	173.1
Net Exports	−134.0	−119.8
Gov't Purchases	744.3	729.2

In the fourth quarter, the implicit price deflator rose to
113.0% of the 1982 average, from 112.1% in the previous
quarter.

Constant-Dollar (Real) GNP

The first paragraph tells you that "the economy expanded at a meager
1.2 percent annual rate in the fourth quarter." What does this mean?

WASHINGTON – The economy expanded at a meager 1.2% annual rate in
the fourth quarter, the Commerce Department said, half the pace estimated by the
agency last month.

Because there's so much focus on the
rate of growth, the GNP revision appears
unusually large. The actual fourth-quarter
GNP figure, however, was only 0.2% less
than the one originally reported. The
agency's latest figure was $3.595 trillion at
an annual rate, adjusted for both inflation
and seasonal changes.

Constant-dollar (real) GNP measures the final output of goods and
services produced in the American economy in one year, without including
the impact of changed prices on the value of those goods. That is, this
year's output (as well as last year's output, next year's, or any year we
wish to measure) is calculated in the prices of the base year (1982). This
eliminates measuring the same thing more than once at various stages
of its production. For instance, bread purchased by the consumer appears
in GNP, but both the flour from which the bread is baked and the wheat
from which the flour is milled are omitted because the value of the bread
comprises the value of all its ingredients.

Thus, the economy's output of *all* goods and services is far greater
than its output of *final* goods and services. We use very little steel, chemi-
cals, or advertising agency services directly. Their value is subsumed in
our purchases of well-promoted Chevrolets and Saran Wrap.

Paragraph 1 refers to a 1.2 percent increase in final output. This measurement was made at a *seasonally adjusted annual rate* in the fourth
quarter. Adjusting for seasonal factors merely means correcting the distortion in the data arising from the fact that the measurement is being taken
during October, November, and December rather than any other quarter.
Obviously, no seasonal adjustment is required when a whole year's data
is measured, but when the year is divided up and data extracted for a
run of months, the risk of distortion attributable to the season is great.
For instance, retail trade is particularly heavy around Christmas and particularly light immediately after the first of the year; you could not make
a useful comparison of the first quarter's retail sales with the last quarter's
without first making a seasonal adjustment.

The reference to "annual rate" shows that the data for the fourth
quarter, which of course covers only three months' activity, has been
multiplied by four to increase it to a level comparable to annual data.

The constant-dollar or real GNP calculation is made in order to compare
the level of output in one time period with that in another without inflation's distorting impact. If the inflation factor were not removed, you

would not know whether differences in dollar value were due to output changes or price changes. Real GNP gives you a dollar value that measures output changes only.

One last point should be made before moving on. The first paragraph referred to the 1.2 percent growth rate as "meager." Three percent or better is good, and more than 5 percent is unsustainable for any length of time. The economy just can't supply (turn out) more than that because of the limits on our productive capacity at any moment. On the other hand, 1.2 percent is barely above the rate of population growth and therefore provides a meager per capita gain.

Current-Dollar (Nominal) GNP

Nominal (current-dollar) GNP includes inflation and is therefore higher than *real* (constant-dollar) GNP, which does not. Distinguishing clearly between these expressions will help you avoid a good deal of confusion.

Before adjustment for inflation but after seasonal adjustment, the nation's total output in the fourth quarter was estimated at an annual rate of $4.062 trillion, up from $4.017 trillion in the third quarter.

The last paragraph of the article informs you that before adjustment for inflation (that is, including current, inflated prices), GNP was $4.062 trillion, considerably more than the real figure (at 1982 prices) of $3.595 trillion, reported in paragraph 6. You can see how rising prices inflate the nominal value of GNP. Both measurements calibrate the same level of output, but the greatly increased value of the current-dollar GNP figure is a direct consequence of the higher level of prices prevailing now.

Rate of Inflation

According to a GNP-based measure known as the deflator, prices rose at an annual rate of 3.3% in the fourth quarter, following an increase at a 2.9% rate in the third quarter. Those figures are unchanged from last month's report.

The third paragraph from the end of the article reports that, "according to a GNP-based measure known as the deflator, prices rose at an annual rate of 3.3 percent in the fourth quarter." This index, known as the *implicit price deflator,* yields the broadest measure of inflation, since GNP is the most broadly based measure of economic activity. It is derived by dividing current-dollar (nominal) GNP, which includes inflation, by constant-dollar (real) GNP, which does not include inflation. Dividing the figure that includes inflation by the figure that does not provides a measurement of price increase.

The more familiar consumer price index includes consumption expenditures only, while the implicit price deflator includes production for business and government use as well. The producer price index, which is explained later in this chapter, covers wholesale prices of goods but not services.

Statistical Summary

Here are some of the major components of the gross national product expressed in seasonally adjusted annual rates in billions of constant (1982) dollars:

	4th. Qtr. 1985	3rd. Qtr. 1985
GNP	3594.8	3584.1
less: inventory change	−6.7	−1.8
equals: final sales	3601.5	3585.8
Components of Final Sales		
Personal Consumption	2330.3	2329.6
Nonresidential Invest.	485.1	473.7
Residential Invest.	175.8	173.1
Net Exports	−134.0	−119.8
Gov't Purchases	744.3	729.2

In the fourth quarter, the implicit price deflator rose to 113.0% of the 1982 average, from 112.1% in the previous quarter.

The statistical summary at the end of the article provides a convenient breakdown of the major GNP components. Note how much more rapidly GNP would have grown had it not been for the continued decline in inventories and net exports.

Now you are ready to put GNP's current performance in historical perspective. Compare it with Chart 7–1 on page 82.

The top graph portrays the actual level of GNP, while the bottom graph depicts quarterly percentage changes at annual rates. When the bottom series is above the zero line, GNP has increased; a drop in GNP is indicated by points below the zero line.

Chart 7-1

Gross National Product (GNP) In Constant (1982) Dollars; Quarterly Change in GNP at Annual Rates

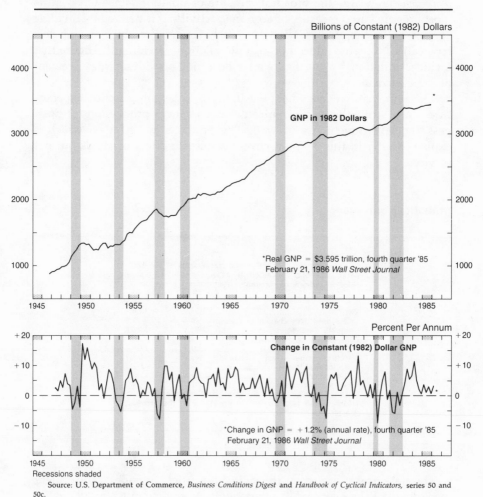

Billions of Constant (1982) Dollars

GNP in 1982 Dollars

*Real GNP = $3.595 trillion, fourth quarter '85
February 21, 1986 *Wall Street Journal*

Percent Per Annum

Change in Constant (1982) Dollar GNP

*Change in GNP = + 1.2% (annual rate), fourth quarter '85
February 21, 1986 *Wall Street Journal*

Recessions shaded

Source: U.S. Department of Commerce, *Business Conditions Digest* and *Handbook of Cyclical Indicators*, series 50 and 50c.

As you look at these graphs, pay special attention to the setback to the growth of GNP during the back-to-back recessions of 1980 and 1981–82. You can also see that GNP has climbed out of that ditch, although it was dented again in 1984.

Industrial production and capacity utilization will mirror GNP's performance, and so you should now become acquainted with these series.

INDUSTRIAL PRODUCTION

The Wall Street Journal reports the Federal Reserve's data on *industrial production* in an article that usually appears midmonth. A typical report was published on April 16, 1986. The headline, accompanying chart, and first paragraph summarize matters, while the article provides detail and commentary. (See page 84.)

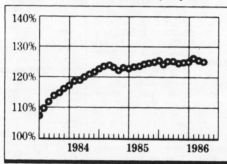

Industrial Production

In percent (1977=100), seasonally adjusted.

INDUSTRIAL PRODUCTION fell to 125.1% of the 1977 average in March, after seasonal adjustment, from a revised 125.7% in February, the Federal Reserve reports.

The Wall Street Journal, *April 16, 1986*

Industrial Production—First Paragraph.

WASHINGTON—Output at the nation's factories, mines and utilities fell 0.5% in March, the second consecutive monthly drop, the Federal Reserve Board said.

Industry Output Dropped Again During March

Decline of 0.5% Followed 0.7% Slide in February; Drilling Cutback a Factor

By ROSE GUTFELD
Staff Reporter of THE WALL STREET JOURNAL.

Industrial Production

WASHINGTON—Output at the nation's factories, mines and utilities fell 0.5% in March, the second consecutive monthly drop, the Federal Reserve Board said.

The decline underscored continued weakness in manufacturing. It followed a revised decline of 0.7% in February, and marked the first two-month decline in the industrial production index since September and October of 1984. The February decline originally was reported as 0.6%.

"The manufacturing sector is getting off to a pretty lousy start this year," said Donald Straszheim, president of Merrill Lynch Economics Inc. in New York.

'Very Sluggish Economy'

"The underlying economy is somewhat weaker than even I thought," said ˉ . at rence Chimerine, chairman ᵒᶠ ⌐ ometrics in Bala-Cyn⌐⌐ ⌐ concentrated very sluggish ᵉ⌐ ⌐⌐g, auto and truck as best." ⌐ steel production, the Fed

The drilling decline reflected cutbacks by energy companies in response to the sharp drop of oil prices in international markets. The price drop is expected to spur spending and economic growth eventually, but in the short term it has seriously damaged some sectors of the economy.

"The oil prices decline will be a fundamental major positive (factor)," said Mr. Straszheim. "But we didn't appreciate how much damage would be done at the outset."

Many economists also expect that the weakness in auto production, which the Fed said reflected poor sales and excessive inventories, will continue in coming months.

Many Expect Pickup

Still, many economists expect industrial

Industrial Production

In percent (1977=100), seasonally adjusted.

INDUSTRIAL PRODUCTION fell to 125.1% of the 1977 average in March, after seasonal adjustment, from a revised 125.7% in February, the Federal Reserve reports.

production to pick up in the second half of the year in response to lower oil prices, falling interest rates and the decline of the dollar over the past year. A lower dollar helps manufacturers, which have been battered by foreign competition, by makin⌐ imports more expensive and U.S ⌐ ⌐⌐y," relatively cheaper.   ⌐sident and

"One should still ⌐ ⌐⌐earson Lehman economy will ⌐ ⌐⌐w York. But he added said A¹¹⌐ ⌐⌐st industrial production report ⌐¹ ⌐⌐rscores that up to now there are really no signs" of the predicted strength.

The report said that output of consumer goods fell 0.7% in March, after declining 0.2% in February. Business equipment production dropped 0.9% last month after a 1.3% decline in February. Mining output, reflecting the drop in drilling, declined 1.1% in March after falling 3% in February. Output at utilities declined 0.1% after rising 1.7%. The numbers are all adjusted for seasonal variations.

The Fed's industrial production index stood at 125.1% of its 1977 average in March, up 0.9% from a year earlier (see chart on page one).

Here is a summary of the Federal Reserve Board's report on industrial production in March. The figures are seasonally adjusted.

	% change from	
	Feb. 1986	March 1985
Total	-0.5	0.9
Consumer goods	-0.7	2.5
Business equipment	-0.9	0
Defense and space	0.6	4.9
Manufacturing only	-0.5	1.6
Durable goods	-1.0	-0.2
Nondurable goods	0.2	4.1
Mining	-1.1	-6.8
Utilities	-0.1	1.1

The industrial production index for March stood at 125.1% of the 1977 average.

The index of industrial production measures changes in the output of the mining, manufacturing, and gas and electric utilities sectors of our economy. Industrial production is a narrower concept than GNP because it omits agriculture, construction, wholesale and retail trade, transportation, communications, services, finance, government, and U.S. activities in the rest of the world. Industrial production is also more volatile than GNP, because GNP, unlike industrial production, includes activities that are largely spared cyclical fluctuation, such as services, finance, and government. The brunt of cyclical fluctuations falls on the mining, manufacturing, and public utilities sectors. Nonetheless, GNP and industrial production move in parallel fashion.

Industrial production is measured by an *index,* a technique that focuses on the relative size and fluctuation of physical output without concern for its dollar value. To construct the index, a base year (1977) is selected to serve as a benchmark and assigned a value of 100.0. (Think of it as 100 percent.) Data for all other months and years is then expressed in relative proportion (numerical ratio) to the data for the base year. For example, according to the caption under the **Industrial Production** chart (see page 83) accompanying the article, industrial production had an index value of 125.1 in March 1986. This means that industrial production in March 1986 was 25.1 percent higher than the average rate of production in 1977.

As with GNP, two graphs are used to illustrate industrial production (see Chart 7–2 on page 86). The top graph displays actual index values, and the second illustrates monthly changes.

Now compare the course of industrial production with GNP, and note that both series have rebounded from the long decline of 1981–82 (see Chart 7–3 on page 87). These developments will be reflected in the rate of capacity utilization and in the efficiency with which the economy is operated.

CAPACITY UTILIZATION

In the third week of each month, *The Wall Street Journal* publishes the Federal Reserve's monthly statistical release on *capacity utilization,* or, as it is often called, the *factory operating rate.* The headline and first paragraph of the March 18, 1986, article inform you of February's rate. (See page 88).

Chart 7–2
Industrial Production Index (1977 = 100); Quarterly Change in Index at Annual Rates

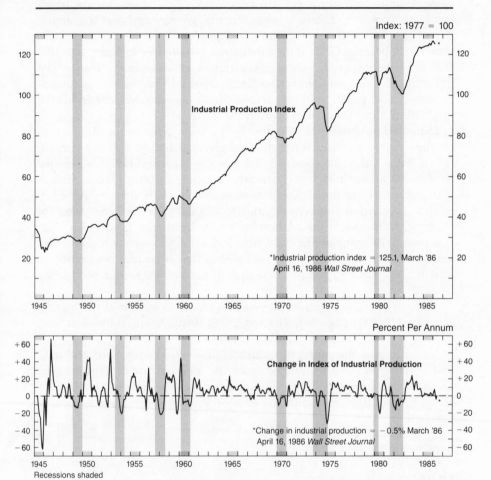

Index: 1977 = 100

Industrial Production Index

*Industrial production index = 125.1, March '86
April 16, 1986 *Wall Street Journal*

Percent Per Annum

Change in Index of Industrial Production

*Change in industrial production = – 0.5% March '86
April 16, 1986 *Wall Street Journal*

Recessions shaded

Source: U.S. Department of Commerce, *Business Conditions Digest* and *Handbook of Cyclical Indicators,* series 47 and 47c.

Chart 7–3
GNP and Industrial Production

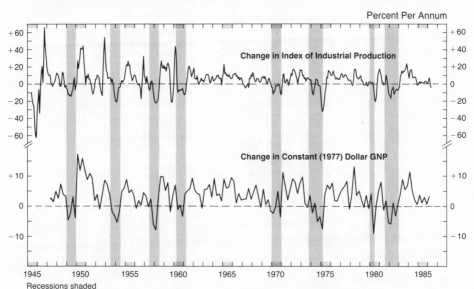

Recessions shaded

Source: U.S. Department of Commerce, *Business Conditions Digest* and *Handbook of Cyclical Indicators,* series 47c and 50c.

Capacity Utilization—First Paragraph.

WASHINGTON—The operating rate for the nation's factories, mines and utilities fell to 80% of capacity in February, the Federal Reserve Board said, tracking the steep drop in industrial production last month.

Capacity utilization is the rate at which manufacturing industry operates, expressed as a percentage of the maximum rate at which it could operate under normal conditions. Putting the matter differently, think of capacity utilization as measuring what manufacturing industry is currently producing compared (in percentage terms) to the most it could produce. Thus, if an industry produces 80 tons of product in a year, while having plant and equipment at its disposal capable of producing

Operating Rate For Industry Fell Last Month to 80%

By a WALL STREET JOURNAL Staff Reporter

Capacity Utilization

WASHINGTON—The operating rate for the nation's factories, mines and utilities fell to 80% of capacity in February, the Federal Reserve Board said, tracking the steep drop in industrial production last month.

The fall in the operating rate, which followed a revised decline in January to 80.6%, also provides further evidence of the detrimental effect the plunge in oil prices is having in some sectors of the economy. The January performance was originally reported as an increase to 80.8%.

The latest rate is down from 80.9% in February 1985.

The operating rate for factories alone stood at 79.9% of capacity last month, down from 80.5% in January. This drop

and the 0.6% decline in industrial production in February indicate that manufacturers have yet to turn the corner after a year of difficulty caused by import competition.

Within the manufacturing category, durable goods makers used 77.1% of capacity, down from 77.9% in January; producers of nondurable goods used 84.1% of capacity, down from 84.6%. Durable goods are items intended to last three years or more.

The operating rate rose for the motor vehicles and parts industry, to 85.7% from 85.5%. The rate for the petroleum products industry fell steeply to 90.7% after rising sharply to 92.5% in January.

The report showed that the nation's mines operated at 77.7% of capacity, down from 80.1% in January. Mining output has been reduced by cutbacks in drilling by oil companies, which have been hurt by the recent sharp drop in oil prices in international spot markets.

The operating rate for utilities rose to 83.5% in February from 82.4% in January. Producers of industrial materials used 79% of capacity in February, down from 79.6% in January.

The Wall Street Journal, *March 18, 1986*

100 tons a year, that industry is operating at 80 percent of capacity; its capacity utilization is 80 percent.

Capacity utilization is a short-run concept determined by a company's current physical limits; at any moment in which capacity utilization is reported, it is assumed that the company's plant and equipment cannot be increased, although labor and other inputs can. This defines the short run. Although manufacturing industry continually adds new plant and equipment, it is useful to snap a photograph at a particular moment to enable measurement and comparison.

What bearing does capacity utilization have on the efficiency or productivity of industry? Consider a hypothetical analogy. Your car operates more efficiently at 50 miles per hour than at 70 if its maximum speed is 80, for you will obtain better gas mileage at the lower speed. Efficiency is expressed as a relationship between inputs (gas gallons) and outputs (miles driven). Your car's engine operates more efficiently at lower speeds—that is, at lower levels of capacity utilization.

You are therefore confronted with the problem of diminishing returns: as your speed increases, you obtain fewer miles for each additional gallon of gas. At 50 miles per hour, you can go 30 miles on an additional gallon of gas; at 52 miles per hour, 29 miles on an additional gallon; at 54 miles per hour, 28 miles; and so on. Your output (miles) per unit of input (gallon) falls as you push toward full capacity utilization (maximum speed).

Likewise, as capacity utilization increases, an industry also reaches the point of diminishing returns. This may be at 70 percent, 80 percent, or 90 percent of capacity utilization, depending on the industry, but the point will ultimately be reached where the percentage increases in output will become smaller than the percentage increases in input. For instance, a 15 percent increase in labor input, once we have passed the point of diminishing returns, may provide only a 10 percent increase in output.

This phenomenon does not develop because of some mystical mathematical relationship. Indeed, you probably know many of the common-sense reasons for it.

First, at low levels of capacity utilization, there is ample time to inspect, maintain, and repair equipment; accidental damage can be held to a minimum; and production increases can be achieved easily in a smoothly efficient plant. Above a certain level of capacity utilization, however, management finds it more difficult to inspect, maintain, and repair equipment because of the plant's heavier operating schedule. Perhaps a second shift of workers has been added or additional overtime scheduled. There is less time for equipment maintenance, and accidental damage becomes inevitable. The labor force is in place and on the payroll, and production does increase, but not as rapidly as does labor input, because equipment frequently breaks down.

Second, as production increases and more labor is hired, the last people hired are less experienced and usually less efficient than the older workers; furthermore, crowding and fatigue can become a problem if more overtime is scheduled. The result: poor work quality and accidental damage. All of this ensures that output will not increase as rapidly as labor input.

Third, low levels of capacity utilization occur at the trough of a recession. Business firms typically suffer a sharp drop in profit, if not actual losses, and under these circumstances, the employer reduces the work force as much as possible—in fact, usually reduces it more than the drop in output, once the decision to cut back has been made. Why more than the drop in output? Because by the trough of recession, the seriousness of the situation is recognized, and industry has embarked on a thorough restructuring. The alarm has sounded and costs (work force) are slashed. That's why recession often generates the sharpest increases in efficiency.

Even after output has begun to recover, an extended period of labor reduction may continue as part of a general cost-cutting program. As recovery boosts capacity utilization, however, hiring additional workers becomes inevitable. When a factory reaches full capacity utilization near the peak of a boom, the cost-cutting program will be long forgotten as

Chart 7–4
GNP, Industrial Production, and Capacity Utilization

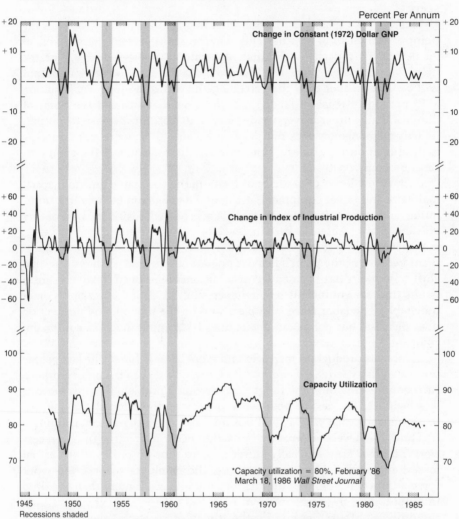

Source: U.S. Department of Commerce, *Business Conditions Digest* and *Handbook of Cyclical Indicators,* series 47c, 50c, and 82.

management scrambles for additional labor in order to meet the barrage of orders. At this point, additions to labor are greater than increments in output, even though (to repeat) output will be rising somewhat.

You can summarize business's decisions regarding labor as follows. During rapid expansion and into economic boom, when orders are heavy and capacity utilization is strained, business will sacrifice efficiency and short-run profits to maintain customer loyalty. Management adds labor more rapidly than output increases to get the job done. But when the recession hits in earnest, and it becomes apparent that orders will not recover for some time, management cuts labor costs to the bone with layoffs and a freeze on hiring. This is especially true during a prolonged recession, such as that of 1981–82, which followed on the heels of an earlier recession (in 1980) and an incomplete recovery. Even after recovery and expansion begin, business will attempt to operate with a reduced labor force in order to reap the benefits of cost cutting in the form of higher profits. Operating efficiency (productivity) improves rapidly, and it will not be threatened until the expansion heats up and boom conditions develop.

Now compare capacity utilization's historical record with that of GNP and industrial production, noting once again the figure reported in the March 18, 1986, *Journal* article and comparing it with the 1981–82 figures (see Chart 7–4 on page 90).

Each of the series examined thus far—GNP, industrial production, capacity utilization—tells the same story. The economy has moved well past phase one (trough to recovery) of the cycle since 1981–82. But the impact of the 1984 minislowdown is clear in all three series. Note especially the plateau in capacity utilization, which lingered long after 1984.

Now you can discern the Fed's reasons for that slowdown. Too rapid an increase in output and capacity utilization, continuing well past the first phase of the cycle, would have eliminated any gain in efficiency created by the slack conditions during and immediately following the 1981–82 recession. The Fed wanted slow, steady growth, not a rush to full capacity utilization, so it held back the economy in 1984 because capacity utilization had improved too quickly—from a 70 percent to an 80 percent rate.

The next series in this chapter, labor productivity and unit labor costs, will provide the statistical measurement needed to calibrate these fluctuations in efficiency.

LABOR PRODUCTIVITY AND UNIT LABOR COSTS

The Wall Street Journal reports the U.S. Department of Labor's preliminary release on *labor productivity* about a month after the end of the

Non-Farm Productivity Fell 0.2% in '85, First Decline Since Recession Year of '82

By Cathy Trost

Staff Reporter of The Wall Street Journal

Labor Productivity

Behind the drop was a sharp revision in the fourth-quarter figure to a 3.1% decline, at an annual rate, compared with the original estimate of 1.8%, the Labor Department said. In either case, it was the steepest drop since the 5% rate in the final quarter of 1981.

The department had originally ~ ~ farm productivity for the ~ ~ fourth-flat. Non-farm pro~ ~ For example, 1984. In the th~ ~ ~tment has reported produc~ ~ ~ly grew at an inflation-ad~ ~ ~ ~.~% annual rate in the fourth quar-~er, half the pace originally estimated.

Output and Hours

In the 1985 fourth quarter, non-farm output grew at a revised annual rate of 1.5%, while hours worked rose at a 4.7% rate. In January, the department had said its estimate of a 1.8% rate of decline reflected a 2.6% annual increase in output and a 4.5% rise in hours worked.

Productivity usually rises steeply in the early stages of a business recovery and then slows as employers hire more workers and increase wages. Productivity in the current economic expansion peaked in the second quarter of 1983, when it spurted at a 7.1% annual rate. As economic growth has slowed, so has productivity.

Some economists cautioned that a weak underlying trend in productivity raises questions about how fast the economy can grow over the next several years. "If the underlying trend remains as weak as it seems to be, then noninflationary growth is likely to be closer to 2% or 2.5%" than the 4% growth rate the Reagan administration is predicting for this year, said Carl Palash, an economist with McCarthy, Crisanti & Maffei Inc., a New York research firm.

"The main question is," said Audrey Freedman, an economist with the Conference Board, "is the long-term trend going to improve?" She said recent studies show that productivity growth in the current recovery has been less than the average for all recoveries since World War II. "Not only are we not returning to any good long-term trend," it has been weakening, she said.

With higher average emplo~ growth in this recovery tha~ ~ur costs "what we've done is n~ ~o annual rate, but with more n~ ~y increase since the very goo~ ~uarter. The department origi-s~i~ ~~timated a 5.4% increase.

Overall business productivity, including farms, grew at a revised annual rate of 0.2% in 1985, slightly less than the 0.3% rate previously estimated. In the 1985 fourth quarter, business productivity declined at a revised annual rate of 3.1%, a sharply steeper drop than the 1.3% annual rate initially projected. That represented the first decline since the 1984 fourth quarter and the largest drop since the 1981 fourth quarter, when it fell 5.5%.

Fourth-quarter manufacturing productivity declined at a 1% annual rate, the first decline in a year and the largest in four years, as output rose at a 2% annual rate and hours worked increased 3%. The department had earlier estimated productivity in this sector declined at a 1.5% annual rate. For the year, manufacturing productivity rose 2.7%, compared with a preliminary estimate of a 2.6% rise and after a gain of 4.9% in 1984.

The department also reported, in a preliminary estimate, that 1985 productivity of nonfinancial corporations, which account for almost 60% of the nation's output, declined 0.1%, the first annual decline in this sector since 1980. Output grew at a 2.8% rate while hours increased at a 3% rate. In 1984, nonfinancial corporations showed a 2.1% gain.

The Wall Street Journal, *February 28, 1986*

quarter, and publishes a revision about a month later. The February 28, 1986, article presents a revision of figures for 1985's fourth quarter, which appeared in preliminary form in late January. (See page 92.)

Labor Productivity—Second and Sixth Paragraphs.

> **Behind the drop was a sharp revision in the fourth-quarter figure to a 3.1% decline, at an annual rate, compared with the original estimate of 1.8%, the Labor Department said. In either case, it was the steepest drop since the 5% rate in the final quarter of 1981.**

> **In the 1985 fourth quarter, non-farm output grew at a revised annual rate of 1.5%, while hours worked rose at a 4.7% rate. In January, the department had said its estimate of a 1.8% rate of decline reflected a 2.6% annual increase in output and a 4.5% rise in hours worked.**

The second and sixth paragraphs inform you that a 1.5 percent improvement in output, combined with a 4.7 percent increase in labor input, drove down output per worker by 3.1 percent for all *nonfarm* business. It's simple subtraction; 1.5 minus 4.7 equals (roughly) negative 3.1.

Chart 7–5 on page 94 presents the record for all business (including farms). The series are similar.

Labor productivity measures output or production per unit of labor input (for instance, output per hour) and is the most important gauge of our nation's efficiency. Its significance cannot be overemphasized, for *per capita real income cannot improve*—and thus the country's standard of living cannot rise—*without an increase in per capita production.*

Unit labor cost measures labor cost per unit of output. Thus, unit labor cost is the *inverse* of labor productivity, since unit labor costs fall as labor productivity rises, and vice versa. Unit labor cost tells you how much added labor is required to produce an additional unit of output.

Chart 7–5
*Productivity: Output per Hour, All Persons, Private Business Sector (1977 =
100); Change in Output per Hour (smoothed)*

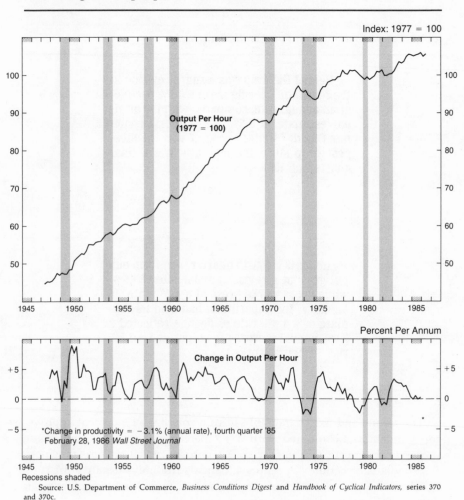

Index: 1977 = 100

Output Per Hour
(1977 = 100)

Percent Per Annum

Change in Output Per Hour

*Change in productivity = −3.1% (annual rate), fourth quarter '85
February 28, 1986 *Wall Street Journal*

Recessions shaded

Source: U.S. Department of Commerce, *Business Conditions Digest* and *Handbook of Cyclical Indicators,* series 370
and 370c.

Because labor is hired for a wage, requiring more labor time to produce
each unit of output will raise labor costs per unit of output, and vice
versa.

Consider, for instance, a factory that assembles hand-held calculators.
If the production of a calculator has required an hour of labor and a
technological innovation permits the production of two calculators per

hour, labor productivity has doubled, from one to two calculators per hour. The output per hour of work is twice what it was.

If the wage rate is $10 per hour, and before the innovation an hour of work was required to complete a calculator, the labor cost per unit of output was then $10. After the innovation, however, two calculators can be produced in an hour, or one calculator in half an hour, so unit labor cost has fallen to $5. Note that as labor productivity doubled, from one to two calculators per hour, unit labor costs were halved, from $10 to $5 per unit of output. The gain in labor productivity drove down unit labor costs without any change in the wage rate.

Now compare the record of labor productivity and unit labor costs, including the decline reported in the *Journal* article, with the other indicators examined so far (see Chart 7–6 on page 96).

GNP, industrial production, and capacity utilization together define the business cycle. Since 1970 their fluctuations have indicated prosperity and recession. You can also see that labor productivity plunged and unit labor costs soared with the peak of each cycle. Then labor productivity improved and unit labor costs declined with recession and into the next recovery. But as soon as expansion got under way, labor productivity's growth began to weaken and unit labor costs began to rise, until productivity slumped and costs peaked at the end of the boom.

And this brings you full circle to the discussion of efficiency included in the earlier investigation of capacity utilization: the economy's efficiency deteriorated with each boom and improved in recession and into recovery. All that this section has done is to provide the labels and devices (labor productivity and unit labor costs) necessary to measure that efficiency. During boom conditions, efficiency (labor productivity) declines and expenses (unit labor costs) mount. During recession the opposite is true.

You can see from the charts that the 1984 minislowdown depressed the growth of productivity, and that productivity advanced fairly slowly afterward due to the Fed's restrictive policies. Indeed, output grew so slowly in 1985 that productivity registered no improvement at all.

If the economy had grown more rapidly, productivity's record might have been better. But the Fed was correct to maintain slack conditions in an effort to prevent a premature peak of the cycle.

Turn now to the object of all this effort to contain costs: producer prices.

PRODUCER PRICES

The *producer price index,* until recently referred to as the wholesale price index, is compiled by the U.S. Department of Labor and shows the changes in price charged by producers of finished goods—changes

Chart 7-6
GNP, Industrial Production, Capacity Utilization, Labor Productivity, and Unit Labor Costs

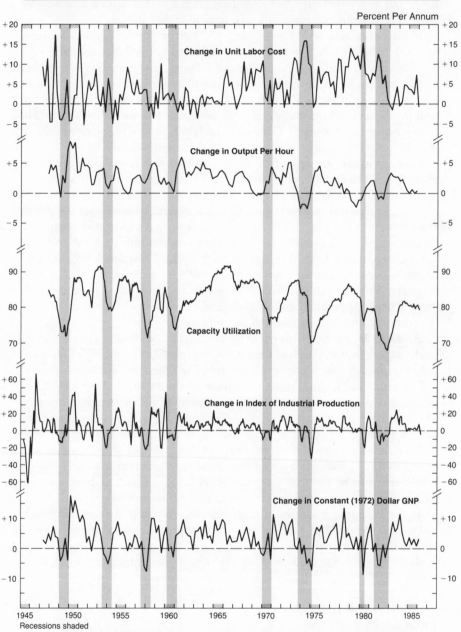

Percent Per Annum

Change in Unit Labor Cost

Change in Output Per Hour

Capacity Utilization

Change in Index of Industrial Production

Change in Constant (1972) Dollar GNP

Recessions shaded

Source: U.S. Department of Commerce, *Business Conditions Digest* and *Handbook of Cyclical Indicators*, series 47c, 50c, 82, and 370c; and Federal Reserve Board.

that are, of course, reflected in the prices consumers must pay. The Labor Department's news release on producer prices is usually published by *The Wall Street Journal* on the third Monday of the month. (See page 98.)

The March 17, 1986, article is an example, and the headline and third paragraph tell you that the producer price index fell 1.6 percent in February. The chart accompanying the article shows the index at 292.3 (1967 = 100).

Producer Prices

In percent (1967=100).

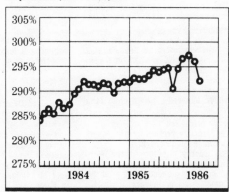

PRODUCER PRICES on finished goods in February, before seasonal adjustments, fell to 292.3% of the 1967 average from 296.2% in January, the Labor Department reports.

The Wall Street Journal, *March 17, 1986*

Producer Prices In February Fell A Record 1.6%

But Good News on Inflation Is Countered by Decline In Industrial Production

By ROSE GUTFELD
Staff Reporter of THE WALL STREET JOURNAL

WASHINGTON — February's record plunge in producer prices brought more good news for consumers on the inflation front, but the month's sharp drop in industrial production suggests the war isn't over for manufacturers.

Fueled by a steep decline in energy prices, producer prices for finished goods fell 1.6% last month, or 17.1% at a compounded annual rate, the Labor Department said. The decline, the steepest since the government began keeping the statistics in 1947, followed a 0.7% drop in January.

Producer Prices —

Energy prices fell 9.4% after droppi· 4.2% in January, reflecting the ·ıl· sharp drop in oil prices in ı· markets. Energy prices ᷄ ᷄erve Board economists generall᷄ ᷄ ᷄actories, mines drop to hold d·᷄ ᷄᷄ last month after ris· more᷄ mon᷄᷄ ᷄᷄% in January. It was the move·ᵉ· ᷄ᵉ since October. The January a᷄ ᷄ ᷄᷄as previously reported as 0.3%. The ᷄.᷄op was fairly broad-based, with the biggest decline coming in mining output, which fell 3% after being unchanged in January.

While economists generally don't expect a sustained decline in output, the report suggests that talk of a resurgence by manufacturers has been premature. "When you average it out, we're not getting much bounce," said Lawrence Chimerine, chairman of Chase Econometrics.

"We saw the beginning of a turnaround and we seem to be backsliding a little bit," said Nariman Behravesh, vice president for U.S. services at Wharton Econometric Forecasting Associates. However, he said he "still feels there's a lot of strength out there."

Several economists suggested that the production drop illustrates the damage the

The Wall Street Journal, *March 17, 1986*

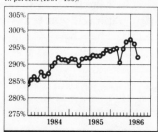

Producer Prices

In percent (1967=100).

PRODUCER PRICES on finished goods in February, before seasonal adjustments, fell to 292.3% of the 1967 average from 296.2% in January, the Labor Department reports.

oil-price plunge is doing in some sector·· of the economy. "I think industrial n· ·· tion indicates that the drop in ᴄ·· beginning to hurt," said S·· ᷄on, or 0.3%, economist with Data ᷄ ᷄᷄on after rising said the big decli᷄ ᷄, the month before to be traced to ·· ᷄nventories equaled 1.36 compani᷄ ᷄ales in January, up from 1.34 ᷄᷄s in December.

The figures in all three reports are adjusted for seasonal variations.

On prices, analysts generally expect further declines in the months ahead. "Because of the oil situation, we are in effect in a deflationary environment for a while," said Mr. Behravesh.

Some upward pressure on prices could result, particularly in the second half of the year, from the drop of the dollar in foreign-exchange markets in the past year. A lower dollar makes imports more expensive.

That, in turn, would aid U.S. manufacturers, however.

Prices of intermediate goods dropped 1.4% in February after falling 0.4% in January. Crude-goods prices fell 5% after declining 1.4% the month before.

Before adjustment for seasonal variation, the Labor Department's index of producer prices for finished goods was 292.3% of its 1967 average, down 1.3% from January and 0.1% below February 1985 (see chart on page one).

The Fed's industrial production index stood at 125.7% of its 1977 average in February, up 1.6% from a year earlier.

The production report showed that utility output rose 1.4% after falling 1.6% in

---

Producer Prices—Second Paragraph.

Fueled by a steep decline in energy prices, producer prices for finished goods fell 1.6% last month, or 17.1% at a compounded annual rate, the Labor Department said. The decline, the steepest since the government began keeping the statistics in 1947, followed a 0.7% drop in January.

Both the article and Chart 7–7 (page 100) confirm that inflation, as measured by the producer price index, has been purged from the economy. The drop since the 1979–80 peak has been dramatic.

You can also see from Chart 7–8 (page 101) that in the 70s the cyclical trends in producer prices mirrored those of unit labor costs. With each boom in output and capacity utilization, productivity dropped and unit labor costs rose, driving producer prices up. Then, when recession hit and output and capacity utilization fell, improved labor productivity and lower unit labor costs were reflected in reduced inflation. The last recession illustrates the principle: inflation's trend followed unit labor costs downward. As the economy's efficiency improved, stable prices followed on the heels of stable costs.

Now, prices got progressively less stable in the 70s, which created problems for all business firms that produced or used commodities. Planning became more difficult as companies attempted to estimate the cost of inputs, or the market price of their output, over the swings of the cycle. For instance, a home builder preparing to develop a subdivision must estimate the future price of lumber before he can advertise home prices to prospective buyers. At the same time, a lumber mill also has to gauge the future price of its product before bidding for the right to log timberland.

As commodity price fluctuations increased, business bought and sold contracts for future delivery in order to protect itself, and investors speculated on price changes, buying and selling futures contracts for profit. And this heightened interest in commodities caused the number of commodities traded on futures markets to grow.

The Wall Street Journal reports *commodity* prices on a daily basis, and each Monday it presents a chart showing indexes of commodity prices over the past year. These indexes cover 12 commodities: wheat, corn,

Chart 7–7
Producer Price Index (1967 = 100); Quarterly Change in Index at Annual Rates
(smoothed)

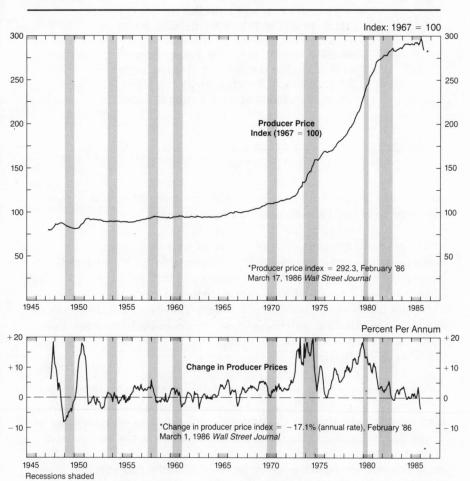

Index: 1967 = 100

Producer Price
Index (1967 = 100)

*Producer price index = 292.3, February '86
March 17, 1986 *Wall Street Journal*

Percent Per Annum

Change in Producer Prices

*Change in producer price index = −17.1% (annual rate), February '86
March 1, 1986 *Wall Street Journal*

Recessions shaded

Source: U.S. Department of Commerce, *Business Conditions Digest* and *Handbook of Cyclical Indicators*, series 334 and 334c; Federal Reserve Board.

soybeans, cattle, hogs, gold, silver, copper, sugar, coffee, cotton, and lumber. Consult the front-page index for easy reference. (See pages 102, 103, 104, and 106.)

"Futures Prices" provides quotes for future delivery of specified amounts of each commodity. Take **Lumber** as an example (see page 104).

This commodity (two-by-fours) is traded on the Chicago Mercantile

Chart 7–8
Changes in Unit Labor Costs and Producer Prices

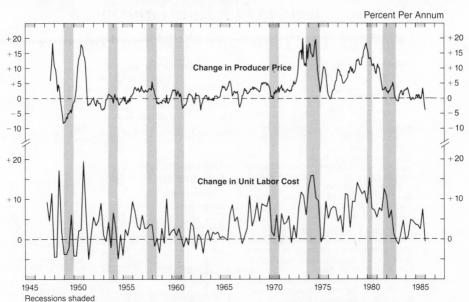

Recessions shaded

Source: U.S. Department of Commerce, *Business Conditions Digest* and *Handbook of Cyclical Indicators*, series 334c; Federal Reserve Board.

Exchange (CME) in contracts of 130,000 board feet at prices quoted in dollars per thousand board feet (boldface heading). The quotations are for delivery in May, July, September, and November 1986 and January and March 1987 (i.e., every two months).

The following information is provided by column.

Open—opening price; that is, $190 per thousand board feet for May 1986 delivery.

High—highest price for trading day.

Low—lowest price for trading day.

Settle—settlement price, or closing price, for trading day.

Change—difference between the latest settlement price and that of previous trading day (decrease of $1.90 for May 1986 delivery).

Lifetime high—highest price ever for the May 1986 contract.

Lifetime low—lowest price ever.

Open interest—number of contracts for delivery outstanding for each month.

COMMODITIES

Farmers Likely to Idle More Land in '86 Than at Any Time Since '83 Crop Plan

FUTURES
MARKETS

By ALBERT R. KARR
And WENDY L. WALL
Staff Reporters of THE WALL STREET JOURNAL

WASHINGTON—U.S. farmers plan to idle more land this year under fo⌐ farm programs than at any ti⌐ ⌐ third massive 1983 "paymen⌐' ⌐ate analysts duction effort, a⌐ ⌐st rebound in farm plantings ⌐ ⌐y won't be enough to re⌐ m⌐ ⌐ trend. And as always, farmers ⌐ll idle their poorest land first, lifting average yields per acre.

Meanwhile, as record numbers of farmers rush to sign up for federal subsidies, the extraordinary complexity of the new farm program has created an administrative nightmare at rural Agriculture Department offices all over the country. Last-minute tinkering with the rules by Congress has caused more frustration.

The amount of farm land idled under federal programs is expected to rise as much as 50% this year. Most analysts expect operators of 85% to 95% of corn and wheat acreage to enroll; that compares with an unusually high sign-up last year of 71% of corn acreage and 74% of wheat land. A projected 40 million to 50 million acres of crop land will lie idle as a result, including five million acres under a new soil-conservation program; that compares with 34 million acres in 1985.

"The only farmers wh⌐ ⌐pring, the program are t⌐ ⌐es last year, ites," most ⌐ ⌐ate. Soybean farm-relig⌐ ⌐illion to 63 million acres, ⌐ with 62.5 million acres in 1985, ⌐ analysts say.

Martin Abel, a Washington agricultural consultant, predicts wheat plantings will fall to between 67 million and 69 million acres, from 75.6 million a year earlier; cotton and rice plantings should drop, too.

Mr. Abel adds that actual plantings are likely to fall below the levels shown by tomorrow's report, which will reflect a survey of farmers' intentions as of March 1. Many more farmers are likely to decide to sign up for federal subsidies by the April 11 deadline.

ment payments will rise. That means farmers outside the program will h⌐ ' by lower prices without any fe⌐ ⌐ acres corn farmer with aver⌐ ⌐ t cover exlosing $121 an ac⌐ ⌐ There's no other up. ⌐ ⌐ ne says.

⌐ ⌐ "v⌐ ⌐s as a result are mobbing ⌐ity Agriculture Department offices.

Dow Jones Commodity Indexes

Weekly averages

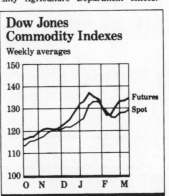

"It's been really hectic—just as bad as t⌐ 1983 PIK program or worse," s⌐ ⌐ Summers, a department⌐ ⌐ies are cennes, Ind.; unde⌐ ⌐ ⌐he program. in-kind, pr⌐ ⌐ any difference if we out g⌐ ⌐embers working, Mr. Sum⌐ ⌐ys. "We'd still have people outside ⌐aiting."

Complicated Program

Administrative tangles have fueled the frustration. Joe Barker, a department official in Dyersburg, Tenn., says the program is the most complicated he has ever had to administer: It has taken him as long as two hours to work through the program for one small farmer. Moreover, Commodity Credit Corp., which funds most farm programs, temporarily ran out of money earlier this month, preventing officials from passing out much-needed payments to farmers.

And with planting only days away in some areas, last-minute congressional tinkering with the farm program has prevented many farmers from lining up credit. Farmers "are trying to get loans

CASH PRICES

Tuesday April 8, 1986
(Quotations as of 4 p.m. Eastern time)

	Tues	Mon	Yr.Ago
GRAINS AND FEEDS			
Alfalfa Pellets, dehy, Neb., ton	82.00	82.00	69.00
Barley, top-quality Mpls., bu	2.40	2.40	2.50
Bran, (Wheat middling) KC ton	78.00	80.00	57.00
Brewer's Grains, Milw. ton	80.00	80.00	45.00
Corn, No. 2 yel. Cent-Ill. bu	bp2.31½	2.32½	2.72
Corn Gluten Feed, Chgo., ton	95.00	95.00	60.00
Cottnsd Meal, Clksdle,Miss. ton	117.5-125.	117.5-30.	80.00
Hominy Feed, Ill., ton	80.00	80.00	72.00
Linseed Meal, Mpls., ton	125.00	125.00	80.00
Meat-Bonemeal 50%-pro, Ill. ton	145.00	145.00	130.00
Oats, No. 2 milling, Mpls., bu	z	1.12	1.70½
Rice, No. 2 milled fob Ark. cwt	16.5-18.0	16.5-18.0	18.00
Rye, No. 2 Mpls., bu	n2.15-.30	2.15-.30	2.37
Sorghum, (Milo) No. 2 Gulf cwt	4.51	4.55	5.39
Soybean Meal, Decatur, Ill. ton	156.00	154.50	117.50
Soybeans, No. 1 yel Cent.-Ill. bu	bp5.22½	5.21	6.01
Sunflwr Sd No. 1 Duluth/Supr cwt	b7.75	7.75	12.95
Wheat, Spring 14%-pro Mpls. bu	r4.18½	4.15¾	4.05½
Wheat, amber durum, Mpls. bu	n3.77	3.77	4.35½
Wheat, No. 2 sft red, St.Lou. bu	h3.59½	3.67	3.70½
Wheat, No. 2 hard KC, bu	3.45¾	3.47½	3.63¼
FOODS			
Beef, 700-900 lbs. Mid-U.S.,lb.fob	.82	.82	.90
Beef, boxed, gross, Mid-US cwt	f86.18	86.22	96.94
Broilers, Dressed "A" NY lb	x.5120	.5137	.5239
Butter, AA, Chgo., lb.	1.38¼	1.38¼	1.41½
Cocoa, Ivory Coast, $metric ton	g2,034	2,032	2,493
Coffee, Brazilian, NY lb.	n2.25	2.25	1.38
Eggs, Lge white, Chgo doz.	.62-.65	.65-.68	.57½
Flour, hard winter KC cwt	9.55	9.45	9.85
Hams, 17-20 lbs, Mid-US lb fob	.55½	.56	.60
Hogs, Iowa-S.Minn. avg. cwt	40.50	38.50	41.50
Hogs, Omaha avg cwt	e38.70	39.00	41.00
Orange Juice, frz con, NY lb.	bz	z	z
Pepper, black, NY lb.	a2.50	2.50	1.75
Pork Bellies, 12-14 lbs Mid-US lb	.47	.46	.59½
Pork Loins, 14-17 lbs. Mid-US lb	.85	.85	.83½
Potatoes, rnd wht, 50 lb., fob	y.70	.70	2.07½
Steers, Omaha choice avg cwt	53.60	53.40	59.81
Steers, Tex.-Okla. ch avg cwt	e54.50	53.50	61.75
Steers, Feeder, Okl Cty, av cwt	63.50	63.00	72.63
Sugar, beet, ref. Chgo-Wst lb fob	.3150	.3150	.3150
Sugar, cane, raw NY lb. del.	z	z	.2083
Sugar, cane, raw, world, lb. fob	.0931	.0918	.0356
Sugar, cane, ref NY lb. fob	.3260	.3260	.3260
FATS AND OILS			
Coconut Oil, crd, N. Orleans lb.	xxn.13	.13	z
Coconut Oil, crd, N. Orleans lb. cif	yyn.13¼	.13¼	.34
Corn Oil, crd wet mill, Chgo. lb.	n.18	.18	.33¾
Corn Oil, crd dry mill, Chgo. lb.	n.17⅝	.17⅝	.34
Cottonseed Oil, crd Miss Vly lb.	a.18	.17	.32
Grease, choice white, Chgo lb.	z	z	.20
Lard, Chgo lb.	b.11½	.12	.23
Linseed Oil, raw Mpls lb.	.30	.30	.33
Palm Oil, ref. bl. deod. N.Orl. lb.	n.14¼	.14½	.32½
Peanut Oil, crd, Southeast lb.	n.23½	.23½	.51
Soybean Oil, crd, Decatur, lb.	.1796	.1826	.3445
Tallow, bleachable, Chgo lb.	b.11	.11	.21
Tallow, bleachable, Mo. River lb.	.09¾	.09¾	.19¾
Tallow, edible, Chgo lb.	.12½	.12½	.23
FIBERS AND TEXTILES			
Burlap, 10 oz. 40-in. NY yd	n.2275	.2295	.3580
Cotton 1 1/16 in str lw-md Mphs lb	.6300	.6300	.6470
Print Cloth, cotton, 48-in NY yd	s.65	.64	.65
Print Cloth, pol/cot 48-in NY yd	t.53	.52	.53
Satin Acetate, NY yd	.75	.71	.65
Sheetings, 60x60 48-in. NY yd	.75	.75	.75
Wool, 64s, Staple, Terr. del. lb.	1.80	1.80	2.10
METALS			
Aluminum ingot lb	p.815	.815	.815
Cobalt cathodes 99.9% NY lb.	ip11.70	11.70	11.70
Copper cathodes lb	p.67-.71	.68-.71	.70½
Copper Scrap, No 2 wire NY lb	k.48¾	.48¾	.49
Lead, lb.	p.18½-.20	.18½-.20	.22½
Mercury 76 lb. flask NY	258.00	250.00	300.00
Nickel plating grade lb	p3.29	3.29	3.29
Steel Scrap 1 hvy mlt Chgo ton	75.0-78.0	75.0-78.0	85.00
Tin Metals Week composite lb.	n.a.	3.5056	5.8849
Zinc High grade lb	p.32-.41	.32-.41	.46
MISCELLANEOUS			
Hides, hvy native strs lb fob	.61	.61	.54
Newspapers, old No. 1 Chgo ton	30.0-35.0	30.0-35.0	.37½
Rubber, smoked sheets, NY lb.	n.38¾	.39	.42¼
PRECIOUS METALS			
Gold, troy oz			
Engelhard indust bullion	339.80	338.05	323.50
Engelhard fabric prods	356.79	354.95	339.68
Handy & Harman base price	339.65	337.90	323.10
London fixing AM 340.65 PM	339.40	337.65	323.10
Krugerrand, whol	a341.00	340.00	335.00
Maple leaf, troy oz.	a352.00	351.00	335.00
Platinum, troy ounce (Contract)	475.00	475.00	475.00
Platinum, troy ounce (Free Mkt.)	426.00	422.00	n.a.
Silver, troy ounce			
Engelhard indust bullion	5.225	5.310	6.615
Engelhard fabric prods	5.591	5.682	7.078
Handy & Harman base price	5.225	5.302	6.670
London Fixing (in pounds)			
Spot (U.S. equiv. $5.3300)	3.6185	3.6015	5.5005
3 months	3.7120	3.6970	5.6725
6 months	3.7960	3.7800	5.8375
1 year	3.9655	3.9500	6.1375
Coins, whol $1,000 face val	a4,440	4,400	6,065

a-Asked. b-Bid. bp-Country elevator bids to producers. h-Terminal elevator truck bids to producers. c-Corrected. d-Dealer market. e-Estimated. f-Carcass equiv. value. g-Main crop, ex-dock, warehouses, Eastern Seaboard, north of Hatteras. i.-f.o.b. warehouse. k-Dealer selling prices in lots of 40,000 pounds or more, f.o.b. buyer's works. n-Nominal. p-Producer price. r-Rail bids. s-Thread count 78x76. t-Thread count 78x54. x-Less than truckloads. y- Maine origin; varies seasonally. z-Not quoted. xx-f.o.b. tankcars. yy- June - July shipment from Philippines.

The Wall Street Journal, *April 9, 1986*

The bottom line provides the estimated volume (number of contracts) for the day as well as the actual volume for the previous trading day. Finally, the total open interest is given, along with the change in the open interest from the previous trading day.

You can see that on April 3, 1986, you could have bought, or sold, a contract for May 1986 delivery of lumber for $24,362 (187.40 × 130).

But keep in mind that your objective is an increase in the contract's price, rather than taking delivery of 130,000 board feet of lumber. Thursday, April 3, 1986, was a bad day for the May 1986 contract because the price fell $1.90 per thousand board feet from the previous day's close. Since a contract is 130,000 board feet, your loss would have been $247 (130 × $1.90 = $247.00).

In order to buy the $24,000 (more or less) contract, your broker may have asked you to put up $1,500 margin (your money) and loaned you

FUTURES PRICES

Thursday, April 3, 1986.
Open Interest Reflects Previous Trading Day.

	Open	High	Low	Settle	Change	Lifetime High	Low	Open Interest
ORANGE JUICE (CTN)–15,000 lbs.; cents per lb.								
May	95.50	95.75	94.00	94.10 – 1.80		162.50	82.60	2,411
July	93.10	94.40	93.10	93.15 – 1.35		157.50	83.50	1,781
Sept	92.30	93.00	92.00	92.05 – 1.45		127.25	82.00	1,089
Nov	92.95	93.00	92.20	92.05 – 1.35		125.00	82.50	474
Jan87	91.85	92.10	91.85	92.10 – .75		113.00	83.75	239
Mar	93.00	93.00	92.00	92.00 – 1.25		122.00	83.90	955
May				92.25 – 1.10		93.30	84.50	680
July	93.00	93.00	92.50	92.50 – 1.50		94.00	84.75	284

Est vol 550; vol Wed 930; open int 7,913, +116.

SUGAR–WORLD (CSCE)–112,000 lbs.; cents per lb.								
May	8.75	8.85	8.55	8.69 – .02		9.26	3.58	38,989
July	8.77	8.82	8.56	8.66 – .04		9.26	3.79	25,468
Sept	8.76	8.78	8.60	8.69 + .01		9.22	4.05	295
Oct	8.80	8.85	8.60	8.68 – .02		9.26	4.02	38,757
Jan87	8.75	8.76	8.75	8.78		9.25	5.65	167
Mar	9.09	9.11	8.95	9.01 + .01		9.50	6.03	13,522
May	9.20	9.24	9.06	9.11		9.66	6.75	3,278
July	9.24	9.35	9.24	9.30 + .02		9.78	7.77	1,218

Est vol 19,782; vol Wed 23,335; open int 121,694, +164.

SUGAR–DOMESTIC (CSCE)–112,000 lbs.; cents per lb.								
May	20.30	20.35	20.30	20.35 – .01		21.90	19.15	395
July	20.50	20.50	20.50	20.55 + .01		21.60	19.35	1,454
Sept	20.60	20.60	20.60	20.60 – .02		21.45	19.35	593
Nov	20.45	20.45	20.45	20.54 – .01		21.29	19.65	292

Est vol 108; vol Wed 102; open int 2,734, –68.

	Open	High	Low	Settle	Change	Lifetime High	Low	Open Interest
Aug	118.00	121.75	117.50	121.75 – 1.75		230.00	107.50	1,400
Sept	121.00	123.00	120.25	123.50 – 1.75		208.00	112.00	294

Actual Thursday; vol 4,048; open int 13,545, n.a..

NY GASOLINE, leaded reg. (NYM) 42,000 gal.; $ per gal.								
May	.3800	.4030	.3800	.3954 + .0007		.7905	.3400	8,043
June	.3800	.3995	.3770	.3910 – .0007		.7870	.3400	5,847
July	.3730	.3950	.3720	.3875 + .0025		.7880	.3390	2,349
Aug	.3775	.3920	.3750	.3835 + .0035		.7820	.3370	944

Est vol 4,682; vol Wed 4,281; open int 17,289, – 1,293.

–WOOD–

LUMBER (CME)–130,000 bd. ft.; $ per 1,000 bd. ft.								
May	190.00	190.20	185.60	187.40 – 1.90		197.00	140.00	3,976
July	183.20	184.00	180.30	181.20 – 1.30		190.90	144.00	3,107
Sept	175.80	176.70	174.30	174.60 – .80		182.40	145.50	1,303
Nov	169.50	170.20	168.00	168.50 – .50		174.50	146.00	1,114
Jan87	172.40	173.30	171.00	172.80 – .20		175.00	150.00	145
Mar	172.50	173.20	170.50	172.80 – 1.90		175.50	153.00	135

Est vol 2,528; vol Wed 2,892; open int 9,791, –16.

Lumber Futures

The Wall Street Journal, *April 4, 1986*

Lumber (CME)—130,000 bd. ft.; $ per 1,000 bd. ft.

	Open	High	Low	Settle	Change	Lifetime High	Lifetime Low	Open Interest
May	190.00	190.20	185.60	187.40	−1.90	197.00	140.00	3,976
July	183.20	184.00	180.30	181.20	−1.30	190.90	144.00	3,107
Sept.	175.80	176.70	174.30	174.60	− .80	182.40	145.50	1,303
Nov	169.50	170.20	168.00	168.50	− .50	174.50	146.00	1,114
Jan 87	172.40	173.30	171.00	172.80	− .20	175.00	150.00	145
Mar	172.50	173.20	170.50	172.80	−1.90	175.50	153.00	135

Est. vol. 2,528; vol. Wed. 2,892; open int. 9,791, −16.

the remainder. Gains and losses can be great when compared to the margin advanced. That's why commodities trading has attracted speculators.

Also, note how close the settlement prices and lifetime high prices were for all months and how distant they were from the lifetime lows. Prices had clearly risen since the contracts began trading on the expectation of stronger demand for lumber. No doubt the drop in mortgage interest rates in early 1986 was responsible for that.

New Indexes of Commodity Futures, Spot Prices With Broader Content Start Today at Dow Jones

By ROBERT D. PRINSKY
Special to THE WALL STREET JOURNAL

NEW YORK – Dow Jones & Co. today begins publication of a new commodity futures index and a companion index of spot commodity prices.

The new Dow Jones commodity indexes substantially update the content of these market indicators. They include such active commodities as gold and soybeans, which weren't traded in futures markets when the previous indexes were formulated. All 12 commodities in the new indexes have equal weights, to avoid giving extra influence to any one.

Like the indexes they replace, the new ones will be published daily in The Wall Street Journal. The futures index will be published hourly during the trading day on the Dow Jones News Service, which also will carry the spot index at the close of markets.

Many Uses

Commodity indexes have a variety of uses. They give an indication of the general trend of futures markets. They enable traders to compare the performance of their own holdings to the general trend. They provide economists with a reading on prices of raw materials generally. Many analysts regard changes in the difference between the futures and spot indexes as an indicator of future price movements.

The hardest part of designing a new index is deciding what it should contain. After consultation with numerous commodity experts, it was determined that the new indexes should be as consistent as possible with the old ones. Thus, they measure prices of 12 widely traded commodities and the futures index calculates prices five months in the future. The spot index measures prices for immediate delivery of the same commodities that are in the futures index.

The old indexes measured only agricultural commodities. The new ones add metals, animals and wood. They don't include financial futures, notably because other indexes of interest and currency rates exist and because financial instruments are of a considerably different nature than raw materials.

The 12 commodities covered are cattle, coffee, corn, corn, cotton, gold, hogs, lumber, silver, soybeans, sugar and wheat.

The base date for the new indexes is Dec. 31, 1974, the day gold trading resumed in the U.S.

To give users an immediate history of the indexes, both have been calculated by Drexel Burnham Lambert Inc. for every trading day since the end of 1974, when both were 100.

The accompanying chart and graph give a seven-year history of the indexes for the last trading day of each month. A complete daily history of the indexes is available from Dow Jones (see below).

The weighting of the indexes is neutral. That is, each commodity's price on a given day is divided by its price on the base date

and the results are totaled. The total is divided by 12 and multiplied by 100 to yield the index.

To estimate the price of a commodity five months in the future, two contract months are used, one expiring in fewer than 150 days and one expiring in more than 150 days. It is assumed that each contract expires on the 15th of the month it relates to.

For each commodity, weights are assigned to the two contracts, based on the number of days between the 150th and the theoretical expiration date of the contract. Then, the price of each contract is multiplied by its weight, the results are added and the sum is divided by the number of days between the expiration dates of the two contracts. The result is the estimated price of the commodity for delivery in exactly five months, or 150 days.

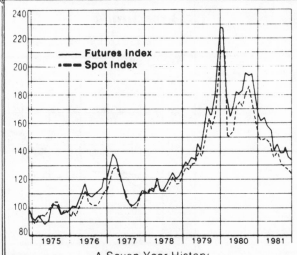

A Seven-Year History

— Futures Index
– – – Spot Index

Month (last trading day)	Futures Index	Cash Index
Dec74	100 00	100 00
Jan75	94 15	94 06
Feb	90 43	89 00
March	95 70	94 78
Apr	91 52	96 30
May	89 26	95 35
June	90 75	98 10
July	98 99	102 39
Aug	102 04	105 11
Sept	100 57	105 46
Oct	95 05	97 22
Nov	95 18	99 51
Dec	96 83	98 06
Jan76	97 64	95 65
Feb	101 46	98 91
Mar	100 29	95 55
Apr	106 08	102 64
May	110 05	106 20
Jun	117 63	112 42
July	109 23	106 02
Aug	107 88	104 98
Sept	108 71	103 26
Oct	110 75	103 74
Nov	113 12	107 63
Dec	121 25	112 91
Jan77	120 77	112 74
Feb	130 65	122 38
Mar	138 91	129 11

Month (last trading day)	Futures Index	Cash Index
May	125 84	123 85
June	115 51	116 61
July	105 97	107 57
Aug	103 15	105 77
Sept	101 72	101 53
Oct	102 14	101 77
Nov	106 64	105 71
Dec	111 58	110 67
Jan78	111 55	112 57
Feb	109 63	112 17
Mar	113 70	115 30
Apr	111 40	114 00
May	120 26	119 71
June	111 85	114 27
July	112 98	113 34
Aug	117 35	116 28
Sept	120 82	118 69
Oct	125 75	123 77
Nov	121 17	118 93
Dec	122 98	119 00
Jan79	126 90	123 18
Feb	133 46	130 58
Mar	131 54	128 78
Apr	136 87	132 48
May	134 91	132 52
June	145 62	141 90
July	140 52	138 86
Aug	154 07	150 20

Month (last trading day)	Futures Index	Cash Index
Sept	172 40	165 32
Oct	166 11	157 52
Nov	177 81	166 00
Dec	200 39	188 58
Jan80	228 11	213 61
Feb	227 21	211 79
Mar	176 46	153 60
Apr	172 12	157 61
June	182 66	172 91
July	180 88	176 02
Aug	183 11	174 47
Sept	196 15	182 18
Oct	194 81	187 09
Nov	195 00	178 84
Dec	181 54	165 63
Jan81	169 50	153 79
Feb	162 90	150 09
Mar	164 49	150 40
Apr	158 92	149 72
May	155 48	147 72
June	140 10	137 68
July	143 82	141 25
Aug	139 75	132 96
Sept	139 85	131 67
Oct	142 01	130 34
Nov	135 88	128 87
Dec	133 79	125 46

COMMODITY INDEXES

	Close	Net Chg.	Yr Ago
New Dow Jones Futures	133 79	- 0 21	Holiday
New Dow Jones Spot	125 46	- 0 23	Holiday
Old Dow Jones Futures	365 97	+ 2 18	Holiday
Old Dow Jones Spot	359 65	+ 2 09	Holiday
Reuter United Kingdom	1614 2	+ 3 6	Holiday

History Available

A seven-year daily history of both indexes, including a history of the five-month prices for each commodity, will be available later this month, priced at $50 a copy. Orders may be sent to Commodity Index, The Wall Street Journal, 200 Burnett Road, Chicopee, Mass. 01021.

Single copies of this article may be ordered at no charge from Dow Jones Educational Service Bureau, P.O. Box 300, Princeton, N.J. 08540.

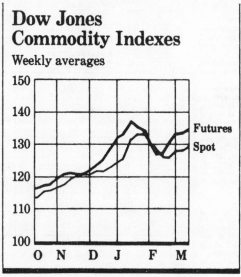

Dow Jones
Commodity Indexes
Weekly averages

The Wall Street Journal, *March 17, 1986*

Dow Jones announced a revision of its commodities indexes in the January 4, 1982, *Wall Street Journal* (see page 105). The article describes the indexes, and the accompanying chart presents them for 1975 through 1981. These indexes are more volatile than the producer price index, and they clearly portray the inflation of the late 1970s, as well as the subsequent deflation. As you can see from the chart accompanying the Monday, March 17, 1986, "Commodities" article above, they remain far below their 1979–80 peak because the forces at work on commodity prices are the same as those at work on producer prices: labor productivity and unit labor costs. As long as the Fed maintains a tight policy, continued slack in the economy will hold all price inflation at bay.

Finally, the sharp rise in commodity prices in the late 70s (see page 105), their collapse in the early 80s, and their continued weakness through the middle of the decade are evidence of the forces of supply and demand at work. Easy credit conditions bloated borrowing, which fueled spending and bid prices upward. As soon as credit tightened and remained tight, borrowing plunged and with it demand and prices.

Oil prices were not responsible for this development. They too were a symptom, not a cause. Their biggest increases came in 1974 and 1979, after the two major bouts of inflation in the 70s had begun. Those inflationary surges would have occurred with or without the increase in oil prices.

Oil prices finally collapsed in 1985–86 for the same reason that all commodity prices suffered in the 80s. Excess capacity had been put in place in response to the high prices and profits of the 70s while demand weakened in the 80s. As supply exceeded demand at current prices, prices plunged. The trauma facing oil producers had the same origins as that facing farmers.

To conclude, this chapter has explored the relationship between production, efficiency, and prices, focusing especially on the first phase of the business cycle. We can summarize the cycle's progress from trough to recovery as follows:

GNP ↓ → Industrial production ↓ → Capacity utilization ↓ → Labor productivity ↑ → Unit labor costs ↓ → Producer prices ↓.

When GNP and industrial production fall, capacity utilization declines. This leads to an increase in labor productivity and a drop in unit labor costs, driving down the rate of inflation as measured by producer prices.

Like the reveler's hangover, recession grips the economy following the bender of boom and inflation. Rest is the only cure, and recovery is marked not by a renewed round of expansion and growth but by a slack period in which steadiness is restored.

The recession of 1981–82 began prematurely with the Fed's tight money policy. This Mickey Finn produced a malaise that required a long recuperation, during which productivity eventually improved and inflation subsided.

The next chapter will examine the benefits reaped from this cooling-off—benefits that in many ways lasted long after the recession had ended.

The Business Cycle Phase Two: From Recovery to Expansion

Inflation is an increase in prices due to excessive spending financed either by borrowing from banks or by the issue of paper money. "Too many dollars chasing too few goods" is a standard way of putting it. Economists are more formal: "Inflation occurs when demand exceeds supply at current prices, and prices are bid up."

Both explanations conjure up a gigantic auction at which customers bid for both goods and services. The more money the customers have to spend, the higher prices go. Where do they get the money? From banks, which create it.

Although we wait and hope for it to subside, we tend to assume that inflation, like death and taxes, is inevitable. In fact, however, chronic inflation is a recent problem. Before the late 1940s, severe inflation was a temporary phenomenon associated with wars. When the federal government's wartime expenditures overshot tax revenues and the government covered the difference by selling bonds to the banking system or by printing paper money, prices increased swiftly.

Except for war-related inflations, prices in America fell more than they rose, until after World War II. As a matter of fact, prices were actually lower in 1914, on the eve of World War I, than they were in 1815, at the end of the Napoleonic Wars and the War of 1812!

Prices dropped during the 19th century because supply grew more rapidly than demand. Business mobilized the technological advances of the Industrial Revolution to produce standard items of consumption in considerably larger quantities at considerably lower cost. Occasionally, prices rose during the upswing of the business cycle, because investment expenditures were financed by bank borrowing or because there were temporary shortages of agricultural commodities, but these increases were more than offset when prices tumbled in recession years as huge additions in supply were brought to market.

Only the Civil War and World Wars I and II provided great inflationary experiences; even the period between World War I and World War II was a time of deflation (falling prices). War brought inflation, and peace brought deflation, because government borrowed and spent more massively in wartime than business borrowed and spent in peacetime. The difference was more a matter of degree than of kind; peacetime investment expenditures and borrowing by farmers, railroads, and manufacturers, though substantial, were usually not large enough to boost the growth in demand beyond the increase in supply, and thus prices fell.

To summarize, prices fell unless there was a rapid increase in demand (spending) financed by bank borrowing or the printing press. Only when outside financing provided a boost did demand take on a life of its own and grow more rapidly than supply. It made little difference whether it was government spending for war or business spending for investment, as long as banks printed bank notes or created demand deposits, or government printed paper money. Once demand grew more rapidly than supply at current prices, and too many dollars chased too few goods, prices rose.

What was responsible for the post–World War II experience? Why have prices risen steadily? The answers lie in consumer spending. This period marked the first time that consumers borrowed continually and prodigiously to finance purchases of luxury goods. The level of activity grew decade after decade, and with each cycle, so that in the 1970s tidal waves of credit roared through the system, rapidly swelling demand to record levels.

It started in the 1920s, a kind of brief test run for the full-scale activity that followed World War II. At first, following World War I, consumers purchased homes and automobiles, but by modern times demand expanded to include kitchen and laundry appliances, furniture and furnishings, and electronic equipment such as television sets and stereos. All were financed by credit, and the terms became more liberal over time, even as interest rates rose. The American consumer was encouraged—

indeed, came to feel obligated—to mortgage the future so that present expenditures could exceed present income, with borrowing covering the difference.

The economy's health thus developed a dependence on the chronic fix of greater consumer expenditures, financed by borrowing. These circumstances were entirely different from the circumstances of the 19th century; during that era, consumers were largely confined to standard items of consumption purchased with current income (not debt), and economic growth was propelled by increased supply, which pushed prices downward. Now the situation is quite different. Full production and employment have become the hostages of ever-larger waves of consumer expenditure on discretionary purchases financed by borrowing.

Unfortunately, these surges in consumer demand always led to their own demise, because expansion brought inflation, which depleted real incomes and generated the downturn of the cycle. Only then did inflation abate, real income recover, and expansion begin anew.

The last chapter examined recession's impact on costs and the attendant decline in the rate of inflation. Now consider the manner in which this decline spurs a recovery in consumer demand. The first statistical series to be examined in this chapter is the consumer price index (CPI), whose fluctuations chart the course of inflation. You'll see that fluctuations in consumer prices are the principal determinant of changes in consumer real income, and that lower inflation means higher real income. This leads to improved consumer sentiment and demand, which drives economic expansion forward. You can gauge the latter through data on auto sales, consumer credit, retail sales, and housing starts, which will serve as the leading indicators of consumer demand.

CONSUMER PRICE INDEX (CPI)

The Bureau of Labor Statistics' CPI release usually appears in *The Wall Street Journal* in the fourth week of the month. In the February 26, 1986, article, the second paragraph informs you of the CPI's increase computed at an annual rate. (See pages 112 and 113.)

Consumer Prices Increased 0.3% During January

Orders for Durable Goods Gained 0.4%, Due Mainly To Rise in Military Items

By ROSE GUTFELD

Staff Reporter of THE WALL STREET JOURNAL

WASHINGTON—Consumer prices rose a moderate 0.3% in January, the Labor Department said, but many economists expect declining oil prices to keep inflation far more subdued in the next few months.

Consumer Price Index

The 0.3% rise in the consumer price index—an increase of 4.1% at a compounded annual rate—followed an increase of 0.4%, or a 4.5% rate, in December. Several economists noted, however, that the report didn't reflect the recent sharp drop in oil prices in international markets.

Declining Gasoline Prices

The report "didn't capture the gasoline prices that we know were declining," said Dorothea Otte, assistant director of the economic forecasting project at Georgia State University. "We're going to see those declines in the February report." The January report shows energy prices rising 0.1% after a 0.4% increase in December.

"Inflation is low and going lower," said Donald Straszheim, president of Merrill Lynch Economics Inc. "Oil is the story and is going to remain the story."

The Labor Department report said food prices rose 0.3% in January after increasing 0.6% in December. Excluding food and energy, January consumer prices increased 0.4% after rising 0.3% in December.

The January rise left the price index for all urban consumers at 328.4% of its 1967 average, before seasonal adjustment, up 0.3% from December and 3.9% above a year earlier (see chart on page one). The index for urban wage earners and clerical workers, a measure that covers half the

population of the all-urban index and is used in adjusting Social Security and other retirement benefits, rose 0.3% in January, after seasonal adjustment, following a 0.4% increase in December. Before adjustment, the index stood at 324.3% of its 1967 average, up 0.3% from December and 3.7% from a year before.

Consumer Prices

In percent (1967 - 100).

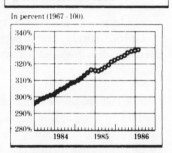

CONSUMER PRICES rose in January to 328.4% of the 1967 average from 327.4% in December before seasonal adjustment, the Labor Department reports.

Here are the seasonally adjusted changes in the components of the Labor Department's consumer price index for January.

	% change from Dec. 1985	Jan. 1985
All items	0.3	3.9
Food and beverage	0.3	2.9
Housing	0.3	4.3
Apparel	-0.3	2.6
Transportation	0.5	2.9
Medical care	0.4	6.9
Entertainment	0.9	3.8
Other	0.9	6.3

January consumer price indexes for various metropolitan areas (1967 equals 100), together with the percentage increases from January 1985, were:

U.S. City Average	328.4	3.9
Chicago	326.3	3.6
Detroit	323.1	3.9
Los Angeles	326.8	4.4
New York	323.1	4.8
Philadelphia	370.3	4.6
Baltimore	332.0	5.3
Boston	327.1	5.7
Cincinnati	343.2	2.5
Denver-Boulder	364.4	3.9
Milwaukee	333.9	2.9
Northeast Pennsylvania	311.6	3.3
Portland	321.3	4.7
St. Louis	322.4	2.9
San Diego	381.9	4.9
Seattle-Everett	327.0	2.3
Washington, D.C.	331.1	5.2

Consumer Prices

In percent (1967 = 100).

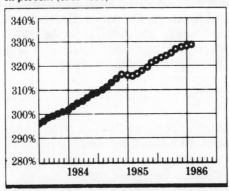

CONSUMER PRICES rose in January to 328.4% of the 1967 average from 327.4% in December before seasonal adjustment, the Labor Department reports.

Here are the seasonally adjusted changes in the components of the Labor Department's consumer price index for January.

	% change from	
	Dec. 1985	Jan. 1985
All items	0.3	3.9
Food and beverage	0.3	2.9
Housing	0.3	4.3
Apparel	−0.3	2.6
Transportation	0.5	2.9
Medical care	0.4	6.9
Entertainment	0.9	3.8
Other	0.9	6.3

January consumer price indexes for various metropolitan areas (1967 equals 100), together with the percentage increases from January 1985, were:

U.S. City Average	328.4	3.9
Chicago	326.3	3.6
Detroit	323.1	3.9
Los Angeles	326.8	4.4
New York	323.1	4.8
Philadelphia	320.3	4.6
Baltimore	332.0	5.3
Boston	327.1	5.7
Cincinnati	333.2	2.5
Denver-Boulder	364.4	3.9
Milwaukee	333.9	2.9
Northeast Pennsylvania	311.6	3.3
Portland	321.3	4.7
St. Louis	322.4	2.9
San Diego	381.9	4.9
Seattle-Everett	327.0	2.3
Washington, D.C.	331.1	5.2

The Wall Street Journal, *February 26, 1986*

CPI—Second Paragraph.

The 0.3% rise in the consumer price index—an increase of 4.1% at a compounded annual rate—followed an increase of 0.4%, or a 4.5% rate, in December. Several economists noted, however, that the report didn't reflect the recent sharp drop in oil prices in international markets.

The *CPI* is designed to compare relative price changes over time. An index must be constructed because consumers purchase such a wide variety of goods and services that no single item could accurately reflect the situation. (See Chart 8–1 on page 115.)

A base year (1967) is selected and assigned an index number of 100.0; and prices for other periods are then reported as percentage changes from this base. For instance, if prices rose 5 percent from this base, the index would be 105.0. If prices fell by 10 percent, the index would be 90.0.

The Bureau of Labor Statistics (BLS) calculates the CPI by compiling a list of the goods and services purchased by the typical consumer, including such items as food, clothing, shelter, public utilities, and medical care. These make up the "market basket." The base-year price of each item is recorded and assigned a weight according to its importance in the basket. Changes in the price of each item are noted, and the percentage change in the total price is reflected in the change of the index number.

The ways consumers spend are continuously shifting because tastes change, as do incomes and the relative prices of goods. New goods and services are frequently introduced. It would be impossible, however, to generate a consistent index of consumer prices if the components of the market basket were constantly changed; a balance must be struck between the need for consistency and the need for an accurate reflection of consumer buying patterns. Therefore, the BLS revises the contents of the market basket only occasionally, after conducting a survey of consumer expenditure patterns.

Contrary to the popular image, the CPI is not really a "cost-of-living" index. The BLS's market basket is fixed; the individual consumer's is not. Substitutions are made with changes in prices and with changes in income. Your cost of living can vary (or can be made to vary) independently of any change in the CPI.

A final point should be made. In the early 80s, the Bureau of Labor Statistics replaced the cost of homeownership with an imputation (or

Chart 8–1
Consumer Price Index (CPI) (1967 = 100); Quarterly Change in Index at Annual Rates (smoothed)

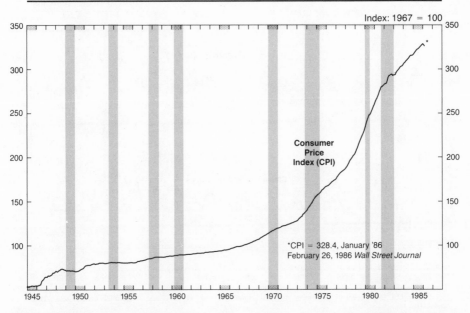

Index: 1967 = 100

Consumer
Price
Index (CPI)

*CPI = 328.4, January '86
February 26, 1986 *Wall Street Journal*

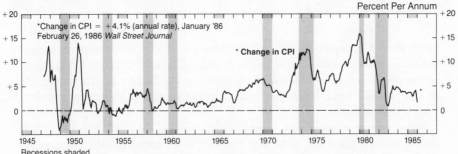

Percent Per Annum

*Change in CPI = +4.1% (annual rate), January '86
February 26, 1986 *Wall Street Journal*

* Change in CPI

Recessions shaded

Source: U.S. Department of Commerce, *Business Conditions Digest* and *Handbook of Cyclical Indicators,* series 320 and 320c.

estimate) of the rental value of owner-occupied homes. The cost of home-ownership, which includes mortgage interest rates and home purchase prices, had swiftly escalated in the late 1970s, so that this component of the CPI was pulling the entire index upward. Many found this an unjustified upward bias. Accordingly, the Bureau of Labor Statistics adjusted the shelter component to estimate the increase in the rental value

Chart 8–2
Change in Producer Prices and in Consumer Prices (smoothed)

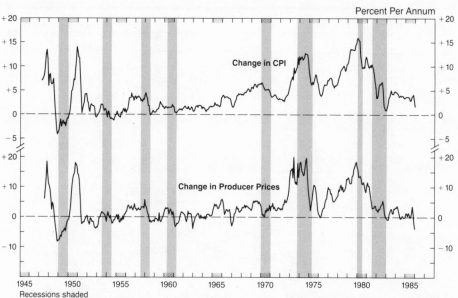

Recessions shaded

Source: U.S. Department of Commerce, *Business Conditions Digest* and *Handbook of Cyclical Indicators*, series 320c and 334c.

of an owner-occupied home, which more closely approximates its usage value than does actual appreciation in price. Ironically, interest rates and home prices fell soon afterward, so that the old index, had it remained in use, would have displayed a downward bias and risen less rapidly than the new index.

Now compare the CPI's recent record to that of the producer price index, making a mental note that the *Journal's* February 26, 1986, report updates Chart 8–2 and confirms inflation's continued abatement. You can see from Chart 8–2 that the CPI's trends have followed the producer price index since World War II.

CONSUMER REAL INCOME AND CONSUMER SENTIMENT

The Fed's tight money policies and ensuing recession forced the rate of inflation down to a moderate level in 1982. Let's now consider the impact of that on economic recovery in general and on the consumer's leading role in particular.

Chart 8–3
Consumer Sentiment: Michigan and Conference Board Surveys

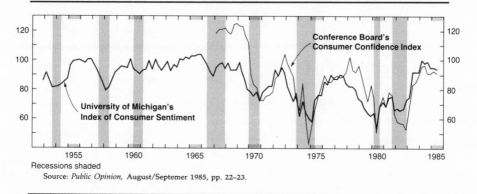

Recessions shaded
Source: *Public Opinion*, August/Septemer 1985, pp. 22–23.

The Institute for Social Research at the University of Michigan compiles the *Index of Consumer Sentiment.* Consumers are asked a variety of questions regarding their personal financial circumstances and their outlook for the future. Responses are tabulated according to whether conditions are perceived as better or worse, and an index is constructed comparing the outcome to that for a base year (1966). *The Wall Street Journal* occasionally reports this index, and the January 31, 1986, article serves as an example. (See pages 118 and 121.) More often, however, the *Journal* publishes the conference Board's index of consumer sentiment. (See the March 7, 1986 article below). A glance at the illustration from the August/September 1985 issue of *Public Opinion* shows you that the Michigan and Conference Board indexes have similar records. (See Chart 8–3 above.)

Consumer Confidence Declined for February

NEW YORK–The Conference Board said its consumer confidence index declined in February to 96.7 from a revised 97.8 in January; the January figure was originally put at 97.3.

The index uses 1985 as a base of 100.

The survey found that while buying plans declined for the second month in a row, "confidence about future business conditions continues to hold at reassuringly high levels."

The Wall Street Journal, *March 7, 1986*

Compare the CPI with the Michigan index (see Chart 8–4 on page 119), and you will find that inflation and consumer sentiment move in opposite directions.

Economic Plus

Consumers Continue Fast Spending Pace Despite Steep Debts

Analysts See Outlays Staying Brisk as Jobs and Incomes Rise, Interest Rates Fall

Are Federal Data Too Grim?

By LINDLEY H. CLARK JR.
And ALFRED L. MALABRE JR.
Staff Reporters of THE WALL STREET JOURNAL.

Despite widespread concern that they may be living beyond their means, consumers by and large remain in sound financial health and are likely to keep spending freely in coming months.

That's the judgment of most analysts who monitor the economy's consumer sector. Consumers' importance in the general business outlook can hardly be overstated because their spending perennially accounts for some two-thirds of overall economic activity. A reasonably vibrant consumer sector in coming months would serve to prolong the current economic expansion, which recently entered its fourth year. (Last month, the index of leading economic indicators rose a strong 0.9%, the government said yesterday. See page 3.)

"All in all, consumers continue to be in an upbeat mood and are likely to remain a positive force in the economy" as 1986 unfolds, remarks Thomas Juster, the director of the University of Michigan's Institute for Social Research. The institute regularly surveys consumers across the country to determine trends in confidence and buying plans.

Reasons for Optimism

A similar assessmen*   ...ier opti-
Schmiedeskamp ·'   .ci of outlays in
and financi·'   ...ere is no question that
zati·   ...rs have recently been in a
...ıg mood. In December, consumer
spending rose 2% from November, the sharpest monthly increase in 11 years. The gain compared with a rise of only 0.7% in November and a 1.3% decline in October.

The Wall Street Journal, *January 31, 1986*

White House spokesman Larry Speakes called the December surge a signal of "a strong first quarter for the nation's economy." And Beryl Sprinkel, the chairman of the President's Council of Economic Advisers, saw it as an indication that "we'll have a pretty good increase in consumer spending this year."

Auto Sales Up

In fact, consumers are continuing to spend freely, latest reports indicate. In the second 10 days of January, for example, new-car sales rose 19% from the year-earlier total, on top of a somewhat smaller year-to-year gain in the first 10 days of the month. Reports from other retailers also suggest brisk business.

And, looking ahead, the nonprofit Conference Board estimates that 34% of con-

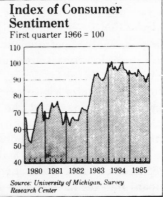

Index of Consumer Sentiment
First quarter 1966 = 100

Source: University of Michigan, Survey Research Center

sumers will purchase a major home appl'
ance within six months, up shar·'
last month's reading of 29 °··   ...ınain
den, who is in ch··   ...ınains read-
search at the ··   ...iıer or later things
its la···   ... similarly, Albert Cox, an
·   ...ı at BIL Management Co., a New
...ɔɪк investment firm, stresses, "You can't have spending running ahead of income indefinitely; eventually, there has to be a catching up."

Recession Danger

Analysts also warn that if the economy should unexpectedly slump, debt-burdened consumers would surely have to retrench sharply. That, in turn, could severely worsen any recession. "The stage is set for a hard fall once the economy turns sour," Mr. Schmiedeskamp says. But precisely

Chart 8–4
Index of Consumer Sentiment and Quarterly Change in CPI

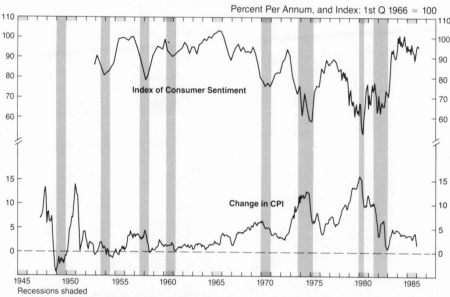

Percent Per Annum, and Index: 1st Q 1966 = 100

Recessions shaded

Source: U.S. Department of Commerce, *Business Conditions Digest* and *Handbook of Cyclical Indicators*, series 58 and 320c.

Consumers are influenced by more than inflation. Employment opportunities, interest rates, and current events all play a role. Consumer psychology is complicated. Yet you can see that the singular impact on inflation has been too strong to overlook since the early 1970s.

There's good reason that inflation and consumer sentiment have demonstrated an inverse relationship in recent years: cyclical swings in inflation have infallibly determined cyclical swings in consumer real income (see Chart 8–5 on page 120). Gains in current-dollar, nominal compensation were wiped out by cyclical increases in inflation, driving real compensation down as the peak of the cycle approached. Real compensation improved only after recession hit, as inflation eased and began to decline. Note the dramatic improvement in real compensation and consumer sentiment after 1980 as inflation slackened due to the recession forced on the economy by the Fed's 1981–82 tight money policy.

Then, when the Fed relaxed its grip and the economy began to recover, consumer sentiment exploded in the most dramatic gains since the construction of the index. You can see (Chart 8–5 on page 120) that by 1983–84 it was in the 100 range and suffered a setback only during the

---

Chart 8–5
Index of Consumer Sentiment, Change in Real Average Hourly Compensation,
Change in Nominal Average Hourly Compensation, and Change in CPI

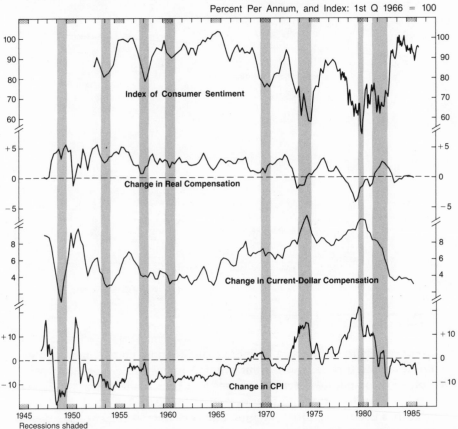

Percent Per Annum, and Index: 1st Q 1966 = 100

Recessions shaded

Source: U.S. Department of Commerce, *Business Conditions Digest* and *Handbook of Cyclical Indicators*, series 58, 320c, 345c, and 346c.

---

minislowdown of 1984. It should remain above 90 as long as growth continues with moderate inflation. (See chart on page 121.)

Before moving on, however, reflect on the robust condition of consumer sentiment today and the spectacular improvement in consumer sentiment between its 1979–80 low and the mid-80s. This turnaround can be explained by comparing the 1955–65 period with 1965–80. Chart 8–5 makes clear that the principal difference between these periods is the moderate rate of inflation in the first decade and the cyclical increase of inflation

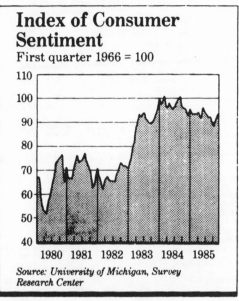

Index of Consumer Sentiment
First quarter 1966 = 100

Source: University of Michigan, Survey Research Center

The Wall Street Journal, *January 31, 1986*

after that. With each boom (1969, 1974, 1979), the rate of inflation hit a new high and the rate of increase in real compensation hit a new low. Although the mid-70s recession was worse than the 1970 recession, the rate of inflation did not drop to as low a number. No wonder consumer sentiment deteriorated for 15 years—inflation and the business cycle were becoming more severe. Consumer real income was slipping, not improving. Now that inflation's grip has been broken and consumer real income can improve, and has improved, consumers are feeling positively upbeat again for the first time in 20 years. The key has been the interruption of the inflationary boom/bust cycle.

Marginal employment adjustments also affect consumer sentiment. This is a fancy term for a longer workweek and more overtime, both of which boost workers' incomes. The Labor Department reports workweek and overtime data with its *monthly employment report,* which *The Wall Street Journal* usually publishes on Monday of the second week. These figures appear in the statistical summary at the end of the article, as in the example drawn from the March 10, 1986, story.

Unemployment Jumped to 7.3% In February

Increase Reflects Weather, Statistical Difficulties; Rise Is Largest Since '80

By ALAN MURRAY
Staff Reporter of THE WALL STREE⌐ ⌐.⌐%
WASHINGTON—The ⌐⌐ ⌐epartment unemployment dur⌐⌐ ⌐⌐t increase since flected stat⌐⌐ ⌐⌐e economy was mired weat⌐⌐ ⌐⌐ (see chart on page one). The ⌐ ⌐rased all the gains made last year in the unemployment picture.

Using a separate measure that includes members of the military among the employed, the February rate rose to 7.2% from 6.6% in January.

Contradictory Evidence

The employment report provided a contradictory array of economic evidence, however. The department's survey of households, used to compile the unemployment rate, showed that total civilian employment in the economy fell 394,000 in February. But a separate survey of business payrolls, which most analysts consider more reliable than the household survey, showed employment rising a healthy 226,000.

"I have looked at some puzzling statistics in my life, but these are about as confusing as any I've ever seen," said Lyle Gramley, chief economist for the Mortgage Bankers Association.

Although interpretation of the February numbers is difficult, they do seem to suggest that the economy isn't expanding as rapidly as many analysts had thought. Even the more-optimistic payroll numbers show a decline of 29,000 jobs in manufacturing industries in February, following increases in each of the previous three months. And the average workweek of nonfarm workers fell 0.2 hours, adding another hint of weakness.

Thus, while the new numbers aren't a cause for concern that the expansion is coming to an end, they do suggest that growth for the moment mightn't be as robust as many government and private analysts had thought. "The cheerleaders are wrong," says Roger Brinner, director of

The Wall Street Journal, March 10, 1986

U.S. forecasting at Data Resources Inc. in Lexington, Mass. "This isn't a boom that's taking off."

President Cites Weather

Asked about the figures at a news conference Friday, President Reagan said a great part of the rise in unemployment "is due to the weather that we've had." The president's top economist, Beryl Sprinkel, told reporters the rise was "largely an aberration," but added that the numb⌐ "still reflect some weakness in ⌐ ⌐ary market." ⌐ ⌐ the labor

Janet Norwood ⌐ ⌐ta for additional partment's P⌐ ⌐⌐ne what is really happcusse⌐ ⌐e economy."

⌐⌐most two-thirds of the rise in unemployment was registered in just three states—California, Texas and Illinois. A quarter of the total rise was concentrated among Hispanics, who account for only

Civilian Unemployment by Groups

In percent, seasonally adjusted

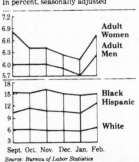

Source: Bureau of Labor Statistics

about 7% of the nation's population. And much of the increase was in farm unemployment, which is included in the household data but not in the payroll survey.

In California, the department said, the rise in joblessness may have reflected problems resulting from the heavy rains in February. In Texas, unemployment appeared to be linked in part to the uncertainty in the oil and gas industry resulting from recent declines in oil prices.

Followed Strong January

The disappo⌐ ⌐y-
ment report fol **Marginal** ng
January report ng
ployment fell to **Employment** rt,
the poor Febru⌐ **Adjustments** ⌐
flected a correc⌐ ⌐ry
numbers.

The Labor Department said 0.1 percentage point of the rise in February's jobless rate was caused by problems resulting from a change in a survey question used to determine whether a person without ⌐ ⌐ should be counted in the labor ⌐ ⌐d you question had read, "I⌐ ⌐ ⌐ne had been why you could n⌐⌐ week if ⌐n⌐ cha⌐

Unemployment Rate

Percent of labor force, seasonally adjusted.

UNEMPLOYMENT in February rose to a seasonally adjusted 7.3% of the labor force from 6.7% the preceding month, the Labor Department reports.

Thus the answer that kept the respondent out of the labor force and off the unemployment rolls changed from a "yes" to a "no." But some of the statisticians who compile the numbers apparently didn't take account of the change and recorded answers incorrectly. That tended to overstate the improvement in unemployment in January, and thus also overstate the deterioration in February.

Average hourly earnings for non-farm workers rose to a seasonally adjusted $8.72 in February from $8.68 in January. The department's hourly earnings index, which excludes wage changes caused by factory overtime and certain shifts within industries, rose to an adjusted 168.5% of its 1977 average from 167.5% in January.

Here are excerpts from the Labor Department's employment report. The figures are seasonally adjusted.

	Feb. 1986	Jan. 1986
	(millions of persons)	
Total labor force	118.8	118.5
Total employment	110.3	110.6
Civilian labor force	117.1	116.8
Civilian employment	108.6	109.0
Unemployment	8.5	7.8
Payroll employment	99.7	99.5
Unemployment:	(percent of labor force)	
All workers	7.2	6.6
All civilian workers	7.3	6.7
Adult men	6.2	5.7
Adult women	6.7	6.1
Teenagers	19.0	18.4
White	6.4	5.7
Black	14.8	14.4
Black teenagers	39.1	41.9
Hispanic	12.3	10.1
Average weekly hours:	(hours of work)	
Total private nonfarm	35.0	35.2
Manufacturing	40.6	40.9
Factory overtime	3.4	3.5

Here are excerpts from the Labor Department's employment report. The figures are seasonally adjusted.

	Feb. 1986	Jan. 1986
	(millions of persons)	
Total labor force	118.8	118.5
Total employment	110.3	110.6
Civilian labor force	117.1	116.8
Civilian employment	108.6	109.0
Unemployment	8.5	7.8
Payroll employment	99.7	99.5
Unemployment:	(percent of labor force)	
All workers	7.2	6.6
All civilian workers	7.3	6.7
Adult men	6.2	5.7
Adult women	6.7	6.1
Teenagers	19.0	18.4
White	6.4	5.7
Black	14.8	14.4
Black teenagers	39.1	41.9
Hispanic	12.3	10.1
Average weekly hours:	(hours of work)	
Total private nonfarm	35.0	35.2
Manufacturing	40.6	40.9
Factory overtime	3.4	3.5

The Wall Street Journal, March 10, 1986

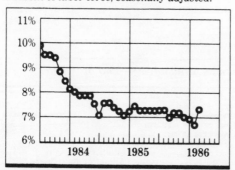

Unemployment Rate

Percent of labor force, seasonally adjusted.

UNEMPLOYMENT in February rose to a seasonally adjusted 7.3% of the labor force from 6.7% the preceding month, the Labor Department reports.

The Wall Street Journal, March 10, 1986

Chart 8–6a
Average Workweek of Production Workers, Manufacturing

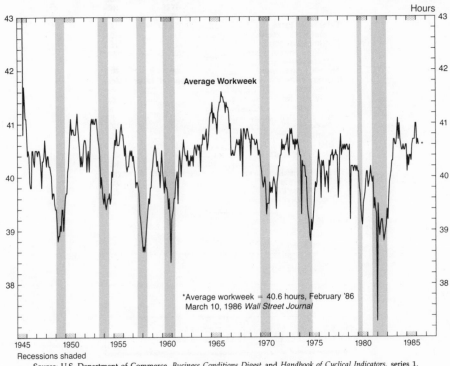

Hours

Average Workweek

*Average workweek = 40.6 hours, February '86
March 10, 1986 Wall Street Journal

1945   1950   1955   1960   1965   1970   1975   1980   1985
Recessions shaded
Source: U.S. Department of Commerce, Business Conditions Digest and Handbook of Cyclical Indicators, series 1.

Marginal Employment Adjustments—End of Article.

Average weekly hours:	(hours of work)	
Total private nonfarm	35.0	35.2
Manufacturing	40.6	40.9
Factory overtime	3.4	3.5

Compare the latest data to Charts 8–6a and 8–6b on this page and page 125, and note that both the workweek and overtime have picked up since their recession lows and rebounded from the 1984 minislow-down. You should also observe that these indicators improve during ex-

Chart 8–6b
Average Weekly Overtime of Production Workers, Manufacturing

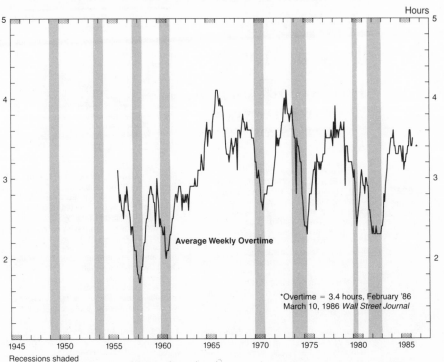

Hours

Average Weekly Overtime

*Overtime = 3.4 hours, February '86
March 10, 1986 *Wall Street Journal*

Recessions shaded

Source: U.S. Department of Commerce, *Business Conditions Digest* and *Handbook of Cyclical Indicators*, series 21.

pansion, flatten with boom conditions, and plummet in recession. The relationship between these indicators and the consumer is probably obvious. True, manufacturing production workers typically have no say over how long their workweek will be or whether they will work overtime. Their employer makes those decisions. Yet the extra income afforded by overtime is welcome and bolsters consumer sentiment early in the expansion, although its effect is exhausted by the time boom conditions develop. Therefore, marginal employment adjustments are a reinforcing element of the business cycle through their impact on consumer sentiment.

The Commerce Department's monthly personal income report appears in *The Wall Street Journal* during the third week. The headline and first paragraph of the March 21, 1986, article inform you that personal income grew by 0.6 percent in February 1986, and the statistical summary accompanying the article puts the current figure at $3.406 trillion. (See pages

Personal Income And Spending Rose in Month

Increases of 0.6% and 0.3% During February Reflect Various Special Factors

By ALAN MURRAY
Staff Reporter of THE WALL STREET JOURNAL

Personal Income {

WASHINGTON—The incomes of Americans grew 0.6% in February while consumer spending rose 0.3%, the Commerce Department said.

The figures appeared to be a solid improvement over January's performance, when incomes rose 0.1% and spending fell 0.4%. But the rise in incomes partly reflected what the department called "special factors" that aren't likely to recur. And the rise in spending was restricted to the services sector, where colder weather led to higher heating bills and the stock market surge led to a spurt in brokerage fees.

Excluding the special factors, incomes rose a moderate 0.4% in both January and February. And excluding services, spending was down in February.

Cautious Consumers

"The heavy debt burden faced ͘   ͘t average household is causing ͘   ͘es and be cautious," said R͘͘   ͘u for inflation, vice president   ͘justed for seasonal "There's   ͘nsumer prices could show a ͘   ͘r February as a result of price ͘uctions in both energy and food, the inflation-adjusted spending figures, which will come out next month, are likely to look significantly better than the unadjusted numbers.

"We're expecting a decline in the consumer price index for February," said Donald Ratajczak, head of the forecasting project at Georgia State University. "When you take that into account, these are decent numbers."

Pleasant Task'

"We have the pleasant task of adjusting our thinking to a situation without infla-

Personal Income

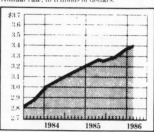

Annual rate, in trillions of dollars.

tion," said Robert Ortner, the Commerce Department's top economist.

The January and February personal income numbers were distorted in part by a sharp drop in farm subsidy payments in January, followed by a partial rebound the following month. A pay raise for the military and cost-of-living adjustments to several pension and income-support programs also affected the statistics.

Wages and salaries in February rose a solid 0.5%, after increasing only 0.3% the previous month. Factory wages, however, fell 0.5% in February, after dropping 0.1% in January.

Savings Rate Increases   . ͘age one).

Because incom͘   ͘ to $2.667 trillion spending gr͘   ͘u in January. sonal ͘   ͘ely, the department also an- ͘ ͘nced revisions to its monthly retail sales figures dating back to January 1983 to take into account new survey data.

The revisions still show that retail sales declined 0.1% in February, as previously reported, but the sales level for the month was a seasonally adjusted $116.81 billion, compared with the previously reported level of $117.27 billion.

For all 1985, the revised numbers show that sales rose 6.3% to $1.374 trillion, rather than 6.2% to $1.378 trillion as previously reported.

Here is the Commerce Department's latest report on personal income. The figures are at seasonally adjusted annual rates in trillions of dollars.

	Feb. 1986	Jan. 1986
Personal income	3.406	3.387
Wages and salaries	2.039	2.029
Factory payrolls	.465	.467
Transfer payments	.503	.502
Disposable personal income	2.902	2.883
Personal outlays	2.766	2.757
Consumption expenditures	2.667	2.659
Other outlays	.099	.098
Personal saving	.136	.126

126 and 127.) The statistical summary at the end of the article also breaks out the major components of personal income and its disposition.

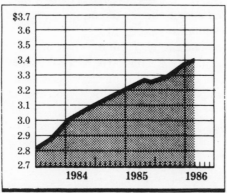

Personal Income

Annual rate, in trillions of dollars.

The Wall Street Journal, *March 21, 1986*

Personal Income—First Paragraph—and Statistical Summary—Last Paragraph.

WASHINGTON—The incomes of Americans grew 0.6% in February while consumer spending rose 0.3%, the Commerce Department said.

Here is the Commerce Department's latest report on personal income. The figures are at seasonally adjusted annual rates in trillions of dollars.

	Feb. 1986	Jan. 1986
Personal income	3.406	3.387
Wages and salaries	2.039	2.029
Factory payrolls	.465	.467
Transfer payments	.503	.502
Disposable personal income	2.902	2.883
Personal outlays	2.766	2.757
Consumption expenditures	2.667	2.659
Other outlays	.099	.098
Personal saving	.136	.126

Personal income is all the income we earn (wages, salaries, fringe benefits, profit, rent, interest, and so on) plus the transfer payments we receive
(such as veterans' benefits, social security, unemployment compensation,
and welfare), less the social security taxes we pay to the government.
Therefore, the federal government's ability to borrow, and pay out to
us in transfer payments more than it receives from us in taxes, provides
a cushion that keeps personal income growing even in recession, when
earned income is down. The huge federal deficits of the 80s, partly due
to the tax cuts earlier in the decade, have helped maintain personal income's growth trend despite heavy unemployment. This has kept a floor
under personal consumption expenditures.

For this reason, as you can see from the chart accompanying the *Journal*
article, and from the historical data too (Chart 8–7 below), personal income
has grown so steadily that it is difficult to use as a cyclical indicator.
As a first step in improving its usefulness, you would have to adjust it
for inflation in order to ascertain trends in real income. But this brings

Chart 8–7
Personal Income

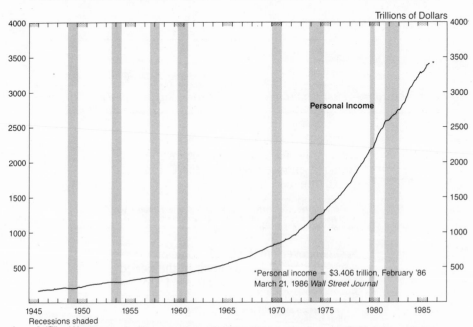

Recessions shaded

Source: U.S. Department of Commerce, *Business Conditions Digest* and *Handbook of Cyclical Indicators*, series 223.

the analysis back to the earlier discussion about the CPI and real income's impact on consumer sentiment. Use the CPI as your test for consumer sentiment, because the two series move in opposite directions.

And here's the nub of this discussion: the relationship between the CPI, real income, and consumer sentiment is what links the recession's reduced inflation rate to the subsequent economic recovery and expansion. You know from the previous chapter's discussion of the first phase of the business cycle (from trough to recovery) that productivity improves in recession and that declining costs drive down the inflation rate as measured by the producer price index. This decline is reflected in the CPI, lifting both consumer real income and consumer sentiment. And that gain in consumer sentiment motivates consumers to begin buying again. What an irony that consumers must wait for recession (and hope not to join the unemployed) to boost their purchasing power before they regain the confidence to resume spending!

Consumer spending's resurgence propels the cycle's second phase (from recovery to expansion). Once the consumer resumes borrowing and spending, all components of demand will eventually advance, propelling the economy's expansion. Therefore, it's time to consider the most important indicators of consumer demand.

CONSUMER DEMAND

Every month, *The Wall Street Journal* publishes articles on four indicators of consumer demand: auto sales, consumer credit, retail sales, and housing starts. Let's examine each in turn.

Around the fifth of the month, *The Wall Street Journal* publishes *automobile sales* data compiled by the manufacturers, such as this April 4, 1986, report. (See page 130.)

Comparison with Same Month, One Year Ago—Third Paragraph.

The seven makers of domestic cars posted sales of 236,735 units in the period March 21-31, a 21.5% decrease from the year-ago period. Domestic sales for the month were off 15.6%.

U.S. Car Sales Slumped 21.5% In Late March

Import Sales Grew in Month Despite Price Increases Tied to Weaker Dollar

By DORON P. LEVIN
Staff Reporter of THE WALL STREET JOURNAL

DETROIT—U.S. auto makers' traditional spring selling season started with a whimper instead of a bang.

Import sales, meanwhile, remained strong in March despite higher prices caused by the weakened U.S. dollar.

Auto Sales— year ago comparison { The seven makers of domestic cars posted sales of 236,735 units in the period March 21-31, a 21.5% decrease from the year-ago period. Domestic sales for the month were off 15.6%.

Sales of import models surged 22.9% in March. Toyota Motor Corp., Mazda Motor Corp., Mitsubishi Motor Corp. and Subaru of America Inc. posted strong gains among the Japanese importers.

General Motors Corp. had the biggest drop among the Big Three in late March as sales slipped 23.7%. Ford Motor Co. sales dropped 19% for the period and Chrysler Corp. sales slumped 22.1%.

The latest decline suggests that auto companies can't sustain strong sales under current market conditions unless they promote their products with some kind of incentives.

"The springtime buyers were pulled into January and February by the incentives," said John H. Hammond, auto analyst for Data Resources Inc. "Others are delaying until new incentives are in place."

Mr. Hammond expects U.S. auto makers to offer a new round of incentives starting April 14, the date GM has set to raise prices 2.9%. GM, he believes, can afford to offer aggressive financing discounts, perhaps as low as 6.9%, because it simultaneously is increasing its revenue from higher prices. GM's production costs also should drop soon as a result of falling energy prices.

Chrysler, Ford and GM have modest incentive programs in effect, variously offering 9.9% financing and as much as $1,-000 in rebates.

Yet the new-car inventory for GM as well as for Chrysler remained uncomfortably swollen, while Ford's appears roughly in balance with sales. That means GM, which already has said it plans some production cuts, may be forced to trim production further and lay off workers if sales don't pick up. Chrysler hasn't cut production yet, but it may be forced to do so.

According to analysts' estimates, GM has an 85-day to 90-day supply of cars; Chrysler has a 90-day supply and Ford has about a 60-day supply. The industry considers a 60-day supply comfortable.

Carl Fischer, owner of Fischer Buick-Subaru in Troy, Mich., sold 107 Buicks in March, compared with 127 Buicks in the year-ago period. But he sold 31 Subarus in the period, compared with 11 last March.

Mr. Fischer attributed soft sales to high Buick prices in comparison with similarly sized Chevrolets and Pontiacs. But recent price increases haven't deterred Subaru buyers.

"People are trying to beat the next price increase," he said. Subaru recently raised prices an additional 4.9% to reflect the stronger yen. "We've been getting close to sticker prices, but I don't think we'll be able to after the next price increase. I think we'll absorb part of the price increase ourselves."

The seasonally adjusted annual rate in March was about seven million domestic cars, down from January's 8.6 million and February's 8.1 million. In the final third of the month, the seasonally adjusted annual rate, according to Commerce Department statistics, stood at 6.7 million cars. } **Auto Sales— seasonally adjusted annual rate**

Imported cars captured a big chunk of the U.S. market in March compared with a year ago, further demonstrating consumer preference for imported products even with price rises. Japanese car companies also were permitted, under voluntary restraints, to import 25% more cars in fiscal year ended April 1.

Imports accounted for 27.5% of the market in March, up from 20.7% a year ago. GM's market share, meanwhile, slipped to 41.3%, including foreign and domestic models, from 43.3% a year ago. Ford slipped to 18.9% from 21.1% and Chrysler dropped to 11.6% from 12.6%.

The Wall Street Journal, *April 4, 1986*

Seasonally Adjusted Annual Data—Third Paragraph from End of Article.

The seasonally adjusted annual rate in March was about seven million domestic cars, down from January's 8.6 million and February's 8.1 million. In the final third of the month, the seasonally adjusted annual rate, according to Commerce Department statistics, stood at 6.7 million cars.

The 15.6 percent decrease for March reported in the third paragraph compares all auto sales with auto sales in the same month one year ago. But you need *seasonally adjusted data at an annual rate* to make a comparison with recent months as well as years past. Thus, the third paragraph from the end of the article reports the March rate of 7.0 million domestically produced automobiles as substantially lower than February's 8.1 million figure. Picture this number on Chart 8–8. (See Chart 8–8 on page 132 and Chart 8–9 on page 133.)

The well-equipped auto, like the well-equipped home, has been a symbol of the American consumer economy since the 1920s. Other countries have copied it and even outdone us in some respects, but we were first. This development, however, did not occur for some time. Indeed, in the effort to mass-merchandise this new convenience, Henry Ford reduced the price of a Model T to $300 in the early 1920s, and provided customers with any color they wanted, as long as it was black. Ford dominated the market until the late 1920s, when General Motors saw the profit potential in continually inflating the product by offering colors, options, and model changes and increased size, weight, and speed. This strategy enabled GM to take the sales lead from Ford; and, from then on, competition in autos meant more (and different) car for more money, not the same car for a lower price. The option of less car for less money was eliminated until the German and Japanese imports arrived.

Ford had grafted 20th-century technology onto 19th-century marketing techniques, driven the price down as far as it could go, and seen sales go flat in the mid-1920s as the market was saturated. GM pioneered the 20th-century marketing technique of product inflation on a mass scale and gambled that the consumer would borrow ever more in order to buy next year's model.

Product inflation boosts sales by cajoling the consumer into buying

Chart 8–8
New Auto Sales, Domestic Type (excluding imports)

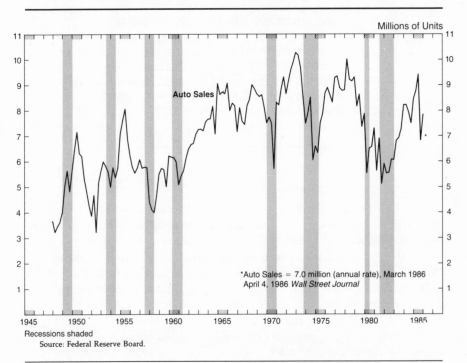

Millions of Units

*Auto Sales = 7.0 million (annual rate), March 1986
April 4, 1986 *Wall Street Journal*

1945   1950   1955   1960   1965   1970   1975   1980   1985
Recessions shaded
Source: Federal Reserve Board.

something new at a higher price. The customer isn't swindled, just convinced by marketing and advertising techniques that he or she needs an improved product for more money. Planned obsolescence is a corollary, because style and model changes, as well as product improvement, aid in persuading the consumer that the present (and still serviceable) model should be replaced with a better, more expensive model, not a lower-cost repeat of the old model.

That set the pattern for American marketing of consumer goods. You can see it in your kitchen, laundry room, and living room, not just your driveway. TV replaced radio, color TV replaced black-and-white TV, and VCRs will soon be perceived as near-compulsory accessories. With each innovation, the price goes up and so does debt.

Glance at the auto sales charts to see this phenomenon in action. You will immediately notice the record sales volume of the 1970s, which looks even more impressive in dollar terms. Part of the growth since the 1950s was pure price inflation, but some was product inflation; that is, we were obliged to buy more car for more money.

Chart 8–9
Personal Consumption Expenditures on Automobiles

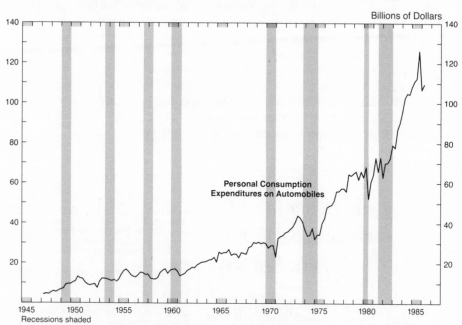

Source: U.S. Department of Commerce, *Business Conditions Digest* and *Handbook of Cyclical Indicators,* series 55.

You can also see that auto sales were a leading indicator of economic activity, turning down as soon as escalating inflation eroded consumer sentiment and recovering quickly when inflation subsided and consumer sentiment improved. Except for the 1984 minislowdown, recent data shows the identical pattern.

This does not mean, however, that the domestic manufacturers will soon reach the 10-million-a-year sales volume they occasionally enjoyed in the 70s. The Fed's tight money policies were responsible for the collapse of auto sales in 1981–82, and the Fed has not permitted installment interest rates to drop back to where they were when the record sales figures were achieved. The manufacturers have had to subsidize interest rates if they wished to push them down to levels that would generate a burst in demand.

On the other hand, some attribute the domestic manufacturers' failure to reach the 10-million mark to their own sloth and shortsightedness.

Product inflation was pushed too far; the love affair is over; fuel is too expensive; the Japanese and Germans do a better job; and so forth. Perhaps. Yet it was not until after World War II that auto sales surpassed rates achieved in the 1920s. The American auto industry has been counted out before, and then revived. It remains to be seen whether or not this is a fully mature industry with no further prospects of expansion.

The Wall Street Journal publishes the Commerce Department's release on *consumer installment debt* in the second week of the month. The first paragraph of the May 13, 1986, *Journal* article provides the figure you need. Changes in consumer credit are an important barometer of consumer activity because of the phenomenon just described: borrowing to finance purchases of autos and other expensive and postponable items.

Consumer Credit
Grew at 8.1% Rate
In March, Fed Says

By a WALL STREET JOURNAL *Staff Reporter*

Consumer
Credit
{
WASHINGTON – Consumer credit expanded a seasonally adjusted $3.71 billion in March, the smallest monthly rise since May 1983, the Federal Reserve Board said.

The expansion was sharply slower than the hefty increases of much of last year. Those rises have led some economists to worry that excessive debt levels would restrain consumer spending.

The March increase, which was at an

The Wall Street Journal, *May 13, 1986*

8.1% annual rate, followed a revised expansion of $5.01 billion, or an 11.1% rate, in February and a $7.66 billion rise, or a 17.2% rate, in January. The February increase was originally reported as $4.97 billion. Credit expanded $2.11 billion in May 1983.

Consumer credit outstanding at the end of March totaled $545.61 billion, up 16.1% from a year earlier.

Auto credit outstanding expanded $1.09 billion in March after rising $2.68 billion in February. Revolving credit increased $1.47 billion after expanding $1.04 billion the month before.

Mobile-home credit rose $232 million in March after increasing $112 million in February. Miscellaneous credit, which includes cash loans and certain retail transactions, expanded $926 million after increasing $1.17 billion in February. All the monthly figures are seasonally adjusted.

Consumer Credit—First Paragraph.

WASHINGTON – Consumer credit expanded a seasonally adjusted $3.71 billion in March, the smallest monthly rise since May 1983, the Federal Reserve Board said.

Chart 8–10
Change in Consumer Installment Credit

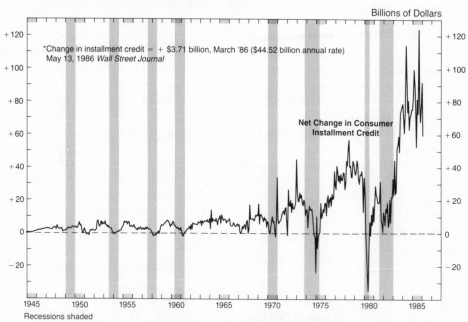

Billions of Dollars

*Change in installment credit = + $3.71 billion, March '86 ($44.52 billion annual rate) May 13, 1986 *Wall Street Journal*

Net Change in Consumer Installment Credit

Recessions shaded

Source: U.S. Department of Commerce, *Business Conditions Digest* and *Handbook of Cyclical Indicators*, series 113.

Now multiply the $3.71 billion reported in the first paragraph of the *Journal* article by 12 (slightly less than $45 billion) to determine the annual rate, and update Chart 8–10 on this page with that figure.

Consumer credit rose gradually and cyclically until the 1970s. Then it exploded. You can see the cyclical maximum of $10 billion in the late 60s, $20 billion in the early 70s, and $50 billion in the late 70s. In the latest expansion, before and after 1984's minislowdown (the Fed's policies hit installment rates, too), installment borrowing blew past $100 billion at an annual rate (Chart 8–10). This series has doubled every half decade for 20 years! No wonder the Fed is concerned; indeed, it's amazing that inflation has not been even more severe in the face of this stimulus to demand.

You can also see the cyclical sensitivity of consumer credit and its reaction to changes in consumer sentiment. Increases in consumer credit trailed off with the surge of inflation in the late 60s, 1973–74, and 1979. Then, with each recession and the return of consumer confidence, consumer credit rebounded.

Until recently, consumer credit was notoriously impervious to the long-run rise in interest rates since World War II. Consumers were primarily concerned with the size of monthly payments, and stretching out the term of the loan was usually regarded as sufficient to mitigate the steady rise in the interest rate. But this piece of conventional wisdom went out the window with the Fed's 1981 tight money policy. Monthly payments became so large that many consumers were forced to forsake consumer credit and postpone purchases of autos and other expensive items. The Fed's tight money policies proved effective once again in 1984, although borrowing bounced back up as soon as the Fed eased off. Consumers' continued willingness to take on ever-larger amounts of debt is one reason the Fed should maintain fairly tight credit conditions for the foreseeable future.

The U.S. Department of Commerce's monthly release on *retail sales* appears in *The Wall Street Journal* around the second week. You can see from the headline, first two paragraphs, and chart accompanying the March 14, 1986, article on page 137 that retail sales made strong progress in the mid-80s.

Retail Sales

In billions of dollars.

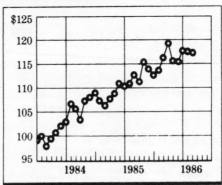

RETAIL SALES fell in February to a seasonally adjusted $117.27 billion from a revised $117.36 billion in January, the Commerce Department reports.

The Wall Street Journal, *March 14, 1986*

Retail Sales Declined 0.1% In February

But Some Expect Rebound Sparked by Lower Rates And Slumping Oil Prices

By Rose Gutfeld

Staff Reporter of The Wall Street Journal

WASHINGTON – Retail sales fell in February for the second consecutive month, the Commerce Department said, but several economists suggested that lower interest rates and oil prices will soon spur consumer spending.

Last month's 0.1% drop, which brought sales to $117.27 billion, followed a revised 0.2% decline in January to $117.36 billion (see chart on page one). The department originally reported the January performance as a 0.1% rise. This marked the first two-month decline since last May and June. The numbers are adjusted for seasonal variations.

While the report clearly showed some weakness, several analysts found reason to cheer. "The reality is a little bit brighter than what the numbers look like," said Sandra Shaber, vice president and economist at Chase Econometrics.

Commerce Secretary Malcolm Baldrige agreed. "Lower interest rates and inflation and strong consumer confidence should sustain a rising trend of sales," he said.

Retail Sales

In billions of dollars.

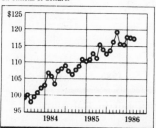

RETAIL SALES fell in February to a seasonally adjusted $117.27 billion from a revised $117.36 billion in January, the Commerce Department reports.

The Wall Street Journal, *March 14, 1986*

However, in reaction to the retail sales report, Mrs. Shaber said that although some concern about consumers' debt load is warranted, people are beginning to "feel richer" as a result of lower gasoline prices, the drop in interest rates and the big rise in the stock market.

As gasoline prices have fallen in response to the recent sharp drop in oil prices, the initial effect on the retail sales figure has been negative. Gasoline-station sales, measured in dollars, fell 2.6% last month after falling 2.4% in January, reflecting lower prices. While lower gasoline prices should give consumers more money to spend on other items, they will also detract from the overall sales gain until they bottom out.

Mrs. Shaber also noted that excluding auto sales, which have risen and fallen sharply in recent months in response to dealer-financing promotions, overall retail sales rose 0.3% last month after falling 0.5% in January. Auto sales fell 1.3% in February after rising 0.8% in January.

Some economists are more pessimistic. "I tend to think the effect of the oil price drop is exaggerated," said Rosalind Wells, chief economist at J.C. Penney Co. She said lower gasoline prices won't "necessarily be immediately translated into spending" on other items. Families "may just drive more," she said.

Department stores posted the biggest sales gain last month, rising 3% after declining 1.7% the month before. Furniture sales rose 2.9% last month after climbing 0.5% in January.

Sales of building materials fell 1.9% in February after increasing 4.4% the month before. Food store sales fell 0.8% after rising 0.2% in January. Sales of apparel and accessory stores increased 0.8% after falling 4.1%.

The Commerce Department's early retail sales estimates, based on a relatively small sample of reports, frequently have been revised substantially as more data is collected. The numbers exclude spending on services, which accounts for a large portion of consumer outlays.

Also, the department is planning to revise its retail sales figures for January 1983 through February 1986. The revised figures will be released next week.

According to the latest report, durable goods sales fell 0.2% in February after rising 0.7% in January. Durable goods are intended to last three years or more. Sales of nondurables were unchanged after falling 0.7% the prior month.

Before seasonal adjustment, retail sales in February totaled $99.69 billion, down from $105.56 billion in January.

Retail Sales—First Two Paragraphs.

WASHINGTON — Retail sales fell in February for the second consecutive month, the Commerce Department said, but several economists suggested that lower interest rates and oil prices will soon spur consumer spending.

Last month's 0.1% drop, which brought sales to $117.27 billion, followed a revised 0.2% decline in January to $117.36 billion (see chart on page one). The department originally reported the January performance as a 0.1% rise. This marked the first two-month decline since last May and June. The numbers are adjusted for seasonal variations.

However, you can see from the historical chart (Chart 8–11, page 139) that retail sales has not been a volatile series and that using retail sales to trace the course of the business cycle is not as easy as using auto sales or consumer credit.

The Commerce Department's monthly release on *housing starts* is usually published in *The Wall Street Journal* between the 17th and the 20th of the month. Always direct your attention to the seasonally adjusted monthly figure, presented at an annual rate. The third paragraph and the chart accompanying the April 17, 1986, story tell you that there were 1.9 million home and apartment unit construction starts in March. (See pages 140 and 141.)

Chart 8–11
Retail Sales

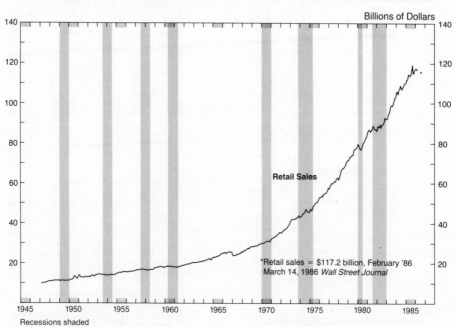

Recessions shaded
Source: U.S. Department of Commerce, *Business Conditions Digest* and *Handbook of Cyclical Indicators,* series 54.

Housing Starts Declined 2.4% Last Month

But Pace of Construction In March Was Vigorous; Operating Rate Dropped

By JoANN S. LUBLIN
Staff Reporter of THE WALL STREET JOURNAL

WASHINGTON—Housing starts slipped 2.4% in March, but the pace marked the third consecutive month of vigorous construction work.

Several economists see a trend in the strong pace that they say should continue at least through the summer.

Builders started work on new houses last month at an annual rate of 1,949,000 units, the Commerce Department reported (see chart on page one). That compared with a revised rate of 1,997,000 units in February, which was 1.8% below January. The department initially said starts had fallen 3.5% in February.

Housing Starts —

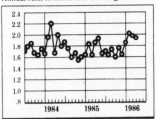

Housing Starts

Annual rate, in millions of dwelling units.

HOUSING STARTS in March fell to a seasonally adjusted annual rate of 1,949,000 units from a revised 1,997,000 units in February, the Commerce Department reports.

The Wall Street Journal, *April 17, 1986*

Last month's housing starts figure was 5.4% above the 1,849,000-unit pace of March 1985. Starts now have exceeded a 1.9 million-unit rate every month this year, the first time since 1978 that starts have been that high for three months in a row. All the figures are adjusted for seasonal variations.

The recent string of relatively strong starts figures "tells me that the housing market is heating up," said Ken Rankin, an economist with Wharton Econometric Forecasting Associates. He and other analysts expect further decreases in mortgage rates to sustain housing construction at close to March's level for a while. Rates on fixed-rate mortgages have tumbled nearly a percentage point since the year began to below 10%, their lowest levels in nearly eight years.

But the tempo of starts activity is likely to be kept from accelerating further by an increasingly weak economy in certain regions, such as oil-dependent areas in the South and Southwest, and overbuilding of apartments. "If it wasn't for the collapse in oil prices, we probably would be at over two million units" for the near future, suggested Edward Yardeni, a senior vice president of Prudential-Bache Securities Inc.

Construction of apartment units, often a volatile indicator, dropped 7.1% in March to a 737,000-unit annual rate after climbing a revised 13.6% in February, the Commerce Department reported. Uncertainty over the proposed federal tax-overhaul bill has caused wide swings in apartment building. There also are high vacancy rates for rental housing in parts of the U.S., which could further depress such construction.

Starts of single-family houses edged up 0.7% last month to a 1,212,000-unit annual rate. Many economists and home builders feel the most bullish about a further pickup in construction of these houses.

Building permits, viewed by some analysts as a precursor of housing activity, advanced 2.4% in March to a 1,846,000-unit annual rate from a revised 1,803,000-unit pace in February. The gain occurred in the West, as permits fell in other regions.

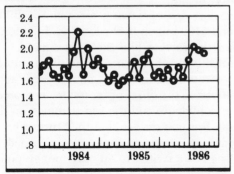

Housing Starts

Annual rate, in millions of dwelling units.

1984　1985　1986

HOUSING STARTS in March fell to a seasonally adjusted annual rate of 1,949,000 units from a revised 1,997,000 units in February, the Commerce Department reports.

The Wall Street Journal, *April 17, 1986*

Housing Starts—Third Paragraph.

Builders started work on new houses last month at an annual rate of 1,949,000 units, the Commerce Department reported (see chart on page one). That compared with a revised rate of 1,997,000 units in February, which was 1.8% below January. The department initially said starts had fallen 3.5% in February.

You can see the record levels of housing starts in the 70s (Chart 8–12 on this page), but the growth of mortgage borrowing is even more impressive (Chart 8–13 on page 143). That growth reflects the increased dollar volume of building activity due to the steep rise in housing prices. It also demonstrates the crucial role of credit in sustaining recent levels of housing activity. In the 50s and 60s, anything over $20 billion was a good year. Then mortgage borrowing reached $60 billion in the boom of the early 70s and $100 billion in the late 70s. Inflation, when propelled by record levels of borrowing like these, becomes an irresistible force.

The cyclical sensitivity of housing starts to consumer sentiment and the availability of mortgage credit is equally striking. Housing starts turned down well before the onset of recession, as soon as rising inflation reduced consumer confidence and the Fed slammed on the brakes, drying up mortgage credit. But you can see that they turned back up even before the recession ended as consumer confidence returned with the decline of inflation and the Fed's switch to an easy money policy.

Chart 8–12
Housing Starts

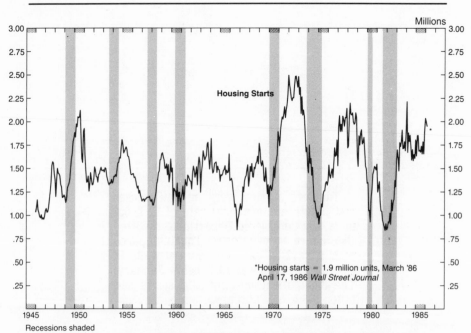

Millions

"Housing starts = 1.9 million units, March '86
April 17, 1986 *Wall Street Journal*

Recessions shaded

Source: U.S. Department of Commerce, *Business Conditions Digest* and *Handbook of Cyclical Indicators*, series 28.

Chart 8–13
Net Change in Mortgage Debt

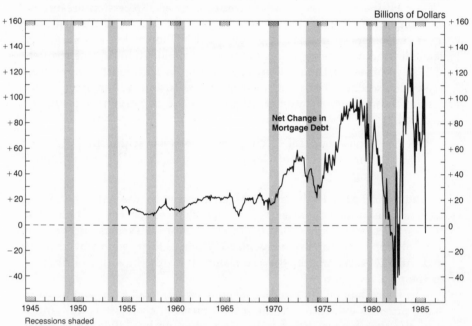

Billions of Dollars

Net Change in Mortgage Debt

Recessions shaded

Source: U.S. Department of Commerce, *Business Conditions Digest* and *Handbook of Cyclical Indicators*, series 33.

Chapter 6 has already reviewed the dramatic impact of the Fed's 1981–82 tight money policy on residential construction. The Fed's policy put a new home beyond the reach of most consumers, and mortgage borrowing and housing starts plunged. Although housing starts and mortgage borrowing have risen once again since the Fed's policies have eased and consumer sentiment has improved, housing starts will not surpass the record levels of the early 70s unless the Fed permits interest rates to remain too low. That would be dangerous, because the flat performance of housing starts, in the 1.6 to 2.0 million range in the mid-80s, is the most reassuring feature of the chart accompanying the article on page 141.

In conclusion, the modern American economy has come to depend on product inflation and ever-larger volumes of debt. These sustain the growth in demand required to maintain production and income at adequate levels. Moreover, consumer debt and consumer demand have been the leading edge of the post–World War II business cycle. Paradoxically, their strong growth led to cyclical problems with inflation, which eventually became chronic and tended to choke off credit, demand, and economic expansion.

The business cycle resumed its course after each recession because of the temporary reduction in the rate of inflation. Reduced inflation encouraged consumers to indulge in a new wave of borrowing and spending, launching another cycle and another round of inflation. In this chapter, you have observed the outlines of this process and you have followed the cycle's second phase (from recovery to expansion) as a chain of events leading from lowered rates of inflation to the expansion of consumer demand.

CPI ↓ → Consumer real income ↑ → Consumer sentiment ↑ → Consumer demand ↑ (Auto sales ↑ + Consumer credit ↑ + Retail sales ↑ + Housing starts ↑).

The 1970s epitomized the process, encouraged by the Fed's alternating tight and easy money policies. Following each recession, the Fed permitted the banks to pump huge amounts of credit into the system, encouraging an explosion of borrowing and demand. Then, as the economy overheated and inflation raced ahead, the Fed slammed on the brakes, contributing to the next recession.

The latest data on auto sales, consumer credit, retail sales, and housing starts provides evidence that the second phase of the cycle is well under way and that expansion is strong. Since inflation has fallen sharply, the excesses of the 70s can be avoided only if the Fed has the resolve to keep interest rates at restrictive levels.

The economy is at an ironic turning point. The irony exists because so many want the Fed to open the floodgates and irrigate the expansion with abundant credit. Under these circumstances, demand will grow too quickly and too soon and will collapse under its own weight before its time. It would be far better to avoid the rapid growth of demand and the resurrection of inflation, the lethal twins that have killed all previous booms. If demand grows slowly because credit is restrained, the expansion will last longer and not be set back so severely by the next recession.

chapter

9

The Business Cycle Phase Three: From Expansion to Peak

*I*f you ask a businessperson why prices rise, he or she will answer, "Rising costs," probably referring to personal experience. When you ask an economist the same question, the response will be, "Demand exceeds supply at current prices, and therefore prices rise," probably referring to the textbook case. These points of view seem to have nothing in common. Yet an analysis of economic expansion shows that they meld into a single explanation.

Currently, all the indicators of economic expansion—auto sales, consumer credit, retail sales, housing starts—are strong. This will initiate broad-based growth as incomes increase in the construction, auto, and other durable goods industries, spilling over and boosting demand for other consumer goods. Boom conditions will intensify as business invests in additional factories and machinery to meet the rush in orders.

As the expansion unfolds, capacity utilization increases with the growth in demand and production. Soon factories move from, say, 70 percent to 90 percent of their rated maximum. Productive facilities strain to meet the demands and retain the loyalty of customers.

Next, high levels of capacity utilization drive labor productivity down and unit labor costs up; efficiency is sacrificed in the name of increased output. Machinery that is always in use cannot be adequately maintained, and so it breaks down. Inexperienced workers often do not make the same contribution as old hands. The amount of labor employed increases more rapidly than output, and as output per worker falls, the labor cost per unit of output rises. This generates a surge in production costs.

Finally, rapidly increasing costs are translated into rapidly increasing prices, and a renewed round of inflation begins.

This third phase of the cycle (from expansion to peak) is the inverse of the first. All the forces that led to a reduction in the rate of inflation are now reversed.

GNP $\uparrow$ $\rightarrow$ Industrial production $\uparrow$ $\rightarrow$ Capacity utilization $\uparrow$ $\rightarrow$ Labor productivity $\downarrow$ $\rightarrow$ Unit labor costs $\uparrow$ $\rightarrow$ Producer price index $\uparrow$.

So the practical (businessperson's) and the theoretical (economist's) explanations of inflation are not at odds. During expansion, demand bids production to a level that is inefficient and costly. The businessperson experiences the increased cost and attributes inflation directly to that experience. The economist sees increased demand as the ultimate cause of the production gain, which drives costs up. Each explanation covers different aspects of the single phenomenon, economic expansion.

The late 1970s illuminate the process graphically. You will need the same statistical series employed in Chapter 7 (Phase One: From Trough to Recovery) to serve as illustrations because this phase of the cycle is the reverse of the first. Since this phase will not occur until the present cycle has unfolded further, you must return to an earlier cycle to find your examples. To illustrate expansion's impact on inflation, look at *GNP, industrial production, capacity utilization, labor productivity* and *unit labor costs,* and the *producer price index.* Each of these statistical series has already been introduced, so excerpts from *The Wall Street Journal* will not be presented again.

THE 1975–1979 ECONOMIC EXPANSION

Although subsequently eclipsed by the 1981–82 recession, the 1974 recession established a postwar record at the time. GNP declined for four quarters, and industrial production tumbled 15 percent. By the spring of 1975, the unemployment rate was over 9 percent.

Like all recessions, however, this one too prepared the way for the subsequent recovery. Capacity utilization fell to a postwar low, and labor productivity began to rise immediately. The resulting decline in unit labor costs cut the rate of inflation.

At the same time, the Federal Reserve System switched from a tight to an easy money policy, reducing interest rates and providing ample credit. A sharp recovery and strong expansion began as the decline in the rate of inflation dramatically improved consumer real income and boosted consumer sentiment. At long last, consumers were pulling ahead of inflation; their pleasure was reflected in demand's rapid increase.

By 1977-78, new housing starts were 2 million annually and domestic automobile sales peaked at more than 10 million. Retail sales and consumer credit provided further evidence of the escalating boom. Consumer installment borrowing hit annual rates of $50 billion.

The evidence of a robust economic expansion was all around as GNP and industrial production surged ahead. Rapid growth in demand, production, and capacity utilization had its inevitable result: the nation's factories and other productive facilities were strained, and increases in the labor force no longer made a proportional contribution to output (see Chart 9-1 on page 148).

In 1979 labor productivity stopped improving and began to fall. As a result, unit labor costs increased steadily, and by early 1980 the rate of inflation, as measured by the producer price index, had reached 15 percent (see Chart 9-2 on page 149).

Declining labor productivity is the focal point of this analysis. Once output is pushed past the point of diminishing returns, unit labor costs become an inevitable problem. Most people believe that the chief culprit in creating this problem is increased wages; wages do play a minor role, naturally, but the fact is that unit labor costs will rise swiftly even if wage gains run well below the rate of inflation (that is, even if real wages are falling).

Falling real wages, coupled with the forward surge in labor costs, creates one of the cruelest features of inflation. Because labor productivity has declined, there is less per capita output and therefore less real income per person. Declining real income pits one segment of American society against another, fighting over a shrinking pie. Labor-management relations become espcially bitter in these periods of boom without prosperity. Employers blame workers' wages for rising labor costs and shrinking profits, while workers blame employers' profits for shrinking real wages; in reality, neither one is actually responsible for the other's misfortune.

In such times, the public's support for wage and price controls becomes insistent (although, of course, management has a greater interest in controlling wages and labor has a greater interest in controlling prices). Yet you can see from this chapter's analysis that rising costs due to reduced efficiency (falling labor productivity) are responsible for the increase in prices that captures everyone's attention. No one's greed is to blame. And therefore controls designed to limit greed are bound to be ineffective.

There have been two recent attempts at wage and price controls: the first under President Nixon in 1971-72 and the second under President Carter in 1979-80. President Nixon's controls were certain to "succeed"

Chart 9–1
GNP, Industrial Production, Capacity Utilization, Labor Productivity, and Unit Labor Costs

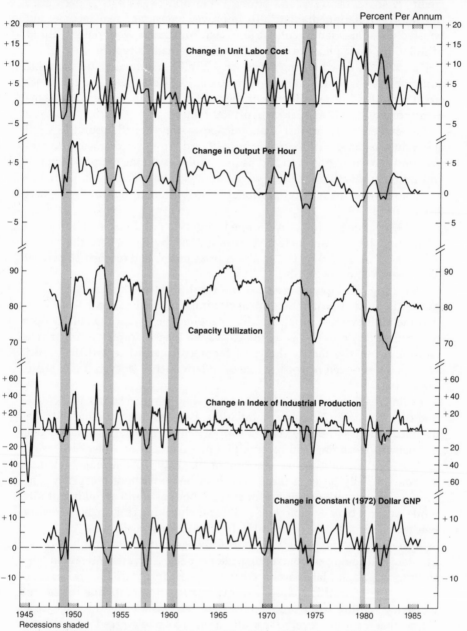

Percent Per Annum

Change in Unit Labor Cost

Change in Output Per Hour

Capacity Utilization

Change in Index of Industrial Production

Change in Constant (1972) Dollar GNP

Recessions shaded

Source: U.S. Department of Commerce, *Business Conditions Digest* and *Handbook of Cyclical Indicators*, series 47c, 50c, 82, and 370c; Federal Reserve Board.

Chart 9-2
Changes in Unit Labor Costs and Producer Prices

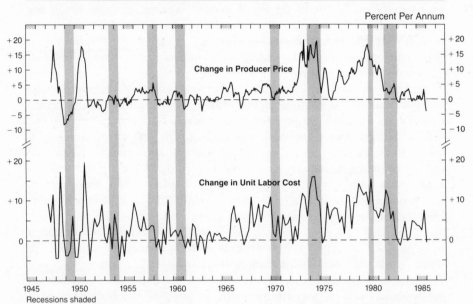

Percent Per Annum

Recessions shaded

Source: U.S. Department of Commerce, *Business Conditions Digest* and *Handbook of Cyclical Indicators*, series 334c; Federal Reserve Board.

because they were implemented during the transition from recovery to expansion while capacity utilization was low and labor productivity high. As a result, the rate of inflation was still falling from its 1970 cyclical peak. It would have continued to decline in any event and remain low until the expansion gained strength. The controls did slightly dampen inflation, but their impact was marginal.

President Carter's controls were bound to fail, just as President Nixon's were bound to succeed, because President Carter's were implemented during the virulent expansion of 1977–79. As labor productivity fell and unit labor costs climbed, business merely passed its increased costs on to the consumer. Rising prices reflected rising costs, not greed, and business did not earn excess profits.

Keep in mind also that more stringent wage controls could not have restrained business costs. Some of the increase in unit labor costs was due to the increase in wage rates, but most of it was due to declining productivity caused by high-capacity utilization. Workers were no more culpable than their employers.

This is an important point. We really can't blame the declines in labor productivity in the 1970s on the American worker, as some are prone to do. Productivity lapses in that decade occurred cyclically, when the economy overheated, and thus they really reflected the limitations of plant and equipment under extreme conditions rather than failures of diligence in the labor force.

And harking back to World War II for an example of successful wage and price controls is not the answer, either. Wage and price (and profit) controls worked then because the economy was on a war footing. About half of the economy's output was devoted to the war effort, much of it under a system of planning and direct resource allocation that operated outside ordinary market relationships. You couldn't bid up the price of a car (none were produced because the auto plants were converted to war production) or buy all the gasoline and steak you wanted (these were rationed). And despite the patriotism aroused by the war effort, black markets arose to subvert the controls. Therefore, it's doubtful whether such a system could work to contain peacetime inflation, for which, unlike war-induced inflation, there is no end in sight.

Imposing wage and price controls during the expansionary phase of the business cycle (as was attempted in the late 70s) is a little like trying to stop the rattle of a boiling kettle by taping down the lid. Demand heats the expansion, and inflation is the natural result. Turning down the heat is the only practical solution.

Finally, there's the question of "supply-side shocks." These are sudden increases in the price of important commodities (imposed by the sellers) or reductions in supply due to forces beyond our control. Some believe that the late 70s' inflation was due to these shocks, but this argument should be taken with a grain of salt. First, any explanation that places the blame on others should be suspect; if you wish to find fault, it is always best to look in the mirror. Second, neither OPEC nor the Russian wheat deal nor the failure of the Peruvian anchovy harvest can explain the price explosions of the 70s. If demand had been weak, prices would have remained stable. After all, prices stopped climbing as soon as recession hit.

And whether you are dealing with free-market farm prices or OPEC, repealing the laws of supply and demand is not easy. Farm prices eased down in the commodity deflation of the 80s, while oil prices collapsed in a matter of months. In both cases, high prices and profits in the 70s had attracted excess capacity (supply). But neither the free market nor the cartel could hold prices up once supply exceeded demand at current prices.

Whether or not the current expansion will generate inflation as virulent as that of 1977–79 remains to be seen. It depends on the Fed, which so far has restrained the growth in demand by restraining the growth in credit. The minislowdown of 1984 demonstrated the Fed's determination to act at the first sign of danger. Yet, recent appointees to the Board of Governors have expressed dissatisfaction with the Fed's restrictive policies. By late 1985 and early 1986 they had already succeeded in relaxing credit at an alarming rate. If demand increases rapidly, generating explosive growth in output and capacity utilization, be prepared for a sharp increase in costs and prices. Only leisurely growth in demand will prevent such a strain and limit inflation.

This chapter has examined expansion's impact on costs and prices during the third phase of the business cycle. Now you can turn to the cycle's last phase, when expansion and inflation lead to the inevitable contraction.

10

The Business Cycle Phase Four: From Peak to Contraction

*I*s the next recession inevitable? Yes, because all economic expansions end in recession. But whether it will be mild or severe depends on the expansion. A strong and rapid expansion, driven by large increases in consumer and business borrowing, that ends in virulent inflation will produce a sharp and severe recession. A mild and gradual expansion, one lacking excessive borrowing and ending with only slight inflation, will produce a mild recession.

Recall from the last chapter that economic expansion generates reduced efficiency and heightened inflation. As production grows, and with it capacity utilization, labor productivity falls. Labor costs increase, driving prices upward. The economy has reached a level of activity that cannot be sustained.

The fourth phase of the business cycle is the inverse of the second. In that phase of the cycle, from recovery to expansion, a declining rate of inflation pushed consumer real income upward, prompting consumers to borrow and spend, thus fueling the economic expansion. Now, in the last phase of the cycle, a rising rate of inflation has the opposite impact on the consumer. Real income falls and consumer sentiment erodes. Consumers become pessimistic when their paychecks don't keep up with inflation, giving them less and less real buying power. They respond by restricting their purchase of deferrable items, especially those requiring heavy borrowing. The downturn in consumer activity will lead to a general contraction in demand, which will continue until the trough of the cycle is reached.

The root cause of the recession, declining productivity, which depressed real wages because rising costs spurred inflation, demands emphasis. It's an important point because some, as the last chapter noted, have incorrectly blamed rapidly rising wages for recent bouts of inflation. As a matter of fact, the charts demonstrate that real wages suffered, rather than improved, whenever inflation heated up. *If rising wages had been responsible for inflation, real wages would have increased.*

The 1980 recession is a good example. You will need the same statistical series developed in Chapter 8 to follow it. Inflation's impact on the consumer will be measured by the *consumer price index (CPI), real compensation,* and *the Index of Consumer Sentiment.* The contraction in consumer expenditures will be measured by the decline in *automobile sales, consumer credit, retail sales,* and *housing starts.*

As you know from Chapter 8, with the exception of real compensation and consumer sentiment, which are reported only occasionally, articles covering all of these series appear regularly in *The Wall Street Journal.* Representative articles were treated in Chapter 8; they need not be reproduced here. This discussion will be limited to an outline of the behavior of these series during the cycle's final phase, as summarized below.

CPI ↑ → Consumer real income ↓ → Consumer sentiment ↓ → Consumer expenditures ↓ (Auto sales ↓ + Consumer credit ↓ + Retail sales ↓ + Housing starts ↓).

By late 1979, rapid increases in the producer price index had pushed the rate of inflation, as measured by the consumer price index, to 15 percent at an annual rate (see Chart 10–1, page 155).

Employee compensation was growing at 10 percent a year, but that was hardly enough to offset the effect of inflation. As you can see, real compensation fell by 5 percent, an even worse erosion than in 1974 (see Chart 10–2, page 156).

The Index of Consumer Sentiment had sunk steadily through 1978 and 1979 as inflation surged upward. In late 1979, it matched 1974's dismal performance. Consumers were discouraged. Their take-home pay was losing the race with inflation, interest rates were high and rising, relief was nowhere in sight, and so they had no cause for anything but pessimism.

Slumping auto sales and housing starts were the first omens of recession. Both declined throughout 1979. Housing starts fell from a 1.8 million

Chart 10–1
Change in Producer Prices and in Consumer Prices (smoothed)

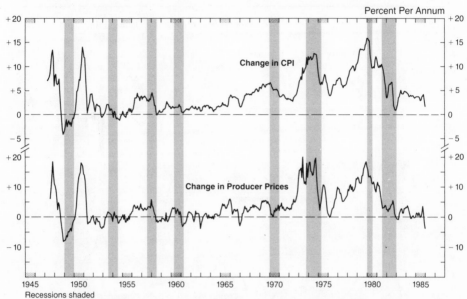

Recessions shaded

Source: U.S. Department of Commerce, *Business Conditions Digest* and *Handbook of Cyclical Indicators*, series 320c and 334c.

annual rate to 1.4 million, and auto sales declined from 9 million to 7 million (see Chart 10–3, page 157, and Chart 10–4, page 158).

In the face of all this, consumer credit remained remarkably strong in 1979, declining only slightly (see Chart 10–5, page 159). Retail sales continued to grow (see Chart 10–6, page 160).

Thus, 1980 began with most of the important leading indicators of consumer activity heading downward or showing weakness. They were beginning to drag the rest of the economy with them.

Interest rates and inflation hit record postwar highs in the first quarter of 1980. The Federal Reserve System clamped down hard on consumer credit, restricting its availability and raising interest rates even higher. This was the proverbial last straw, and in the second quarter, consumer credit fell more steeply than at any other time in the postwar period.

Chart 10–2
*Index of Consumer Sentiment, Change in Real Average Hourly Compensation,
Change in Nominal Average Hourly Compensation, and Change in CPI*

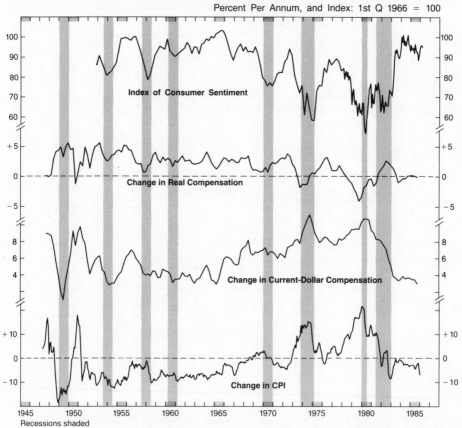

Percent Per Annum, and Index: 1st Q 1966 = 100

Source: U.S. Department of Commerce, *Business Conditions Digest* and *Handbook of Cyclical Indicators*, series 58,
320c, 345c, and 346c.

All consumer activities that had come to depend on consumer credit were
affected: auto sales, retail sales, and housing starts plunged. The Fed's
action had brought the entire process to a head and hastened the recession
that had been inevitable for over a year.

In summary, the developments were typical of the cycle's fourth phase
(from peak to contraction). Rapidly rising inflation depressed consumer
real income and consumer sentiment, bringing on a collapse in consumer
demand.

Chart 10–3
New Auto Sales, Domestic Type (excluding imports)

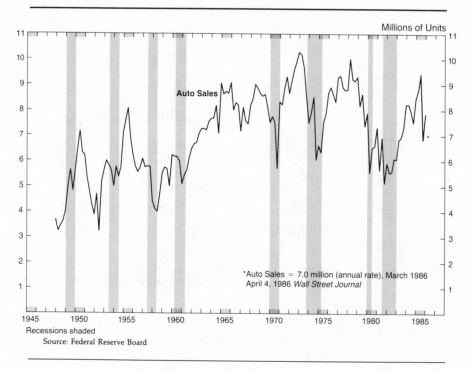

Millions of Units

Auto Sales

*Auto Sales = 7.0 million (annual rate), March 1986
April 4, 1986 *Wall Street Journal*

1945   1950   1955   1960   1965   1970   1975   1980   1985

Recessions shaded
Source: Federal Reserve Board

There was no human villain in this drama. Blame the inanimate forces of credit and inflation, which periodically swept over the economy to leave recession's wreckage behind. The Fed finally came to grips with the problem in 1981 when, in its attempt to bring inflation under control, it tightened credit sufficiently to turn recovery into recession. That is why the 1980 recession, rather than the 1981–82 experience, was used as an illustration of the cycle's fourth phase: the most recent recession was engineered by the Fed to reduce inflation, while the recession of 1980 was a more natural outcome of cyclical developments.

Although all factors of production bore the burden of inflation in the form of declining real income, there is no doubt who bore the burden of recession: the unemployed. Their loss of income is not shared by the rest of us as the economy contracts. Moreover, unemployment hits hardest those industries that depend heavily on big-ticket consumer expenditures

Chart 10–4
Housing Starts

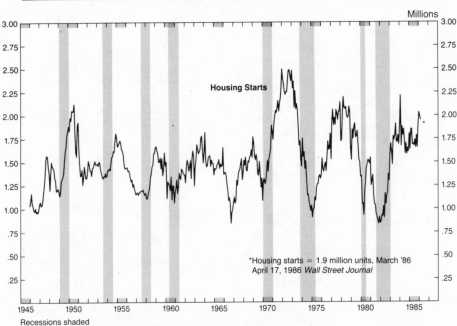

Recessions shaded

Source: U.S. Department of Commerce, *Business Conditions Digest* and *Handbook of Cyclical Indicators*, series 28.

financed by borrowing. It is worst in construction, autos, and other durable goods industries and in the steel and nonferrous metal industries. Workers in communications, services, finance, and government are largely spared.

Through no fault of their own, therefore, workers (and their families) in a narrow band of industries must bear most of the cycle's burden. They are not responsible for the economy's fluctuations, but they are the chief victims in every downturn. Someone must build the homes and cars and mill the lumber and steel. Yet, as if caught in a perverse game of musical chairs, those who do are always left without a seat when the music stops.

This chapter completes the analysis of the four phases of the business cycle. The statistical series particularly useful in charting the persistent rise and fall of the cycle's course are now familiar to you. More important, you now comprehend the inevitability of these phases. There *must* be a recession in the future, and there *must* be a recovery after that, . . .

Chart 10–5
Change in Consumer Installment Credit

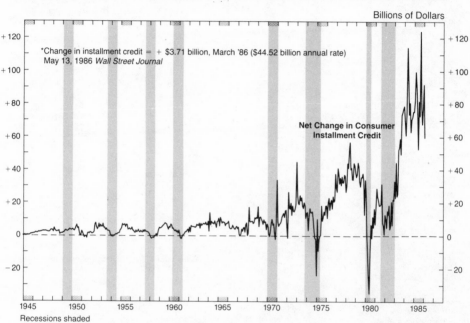

Billions of Dollars

*Change in installment credit = + $3.71 billion, March '86 ($44.52 billion annual rate)
May 13, 1986 Wall Street Journal

Net Change in Consumer Installment Credit

Recessions shaded

Source: U.S. Department of Commerce, *Business Conditions Digest* and *Handbook of Cyclical Indicators*, series 113.

and so on. The statistical series you have examined so far are your surveyor's tools.

Now it's time to examine the cycle's impact on other economic indicators, such as inventory accumulation, business capital expenditures, profits and the stock market, and America's international transactions. They play a role in reinforcing the cycle, or generating income from it, or transmitting our cycle to the rest of the world.

Chart 10–6
Retail Sales

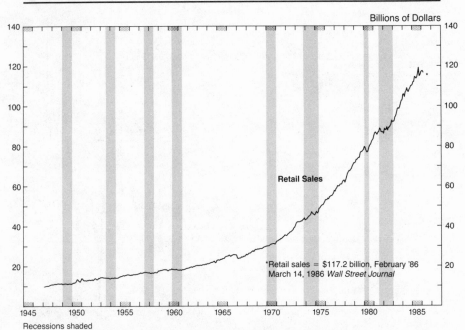

Billions of Dollars

Retail Sales

*Retail sales = $117.2 billion, February '86
March 14, 1986 *Wall Street Journal*

Recessions shaded

Source: U.S. Department of Commerce, *Business Conditions Digest* and *Handbook of Cyclical Indicators,* series 54.

11

Inventories

*I*nventories are stocks of goods on hand—raw materials, goods in process, or finished products. Individual businesses use them to bring stability to their operations, and yet you'll see that they actually have a destabilizing effect on the business cycle.

Businesses view inventories as a necessary evil. A manufacturer, wholesaler, or retailer can't live from hand to mouth, continually filling sales orders from current production. Stocks of goods "on the shelf" are a cushion against unexpected orders and slowdowns in production. On the other hand, inventories are an investment in working capital and incur an interest cost. If the firm borrows capital to maintain inventories, the direct interest cost is obvious. Even if the firm has not borrowed, however, working capital tied up in inventories represents an interest cost. Any funds invested in inventories could have earned the going interest rate in the money market, and this loss can substantially crimp profits.

Therefore, business attempts to keep inventories at an absolute minimum consistent with smooth operations. For a very large business, literally millions of dollars are at stake. This is why you see modern automated cash registers in large chain supermarkets and retail establishments. These cash registers came into use, not chiefly because they record your purchases more quickly (which of course they do), but because they also tie into a computer network, which keeps track of inventories of thousands of items on a daily basis.

But why do inventories exacerbate the business cycle?

Consider the upswing of the cycle first. As demand increases rapidly, businesses must boost production to meet the growing volume of orders. If they are not quick enough, and sales grow more rapidly than output, an unplanned drawdown of inventories will occur as orders are filled. This is known as *involuntary inventory depletion*. If inventories are severely depleted, shortages can result and sales may be jeopardized. To protect itself against such developments once it is confident of the unfolding expansion, business will expand output and defensively accumulate inventories more rapidly than its sales are growing. Since all firms are stockpiling to prevent shortages, industrial production increases more vigorously than it otherwise would, accentuating the cyclical expansion and the swift rise in capacity utilization. This, of course, hastens the inevitable decrease in labor productivity and increase in unit labor costs associated with this phase of the cycle. Hence, inventory accumulation adds to the inflationary pressures.

Now consider the downswing of the cycle. No firm willingly maintains production in a sales slump because unsold goods would pile up on the shelf. As sales weaken and fall, business curtails production in order to prevent *involuntary inventory accumulation*. Indeed, once business recognizes the severity of the slump, it will begin to liquidate the large volume of (now unnecessary) inventories built up during the previous expansion. These stockpiles of goods are no longer needed and can be disposed of. But as goods are sold from inventories, output and employment are reduced more than sales, since orders can be filled from inventories rather than from current production. This aggravates the cycle's downturn.

Thus, inventories play an important destabilizing role in the cycle through their influence on industrial production, boosting output during expansion and depressing it during slump. Now, this destabilizing influence is compounded by inventory's impact on inflation. When rapid expansion is heightened by inventory accumulation, contributing to inflationary pressures, business firms increase their inventory buildup to take advantage of rising prices. And when inventory liquidation in a recession contributes to deflationary pressures, falling prices can trigger a panic sell-off, which drives prices down even more steeply.

Here's how it works. Business stockpiles goods during the expansionary phase of the cycle to prevent involuntary inventory depletion and shortages, and prices start to rise. Firms quickly discover that goods held in inventory increase in value along with the general rise in prices. They have an incentive to buy now while prices are low, hold the goods in inventory, and sell them later at higher prices and profits. If prices are rising rapidly enough, widespread speculation can set in, which adds to the general increase in production and reinforces the inflation.

Recall, for example, the rapid increase in sugar prices in 1973–74. Sugar manufacturers and industrial users of sugar (canners, soft drink bottlers, confectioners, and bakers) produced sugar and sweetened products and held them in inventory while their prices were low, hoping to make large profits from sales when their prices increased. This speculative stockpiling contributed to the price increase by bidding up production (and costs) out of proportion to sales.

Of course, when the inevitable contraction comes, liquidation of the inventory overhang helps halt the inflationary spiral. Businesses panic when faced with the prospect of selling at a price that will not recoup interest costs. If sufficiently severe, the sell-off can force prices down. More important, output plummets and layoffs mount as orders are filled from the shelf. Liquidation continues until inventories are in proper relation to sales.

Thus, speculative inventory accumulation and liquidation become a self-fulfilling prophecy. Firms pile up inventories in anticipation of a price increase, and the large volume of orders bids prices upward. When the recession begins, firms sell inventories in haste, afraid of a drop in prices, and the sell-off forces prices downward.

Now you understand why inventories and their relationship to sales are such important economic indicators. They not only confirm the stage of the cycle, they also provide advance warning of turning points and of the strength or severity of impending boom and bust.

The cyclical experience of the early 1970s will serve as an illustration. This will be followed by an examination of recent developments.

To begin with, *The Wall Street Journal* publishes the Commerce Department's inventory and sales data around the middle of each month. The April 15, 1986, article is representative. (See page 164.)

Look for the following: *inventories, sales,* and *the inventory-sales ratio.*

Inventories and sales are straightforward concepts. The inventory-sales ratio tells you how many months it would take to sell off inventories at the prevailing sales pace. You can calculate the ratio by dividing monthly inventory by monthly sales. Typically, inventories have been roughly 1½ times sales over the cycle. A rise in the ratio indicates that inventories are growing out of proportion to sales and that inventory liquidation and recession are imminent. A fall in the ratio informs you that sales are outpacing inventory growth and that economic expansion is under way. This is a key indicator; you should follow it closely.

Return to the *Journal* article after examining the inventory cycle of the early 1970s. This cycle concluded with a good example of inventory accumulation and speculation followed by inventory liquidation. To trace these events, follow the steep rise in inventories from 1972 through 1974 and the 1975 liquidation; note the decline in the inventory-sales ratio in 1971–72 and the increase in 1973 and 1974 (see Chart 11–1 on page 166); and note that the inventory and sales curves are nearly congruent, with inventories lagging behind sales by a year or so.

You can observe the decline of the inventory-sales ratio as the business cycle moved from recovery to expansion in 1971–72. Sales were expanding, but it was still too early for business to rebuild inventories.

As increasing demand boosted sales, 1973 displayed all the symptoms of the expansion-to-peak phase of the cycle: strong and rapidly growing sales, strained capacity utilization and slower deliveries, and a rising rate of inflation. Under these circumstances, business sought to defend itself against possible shortages by adding to inventories more rapidly than sales grew. The long decline in the inventory-sales ratio was reversed, and speculation began. Business boosted inventories in the expectation of rising prices, hoping to make a profit as goods increased in value. This intensified inflationary pressures (recall sugar) as a share of produc-

Inventory Building Didn't Much Help Growth in Quarter

By ROSE GUTFELD
Staff Reporter of THE WALL STREET JOURNAL

WASHINGTON -- Business inventories were essentially unchanged in February after edging up a revised 0.3% in January, the Commerce Department said. The report suggests that first-quarter growth wasn't aided much by inventory building.

The January figure originally was reported as a 0.7% rise.

Separately, the Federal Reserve Board said that consumer credit expanded $4.97 billion in February, or at an 11% annual rate, after rising a revised $7.66 billion in January, or at a 17.2% rate. The Fed had previously reported a $6.88 billion rise for January.

The latest rise is modest compared with the hefty increases of much of last year.

Some economists have hoped that sluggish first-quarter economic growth benefited from business efforts to rebuild inventories. The lack of substantial inventory building "takes away the factor that looks like it might carry you in the first quarter," said Maury Harris, vice president and chief economist for PaineWebber Group Inc.

Business sales fell $4.77 billion, or 1.1%, in February to $427.18 billion after falling $840 million, or 0.2%, to $431.96 billion in January. Inventories equaled 1.37 months of sales in February, compared with 1.35 months in January.

February inventories totaled $585.13 billion, compared with $584.97 billion in January.

Some analysts suggested that the weak inventory growth in dollar terms reflected lower prices for many items. Also, some economists suggested that manufacturers are well-positioned for the expected pickup in economic growth.

"Manufacturers have been maintaining a tight posture and are poised to boost inventories when demand picks up," said Robert Dederick, chief economist for Northern Trust Co.

The inventories and credit figures are adjusted for seasonal variations but aren't adjusted for inflation.

Inventories declined for manufacturers, rose for retailers and fell slightly for wholesalers. Sales fell for manufacturers and wholesalers, while retail sales rose slightly.

According to the Fed's report, consumer credit outstanding at the end of February totaled $543.46 billion, up 17.3% from a year earlier.

Auto credit outstanding expanded $2.54 billion in February after rising $4.18 billion in January. Revolving credit rose $1.04 billion after increasing $1.39 billion.

Mobile-home credit rose $194 million in February after decreasing $90 million the month before. Miscellaneous credit, which includes cash loans and certain retail transactions, expanded $1.21 billion after rising $2.18 billion.

Here is a summary of the Commerce Department's report on business inventories and sales in February. The figures are in billions of dollars, seasonally adjusted:

	(billions of dollars)		
	Feb 1986	Jan 1986	Feb 1985
Total business inventories	585.13	584.97	578.54
Manufacturers	279.51	280.36	286.15
Retailers	169.07	167.99	159.48
Wholesalers	136.55	136.62	132.92
Total business sales	427.18	431.96	418.22
Inventory/sales ratio	1.37	1.35	1.38

Sales and Inventory/ Sales Ratio {

Inventories {

Statistical Summary

Sales and Inventory-Sales Ratio—Sixth Paragraph.

Business sales fell $4.77 billion, or 1.1%, in February to $427.18 billion after falling $840 million, or 0.2%, to $431.96 billion in January. Inventories equaled 1.37 months of sales in February, compared with 1.35 months in January.

Inventories—Seventh Paragraph.

February inventories totaled $585.13 billion, compared with $584.97 billion in January.

Statistical Summary—End of Article.

Here is a summary of the Commerce Department's report on business inventories and sales in February. The figures are in billions of dollars, seasonally adjusted:

	(billions of dollars)		
	Feb 1986	Jan 1986	Feb 1985
Total business inventories	585.13	584.97	578.54
Manufacturers	279.51	280.36	286.15
Retailers	169.07	167.99	159.48
Wholesalers	136.55	136.62	132.92
Total business sales	427.18	431.96	418.22
Inventory/sales ratio	1.37	1.35	1.38

tion went on the shelf instead of satisfying consumer demand. You can see that the inventory run-up dwarfed all other postwar increases up to that point.

As the cycle's peak approached, in 1974, sales stopped growing. Unplanned inventory accumulation became a problem; the inventory-sales ratio rose even more rapidly; and business firms had to deal with ever-larger stockpiles of goods. Sensing that a sell-off was around the corner, they tried to bring inventories under control. Unfortunately, this was

Chart 11–1
*Manufacturing and Trade Sales and Inventories, Inventory-Sales Ratio
(monthly basis), and Change in Book Value of Manufacturing and Trade
Inventories*

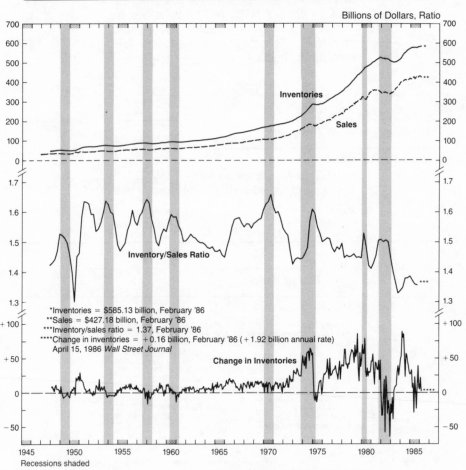

Billions of Dollars, Ratio

*Inventories = \$585.13 billion, February '86
**Sales = \$427.18 billion, February '86
***Inventory/sales ratio = 1.37, February '86
****Change in inventories = +0.16 billion, February '86 (+1.92 billion annual rate)
April 15, 1986 *Wall Street Journal*

Recessions shaded

Source: U.S. Department of Commerce, *Business Conditions Digest* and *Handbook of Cyclical Indicators*, series 31, 56, and 71; and Federal Reserve Board.

more easily said than done. Orders had to be canceled and production
curtailed more than once because business underestimated the situation's
severity.

But beginning in late 1974 and continuing into 1975, inventory liquidation finally began. Under panic conditions, business desperately dumped

goods on the market. Despite the sell-off, you'll notice that the inventory-sales ratio remained high until early 1975. This is evidence of the collapse in sales and the recession's severity—the reason business went to such lengths to unload its stocks of goods.

Other postwar recessions had been mild by comparison. Industrial production plunged as business firms cut output severely and filled the meager volume of orders from their overstocked inventories. Two million workers were laid off between the fall of 1974 and the spring of 1975, and the unemployment rate brushed 10 percent. There is no doubt that inventory accumulation and liquidation played a key role in the cycle's severity.

Unlike the cycle of the early 70s, the 1981–82 recession can't be used as a typical example of inventory accumulation and liquidation because of the Fed's role in aborting the 1981 recovery. Sales were doing well and the inventory-sales ratio was low when the Fed's tight money policy clamped a vise on the economy in 1981. Sales shrank and involuntary inventory accumulation drove up both inventories and the inventory-sales ratio. As soon as possible, business began a massive inventory liquidation program that continued through early 1983. As you can tell from Chart 11–1 on page 166, the worst recession since World War II was accompanied by the most severe bout of inventory liquidation.

Recovery began as soon as the Fed provided easier credit conditions. And you can see that business did not wait long before it began restocking its depleted inventories. By early 1984 inventory accumulation set a new record. Yet sales were so strong that the inventory-sales ratio declined throughout 1983 and remained low in 1984. There was no indication that inventory growth had outstripped sales or that the economy was near a cyclical peak.

Nevertheless, the Fed was concerned that the recovery and expansion were proceeding too rapidly. It fine-tuned the slowdown of mid-84, and inventory accumulations began to subside. By 1985 and early 1986 inventory accumulation was down to a moderate level.

To a large extent, the inventory run-up of 1984 and the subsequent drop to a moderate pace in 1985–86 were a one-time reaction to severe inventory depletion during the 1981–82 recession. These developments were not part of the ordinary cyclical scene; they were a reaction to the credit conditions imposed on the economy by the Fed. In a way, the decks were cleared for a resumption of the normal cyclical patterns by the second half of the 80s.

Return to the April 15, 1986, *Journal* article on pages 164 and 165. It informs you that the inventory-sales ratio was 1.37, and you will observe from Chart 11–1 on page 166 that the ratio had fallen to a historic low by the mid-80s. This is partly a consequence of the improved technology that enables business to keep a closer watch over its inventories. But it's also a sign of a lean economy, a cyclically low ratio that tells us

that businesses had not accumulated inventories in anticipation of shortages and inflation. In early 1986, the expansion still had a way to go.

How long will the inventory-sales ratio remain low, and how long
will it be before inventory accumulation exacerbates the expansion and
contributes to the next recession? That depends on the strength of the
expansion as determined by the growth in consumer demand. If demand
grows too quickly and inflation speeds up, business will begin stockpiling
for self-protection and speculation, and the inventory-sales ratio will start
to climb. This will be a dead giveaway that inventory accumulation is
contributing to boom conditions and that the peak of the cycle cannot
be far off. On the other hand, if the expansion is restrained, the inventory-
sales ratio should remain flat for a long time. In that case, inventory
accumulation will not aggravate the expansion and the business cycle
will not be brought to a peak prematurely.

12

Business Capital Expenditures

*B*usiness's expenditures on factories, warehouses, offices, machinery, and equipment, like its accumulation of inventories, reinforce the business cycle; they do not lead it. Business waits for its signal from the economy before committing its capital. Similarly, only after the expansion is over does business begin to cut back on capital expenditures in anticipation of reduced sales.

There are five principal factors influencing decisions to spend on new plant and equipment.

First, the rate of capacity utilization must be high. Putting it simply, if sales are strong, business will invest in new machinery and equipment in order to have the capacity necessary to fill the orders. During a recession, however, the rate of capacity utilization is low and business has more than enough plant and equipment on hand to satisfy the low volume of orders. Why add to plant and equipment when the existing level is already more than adequate?

Second, old facilities, whether fully utilized or not, will be scrapped and replaced by new if operating costs can be sufficiently reduced through innovation in the process of production. Competition leaves business no choice: if equipment is no longer cost-effective, it must be replaced even though it could still be used.

Third, new plant and equipment may be required to produce a new or redesigned product even if existing facilities are operating at full capacity and have a continued useful life. Model and style changes have forced the automobile industry to spend billions replacing still-functional equipment, for instance.

Fourth, spending on plant and equipment is sensitive to current and anticipated profits. Business will invest in additional facilities if it expects long-range profit growth beyond any short-run cyclical fluctuation. In addition, profits plowed back into the business provide the cash flow necessary to finance capital expenditures. A recession will limit business's ability to finance capital expenditures; an expansion will generate the necessary cash flow.

The final factor is interest rates. Business must borrow to finance plant and equipment expenditures if internally generated funds are not adequate. When interest rates are very high the cost of borrowing may be prohibitive, and so business firms postpone or cancel their capital expenditure plans. Or they may feel that for the time being they can get a better return by investing their own funds at high rates of interest than by making expenditures on new productive facilities.

Keep these factors in mind when evaluating business's capital expansion plans and their role in the current cycle. You can keep abreast of capital expenditures by following three series published monthly in *The Wall Street Journal:* the Commerce Department report on new orders for nondefense capital goods, the National Machine Tool Builders' Association report on machine tool orders, and the F. W. Dodge report on building awards.

The Wall Street Journal publishes preliminary data for *nondefense capital goods,* such as the May 23, 1986, release, on the Thursday or Friday of the next-to-the-last week of the month, and the final report appears about a week later. You will have to keep your eyes open for these figures because they are part of an overall report on *durable goods.* (See page 171.)

The revised data, appearing a week later, is included with a general release on *factory orders.* The June 3, 1986, article is a good example. (See page 172.)

This series presents new orders received by manufacturers of durable goods other than military equipment. (*Durable goods* are defined as those having a useful life of more than three years.) Nondefense capital goods represent approximately one fifth to one third of all durable goods production. The series includes engines; construction, mining, and materials handling equipment; office and store machinery; electrical transmission and distribution equipment and other electrical machinery (excluding household appliances and electronic equipment); and railroad, ship, and aircraft transportation equipment. Military equipment is excluded because new

Durables Orders Declined Again During April

By Rose Gutfeld
Staff Reporter of The Wall Street Journal

WASHINGTON—New orders for big-ticket factory goods fell 0.8% in April, the Commerce Department said, offering little sign of a rebound for ailing manufacturers.

The decline, the third consecutive monthly drop and the seventh in the past 10 months, followed a revised decline of 2.2% in March. The March drop was previously reported as 2.1%.

"The report is a fairly dismal statement on the durable-goods and capital-goods sectors," said Allen Sinai, senior vice president and chief economist at Shearson Lehman Brothers Inc. "It is consistent with continuing weakness in the production side of the economy."

Jerry Jasinowski, chief economist for the National Association of Manufacturers, said the order decline "reflects the weak demand situation that we're seeing overall."

Excluding a 27.2% drop in defense orders, which move erratically from month to month, orders rose 2.1%. A Commerce Department analyst said orders increased

The Wall Street Journal, *May 23, 1986*

for motor vehicles and parts, fabricated metals, lumber and furniture, which aren't broken out in this initial report on the orders.

But declines were shown in the report's three biggest categories: primary metals, machinery and transportation equipment. Orders for non-defense capital goods, considered a major barometer of business investment, fell 3.7% after falling 5.6% in March.

Commerce Secretary Malcolm Baldrige acknowledged in a statement that "April orders stand 2.5% below their first-quarter average." But he said, "Though durable-goods production has not yet picked up, the housing sector and financial markets continue to signal faster economic growth."

Durable goods are items intended to last three years or more.

The durable-goods figures are adjusted for seasonal variations but not for inflation. Mr. Sinai noted that the figure would look better if declining prices were taken into account.

The decline in new orders brought them to $104.31 billion from $105.17 billion in March (see chart on page one). Orders for non-defense capital goods declined to $26.04 billion from $27.03 billion. } Non-defense Capital Goods

Shipments of durable goods increased 2.8% to $105.58 billion, after falling 2.7% to $102.69 billion in March. The rise, the largest since last August, when shipments also rose 2.8%, reflected a sharp increase in shipments of motor vehicles and parts.

The backlog of orders declined 0.4% to $358.81 billion after rising 0.7% to $360.08 billion in March.

orders for such equipment do not respond directly to the business cycle. Note that the April figure was $26.04 billion, which was revised to $26.08 billion on June 3. Both reports tell you that April's data was a decrease from the preceding month.

These figures, together with Chart 12–1 on page 173, provide a good illustration of the relationship between capacity utilization (see Chart 7–4 on page 90) and equipment expenditures. Orders for nondefense capital goods expanded swiftly as capacity utilization rose rapidly through early 1984. Then, capacity utilization leveled off at 80 percent during the mid-80s, and nondefense orders stopped growing.

Machine tools are used to shape parts for all durable goods; therefore, orders for new machine tools reliably herald industry's plans to add to plant and equipment. The National Machine Tool Builders' Association

Factory Orders Rose Slim 0.1% During April

Non-Defense Sector Gained 1.6%; Building Outlays Advanced 0.8% in Month

By ROSE GUTFELD
Staff Reporter of THE WALL STREET JOURNAL

WASHINGTON—New orders for factory goods rose a small 0.1% in April, the Commerce Department said, while strong residential building paced a 0.8% advance in construction spending.

The orders increase, which occurred despite a sharp drop in defense orders, followed a revised 2.8% decline in March and a 1.3% drop in February. The March decline was originally reported as 2.3%. Excluding defense orders, which move erratically from month to month, orders increased 1.6% in April.

The rise in orders doesn't signal a turnaround for manufacturers, according to many economists. "It's a small increase," noted Lawrence Chimerine, chairman of Chase Econometrics in Bala Cynwyd, Pa. "It's better than a decline. But there's still no apparent upturn in the manufacturing sector."

"It's no clear signal that the manufacturing industry is on the mend," said Kathleen Cooper, chief economist at Security Pacific National Bank in Los Angeles. "It's a small plus but it's nothing to write home about."

Durables Orders Slip

The latest report showed that durable goods orders fell 0.2% in April, less than the 0.8% drop reported last month in the department's advance report on orders for big-ticket factory goods. Orders for durable goods, items intended to last three years or more, fell 2.7% in March and 0.6% in February.

Orders for nondurables rose 0.4% in April after declining 3% in March and 2.1% in February.

The construction spending report showed a continued split within the industry: Residential building remains strong while nonresidential construction is weak.

Followed March Decline

The overall rise in April followed a revised 1.4% drop in March and a 1% increase in February. The department previously put the March drop at 1.2%.

Outlays for residential building rose 2.6% in April after increasing a revised 0.2% in March and 2.3% in February. Robert Ortner, the Commerce Department's chief economist, predicted that residential construction would continue to rise and would be the strongest sector of the economy for the year.

Spending for nonresidential construction fell 1.4% in April after declining 5.2% in March and 0.2% in February.

The rise in factory orders brought them to $193.18 billion from $193 billion in March (see chart on page one). Orders for non-defense capital goods, considered a barometer of business investment, fell 1.8% in April after declining 7.3% in March.

Factory Inventories Fall

Manufacturers' inventories fell 0.1% in April to $279.2 billion after rising 0.1% to $279.57 billion in March. Factory shipments rose 2% in April to $194.92 billion after falling 2.7% to $191.05 billion in March. The backlog of orders declined 0.5% in April to $368.72 billion after increasing 0.5% in March to $370.46 billion.

The April rise in construction spending brought it to an annual rate of $356.7 billion from $353.9 billion in March.

Measured in 1977 dollars to eliminate the effects of inflation, construction spending in April was unchanged from March at $204.6 billion.

Figures in both reports are seasonally adjusted.

Here are the Commerce Department's latest figures for factory orders in billions of dollars, seasonally adjusted.

	April 1986	March 1986	% Chg.
All industries	193.18	193.00	+ 0.1
Durable goods	104.51	104.68	− 0.2
Nondurable goods	88.67	88.31	+ 0.4
Capital goods industries	33.81	36.99	− 8.6
Non-defense	26.08	26.54	− 1.8
Defense	7.74	10.45	− 25.9

} Non-defense Capital Goods

Here are the Commerce Department's figures for construction spending in billions of dollars at seasonally adjusted annual rates.

	April 1986	March 1986	April 1985
Total new construction	356.7	353.9	341.9
Residential	159.6	155.5	146.5
Nonresidential	86.3	87.5	91.2
Public	69.4	69.0	59.9

The decline in new orders brought them to $104.31 billion from $105.17 billion in March (see chart on page one). Orders for non-defense capital goods declined to $26.04 billion from $27.03 billion.

June 3, 1986—Final Report—Statistical Summary at End of Article.

	April 1986	March 1986		% Chg.
All industries..............	193.18	193.00	+	0.1
Durable goods	104.51	104.68	−	0.2
Nondurable goods	88.67	88.31	+	0.4
Capital goods industries....	33.81	36.99	−	8.6
Non-defense	26.08	26.54	−	1.8
Defense	7.74	10.45	−	25.9

Chart 12–1
Nondefense Orders of Capital Goods

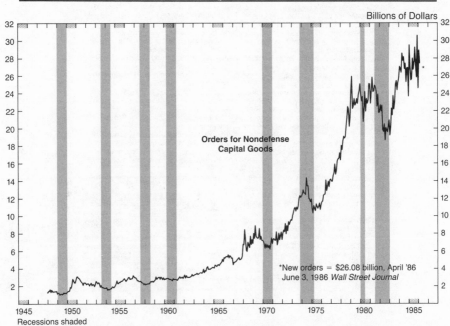

Billions of Dollars

Orders for Nondefense Capital Goods

*New orders = $26.08 billion, April '86
June 3, 1986 *Wall Street Journal*

Recessions shaded

Source: U.S. Department of Commerce, *Business Conditions Digest* and *Handbook of Cyclical Indicators*, series 24.

reports data for *new machine tool orders,* which is published by *The Wall Street Journal* around the last Monday of each month, just after the Commerce Department's preliminary release on new orders for nondefense capital goods. Take a look at the March 31, 1986, *Journal* article below.

You can see from the second paragraph that new machine tool orders were $211.1 million in February 1986, 11 percent less than new machine tool orders a year earlier. Compare these figures with the data in Chart 12–2 on page 176. While machine tool orders recovered from their reces-

---

Machine Tool Orders Rose 11% During February

By RALPH E. WINTER
Staff Reporter of THE WALL STREET JOURNAL.
Machine tool orders have recovered from the low levels of December and January, but there is no sign that producers of durable goods are beginning aggressive machinery-purchase programs.

{ Machine Tool Orders } February orders for machine tools, which are used in making most metal parts, totaled $211.1 million, up 11% from January's $190.8 million, according to the National Machine Tool Builders' Association. But last month's bookings still lagged 11% behind the $237.5 million of February 1985.

Furthermore, Japanese competitors have been pouring machine tools into the U.S. market recently, some U.S. executives complain, apparently trying to establish a higher sales base in the event that a "voluntary" quota system is established.

"We are seeing a modest improvement in orders, with aerospace and automotive the strongest segments of the market," said George S. Carper, group vice president, machine tools, at Cincinnati Milacron Inc., the nation's largest machine tool maker. "We're cautiously optimistic about orders for the remainder of 1986."

Mr. Carper said Milacron has received some orders recently that it had been anticipating for a while, but that there are others being held up. Prospective buyers have discussed the purchases in detail, but appear to be holding back on signing, he said.

February orders for lathes, machining centers, grinders, boring mills, milling machines and other machines to shape parts by cutting rose to $168.8 million, the association said, a gain of 3.1% from $163.8 million a year earlier and a 25% rise from the weak $135 million of January.

Orders for metal-forming presses and other machines to shape metal with pres-

sure fell, however, to $42.3 million, down 43% from $73.8 million in February 1985 and down 24% from $55.8 million in January. Sharply higher cancellations of previously placed orders accounted for part of the decline.

While the declining value of the U.S. dollar has resulted in price increase announcements by importers of some machine tools, it hasn't lessened competition from Japanese-made machining centers and lathes, according to U.S. producers. In fact, some Japanese producers appear to be dumping these machines into the U.S. at substantial discounts because they fear a quota system may be put into effect, said Richard T. Lindgren, president and chief executive officer of Cross & Trecker Corp., Bloomfield Hills, Mich.

"We're seeing very, very strong pricing competition as they (the Japanese) proceed to dump their product," said Mr. Lindgren. "They seem to be trying to get as high a sales base as they can for a quota, if a quota is in the cards."

Japanese trade publications have speculated that Japanese machine tool companies may be pressured to agree to export quotas to avoid some protective action by the U.S. government. U.S. machine tool builders have been seeking U.S.-imposed quotas on the ground that high imports of machine tools are weakening an industry essential to arms production.

The Japanese publications also said capacity in the Japanese machine tool industry exceeds current relatively sluggish demand in Japan, and that sales in the rest of Asia are below expectations, which puts further pressure on Japanese machine tool companies to sell to the U.S.

Comparative new orders for metal-cutting machines:	Feb. 1986	Jan. 1986	Feb. 1985
Domestic	$161,150,000	$124,750,000	$148,050,000
Foreign	7,650,000	10,250,000	15,700,000
Total	168,800,000	135,000,000	163,750,000
2-month total for 1986: $303,800,000; for 1985: $301,500,000.			
Metal-forming machine orders:			
Domestic	$38,100,000	$50,200,000	$69,550,000
Foreign	4,200,000	5,550,000	4,200,000
Total	42,300,000	55,750,000	73,750,000
2-month total for 1986: $98,050,000; for 1985: $147,450,000.			
Comparative shipment figures for metal-cutting machines:			
Domestic	$109,550,000	$74,050,000	$98,950,000
Foreign	14,400,000	17,450,000	9,350,000
Total	123,950,000	91,500,000	108,300,000
2-month total for 1986: $215,450,000; for 1985: $198,050,000.			
Metal-forming machine shipments:			
Domestic	$76,000,000	$50,800,000	$52,700,000
Foreign	2,600,000	3,550,000	5,250,000
Total	78,600,000	54,350,000	57,950,000
2-month total for 1986: $132,950,000; for 1985: $106,000,000.			

] Statistical Summary

The Wall Street Journal, *March 31, 1986*

New Orders for Machine Tools—Second Paragraph.

February orders for machine tools, which are used in making most metal parts, totaled $211.1 million, up 11% from January's $190.8 million, according to the National Machine Tool Builders' Association. But last month's bookings still lagged 11% behind the $237.5 million of February 1985.

Statistical Summary—End of Article

Comparative new orders for metal-cutting machines:

	Feb. 1986	Jan. 1986	Feb. 1985
Domestic	$161,150,000	$124,750,000	$148,050,000
Foreign	7,650,000	10,250,000	15,700,000
Total	168,800,000	135,000,000	163,750,000

2-month total for 1986: $303,800,000; for 1985: $301,500,000.

Metal-forming machine orders:

Domestic	$38,100,000	$50,200,000	$69,550,000
Foreign	4,200,000	5,550,000	4,200,000
Total	42,300,000	55,750,000	73,750,000

2-month total for 1986: $98,050,000; for 1985: $147,450,000.

Comparative shipment figures for metal-cutting machines:

Domestic	$109,550,000	$74,050,000	$98,950,000
Foreign	14,400,000	17,450,000	9,350,000
Total	123,950,000	91,500,000	108,300,000

2-month total for 1986: $215,450,000; for 1985: $198,050,000.

Metal-forming machine shipments:

Domestic	$76,000,000	$50,800,000	$52,700,000
Foreign	2,600,000	3,550,000	5,250,000
Total	78,600,000	54,350,000	57,950,000

2-month total for 1986: $132,950,000; for 1985: $106,000,000.

---

sion lows, they remained at half the peak levels reached in the late 70s. And as the text of the March 31, 1986, article makes clear, imports were as much to blame as the low level of capacity utilization.

You have examined two sources of data on *equipment* expenditures. Turn now to a series on *plant* expenditures. F. W. Dodge's report on building awards is published by *The Wall Street Journal* at the turn of the month, as in the March 4, 1986, article. (See page 177.)

Focus on the third paragraph from the end of the article, which reports *nonresidential building,* including factories, offices, and retail and wholesale establishments. You can ignore the data on residential building because

Chart 12–2
Machine Tool Orders

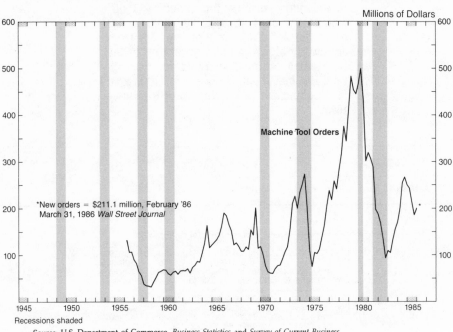

Recessions shaded

Source: U.S. Department of Commerce, *Business Statistics* and *Survey of Current Business.*

this refers to home construction, which has already been covered in Chapters 8 and 10, and on nonbuilding construction because this covers mostly government projects, such as roads and bridges, rather than business plant.

You can use the *Journal* article in tandem with Chart 12–3 on page 178. Both reinforce earlier observations that expansion will have to be well under way before business contracts for additional factories, offices, and wholesale and retail establishments.

In conclusion, the data in the *Journal* articles, along with Charts 12–1 through 12–3, illustrate the point that capital expenditures, like inventory accumulation, reinforce the cycle rather than initiate it. Business responds to consumer orders by adding plant and equipment. As the expansion develops into the peak of the cycle and productive capacity is strained, business adds facilities and equipment. Their completion swells the level of demand and contributes to generally inflationary conditions.

After recession begins, some of the investment projects are canceled, but most are completed, and these expenditures ease the downturn. Time elapses before a new cycle's expansionary phase encourages another round

January Building Contracts Fell 14%
As Nonresidential Activity Plunged

By Paula Schnorbus
Staff Reporter of The Wall Street Journal.

NEW YORK—New construction contracts awarded in January plunged 14% from the previous month because of sharp reductions in nonresidential building and public works.

F.W. Dodge Co., a forecasting unit of McGraw-Hill Inc., said the value of January's contracts fell to a seasonally adjusted annual rate of $195.9 billion from December's $227.95 billion. That brought the Dodge index to a two-year low of 139, down from 162 in both November and December. The index compares current contracting with a 1977 base of 100.

"January's contracts revealed an acceleration of the decline of new construction activity that has been under way since the building cycle reached its peak last October," said George A. Christie, vice president and chief economist for F.W. Dodge.

Falling interest rates have promoted home building, Mr. Christie said, but "weak business capital spending and federal budget slashing mean less nonresidential construction in 1986."

So-called non-building projects, or those involving public works and utilities, dropped the most—23% to a rate of $32.78 billion in January from $42.31 billion in December.

"Because 90% of non-building construction depends on public funding, a commitment to Gramm-Rudman deficit targets translates into an extended squeeze on in-

The Wall Street Journal, *March 4, 1986*

frastructure work," Mr. Christie said, referring to the new federal deficit-reduction law.

Nonresidential building contracts fell 16% to a seasonally adjusted annual rate of $64.64 billion in January from $77.19 billion a month earlier. Contracts for office buildings kept the commercial-industrial segment from dropping more than 13% even though contracting for factories, stores and warehouses showed "sharp declines." Institutional building also felt the public funding crunch, falling 18%.

Residential building contracts had the smallest decrease in January, falling 9%, to an annual rate of $98.48 billion from $108.45 billion in December. A gain in single-family housing contracts was more than offset by weakness in contracts for multifamily housing, hotels and motels.

The West felt the overall contracting decline the most, posting an 18% drop. The Northeast and North Central regions fell 12% and 10%, respectively, and the South slipped 8%.

	a-Jan. '86 Construction Contract Val (000,000)	Seasonally Adjusted % Change From Prev. Month
Nonresidential bldg.	$ 64,643	- 16
Residential building	98,479	- 9
Non-building constr.	32,779	- 23
Total construction	$195,901	- 14

a-Monthly construction contract values are reported on an annualized, seasonally adjusted basis

	1 Mo. 1986 (000,000)	1 Mo. 1985 (000.000)	Cumulative % Chg
Nonresidential bldg.	$ 4,998	$ 5,919	- 16
Residential building	6,622	6,684	
Non-building constr.	2,060	2,551	- 19
Total construction	$13,680	$15,154	- 10

Nonresidential Building

Statistical Summary

Nonresidential Building—Third Paragraph from End of Article.

Nonresidential building contracts fell 16% to a seasonally adjusted annual rate of $64.64 billion in January from $77.19 billion a month earlier. Contracts for office buildings kept the commercial-industrial segment from dropping more than 13% even though contracting for factories, stores and warehouses showed "sharp declines." Institutional building also felt the public funding crunch, falling 18%.

Statistical Summary—End of Article.

	a-Jan. '86 Construction Contract Val. (000,000)	Seasonally Adjusted % Change From Prev. Month
Nonresidential bldg.	$ 64,643	– 16
Residential building	98,479	– 9
Non-building constr.	32,779	– 23
Total construction	$195,901	– 14

a-Monthly construction contract values are reported on an annualized, seasonally adjusted basis.

	1 Mo. 1986 (000,000)	1 Mo. 1985 (000,000)	Cumulative % Chg
Nonresidential bldg.	$ 4,998	$ 5,919	-- 16
Residential building	6,622	6,684	....
Non-building constr.	2,060	2,551	– 19
Total construction	$13,680	$15,154	– 10

Chart 12–3
Nonresidential Building

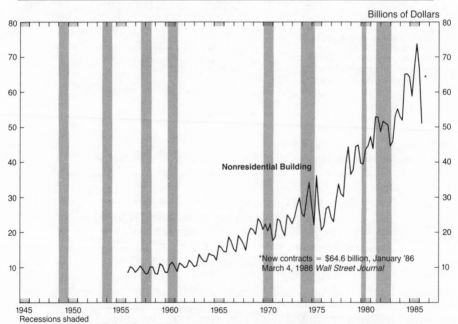

Billions of Dollars

*New contracts = $64.6 billion, January '86
March 4, 1986 *Wall Street Journal*

Recessions shaded

Source: *Dodge Construction Potentials*, McGraw-Hill Information Systems Company; and U.S. Department of Commerce, *Business Statistics* and *Survey of Current Business*.

of capital expenditures. Until this occurs, the depressed level of plant and equipment expenditures holds demand down and prevents the economy from heating up too quickly. When capital expenditures do recover, the economy is once again approaching the cycle's peak.

Returning one last time to the articles and charts for an overview of the process, note that low levels of capacity utilization are depressing capital expenditures. That's why, despite the other evidence of expansion, nondefense orders for capital equipment, machine tool orders, and non-residential construction have not yet recovered. As capacity utilization improves, however, they will improve, contributing to the general expansion of demand and economic activity.

13

Profits and the Stock Market

You would expect the stock market to be a good barometer of economic activity because it reflects the value of owning the business firms responsible for most of our economy's output. The *Dow Jones Industrial Average* is the most widely followed indicator of stock market activity.

The Dow represents share prices of 30 blue-chip industrial corporations, chosen because their operations cover the broad spectrum of industrial America.

30 Stocks in Industrial Average

Allied-Signal	General Electric	Navistar International
Aluminum Co of America	General Motors	Owens-Illinois
American Can	Goodyear	Philip Morris
American Express	Inco	Procter & Gamble
American Telephone & Telegraph	IBM	Sears Roebuck
Bethlehem Steel	International Paper	Texaco
Chevron	McDonald's	Union Carbide
Du Pont	Merck	United Technologies
Eastman Kodak	Minnesota Mining &	United States Steel
Exxon	Manufacturing	Westinghouse Electric
		Woolworth

Dow Jones also publishes indexes for public utilities and transportation companies, and there are broader stock market barometers that measure changes in the average price of 500 shares (Standard & Poor's index of 500 stocks), or even all of the shares traded on the New York Stock Exchange (NYSE). Yet the Dow Industrials is the most closely watched average because it was first and because its handful of blue-chip companies does reflect stock market activity with surprising precision.

A corporation must meet minimum qualifications, such as capital invested and trading activity in its shares, to be listed on the NYSE. Companies engaged in agriculture, services, construction, trade, and finance are usually too small to be publicly traded on the NYSE. Industrial corporations make up the majority of the companies listed there, and the companies in the Dow are among the biggest and most widely traded of these.

Corporations issue stock to raise capital; investors buy shares of it in order to earn dividends and to enjoy a capital gain if the stock's price rises. The ability of a corporation to pay dividends and the potential for increase in the value of a share of stock depend directly on the profits earned by the corporation: the greater the flow of profit, the higher the price investors will pay for that share of stock. Fluctuations in the Dow precede those in the economy, because investors buy shares of stock in order to take advantage of future profit potential. They will bid up stock prices when that potential looks promising and sell their holdings and drive stock prices down when the outlook turns gloomy.

That's how you would expect the capitalist system to operate. The ownership value of assets depends on the income they generate, because potential buyers will pay a higher price for them if they engender a rising stream of income. The value of farmland reflects profits that can be reaped by raising crops on it, and the value of an apartment building reflects rents that can be collected. Similarly, the value of a share in the ownership of a corporation ultimately depends on the ability of that corporation to create profits. Note that the value of an asset depends not only on the income it is currently earning but also on its potential for greater earnings and on investors' willingness to pay for them.

The broad line of industrial companies represented by the Dow enjoys an improvement in earnings during the expansionary phases of the cycle and suffers a decline in earnings when the economy slips into recession. Because these companies represent the backbone of industrial America, their fortunes are intimately tied to the swings of the business cycle. Thus, the Dow moves in anticipation of the cycle as investors gauge not only the profit potential of these corporations but also future cyclical prospects for the economy as a whole.

A corporation's profit is the most important measure of its success because profit indicates the effectiveness and efficiency with which its assets are managed and employed. Profits calibrate the ability of a firm to make and sell its product for more than the cost of production. Profit means that the firm has efficiently combined the labor, material, and capital necessary to produce and market its product at a price that people will pay and that will provide the owners with the financial incentive to expand the operation. When costs exceed revenues and the firm takes a loss, the amount society is willing to pay for the firm's product no longer justifies the cost of producing it.

Therefore, you should now explore the various statistical series on profits and profitability and the stock market averages so that you can understand their role in the business cycle.

PROFITS AND PROFITABILITY

The Wall Street Journal survey of corporate profits for over 500 corporations appears about a month after the close of the quarter. The second paragraph of the February 24, 1986, report for the fourth quarter of 1985 states that profits fell 13 percent from the same period a year earlier. (See Page 184.)

The *Commerce Department's quarterly survey of profits,* usually included in the GNP article, appears about 20 days later and covers a much larger sample. Examine the March 20, 1986, report, especially the next-to-last paragraph. (See page 186.)

Don't be confused by different comparisons. Profits were 6 percent higher in the fourth quarter of 1985 than in the *third quarter* according to the Commerce Department survey, but 15 percent lower in the fourth quarter than in the *same quarter one year earlier* according to *The Wall Street Journal* survey. Be sure you understand which time periods are being compared.

Compare fourth-quarter 1985 profits of $149.5 billion with the postwar record of profits in Chart 12–1. (See page 187). You can see that profits deteriorated in the 1981–82 recession, following a meager recovery from the 1980 recession. How will profits perform during the current recovery and expansion? Will they rebound to record highs? The answers to these questions are found in an examination of profits over the business cycle.

Profits measure efficiency by comparing revenues to costs. Recall that the economy's efficiency improves during the early phases of the cycle and deteriorates during the latter phases. Thus, profits grow during recovery and expansion and deteriorate during peak and contraction.

A bit of logic should reveal the relationship between general changes in economic efficiency over the cycle and the specific measurement of profit. Efficiency rises early in the cycle because factories are operating with excess capacity and producing less than maximum output. The general reduction in costs due to enhanced productivity increases the spread

Weak Earnings

Corporate Profits Fell 13% in Fourth Period; Huge Write-Offs Hurt

Survey Finds Many Groups With Declines or Losses; Productivity Down a Bit

But an Upturn Is Anticipated

A WALL STREET JOURNAL News Roundup

A flood of corporate write-offs and a drop in productivity held fourth-quarter profits below the year-earlier level for the fourth period in a row. Analysts generally expect earnings to look much better this year.

In the three months ended Dec. , af ter-tax earnings on continuing operations of 494 major corporations fell 15% from a year earlier, according to a Wall Street Journal survey. Net income slid 13%, compared with declines of 5% in the third quarter, 14% in the second and 11% in the first.

Most of the corporate write-offs reflected divestment of companies' less profitable assets. Write-offs, as a sign of corporate weaknesses, used to depress stock prices, but investors now seem to regard them as indications of improved future profits.

Lacy Hunt, the chief economist at the investment firm of CM&M Group, thinks that the investors are right. "There's no question," he says, "but that the write-offs are clearing the way for big profits gains this year." Mr. Hunt expects after-tax profits this year to rise 19% from 1985. The four dozen economists interviewed monthly by Blue Chip Economic Indicators, a Sedona, Ariz., newsletter, see a gain of more than 9% this year.

Rising Profitability

"With an improvement in sales this year, the efforts to impr yment. ity and reduce costs w   t rose 3.4% bottom line in   with a 2.3% gain in First In   justed gross national prod   Blue Chip forecasters on the average expect real GNP to rise 3.1% this year.

Although the sharp drop in oil prices will help profits of many companies by holding down costs, the price decline obviously hurts the banks with large loans to oil producers, either here or abroad. It also isn't good for companies in the oil industry. "While we believe a significant improvement in corporate profitability is emerging currently, it will be restrained, on a pretax basis, by inventory losses coming from the decline in oil prices," says Alan Greenspan, a New York consultant.

In the latest quarter, writeoffs at individual companies dragged down net income in many industry groups. The unusually stable telephone companies, for example, posted a fourth-quarter decline from a year earlier because of GTE's $1.3 billion charge and a big write-off at United Telecommunications. A $223 charge at Avon Products similarly hit the soap and cosmetics group. The railroads were depressed by a $954 million pretax charge at CSX Corp. Schlumberger's $486 million write-off pushed the already-ailing oil-field services group deep into the red in the quarter. Big charges held down the building-materials producers despite the

Quarterly Profit Changes On a Year-to-Year Basis
In percent

strength in home building, and the chemical industry's reports showed a wide   ex of special charges.

Special items help   incentives however. A $34   od.

Pan Am

G   al Motors' net surged 43% from   strike-plagued year-earlier quarter to $1.25 billion. GM's aggressive U.S. auto output schedule contributed to the increase because auto makers record sales revenue when cars are sold to dealers, not when dealers sell them to consumers.

Ford's net slipped a little to $720 million despite a 5% gain in sales; its U.S. auto production was hampered by problems at

Fourth-Quarter Profits—Second Paragraph.

In the three months ended Dec. 31, af
ter-tax earnings on continuing operations
of 494 major corporations fell 15% from a
year earlier, according to a Wall Street
Journal survey. Net income slid 13%, compared with declines of 5% in the third
quarter, 14% in the second and 11% in the
first.

between prices and costs, known as the *profit rate* or profit per unit of
output. As sales increase, total profit grows because of both higher output
and higher profits per unit of output.

Efficiency deteriorates late in the cycle as factories strain to produce
maximum output. Costs rise as productivity falls, and industry is forced
into a "profit squeeze," meaning that costs push up against prices. Total
profits fall as sales volume stops growing, or actually contracts, and profit
per unit of output (the profit rate) falls.

The top graph in Chart 13–2 on page 188 gives a bedrock picture of
real profits, stripped of inflationary gains. It portrays the quality of profits
by removing inventory profits swollen by inflation and by taking into
account the replacement cost of depreciating plant and equipment (rather
than the unrealistically low original cost). The bottom graph portrays
the ratio of price to unit labor cost, that is, the relative strength of prices
and unit labor cost. This informs you of the extent of labor cost's encroach-
ment on prices and of business's ability to hold down labor costs in
relation to the prices received.

Each of the cycles in the 1970s demonstrates the same sequence of
events. Start with a typical recovery and expansion such as the recovery
and expansion of 1971–72 or 1975–77. Unit labor cost was kept down
by good gains in labor productivity due to modest levels of capacity
utilization. As a result, the ratio of price to unit labor cost (our proxy
for the term *profit margins*) improved and held up well. Since sales volume
and output were growing, total real profits grew sharply.

Then, in 1973 and 1978–79, as production and capacity utilization
peaked, labor productivity declined and unit labor cost increased. As a
result, the ratio of price to unit labor cost fell as profit margins were
pinched. Since, at the peak of the cycle, sales and output had also stalled,
real profits tumbled and continued to fall throughout the ensuing recessions of 1974–75 and 1980.

GNP Increased At 0.7% Rate In 4th Period

Pace Was Below Estimates; 2.2% Rise Posted for '85 While Profits Fell 2.2%

By ALAN MURRAY
Staff Reporter of THE WALL STREET JOURNAL
WASHINGTON — The U.S. economy ended 1985 on an even weaker footing than previously thought, growing at an inflation-adjusted annual rate of only 0.7% in the fourth quarter, according to revised C- merce Department figures.   af-
The growth in the v?¹`
total output, or g⌐⌐   ...ilation-adjusted
less than ᵗʰ   _ ,o from 1984 after surg-
anᵈ   ₁984. The department had pre-
...₁y reported a 2.3% increase for all 1985.
The department also said after-tax corporate profits fell 2.2% in 1985, reflecting the general weakness in the economy during the year. For the fourth quarter, however, after-tax profits rose 6% because of a surge in the profits companies reported from their inventories.

Many Analysts Optimistic
Despite the weak fourth-quarter GNP growth, many analysts are optimistic that the economy will begin to improve in the current quarter. "This doesn't change the outlook much," said Robert Wescott, an economist with Wharton Econometric Forecasting Associates. "We still expect a strong rebound in the first quarter."
The revision in fourth-quarter growth resulted from new data indicating that the December surge in imports was much larger than previously reported. Many analysts expect that the nation's trade problems, which held back economic growth throughout 1984 and 1985, will begin improving later this year as a result of declines in the dollar's value.
The department's first estimate of first-quarter growth will be released next month. The agency formerly gave a "flash" GNP estimate for the current quarter in the third month of each period but stopped the practice because it said the number was unreliable.

The Wall Street Journal, *March 20, 1986*

The 2.2% decline in after-tax profits last year left them at $140.9 billion, following a strong 10.9% rise in 1984 to $144 billion. Many analysts believe the profit outlook for this year is bright, except for companies in the oil business, which will be hurt by dropping oil prices. Other corporations still face only small increases in wages and costs, and are likely to feel less competition this year from imports because of the dollar's drop.

Improving Trends Seen
"Clearly the underlying profit trends are improving," said Alan Greenspan, a New York economic consultant. "The outlook for this year in non-energy earnings is quite good."
"We could easily be seeing nʳ⌐`   . ᵤy 15⌐ this year," Mr. Wᵉ⌐   ...ᵤ.
While after-tᵃᵛ   .ᵤ declined last year, the dᶜ⌐   .ᴵᵗ s measure of before-tax ⌐·   .ᵤin current production—which .   ...ᵢ₀ account the benefits companies get from generous tax depreciation allowances, and also makes inflation adjustments to inventories—rose a solid 8.7% to $297 billion after jumping 27.8% in 1984 to $273.3 billion. The department's measure of corporate cash flow, which is also adjusted to take into account depreciation and inventories, rose 10.7% last year to $396.8 billion from $358.2 billion.
Before-tax profits without the depreciation and inventory adjustments fell 4.5% last year to $226.8 billion from $237.6 billion in 1984.
The 6% rise in fourth-quarter after-tax profits brought them to a $149.5 billion annual rate, following a 3.4% increase in the third quarter to a $141.1 billion rate. But the department's measure of profits from current production, which most analysts consider a more accurate measure of underlying profit trends, showed no change in the fourth quarter, following a 7.3% rise in the third quarter.
Profits before taxes increased 4.9% in the fourth quarter, following a 4.5% rise in the third quarter. The department's measure of the cash flow generated by current production was unchanged in the fourth quarter after growing 4.9% in the third period.

Here are some of the major components of the gross national product expressed in seasonally adjusted annual rates in billions of constant (1982) dollars:

	4th Qtr. 1985	3rd Qtr. 1985
GNP	3590.8	3584.1
less: inventory change	− 6.3	− 1.8
equals: final sales	3597.1	3585.8
Components of Final Sales		
Personal Consumption	2330.4	2329.6
Nonresidential Invest.	486.5	473.7
Residential Invest.	175.5	173.1
Net Exports	− 140.8	119.8
Gov't Purchases	745.5	729.2

In the first quarter, the implicit price deflator rose to 113.0% of the 1982 average, from 112.1% in the previous quarter.

— Corporate Profits

Corporate Profits—Next-to-Last Paragraph.

The 6% rise in fourth-quarter after-tax profits brought them to a $149.5 billion annual rate, following a 3.4% increase in the third quarter to a $141.1 billion rate. But the department's measure of profits from current production, which most analysts consider a more accurate measure of underlying profit trends, showed no change in the fourth quarter, following a 7.3% rise in the third quarter.

Chart 13–1
Corporate Profits after Taxes

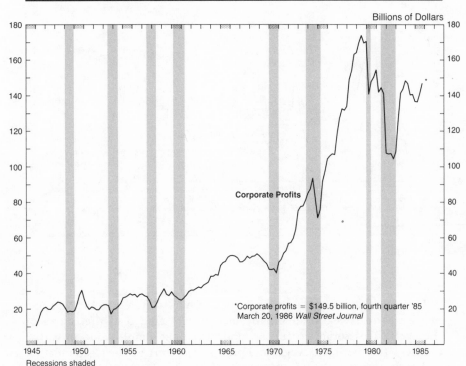

Billions of Dollars

Corporate Profits

*Corporate profits = $149.5 billion, fourth quarter '85
March 20, 1986 *Wall Street Journal*

1945   1950   1955   1960   1965   1970   1975   1980   1985

Recessions shaded

Source: U.S. Department of Commerce, *Business Conditions Digest* and *Handbook of Cyclical Indicators*, series 16.

Chart 13-2

Corporate Profits in 1982 Dollars with Inventory Valuation and Capital Consumption Adjustment; and Ratio, Price to Unit Labor Cost, Nonfarm Business

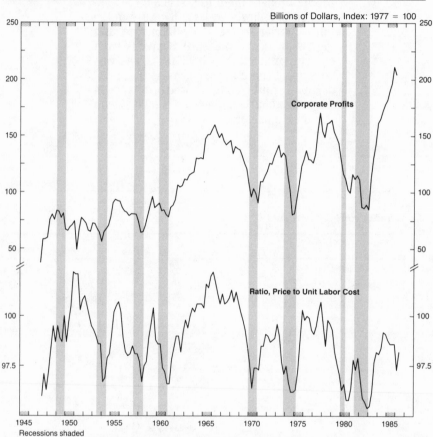

Billions of Dollars, Index: 1977 = 100

Recessions shaded

Source: U.S. Department of Commerce, *Business Conditions Digest* and *Handbook of Cyclical Indicators*, series 26 and 80.

Observe that after the mid-60s, real profits suffered from the same malaise as real wages; all improvements were eroded in the course of the cycle. This serves to further underscore the point, made in earlier chapters, that both real wages and profits were hurt by the steep inflation and cyclical instability of 1965–80. Profits' poor performance cannot be blamed on workers' wages, nor can wages' poor performance be blamed on profits. Both were victims of the cycle's debilitating impact on productivity.

Chapter 9 discussed wage and price controls, and Chart 13–2 illustrates the foolishness of this adventure. The rate of inflation declined in 1971–72, during President Nixon's controls, despite rising real wages, a rising ratio of price to unit labor cost, and rising real profits. Since real wages and profits were rising, what use were the wage and price controls? Inflation subsided, not because of the controls, but because of *improved productivity brought about by the recovery phase of the business cycle*. The rate of inflation increased in 1979–80, during President Carter's controls, despite falling wages, a falling ratio of price to unit labor cost, and falling real profits. Since real wages and profits were falling, why weren't controls effective in limiting greed? Because the inflation was due to *cyclical expansion's negative impact on productivity*, which boosted costs. Controls could not stem the rising spiral of prices.

To summarize, profits, when calculated for the entire economy, measure efficiency, not greed. Prices simply can't be controlled by limiting profits.

You can see in Chart 13–2 that real profits improved substantially in the mid-80s, and you can predict with confidence that they will continue to improve during this expansion as profit margins and sales volume grow. Low rates of capacity utilization have boosted labor productivity and cut unit labor costs, providing an increased spread between prices and costs. As production grows, total profits should grow, too.

If the expansion continues to be mild and gradual, and capacity utilization does not rise quickly and intensify cost pressures, real profits should continue to grow over a number of years and, like real wages, continue to climb out of the low range of the 1970s. But don't forget that while most companies will follow this (or any) trend, a few will not; as you well know, the profits of an individual business can be dramatically affected upwards or downwards by the quality of its management and of its products or services, as well as by sheer luck. Even if you believe you know which direction the market will take, be careful of assuming that any given company will follow.

But suppose you do wish to monitor the earnings of a particular company rather than all corporations? You can do so by using *The Wall Street Journal's* **Digest of Earnings Reports**, listed as "Earnings Digest" in the front-page index. (See page 190.)

Take **GTE Corporation** as an example (last column, second from the top). As you can see, the statement is a report for the quarter ending March 31 as compared with figures for the same period one year earlier (see page 191). Look for these figures: revenues, net income (profit), and net income (earnings) per share (that is, total earnings divided by total shares of stock outstanding), and as you can tell, GTE's sales revenue and profits improved. (A digest of these figures for GTE is presented at

DIGEST OF EARNINGS REPORTS

— — Highlights — —

Selected summaries for the quarter ended March 31, 1986 unless noted. Percentage changes are from the corresponding year-ago quarter. Operating net excludes the results from discontinued operations and extraordinary items where applicable.

Company	Revs (in mil.)	% Chg.	Oper. net (in thou.)	% Chg.
Bankers Trust NY Corp.	....	....	$115,950	+ 25.3
Caterpillar Tractor (b)	$1,735.0	+ 17.6	111,000	a
Champion International	1,122.3	− 31.8	22,001	− 49.7
Citicorp	....	....	270,000	− 2.5
GTE Corp.	3,954.2	+ 8.3	282,814	+ 3.5
IC Industries Inc.	1,024.5	+ 3.3	31,100	+ 26.9
Manufacturers Hanover	....	....	102,100	+ 1.9
Northrop Corp.	1,300.0	+ 18.2	39,300	− 13.6
Nynex Corp.	2,670.0	+ 6.0	296,500	+ 15.2
PPG Industries Inc.	1,137.1	+ 9.8	69,200	− 13.9
Scott Paper Co.	801.4	+ 15.1	39,100	− 7.1
Security Pacific Corp	....	....	c87,900	+ 19.6

a-Year earlier loss. b-For the quarter ended March 26. c-Includes pretax gain of $34.7 million.

AFFILIATED BNKSHRS COLO (O)
Quar Mar 31: 1986 1985
Net Income $2,335,433 $4,276,776
Shr earns:
Net income . .22 .41

ALASKA AIR GROUP INC. (N)
Quar Mar 31: 1986 1985
Revenues $98,786,000 $82,900,000
Net Income 4,849,000 c1,607,000
Shr earns (primary):
Net income c.14
Shr earns (fully diluted):
Net income c.13
c-Income.

ALLIS-CHALMERS CORP. (N)
Quar 785
Sales .. 143,000
Loss cnt 315,000
Loss dis 255,000
Net loss 570,000
a-Restated to reflect discontinued operations.

AMERICAN FLETCHER CORP. (O)
Quar Mar 31: 1986 1985
Net Income $10,469,000 $7,107,000
Shr earns (primary):
Net income .. 1.08 a.75
Shr earns (fully diluted):
Net income .. 1.08 a.74
a-Adjusted for a two-for-one stock split paid in May 1985.

AMERICAN PACESETTER (Pa)
Year Dec 31: 1985 a1984
Revenues $79,588,000 $92,388,000
Inco cnt op 436,000 d2,093,000
Loss dis op 829,000 b427,000
Net loss 393,000 2,492,000
Shr earns:
Inco cnt op .. .22
Quarter:
Revenues 22,811,000 29,689,000
Loss cnt op 250,000 b109,000
Loss dis op 342,000 b85,000
Net loss 592,000 b194,000
Shr earns:
Loss cnt op . b.06
Net loss b.10
a-Restated. b-Income. d-Loss.

ARGO PETROLEUM CORP. (A)
Year Dec 31: 1985 a1984
Revenues $22,572,000 $26,286,000
Loss cnt op .. b33,260,000 95,000
Loss dis op 3,549,000 526,000
Net loss 36,809,000 621,000
Quarter:
Revenues 5,167,000 6,832,000
Loss cnt op .. b31,846,000 419,000
Loss dis op 1,249,000 187,000
Net loss 33,095,000 606,000
a-Restated. b-Includes a charge of $30,902,000 from write-down of oil and gas properties.

ARTHUR J. GALLAGHER & CO. (O)
Quar Mar 31: 1986 1985
Revenues $24,541,000 $19,332,000
Net income 3,705,000 3,125,000
Avg shares 4,517,000 4,480,000
Shr earns (com & com equiv):
Net income .. .82 .70

ATHENS FED'L SAVINGS BNK (O)
Quar Mar 31: 1986 1985
Net Income $931,294 $725,550
Shr earns:
Net income . .69 a.55
a-Adjusted for a three-for-two stock split paid in August 1985.

COMERICA INC. (O)
Quar Mar 31: 1986 a1985
Income $13,059,000 $15,706,000
Acctg adl 3,832,000
Net income 13,059,000 19,540,000
Avg shares 10,430,649 10,370,341
Shr earns (primary):
Income 1.12 1.36
Net income .. 1.12 1.73
Shr earns (fully diluted):
Income 1.08 1.29
Net income . 1.08 1.64
a-Restated.

COMMAND AIRWAYS (O)
Quar Feb 28: 1986 1985
Revenues $3,469,852 $3,510,545
Net loss 1,034,490 282,330
9 months:
Revenues 11,731,903 11,494,244
Net loss 1,269,356 a143,325
Shr earns:
Net loss a.10
a-Income.

COMMERCE UNION CORP. (O)
Quar Mar 31: 1986 a1985
Net income $6,906,372 $5,541,630
bAvg shares .. 11,547,152 10,457,552
Shr earns (primary):
bNet income .. .60 .53
Shr earns (fully diluted):
bNet income .. .54 .46
a-Restated. b-Adjusted to reflect a two-for-one stock split payable in May 1986.

COMMERCIAL NATIONAL (O)
Quar Mar 31: 1986 1985
Net income $1,119,000 $3,175,000
Shr earns:
Net income . .27 .76

ELDORADO BANCORP. (O)
Quar Mar 31: 1986 1985
Net income $364,000 $307,000
Avg shares 1,566,273 1,655,769
Shr earns:
Net income . .23 .19

ELECTROMAGNETIC SCI (O)
Quar Mar 31: 1986 1985
Sales $9,608,000 $7,636,000
Net income 917,000
Shr ear
Net ir .19

ENGRA ....
Quar Mar 29: 1986 1985
Sales $26,690,000 $25,164,000
Net income 845,000 966,000
Shr earns:
Net income . .17 a.20
a-Adjusted for a five-for-four stock split paid in March 1986.

ENSERCH CORP. (N)
Quar Mar 31: 1986 1985
Revenues $811,851,000 $980,908,000
Net income 18,151,000 45,978,000
Shr earns:
Net income . .23 .69

EVERGOOD PRODUCTS CORP. (O)
Year Dec 31: 1985 1984
Sales $14,627,000 $17,877,000
Net loss 476,000 a644,000
Shr earns:
Net loss a.45
a-Income.

EXCHANGE INTERNATIONAL (O)
Quar Mar 31: 1986 1985
Net income $2,566,000 $2,325,000
Shr earns:

GREAT LAKES FOREST PROD (T)
Quar Mar 31: 1986 1985
Sales $141,706,000 $148,162,000
Net loss 470,000 a4,838,000
Shr earns:
Net loss b.25
a-Income. b-Income; adjusted for a four-for-one stock split paid in May 1985.
Amounts in Canadian dollars.

GTE CORP. (N)
Quar Mar 31: 1986 1985
Revenues $3,954,239,000 $3,651,554,000
Net income . 282,814,000 273,170,000
Avg shares . 212,995,000 205,206,000
Shr earns (primary):
Net income .. 1.29 1.29
Shr earns (fully diluted):
Net income .. 1.25 1.24

HAWAIIAN ELECTRIC INC. (N)
Quar Mar 31: 1986 1985
Revenues $162,263,000 $163,796,000
Net income 10,896,000 9,146,000
Avg shares 16,669,946 16,172,736
Shr earns:
Net income . .66 .57
12 months:
Revenues 646,800,000 674,280,000
Net income 40,790,000 36,148,000
Shr earns:
Net income . 2.48 2.28

HEART FED'L S&L ASSOC (O)
Quar Mar 31: 1986 1985
Net income $1,321,000 $159,000
Shr earns:
Net income . .62 a
a-Common share earnings not shown; company converted to stock form from a mutual association on December 3, 1985.

the top of the page under **Highlights,** a summary of the revenues and earnings of a few selected companies.)

GTE CORP. (N)

Quar Mar 31:	1986	1985
Revenues	$3,954,239,000	$3,651,554,000
Net income	282,814,000	273,170,000
Avg shares	212,995,000	205,206,000
Shr earns (primary):		
Net income	1.29	1.29
Shr earns (fully diluted):		
Net income	1.25	1.24

Company	Revs (in mil.)	% Chg.	Oper. Net (in thou.)	% Chg.
GTE Corp.	3,954.2	+ 8.3	282,814	+ 3.5

THE STOCK MARKET

Each day, on the third from the last page, the *Journal* publishes in chart form a detailed summary of the **Dow Jones Averages** over the past six months. It records the progress of the 30 industrials, the 20 stocks in the transportation average, and the 15 stocks in the utility average, as well as trading volume.

At the bottom you'll find the *divisors* used to compute the Dow averages. Look at the example drawn from the edition of Monday, April 14, 1986, and the blowup of the divisor information at the bottom. (See pages 192, 193, and 194.) The divisor was 1.008 on the previous trading day—Friday, April 11. It is now less than 1.0.

The divisor is needed for two reasons. First, companies sometimes split their stock (say, two for one) when they feel the price has risen so high that investors may be discouraged from purchasing it.

Now, suppose you are calculating the average of a group of 30 stocks (such as the Dow) by adding the share prices of all of them and dividing by 30. If (to make the arithmetic simple and the point clear) each of the 30 were selling at $100, obviously the average would be $100. However, if each of the 30 happened to split two for one, then each would be worth $50 per share; that is, the average price per share of these 30 stocks would suddenly be $50, not $100. Clearly it makes no sense to reduce the average because of such splits, since someone who owns the stock has exactly as much equity after a split as before it.

Lowering the divisor from 30 to 15 is one solution: 30 shares at $50 each ($1,500) divided by 15 (not 30) keeps the average at 100. And as the stocks split in the future, you would continue to lower the divisor.

THE DOW JONES AVERAGES ®

High
Close
Low

Industrials

30 STOCKS IN INDUSTRIAL AVERAGE

Allied-Signal	General Electric	Owens-Illinois
Aluminum Co	General Motors	Philip Morris
Amer Can	Goodyear	Procter & Gamb
Amer Express	Inco	Sears Roebuck
Amer T&T	IBM	Texaco
Bethlehem Steel	Inter Paper	Union Carbide
Chevron	McDonalds	United Technologies
DuPont	Merck	US Steel
Eastman Kodak	Minnesota M&M	Westinghouse El
Exxon	Navistar Inter	Woolworth

a-The Dow Jones Industrial Average and the 65-stock Composite Average reflect the Philip Morris Cos. 2-for-1 common stock split.
This changed the divisor for the 30 industrials to 1.008 from 1.044 and that for the 65 stocks to 4.387 from 4.480.

Divisor

DOW JONES 65 COMPONENTS

	– P/E Ratios –		Dividend Yields	
	Apr. 11,	Yr. Ago	Apr. 11,	Yr. Ago
Industrials	18.6	11.1	3.64	4.82
Transportation	16.6	9.6	2.04	2.44
Utilities	10.3	7.4	7.61	8.85

Price earnings ratios are based on per share earnings for the 12 months ended December 31, 1985 of 96.11 for the 30 Industrials; 47.27 for the 20 transportation issues; 18.27 for the 15 utilities.

Transportation

20 STOCKS IN TRANSPORTATION AVERAGE

AMR Corp	Delta Air Lines	Pan Am Corp
Amer President	Eastern Air Lines	Santa Fe So Pacific
Burlington North	Federal Express	TWA
Canadian Pacific	Leaseway Transp	UAL Inc.
Carolina Freight	Norfolk Southern	Union Pac Corp
Consolid Freight	NWA Inc	USAir Group
CSX Corp	Overnite Transp	

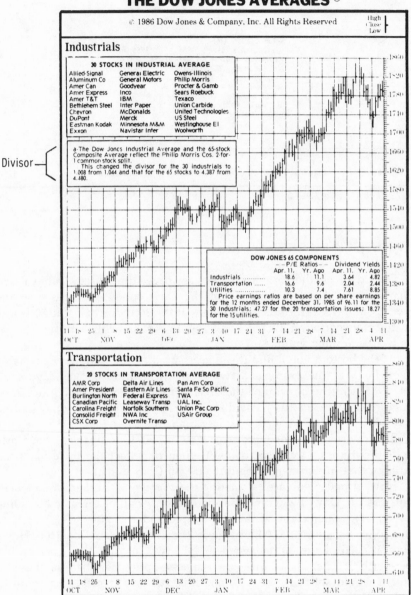

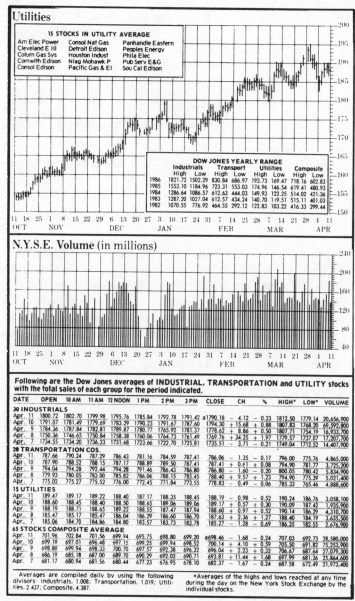

Utilities

15 STOCKS IN UTILITY AVERAGE

Am Elec Power	Consol Nat Gas	Panhandle Eastern
Cleveland E Ill	Detroit Edison	Peoples Energy
Colum Gas Sys	Houston Indust	Phila Elec
Comwlth Edison	Niag Mohawk P	Pub Serv E&G
Consol Edison	Pacific Gas & El	Sou Cal Edison

DOW JONES YEARLY RANGE

	Industrials		Transport		Utilities		Composite	
	High	Low	High	Low	High	Low	High	Low
1986	1821.72	1502.29	830.84	686.97	193.73	169.47	718.16	602.83
1985	1553.10	1184.96	723.31	553.03	174.96	146.54	619.41	480.93
1984	1286.64	1086.57	612.63	444.03	149.93	122.25	514.02	421.36
1983	1287.20	1027.04	612.57	434.24	140.70	119.51	515.11	401.03
1982	1070.55	776.92	464.55	292.12	122.83	103.22	416.33	299.44

N.Y.S.E. Volume (in millions)

Following are the Dow Jones averages of INDUSTRIAL, TRANSPORTATION and UTILITY stocks with the total sales of each group for the period indicated.

DATE	OPEN	10 AM	11 AM	12 NOON	1 PM	2 PM	3 PM	CLOSE	CH	%	HIGH*	LOW*	VOLUME
30 INDUSTRIALS													
Apr. 11	1800.72	1802.70	1799.98	1795.76	1785.84	1792.78	1791.42	a1790.18	− 4.12	− 0.23	1812.50	1779.14	20,656,900
Apr. 10	1791.07	1781.49	1779.69	1783.29	1790.23	1791.67	1787.60	1794.30	+ 15.68	+ 0.88	1807.83	1768.20	69,592,800
Apr. 9	1784.36	1787.84	1782.81	1789.87	1780.77	1765.92	1781.37	1778.62	+ 8.86	+ 0.50	1807.71	1754.19	16,933,700
Apr. 8	1750.36	1746.65	1750.84	1758.38	1760.06	1764.73	1761.49	1769.76	+ 34.25	+ 1.97	1779.57	1737.07	17,207,700
Apr. 7	1734.55	1734.20	1736.23	1731.68	1723.66	1722.70	1725.81	1735.51	− 3.71	− 0.21	1749.04	1712.52	14,407,900
20 TRANSPORTATION COS.													
Apr. 11	787.66	790.24	787.29	786.43	781.16	784.59	787.41	786.06	− 1.35	− 0.17	796.05	775.76	4,865,000
Apr. 10	787.90	788.52	788.15	787.17	788.89	789.50	787.41	787.41	+ 0.61	+ 0.08	794.90	781.77	3,725,200
Apr. 9	794.04	794.28	792.44	794.28	791.46	786.43	786.80	786.80	− 1.60	− 0.20	800.05	780.42	5,834,900
Apr. 8	779.93	780.05	783.00	785.82	786.06	788.15	785.45	788.40	+ 9.57	+ 1.23	794.90	775.39	5,021,400
Apr. 7	775.02	775.27	775.52	776.00	772.45	771.84	773.55	778.83	− 0.49	− 0.06	785.33	765.46	4,888,600
15 UTILITIES													
Apr. 11	189.47	189.17	189.22	188.40	187.17	188.35	188.45	188.19	− 0.98	− 0.52	190.24	186.76	3,058,100
Apr. 10	188.60	188.45	188.40	188.50	188.65	189.06	189.06	189.17	+ 0.57	+ 0.30	190.09	187.42	1,935,900
Apr. 9	188 19	188.71	188.65	189.22	188.55	187.47	187.94	188.60	+ 0.97	+ 0.52	190.14	186.29	4,310,700
Apr. 8	185.47	185.17	185.47	186.04	186.29	186.60	186.70	187.63	+ 2.36	+ 1.27	188.40	184.19	3,635,500
Apr. 7	185.06	184.70	184.86	184.80	183.57	183.73	183.78	185.27	− 1.28	− 0.69	186.35	182.55	2,676,900
65 STOCKS COMPOSITE AVERAGE													
Apr. 11	701.96	702.84	701.56	699.94	695.75	698.80	699.20	a698.46	− 1.68	− 0.24	707.03	692.73	28,580,000
Apr. 10	699.19	697.01	696.48	697.15	699.25	699.94	698.52	700.14	+ 4.10	+ 0.59	705.50	691.82	75,253,900
Apr. 9	698.80	699.94	698.33	700.70	697.57	692.38	696.32	696.04	+ 2.23	+ 0.32	706.67	687.64	27,079,300
Apr. 8	686.19	685.18	687.00	689.70	690.29	692.02	690.71	693.81	+ 11.44	+ 1.68	697.99	681.36	25,864,600
Apr. 7	681.17	680.94	681.56	680.44	677.23	676.95	678.10	682.37	− 1.67	− 0.24	687.58	672.49	21,973,400

Averages are compiled daily by using the following divisors: Industrials, 1.008; Transportation, 1.019; Utilities, 2.437; Composite, 4.387.

*Averages of the highs and lows reached at any time during the day on the New York Stock Exchange by the individual stocks.

Divisor

The Wall Street Journal, *April 14, 1986*

The Dow closed at 1790.18 ($1,790.18) on April 11. This "average" was virtually the *sum* of the 30 stocks in the Dow, reduced slightly by a divisor that was barely above 1, because these stocks have split so frequently.

Divisors —

a-The Dow Jones Industrial Average and the 65-stock Composite Average reflect the Philip Morris Cos. 2-for-1 common stock split.
This changed the divisor for the 30 industrials to 1.008 from 1.044 and that for the 65 stocks to 4.387 from 4.480.

Averages are compiled daily by using the following divisors: Industrials, 1.008; Transportation, 1.019; Utilities, 2.437; Composite, 4.387.

To see this operation in more detail, let's look at the Dow a few days later (April 18, 1986, *Journal,* see page 195). But this time, to make the arithmetic clearer, let's break out all 30 companies in the Dow and add up their prices. The total comes to $1,869.875, and when you divide that by 1.008, you get 1855.03—the Dow average for April 17.

Another, though less important, reason for the divisor is that occasionally Dow Jones will replace one of the 30 industrial stocks with another. Here, too, it wouldn't make sense to change the average; just because one stock is substituted for another doesn't mean the market itself has changed at all. Therefore, the divisor will be adjusted at the same time, to keep the average constant.

The **Markets and Money** charts on the next to the last page of the *Journal* provide a record of the industrial average over the past five trading days as well as a chart covering the last two years (see page 196).
The remaining charts cover short-term interest rates (federal funds), long-term bond prices, and the dollar's value. You can observe the strong relationship between 1985 stock and bond prices in the example drawn from the April 14, 1986, *Journal.*

The **Stock Market Data Bank** (see pages 197 through 200) appears directly below **Markets and Money** and presents a comprehensive summary of stock market activity in five sections: **Major Indexes, Most Active Issues, Diaries, Percentage Gainers and Losers,** and **Breakdown of Trading in NYSE Stocks.**

Major Indexes lists the Dow averages as well as a variety of other indexes. These permit you to compare the performance of your own investments with the broadest gauges of stock market activity. For instance, you can see in the examples on pages 197 and 199, drawn from the April

April 17, 1986, Closing Stock Prices

Company	Price
Allied-Signal	$ 51.125
Alcoa	42.5
American Can	73.875
American Express	67.125
AT&T	24.75
Bethlehem Steel	19.25
Chevron	38.125
Du Pont	76.625
Eastman Kodak	59.5
Exxon	57.875
General Electric	78.5
General Motors	82.875
Goodyear	32.75
Inco	15.75
IBM	154.625
International Paper	60.625
McDonald's	104.
Merck	179.25
Minnesota Mining & Manufacturing	102.75
Navistar	11.
Owens-Illinois	76.25
Philip Morris	67.75
Procter & Gamble	76.5
Sears	48.375
Texaco	32.5
Union Carbide	25.5
U.S. Steel	19.625
United Tech.	52.875
Westinghouse	56.875
Woolworth	80.75
Total	$1869.875

$$\frac{1869.875}{1.008} = 1855.03 \text{ (Dow average on April 17, 1986)}$$

$$\frac{\text{Sum of stock prices}}{\text{Divisor}} = \text{Dow Jones Industrial Average}$$

14, 1986, *Journal,* that the composite index of all stocks traded on the New York exchange fell 0.15 percent on April 11, 1986, and the Standard & Poor's 500 fell 0.20 percent, while the Dow industrials fell 0.23 percent.

Most Active Issues lists the day's most heavily traded stocks on the three major markets: New York Stock Exchange (NYSE), National Association of Security Dealers Automated Quotation (NASDAQ) system in the over-the-counter (OTC) market, and the American Stock Exchange (AMEX). For instance, over 5 million shares of Navistar (formerly International Harvester) changed hands. (See pages 197 and 199.)

The **Diaries** provide other important measures of the day's trading activity: advances versus declines, new highs versus new lows, and the

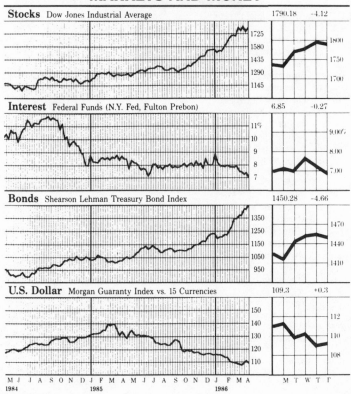

MARKETS AND MONEY

Stocks Dow Jones Industrial Average   1790.18   -4.12

Interest Federal Funds (N.Y. Fed, Fulton Prebon)   6.85   -0.27

Bonds Shearson Lehman Treasury Bond Index   1450.28   -4.66

U.S. Dollar Morgan Guaranty Index vs. 15 Currencies   109.3   +0.3

M J J A S O N D J F M A M J J A S O N D J F M A   M T W T F
1984   1985   1986

The Wall Street Journal, *April 14, 1986*

volume of the stocks advancing and declining. On April 11, 1986, 815 advanced and 817 declined on the New York exchange. Those that advanced were a bit more actively traded—65,925,000 to 61,129,000. These figures are not inconsistent with the slight decline in the Dow that day, but the huge margin of stocks that hit new highs (186) over those that hit new lows (6) is a sign of a market with upward strength. (See pages 197 and 199.)

Percentage Gainers and Losers don't require a great deal of elaboration; just remember that the biggest *percentage* changes usually occur in low-priced stocks. Raymark fell 19 percent in a single day (ouch!) on a drop of $2.375 to $10.125 on the New York exchange. As an investor, you want to know the percentage performance of your stocks. (See pages 198 and 200.)

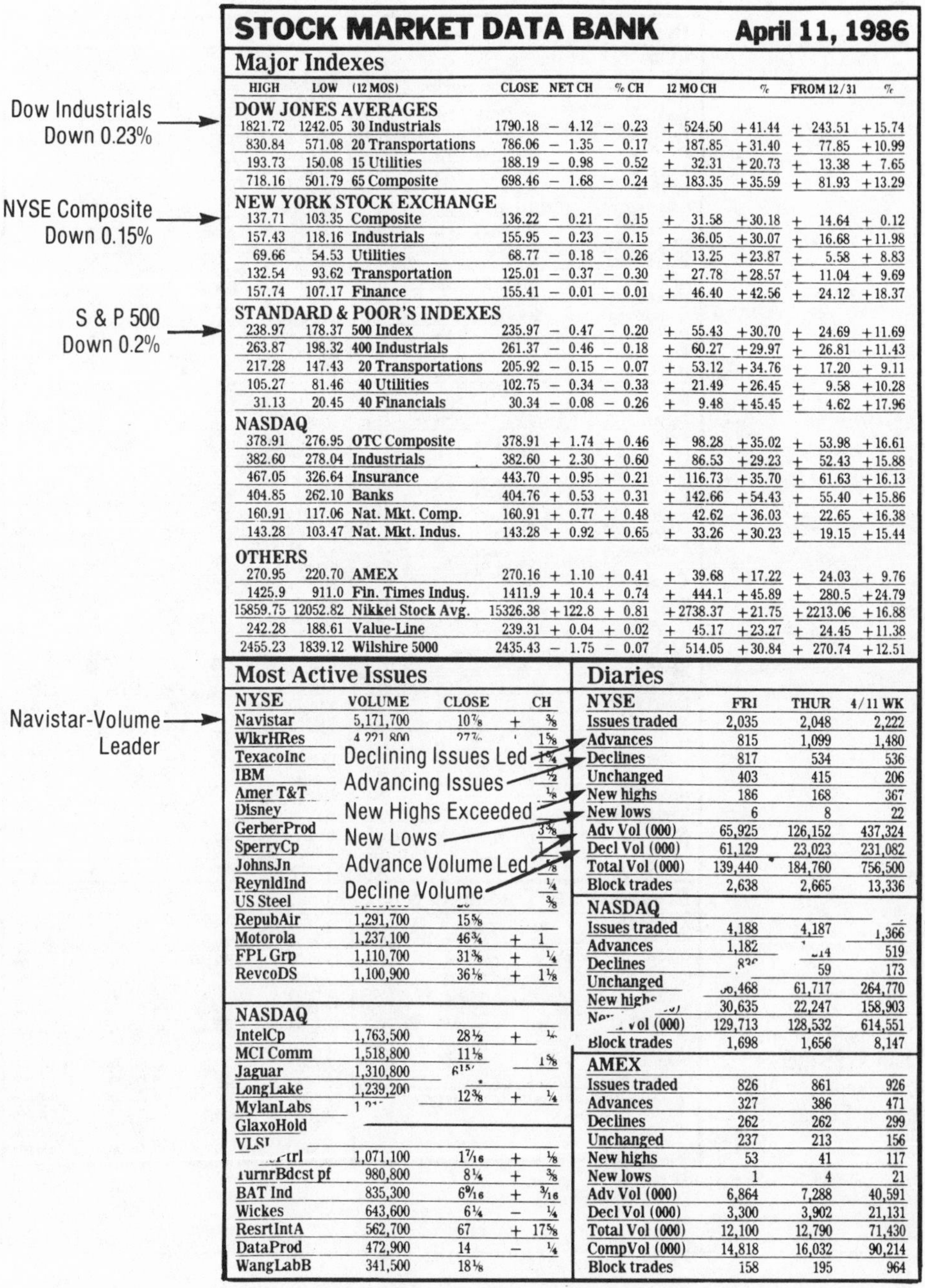

Dow Industrials Down 0.23% →

NYSE Composite Down 0.15% →

S & P 500 Down 0.2% →

Navistar-Volume Leader →

STOCK MARKET DATA BANK   April 11, 1986

Major Indexes

HIGH	LOW	(12 MOS)	CLOSE	NET CH	% CH	12 MO CH	%	FROM 12/31	%
DOW JONES AVERAGES									
1821.72	1242.05	30 Industrials	1790.18	− 4.12	− 0.23	+ 524.50	+41.44	+ 243.51	+15.74
830.84	571.08	20 Transportations	786.06	− 1.35	− 0.17	+ 187.85	+31.40	+ 77.85	+10.99
193.73	150.08	15 Utilities	188.19	− 0.98	− 0.52	+ 32.31	+20.73	+ 13.38	+ 7.65
718.16	501.79	65 Composite	698.46	− 1.68	− 0.24	+ 183.35	+35.59	+ 81.93	+13.29
NEW YORK STOCK EXCHANGE									
137.71	103.35	Composite	136.22	− 0.21	− 0.15	+ 31.58	+30.18	+ 14.64	+ 0.12
157.43	118.16	Industrials	155.95	− 0.23	− 0.15	+ 36.05	+30.07	+ 16.68	+11.98
69.66	54.53	Utilities	68.77	− 0.18	− 0.26	+ 13.25	+23.87	+ 5.58	+ 8.83
132.54	93.62	Transportation	125.01	− 0.37	− 0.30	+ 27.78	+28.57	+ 11.04	+ 9.69
157.74	107.17	Finance	155.41	− 0.01	− 0.01	+ 46.40	+42.56	+ 24.12	+18.37
STANDARD & POOR'S INDEXES									
238.97	178.37	500 Index	235.97	− 0.47	− 0.20	+ 55.43	+30.70	+ 24.69	+11.69
263.87	198.32	400 Industrials	261.37	− 0.46	− 0.18	+ 60.27	+29.97	+ 26.81	+11.43
217.28	147.43	20 Transportations	205.92	− 0.15	− 0.07	+ 53.12	+34.76	+ 17.20	+ 9.11
105.27	81.46	40 Utilities	102.75	− 0.34	− 0.33	+ 21.49	+26.45	+ 9.58	+10.28
31.13	20.45	40 Financials	30.34	− 0.08	− 0.26	+ 9.48	+45.45	+ 4.62	+17.96
NASDAQ									
378.91	276.95	OTC Composite	378.91	+ 1.74	+ 0.46	+ 98.28	+35.02	+ 53.98	+16.61
382.60	278.04	Industrials	382.60	+ 2.30	+ 0.60	+ 86.53	+29.23	+ 52.43	+15.88
467.05	326.64	Insurance	443.70	+ 0.95	+ 0.21	+ 116.73	+35.70	+ 61.63	+16.13
404.85	262.10	Banks	404.76	+ 0.53	+ 0.31	+ 142.66	+54.43	+ 55.40	+15.86
160.91	117.06	Nat. Mkt. Comp.	160.91	+ 0.77	+ 0.48	+ 42.62	+36.03	+ 22.65	+16.38
143.28	103.47	Nat. Mkt. Indus.	143.28	+ 0.92	+ 0.65	+ 33.26	+30.23	+ 19.15	+15.44
OTHERS									
270.95	220.70	AMEX	270.16	+ 1.10	+ 0.41	+ 39.68	+17.22	+ 24.03	+ 9.76
1425.9	911.0	Fin. Times Indus.	1411.9	+ 10.4	+ 0.74	+ 444.1	+45.89	+ 280.5	+24.79
15859.75	12052.82	Nikkei Stock Avg.	15326.38	+122.8	+ 0.81	+ 2738.37	+21.75	+2213.06	+16.88
242.28	188.61	Value-Line	239.31	+ 0.04	+ 0.02	+ 45.17	+23.27	+ 24.45	+11.38
2455.23	1839.12	Wilshire 5000	2435.43	− 1.75	− 0.07	+ 514.05	+30.84	+ 270.74	+12.51

Most Active Issues

NYSE	VOLUME	CLOSE	CH
Navistar	5,171,700	10⅝	+ ⅜
WlkrHRes	4,221,800	27⅞	+ 1⅝
TexacoInc		Declining Issues Led	1%
IBM			− ½
Amer T&T		Advancing Issues	− ⅛
Disney		New Highs Exceeded	
GerberProd			3⅛
SperryCp		New Lows	1
JohnsJn		Advance Volume Led	⅝
ReynldInd		Decline Volume	¼
US Steel			⅜
RepubAir	1,291,700	15⅝	
Motorola	1,237,100	46¾	+ 1
FPL Grp	1,110,700	31⅜	+ ¼
RevcoDS	1,100,900	36⅛	+ 1⅛

NASDAQ			
IntelCp	1,763,500	28½	+ ¼
MCI Comm	1,518,800	11⅛	
Jaguar	1,310,800	6¹⁵	1⅜
LongLake	1,239,200		
MylanLabs	1	12⅜	+ ¼
GlaxoHold			
VLSI			
...rtrl	1,071,100	1⁷⁄₁₆	+ ⅛
TurnrBdcst pf	980,800	8¼	+ ⅜
BAT Ind	835,300	6⁹⁄₁₆	+ ³⁄₁₆
Wickes	643,600	6¼	− ¼
ResrtIntA	562,700	67	+ 17⅝
DataProd	472,900	14	− ¼
WangLabB	341,500	18⅛	

Diaries

NYSE	FRI	THUR	4/11 WK
Issues traded	2,035	2,048	2,222
Advances	815	1,099	1,480
Declines	817	534	536
Unchanged	403	415	206
New highs	186	168	367
New lows	6	8	22
Adv Vol (000)	65,925	126,152	437,324
Decl Vol (000)	61,129	23,023	231,082
Total Vol (000)	139,440	184,760	756,500
Block trades	2,638	2,665	13,336

NASDAQ			
Issues traded	4,188	4,187	1,366
Advances	1,182		519
Declines	82°	59	173
Unchanged	₀₀,468	61,717	264,770
New highs	30,635	22,247	158,903
N... vol (000)	129,713	128,532	614,551
Block trades	1,698	1,656	8,147

AMEX			
Issues traded	826	861	926
Advances	327	386	471
Declines	262	262	299
Unchanged	237	213	156
New highs	53	41	117
New lows	1	4	21
Adv Vol (000)	6,864	7,288	40,591
Decl Vol (000)	3,300	3,902	21,131
Total Vol (000)	12,100	12,790	71,430
CompVol (000)	14,818	16,032	90,214
Block trades	158	195	964

Percentage Gainers . . . and Losers

Raymark Down 19.0%

NYSE	CLOSE	CH	% CH		CLOSE	CH	% CH
ElTorito	17[illegible]	[illegible]	15.0	Raymark	10⅛	– 2⅜	– 19.0
WstCoNA	7[illegible]	[illegible]	14.8	McLean wt	2⅛	– ¼	– 10.5
YorkIntl	16[illegible]	[illegible]	13.0	DeltonaCp	9	– 1	– 10.0
vjChrtCo pf	2⅜	+ ¼	+ 11.8	Pennzoil	51⅛	– 4⅜	– 7.9
FairCom	13¼	+ 1⅜	+ 11.6	WilcoxGbs	15⅝	– 1⅛	– 6.7
EntexInc	24¼	+ 2¼	+ 10.2	GenlDevl wt	8	– ½	– 5.9
IntlRect	9⅝	+ ⅞	+ 10.0	InexcoOil	4	– ¼	– 5.9
GoldnNug wt	2⅞	+ ¼	+ 9.5	CapCities	215¼	– 13¼	– 5.8
CntrCred	15¼	+ 1¼	+ 8.9	FedSignl	21½	– 1¼	– 5.5
UnileverPlc	96⅛	+ 7⅛	+ 8.0	BerkeyInc	6⅝	– ⅜	– 5.4
PSInd 4.16pf	10½	+ ¾	+ 7.7	ComdreInt	7	– ⅜	– 5.1
LTV Corp	9⅛	+ ⅝	+ 7.4	Micklbry	4⅝	– ¼	– 5.1
ParkEl	16⅝	+ 1⅛	+ 7.3	EnterraCp	7⅛	– ⅜	– 5.0
GerberProd	51½	+ 3⅜	+ 7.0	ImpCpAm	12	– ⅝	– 5.0
RevereCopr	17¼	+ 1⅛	+ 7.0	Cooprvsn	26⅞	– 1⅜	– 4.9
LLC Corp	2	+ ⅛	+ 6.7	ElcorCp	12⅛	– ⅝	– 4.9
WlkrHRes	27⅞	+ 1⅝	+ 6.2	GF Corp	4⅞	– ¼	– 4.9
OTC							
Pelsart ADR	2⅞	+ 1 3/32	+ 61.4	InstClinPh	4	– 3¼	– 44.8
FrnklnCon	2 1/16	+ 9/16	+ 37.5	VistaF 88wt	2½	– 1	– 28.6
ChalngrInt	6⅜	+ 1⅝	+ 34.2	NBL Roman	4½	– 1	– 18.2
MarcomTel un	3¼	+ ¾	+ 30.0	VistaF 86wt	6¼	– 1⅜	– 18.0
Fngmtx wt	4½	+ 1	+ 28.6	Kevlin	4	– ¾	– 15.8
SaharaRsrt	5	+ 1	+ 25.0	VistarFilm	3 11/16	– 11/16	– 15.7
CmclProg wt	7¾	+ 1½	+ 24.0	ContlDta un	4⅛	– ¾	– 15.4
PowellInd	2	+ ⅜	+ 23.1	VistaF un	83	– 15	– 15.3
Zymos	2⅜	+ 7/16	+ 22.6	ArtelCom	3½	– ⅝	– 15.2
AdvMed un	3¼	+ ½	+ 18.2	MetCoilSys	5¾	– 1	– 14.8
Synbiotics	13¼	+ 2	+ 17.8	SpecltyCompst	4¾	– ¾	– 13.6
US Capit	3⅜	+ ½	+ 17.4	IBI Security	2⅞	– ⅜	– 11.5
AMEX							
ResortsA	66¾	+ 17⅜	+ 35.2	SanCarlos	2⅝	– ⅜	– 12.5
ResortsB	69	+ 16⅞	+ 32.4	ActonCp	2¼	– ¼	– 10.0
Lionel wtB	2	+ ⅜	+ 23.1	MtgeRty wt	3⅜	– ⅜	– 10.0
NW WldPict	18⅜	+ 2⅜	+ 14.8	Kidde wt	4½	– ⅜	– 7.7
WellsAmerican	2	+ ¼	+ 14.3	Openheimer	13¾	– 1⅛	– 7.6
Lionel wtA	2⅛	+ ¼	+ 13.3	DeRoseInd	4⅝	– ⅜	– 7.5
DiagRetB	9¼	+ 1	+ 12.1	SeligAsc	13⅞	– 1	– 6.7
OrioleHmA	10⅝	+ 1	+ 10.4	CahmpHom	2 13/16	– 3/16	– 6.3
WwdeEng pf	6⅞	+ ⅝	+ 10.0	WstDigital	11¼	– ¾	– 6.3
Ampal	2⅞	+ ¼	+ 9.5	BarnesEng	3⅞	– ¼	– 6.1
Vicon	6	+ ½	+ 9.1	WinnEntA	3⅞	– ¼	– 6.1
EngyDevLp	9⅛	+ ¾	+ 9.0	SceptreResc	2	– ⅛	– 5.9

Breakdown of Trading in NYSE Stocks

BY MARKET	FRI	THUR	WK AGO
New York	139,440,000	184,760,000	147,270,000
Midwest	11,056,300	12,543,900	10,657,200
Pacific	6,370,000	6,301,600	6,080,400
NASD	5,523,190	3,665,380	5,959,820
Phila	2,196,400	2,529,400	3,099,400
Boston	2,081,900	1,999,800	1,775,600
Cincinnati	157,500	291,900	174,800
Instinet	699,800	179,300	104,700
Composite	167,525,090	212,271,280	175,121,920

Composite Volume of All NYSE Stocks Traded on All Exchanges

Block trades are trades of 10,000 shares or more.

½-HOURLY	FRI	THUR	WK AGO
9:30-10	23,260,000	67,940,000	19,540,000
10-10:30	15,170,000	14,230,000	14,370,000
10:30-11	13,150,000	9,920,000	11,120,000
11-11:30	15,670,000	10,340,000	8,050,000
11:30-12	8,810,000	8,820,000	8,200,000
12-12:30	8,370,000	10,550,000	7,930,000
12:30-1	10,940,000	9,470,000	7,080,000
1-1:30	5,190,000	10,780,000	14,170,000
1:30-2	6,320,000	6,420,000	11,880,000
2-2:30	6,750,000	6,910,000	12,860,000
2:30-3	6,880,000	7,570,000	8,330,000
3-3:30	7,910,000	9,890,000	7,750,000
3:30-4	11,020,000	11,920,000	15,990,000

The Wall Street Journal, *April 14, 1986*

Major Indexes

HIGH	LOW	(12 MOS)	CLOSE	NET CH	% CH	12 MO CH	%	FROM 12/31	%
DOW JONES AVERAGES									
1821.72	1242.05	30 Industrials	1790.18	− 4.12	− 0.23	+ 524.50	+41.44	+ 243.51	+15.74
830.84	571.08	20 Transportations	786.06	− 1.35	− 0.17	+ 187.85	+31.40	+ 77.85	+10.99
193.73	150.08	15 Utilities	188.19	− 0.98	− 0.52	+ 32.31	+20.73	+ 13.38	+ 7.65
718.16	501.79	65 Composite	698.46	− 1.68	− 0.24	+ 183.35	+35.59	+ 81.93	+13.29
NEW YORK STOCK EXCHANGE									
137.71	103.35	Composite	136.22	− 0.21	− 0.15	+ 31.58	+30.18	+ 14.64	+ 0.12
157.43	118.16	Industrials	155.95	− 0.23	− 0.15	+ 36.05	+30.07	+ 16.68	+11.98
69.66	54.53	Utilities	68.77	− 0.18	− 0.26	+ 13.25	+23.87	+ 5.58	+ 8.83
132.54	93.62	Transportation	125.01	− 0.37	− 0.30	+ 27.78	+28.57	+ 11.04	+ 9.69
157.74	107.17	Finance	155.41	− 0.01	− 0.01	+ 46.40	+42.56	+ 24.12	+18.37
STANDARD & POOR'S INDEXES									
238.97	178.37	500 Index	235.97	− 0.47	− 0.20	+ 55.43	+30.70	+ 24.69	+11.69
263.87	198.32	400 Industrials	261.37	− 0.46	− 0.18	+ 60.27	+29.97	+ 26.81	+11.43
217.28	147.43	20 Transportations	205.92	− 0.15	− 0.07	+ 53.12	+34.76	+ 17.20	+ 9.11
105.27	81.46	40 Utilities	102.75	− 0.34	− 0.33	+ 21.49	+26.45	+ 9.58	+10.28
31.13	20.45	40 Financials	30.34	− 0.08	− 0.26	+ 9.48	+45.45	+ 4.62	+17.96

Dow Industrials Down 0.23%

NYSE Composite Down 0.15%

S&P 500 Down 0.2%

Most Active Issues

NYSE	VOLUME	CLOSE	CH	
Navistar	5,171,700	10⅞	+	⅜
WlkrHRes	4,221,800	27⅞	+	1⅝
TexacoInc	2,520,000	32⅝	+	1¾
IBM	2,224,700	149¾	−	½

Navistar Volume Leader

Diaries

NYSE	FRI	THUR	4/11 WK
Issues traded	2,035	2,048	2,222
Advances	815	1,099	1,480
Declines	817	534	536
Unchanged	403	415	206
New highs	186	168	367
New lows	6	8	22
Adv Vol (000)	65,925	126,152	437,324
Decl Vol (000)	61,129	23,023	231,082
Total Vol (000)	139,440	184,760	756,500
Block trades	2,638	2,665	13,336

Declining Issues Led Advancing Issues

New Highs Exceeded New Lows

Advance Volume Led Decline Volume

Raymark Down 19.0%

and Losers

	CLOSE	CH	% CH
Raymark	10⅛	− 2⅜	− 19.0
McLean wt	2⅛	− ¼	− 10.5
DeltonaCp	9	− 1	− 10.0
Pennzoil	51⅛	− 4⅜	− 7.9

Raymark Down 19.0%

The **Breakdown of Trading in NYSE Stocks** presents trading volume that occurs on *all* stock exchanges of securities listed on the New York Stock Exchange, as well as trading volume by half hours. The composite volume of 167,525,090 shares for Friday, April 11, 1986, was for all NYSE stocks traded on all exchanges.

Breakdown of Trading in NYSE Stocks

BY MARKET	FRI	THUR	WK AGO
New York	139,440,000	184,760,000	147,270,000
Midwest	11,056,300	12,543,900	10,657,200
Pacific	6,370,000	6,301,600	6,080,400
NASD	5,523,190	3,665,380	5,959,820
Phila	2,196,400	2,529,400	3,099,400
Boston	2,081,900	1,999,800	1,775,600
Cincinnati	157,500	291,900	174,800
Instinet	699,800	179,300	104,700
Composite	167,525,090	212,271,280	175,121,920

Block trades are trades of 10,000 shares or more.

Composite Volume of All NYSE Stocks Traded on All Exchanges

NYSE Highs/Lows (listed in the front-page index) presents another daily indicator of market strength or weakness that was discussed earlier as a Diaries component. You saw that 186 stocks hit new highs for the past 52 weeks on April 11, 1986, while 6 hit new lows. NYSE Highs/Lows lists these stocks (see page 201).

Odd-Lot Trading reports each day on stock purchases and sales by small investors who conduct transactions of fewer than 100 shares (see

NYSE HIGHS/LOWS

Friday, April 11, 1986
NEW HIGHS – 186

AFG Ind	DetE 7.36pf	LIL Co pfT	PSEG 2.17pf
ANR 2.12pf	DiGiorgio	LIL Co pfO	PSEG 7.40pf
AetnaLf pfC	Donaldson	LongsDrug	RevcoDS
AlaP 9.44pf	DukeP pfA	LaPwL t 19.20pf	Revlon
AlaP 8 16pf	Eastn Util	LaPwL t pf	RoyalDutch
AmBrands	EmersRad	ManorCre s	RyderSyst
AmBrd 2.67pf	Entexinc	Marine Mid	StJos LtPw
AmCapCv	FMC	Marshind	SntaFeEP n
Am Home	FMCCp pf	McDonalds	SeaLand
AmWatr Wk s	FPL Grp	Mellon 1.00pf	SealedAir
ArizPSv 2.58pf	FederDStr	MetE 8.12pf	SherwinWm s
Arvin s	FstBkSv	MetE d pfG	SmithBeck
Avon Prod	FtBnkFla s	MetEd pfI	SourceCap pf
BancOne s	FstVaBks	MooreCorp s	SCarEG pt
Bandag Inc	FleetFnGp	Morgan JP	SouJer Ind
BankNY	FordMot	Motorola	SoRv 2.60pf
BarnesGp	Gannett	NAFCO Fncl	StPacCp s
BearStrns n	GapInc s	Nashua Cp	SuaveShoe
Beatrice	GMtr 3.75pf	NatGypsum s	TECO
BectonDick s	GenMot Spf	Navstr wtB	Textn 1.40pf
Benef 4.30pf	GnMofr E	Navstr prfC	ThermoEl s
Benequity n	GaPacif	NYS 8.48pf	Toled 3.75pf
BosE 8.88pf	GerberProd	NiM 4.10pf	TolEd 8.84pf
BristMy pf	GleasnC	NiMo 7.72pf	ToroCo
BklynUGs pf	GreenTree	OccldPtri wi	ToysRUs
BrownGrp	Hartmarx	Ohio Edison	UDC Dev n
Celanese	Heinz s	OhEd 7.36pf	UnCarbde s
Cert-teed	IndM 7.08pf	OhEd 8.20pf	UnEl 4.50pf
ChmNY pf	IntcapSec	OhEd 9.12pf	UnEl 2.13pf
Cinn Bell	Interst Pw	OhEd 8.64pf	UnEl 2.72pf
CircleK s	JohnsJn	OhPw 2.27pf	Uniroval pf
Coachman	KCPL 4.35pf	OutbdMar	UtiliCorp
ColGas pfB	KCPL 2.33pf	Owenslil	UtiliCo 2.44pr
CwE 1.90pf	KC Sthn pf	PaylessCash	VaEP 7.72pf
CwE 7.24of	KansPL 2.32pf	PaPL 8.40pr	Wacknhut
ConnNG	Koopers pf	PaPL 11pr	Walgreen s
ConEd4 65pf	LaQuinta	PetrieStr s	WlkrHRes g
ConEd SpfA	Lear Siegler	PhEl 8.75pf	Warnaco
CnPw 7.68pf	LehVallnd	Pilsbury	Wash WatP
CntrCred	Limited s	Potom Elec	WellsFar Co
DartKrft s	LoewsCp	PotEl 2.44pf	Wendy
DaytPL pfD	LIL Co	PotEl 4.50pf	Weyerhsr
DaytPL pfF	LIL Co pfE	PrimeMotr s	Weyerhsr pf
Deltona Cp	LIL Co pfJ	PSInd 4.16pf	WhitCn pfC
DetE 5 50pf	LIL Co pfX	PSInd 9.60pf	YorkIntl n
DetE 7.68pf	LIL Co pfV	PSEG 4.30pf	
DetE 7.45pf	LIL Co pfU	PSEG 5.28pf	

NEW LOWS 6

Augat	Ensrch dp pf	FogoProd	US Steel
BritTelEn	FtBTx adi ofB		

s Split or stock dividend of 25 per cent or more in the past 52 weeks. High-low range is adjusted from old stock. n-New issue in past 52 weeks and does not cover the entire 52 week period.

the front-page index). These transactions are referred to as odd lots (round-lots are trades of 100 shares). Small investors use odd lots because their stock portfolios are small and they cannot afford to deal in round lots. For instance, IBM closed at $149.75 on April 11, 1986, putting the cost of a round-lot purchase at $14,975 ($149.75 × 100) and out of the reach of many small investors.

Many market analysts used to believe that odd-lot transactions were a contrary indicator, because they saw the small investor as a market follower who buys more as the market peaks and sells more as it bottoms out (the opposite of the savvy, big-time trader who gets in at the bottom and out at the top). Therefore, according to this wisdom, a high ratio of odd-lot buying to selling is a sign that the market is near a peak (time to sell), while the opposite indicates a market trough (time to buy).

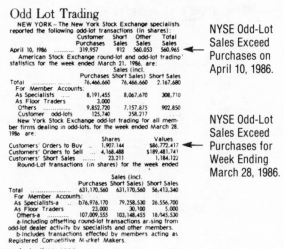

Odd Lot Trading

The Wall Street Journal, *April 14, 1986*

However, since a great many small investors in recent years have abandoned odd lots in favor of mutual funds, this omen has become less significant to analysts.

You can see in the excerpt from the April 14, 1986, edition of the *Journal* that odd-lot sales (560,965 shares) exceeded odd-lot purchases

(319,957) on April 10, 1986, in NYSE trading. For the entire week ended March 28, 1986, shares sold (4,168,488) also exceeded shares purchased (1,907,144). Since the odd-lot trader was a net seller in a rising market, those who view odd-lot statistics as a contrary indicator would say that the market had not peaked.

So much for the stock market averages and indicators. You may wish to purchase shares of stock and follow their progress. Here's how you do it.

Suppose you own some shares of Anheuser-Busch. Turn to the daily listing of **New York Stock Exchange Composite Transactions** in *The Wall Street Journal*. You'll find a reference to all exchanges in the index on the front page.

In the accompanying April 14 excerpt, (pages 204 and 205), columns 1 and 2 tell you the highest and lowest value of one share of the stock in the past 52 weeks, expressed in dollars and fractions of a dollar. Thus, Anheuser-Busch stock was as low as 26 3/8 dollars ($26.375) and as high as 49 3/8 dollars ($49.375) in the year preceding April 11, 1986.

(1)	(2)	(3)	(4)	(5)	(6)	(7)	(8)	(9)	(10)
52 Weeks				Yld	P-E	Sales			Net
High	Low	Stock	Div.	%	Ratio	100s	High	Low	Close	Chg.
49⅜	26⅜	Anheus	s .80	1.7	17	3200	48⅜	47⅝	48	+¼

Footnotes are listed next to the company name. In this case, the *s* indicates that there has been a stock split or stock dividend. That is, within the past year shareholders received additional shares in some fixed ratio (say, two for one or three for two) with the appropriate adjustment in the stock's price, or else a dividend was paid to shareholders in the form of more stock rather than cash, usually with a price adjustment.

The third column of data reports the latest annual cash dividend (of 80 cents per share). The dividend is expressed as a percentage of the closing price in the following column ($0.80/$48.00 = 1.7 percent).

Column 5 reports the price-earnings (P-E) ratio, which is obtained by dividing the price of the stock by its earnings per share. (This important statistic is discussed in detail later in this chapter.) On April 11, 1986, Anheuser-Busch's stock was worth 17 times the profits per share of stock.

The sixth column informs you of the number of shares traded that day, expressed in hundreds of shares. Thus, on April 11, 1986, 320,000 shares of Anheuser-Busch stock were traded. If a *z* appears before the number in this column, the figure represents the actual number (not hundreds) of shares traded.

Columns 7, 8, and 9 tell you the stock's highest, lowest, and closing (last) price for the trading day. (Note in the caption under the date in the illustration that these quotes are a composite of transactions on the NYSE and the other exchanges listed. The closing price on the Pacific

NEW YORK STOCK EXCHANGE COMPOSITE TRANSACTIONS

Friday, April 11, 1986

Quotations include trades on the Midwest, Pacific, Philadelphia, Boston and Cincinnati stock exchanges and reported by the National Association of Securities Dealers and Instinet

Anheuser Busch →

52 Weeks High	Low	Stock	Div.	Yld %	P-E Ratio	Sales 100s	High	Low	Close	Net Chg.
31	18	Anlog		..	38	120	29⅜	29	29¼	+ ⅜
30¼	20⅝	Anchor	1.48	5.0	129	145	30	29½	29¾	.....
61¼	35⅝	AnClay	.33j	..	33	795	57	56⅛	57	.....
16½	9⅛	AndrGr	.21	1.4	17	80	15¾	15½	15½	− ⅛
29⅜	20⅛	Angelic	.60	2.1	15	317	28½	28⅛	28½	+ ¼
49⅜	26⅜	Anheus	s.80	1.7	17	3200	48⅜	47⅝	48	+ ¼
96½	56¾	Anheu	pf3.60	3.8	..	50	94¾	93½	94¾	+ 1¼
25⅜	13½	Anixtr	.28	1.1	23	168	25	24½	25	+ ¼
19⅛	10¼	Anthem	.04	.2	38	115	17¼	16⅝	16⅞	+ ⅝
18	11	Anthny	.44b	2.7	16	55	16½	16⅜	16⅜	− ⅛
13⅜	8⅜	Apache	.28	3.1	24	150	9	8⅞	9	.....
2	1-16	ApchP	wt	..	..	54	5-64	9-128	9-128	− 1-64
19⅞	10⅞	ApcP	un1.40	11.	..	859	13	12½	12½	− ¼
84⅜	59	ApPw	pf7.40	8.9	.	z110	83¼	83¼	83¼	+ 1¼
27½	24¼	ApPw	pf2.65	10.	..	2	26	26	26	+ ¼
34⅜	31	ApPw	pf4.18	13.	..	10	33⅛	32¾	33⅛	.....
32	28½	ApPw	pf3.80	12.	..	9	30⅝	30⅜	30⅝	+ ½
19½	12	ApplMg		..	28	76	17½	16¾	17	+ ¼
30⅜	19¼	ArchDn	.14b	.5	13	2701	26⅛	25⅝	25⅞	+ ¼
31⅞	27¾	ArlP	pf 3.58	11.	..	42	u32⅛	31⅝	32	+ ⅜
105	94	AzPpf	10.70	10.	..	z100	102¼	102¼	102¼	.....
42½	18	ArkBst	.60	1.5	14	479	40⅝	39½	40⅛	+ ½
24¼	16	Arkla	1.08	6.1	13	950	17¾	17½	17⅝	+ ⅛
15⅝	10⅝	Armada		..	..	13	10⅝	10⅝	10⅝	.....
12	6⅞	Armco		..	13	1546	9⅜	9⅛	9¼	− ⅜
26½	15½	Armc	pf2.10	9.1	..	15	23½	23⅛	23⅛	− ⅝
20⅜	13½	ArmsRb	.48	3.0	18	6167	16⅜	16	16	− ½
62	31⅞	ArmWin	1.30	2.1	15	760	61¾	60⅞	61¾	+ ¾
18	11¼	ArowE	.20	1.3	..	437	15¼	14⅝	15¼	+ ¼
30⅜	19¾	Artra	.22	.8	..	71	29¼	29	29⅛	+ ¼
28⅞	14¼	Arvin	s .64	2.2	13	190	u29½	28⅞	29⅛	+ ¼
27¾	15¾	Asarco		..	..	930	20⅜	20¼	20⅜	− ⅛
56	28⅝	AshlOil	1.60	3.2	10	1344	50⅜	49⅝	50⅜	+ ½
54¼	41⅞	AshlO	pf4.50	9.3	..	7	48⅜	48¼	48¼	.....
45½	28¾	AsdDG	s1.40	3.1	15	2267	45	43¾	44¾	+ ½
144¾	91¾	AsdD	pf4.75	3.3	..	2	142	142	142	+ 2⅛
23½	16⅜	Athlone	1.60	8.0	..	17	20⅜	20⅛	20⅛	− ¼
36¼	25¼	AtCyEl	2.58	7.3	12	212	35⅝	35⅜	35½	.....
67⅞	47⅞	AtlRich	4	7.5	..	6042	54⅜	53½	53½	− ½
455	325	AtlRc	pf 3	.8	..	2	366¼	366¼	366¼	+ 12
162	114¾	AtlRc	pf2.80	2.2	..	3	129⅜	129	129	.....
16⅞	10⅛	AtlasCp		..	..	42	14⅛	13½	13⅞	− ⅜
26⅛	11¼	AudVd	s	..	25	71	21⅜	21⅛	21⅜	+ ⅛
27½	19⅜	Augat	.40	2.0	29	2232	20⅝	d19¼	19⅞	+ ¼
70⅞	41½	AutoDt	.68	1.0	25	714	68	67	67¾	+ ¾
5¼	3⅛	Avalon	n.05e	1.4	..	40	3½	3⅜	3½	.....
39⅛	24⅜	AVEMC	.60	1.6	15	4	37⅞	37¾	37⅞	− ⅛
47½	30	Avery	.68	1.5	18	464	44½	44⅛	44⅜	− ⅛
40⅜	27	Avnet	.50	1.4	40	1486	37½	36⅝	37	+ ⅝
34	17⅞	Avon	2	5.8	..	9023	u35	33½	34⅝	+ 1⅛
27⅜	16⅛	Aydin		..	27	64	23⅞	23½	23⅜	− ⅜

52 Weeks High	Low	Stock	Div.	Yld %	P-E Ratio	Sales 100s	High	Low	Close	Net Chg.
32⅜	18	Chelsea	.72	2.6	11	159	28	27¼	27¾	+ ¾
39¼	26⅜	Chemed	1.56	4.1	15	197	38⅞	37¾	38	− ⅜
55¼	33¼	ChmNY	2.60	4.8	7	3725	55⅛	53⅜	53⅞	− ⅜
54½	34½	ChNY	pf1.87	3.4	..	1	u54⅝	54⅝	54⅝	+ 1
56¾	52⅛	ChNY	pf5.67e	11.	..	200	52⅞	52⅞	52⅞	− 1⅞
45⅛	32¼	Chespk	1.24	2.9	18	100	42⅞	42⅛	42½	+ ⅛
48½	31	ChesPn	2	4.3	20	2531	46⅜	45¾	46	+ ⅛
40¾	33⅝	Chevrn	2.40	6.2	9	6481	38⅞	38	38¾	+ ¾
154	124	ChiMlw		..	..	6	146¾	146¼	146¼	− ¾
39⅞	19⅜	ChiPnT		..	..	845	37¾	36¾	37½	+ ½
14⅜	7⅝	ChkFull	.24t	2.2	..	66	11¼	10⅞	10⅞	− ⅜
64	44¾	ChrisCr	1.24t	2.0	24	120	61	60⅝	60¾	+ ½
13⅛	6¾	Christn		..	..	9	7⅛	7	7⅛	.....
20⅝	9¾	Chroma		..	..	81	19⅝	19½	19⅝	+ ⅛
47⅛	22¼	Chrys	s	..	4	8100	43	40½	40⅝	− 2
77⅝	38	Chubb	s1.56	2.1	38	749	73½	72⅛	72¾	+ ½
84¾	50¾	Chubb	pf4.25	5.4	..	24	79	78	78¼	+ ½
20¼	14⅜	Churchs	.44	2.6	27	921	17⅛	16¾	17	.....
9¼	4⅞	Chyron	.10	1.7	26	165	6⅜	6	6	− ¼
31¾	22¼	Cilcorp	2.28	7.3	11	276	31⅝	31¼	31¼	− ½
70	43⅛	CinBell	3.52	5.0	11	204	u70⅛	69⅝	69⅞	− ⅛
25⅞	14¾	CinGE	2.16	8.5	8	1312	25⅞	25½	25½	− ¼
49	34	CinG	pf 4.75	9.8	..	z120	48½	48½	48½	+ ¼
100	64	CinG	pf 9.28	9.3	..	z100	100	100	100	.....
99	66	CinG	pf 9.52	9.7	..	z3260	98½	98½	98½	.....
25⅞	15⅛	CinMil	.72	3.0	..	190	24⅝	24	24¼	− ⅛
27¾	19⅛	CirclK	s .50	1.7	16	3190	u28⅝	27⅝	28⅝	+ ⅞
43	18⅝	CirCity	.10	.3	22	704	39¾	39	39⅜	+ ⅛
40⅛	22⅛	Circus		..	19	229	39⅜	38⅜	38¾	− ⅛
63¾	40	Citicrp	2.46	4.0	9	3807	62	60⅞	61¼	− ⅛
89	77¼	Citcp	pf6.53e	7.5	..	592	87	86⅞	87	+ ¼
102	92½	Citcp	pfA8e	7.9	..	30	100¾	100¾	100¾	+ ⅜
8⅞	6⅝	Clabir	.72	10.	..	95	7⅛	6⅞	7	.....
19¾	6⅞	ClairS	s .10	.9	25	3213	11½	11	11⅜	+ ⅜
32¾	20⅛	ClarkE		..	..	726	22⅝	22½	22½	− ⅛
26¼	8½	ClayH	s	..	26	152	26	25⅜	25½	− ¼
22	15½	ClvClf	1	5.7	12	369	18⅛	17⅜	17⅝	+ ¼
23	19¾	ClvCl	pf 2	9.1	..	10	22¼	21⅞	21⅞	− ⅜
29¼	20	ClevEl	2.64	9.1	8	2822	29⅛	28⅝	29	+ ⅜
75½	56⅝	ClvEl	pf7.40	9.9	..	z100	74¾	74¾	74¾	.....
58¼	33⅝	Clorox	1.36	2.4	16	914	56⅞	55½	56¾	+ 1½
27⅞	19⅞	ClubMd	.20	.8	24	118	26⅛	25⅞	25⅞	+ ¼
20⅛	9⅞	Coachm	.40	2.0	44	503	u20¼	19⅞	20	.....
40	28	Coastl	s .40	1.2	9	1458	32⅞	32¼	32¾	+ ½
30	25½	Cstl	pf 2.11	7.6	..	122	27¾	27¾	27¾	+ ¼
110	66	CocaCl	3.12	3.1	18	3525	102	99⅜	100¼	− ¾
21½	13⅜	Coleco		..	4	536	17⅞	17½	17½	− ¼
40	26⅛	Colemn	1.20	3.0	27	95	39⅝	39¼	39½	+ ¼
39¼	23⅛	ColgPal	1.36	3.6	27	1257	38½	38	38⅛	.....
39⅞	18⅜	ColAlk	.80	2.1	13	324	38½	37⅞	38¼	.....
16⅝	11½	ColFds	.12	.8	17	1772	16⅛	15½	15⅞	− [illegible]

The Wall Street Journal, *April 14, 1986*

Stock Exchange in San Francisco rather than the closing price on the NYSE may be listed because trading ends later in San Francisco than in New York due to the time-zone difference.) Thus, on April 11, Anheuser-Busch stock traded as high as 48⅜ and as low as 47⅝ before closing at 48.

The last column provides the change in the closing price of the stock from the price at the close of the previous day. You can see that this stock closed on April 11 at a price 25 cents higher than the previous closing price.

Shares of other, usually smaller, companies than those traded on the NYSE are traded on the *American Stock Exchange (AMEX).* Information on that exchange is published by *The Wall Street Journal* in a form identical

	52 Weeks High	Low	Stock	Div.	Yld %	P-E Ratio	Sales 100s	High	Low	Close	Net Chg.
	31	18	Anlog		..	38	120	29⅜	29	29¼	+ ⅜
	30¼	20⅝	Anchor	1.48	5.0	129	145	30	29½	29¾	.....
	61¼	35⅝	AnClay	.33j	..	33	795	57	56⅛	57	.....
	16½	9⅛	AndrGr	.21	1.4	17	80	15¾	15½	15½	− ⅛
	29⅝	20⅛	Angelic	.60	2.1	15	317	28½	28⅛	28½	+ ¼
Anheuser Busch →	49⅜	26⅜	Anheus	s.80	1.7	17	3200	48⅜	47⅝	48	+ ¼
	96½	56¾	Anheu	pf3.60	3.8	..	50	94¾	93½	94¾	+1¼
	25⅜	13½	Anixtr	.28	1.1	23	168	25	24½	25	+ ¼
	19⅛	10¼	Anthem	.04	.2	38	115	17¼	16⅝	16⅞	+ ⅝
	18	11	Anthny	.44b	2.7	16	55	16½	16⅜	16⅜	− ⅛

AMERICAN STOCK EXCHANGE COMPOSITE TRANSACTIONS

Friday, April 11, 1986

'Quotations include trades on the Midwest, Pacific, Philadelphia, Boston and Cincinnati stock exchanges and reported by the National Association of Securities Dealers and Instinet

52 Weeks High	Low	Stock	Div.	Yld %	P-E Ratio	Sales 100s	High	Low	Close	Net Chg.
32¾	23⅝	FltGE pf	4	12.	..	11	u34¼	33	34¼	+1½
61½	36⅝	FlaRck	.90	1.7	11	7	53⅝	53¼	53⅝	+ ⅛
30⅞	21	Fluke	1.14t	4.4	15	39	26	25½	26	+ ½
16⅞	9¼	Foodrm		..	8	26	16⅞	16½	16½	− ¼
9⅝	7	FooteM		..	..	13	8⅝	8⅝	8⅝	− ⅛
33⅛	28⅛	Foote pf		..	..	6	30¾	30⅜	30½	+ ½
9¼	5⅛	FthillG		..	..	202	6¾	6⅝	6⅝	− ⅛
141½	91¼	FordCn	g12e	..	..	z340	128½	126	126	−1½
39⅜	17⅝	ForestL		..	38	250	38½	37⅝	38	+ ⅛
2	15-16	Fotomt		..	..	84	1⅛	1	1	− ⅛
54	33¾	Frantz	1	2.3	..	4	43⅞	43⅞	43⅞	+ ⅜
8⅝	5⅜	FrdHly		..	96	28	8⅝	8⅜	8⅝	+ ⅜
30¼	19½	FreqEl		..	20	98	30¼	29¾	30	− ¼
10⅛	7⅝	Friedm	.28b	2.9	14	8	9½	9½	9½	.....
11	4¾	FriesE s		..	18	150	10⅛	9⅝	9⅝	− ¼
33⅛	20	Frischs	.22b	.7	43	1	32	32	32	− ¼
13⅜	5¾	FurVlt s	.20	1.9	28	47	10¾	10⅝	10⅝	.....
		− G−G−G −								
6	4	GRI		..	..	14	5⅝	5½	5½	.....
3½	1¾	GTI		..	..	7	2½	2⅜	2⅜	− ⅛
16½	10¼	GalaxC		..	14	55	15⅝	15¼	15⅝	+ ⅛
2¾	½	GalxyO		..	13	87	⅞	¾	¾	− ⅛
30¼	22⅝	Garan	.60	2.4	20	2	25⅛	25⅛	25⅛	.....
12½	5¼	GatLit		..	..	42	6⅞	6½	6⅝	− ⅛
15	11	GelmS		..	45	3	13⅝	13⅝	13⅝	− ⅛
4	15-16	Gemco		..	..	46	1⅜	1¼	1¼	− ⅛
18¼	11½	GDefns	.88	5.9	11	384	15⅛	15	15	.....
19⅛	13⅜	GnMicr	.10b	.7	15	2	15⅜	15⅜	15⅜	.....
7⅛	3⅞	Genisco		..	81	7	6⅝	6½	6½	− ⅛
14⅜	9⅛	GenvDr	.20	1.6	17	19	12¾	12½	12¾	− ¼
14⅞	10¾	GeoRes		..	7	2	14½	14⅜	14⅜	− ¼
12⅞	10	GeoRs pf	1	8.2	..	4	12⅛	12	12⅛	+ ⅛
26⅞	18⅜	GianF s	.50	1.9	14	318	26½	26⅛	26⅜	.....
20	9	GntYl	g.25e	1.6	..	120	16¼	15½	16⅛	+ ½
48¼	30½	Glatflt	1	2.1	15	28	47¾	47⅛	47⅝	− ⅛
36⅜	26½	Glnmr	1b	3.2	30	27	32	31½	31½	− ⅜
4⅛	2¾	GlobNR		..	35	9	3⅛	3	3⅛	.....
5⅝	3	GoldW		..	..	466	5	4⅞	5	.....
1⅛	½	GldFld		..	..	126	⅝	9-16	9-16	.....
24¼	17½	GorRp s	.80	3.5	16	4	23¼	23	23	.....
31⅝	23⅛	GouldT	2.87t	9.2	11	36	31¼	31¼	31¼	+ ¼
12¾	6¾	Graham		..	..	2	9⅝	9⅝	9⅝	− ⅛
9⅜	2¼	GrahMc	1.10e	44.	31	157	2⅝	2¼	2½	+ ⅛
22⅞	16½	GrndAu	.40	2.1	14	81	19⅜	18¾	19⅛	.....
10⅝	7¾	Grant		..	28	70	9⅜	9¼	9¼	− ⅛
14⅛	8⅞	GrTech		..	15	22	10⅜	10⅛	10⅛	.....
44¼	32¾	GrtLkC	.52	1.3	21	1241	40	37¾	39¾	+2⅛
36	19½	Greenm		..	18	44	30⅛	29⅝	29⅝	− ¼
15	8⅞	Greiner	.98t	7.1	13	9	13⅞	13¾	13¾	− ¼
14⅞	9¼	GrdCh	.50b	3.6	13	13	14	13⅞	14	.....
12⅜	10¼	GlfCda	n.52	..	..	179	11¾	11⅝	11⅝	− ⅛
5⅛	2½	MrthOf		..	..	8	4¾	4⅝	4⅝	.....
24⅝	8⅝	MarkIV		..	20	38	24⅜	23⅝	23⅝	− ⅜
23	21⅜	Marm	pf2.35	11.	..	8	22¼	22⅛	22⅛	− ⅛
83	25⅛	MartPr	.05e	.1	36	15	53¼	52¾	53¼	+ ⅛
37¾	15½	Masind	.20a	.5	10	73	u38¼	37⅛	38¼	+1
6¾	4¾	Matec		..	20	12	5⅝	5¼	5⅝	.....
17¾	9⅝	MatRsh	.12	1.0	138	431	12½	11⅞	12⅜	+ ¾
22¼	13	MatSci		..	10	59	19⅞	19⅝	19⅝	− ⅛
26⅝	15½	Matrix s		..	22	448	21⅛	20⅞	21	+ ⅛
16⅜	3¾	MayEng	.40	10.	..	34	4	3⅞	3⅞	− ⅛
27½	18¼	Mayflw	.80	3.0	14	45	26⅝	26⅛	26⅝	+ ⅜
6⅜	3¼	McDow		3.2	..	1	4⅛	4⅛	4⅛	− ⅛
11½	4⅜	McFad		..	8	66	5	4⅞	5	+ ⅛
92¼	72	Media	1.16	1.3	20	19	92	91¼	92	+ ¾
18⅞	10⅝	Mediq s	.16	1.0	18	188	15⅞	15⅛	15¼	− ⅝
16⅜	6½	MercSL	.30r	2.1	6	53	14⅜	13⅞	14⅛	.....
25⅜	13½	MetPro	.15	1.0	18	15	14⅜	14¼	14⅜	+ ¼
20½	11	Metex s		..	10	2	14½	14½	14½	.....
6⅞	3¼	MchGn		..	8	123	4½	4⅜	4½	+ ⅛
12	8⅛	MidAm	.20	2.3	30	2	8⅞	8⅞	8⅞	.....
34⅜	23½	Midlnd	.40	1.2	19	2	33½	33¼	33½	.....
57	42	MinP pf	5	8.8	..	z375	57	55½	57	+1¼
9½	7⅛	MissnW	.28	3.1	54	6	9⅛	8⅞	9⅛	.....
15¾	9⅛	MtchlE	.24	2.2	11	1370	10¾	10⅜	10¾	+ ¼
23⅛	9¾	MonMg	.60a	2.5	14	18	u23¾	23¼	23¾	+ ¾
52½	36	MonP	pf4.50	9.2	..	z10	49	49	49	.....
20⅜	14¼	MoogB	.20	1.1	16	10	18¼	18⅛	18⅛	− ⅜
20½	13⅞	MoogA	.28	1.5	16	62	18½	18	18¼	− ⅛
24¼	15¾	MMed n		..	15	27	22	21¾	21¾	− ⅛
4⅜	1½	MtgRt wt		..	..	90	3⅝	3⅜	3⅜	− ⅜
20¼	16⅜	MtgGth	1.60	8.1	13	47	20	19¾	19⅞	+ ⅛
10	8	MtgPl n	1	10.	..	73	9⅝	9⅜	9⅝	+ ⅛
2¼	1⅛	Mortrn		..	..	76	1⅜	1¼	1⅜	+ ⅛
5-16	⅛	Mortr rt		..	..	35	7-32	3-16	7-32	.....
12⅛	7⅞	Motts	.05l	..	..	5	9⅞	9⅞	9⅞	.....
8⅜	3⅞	MtMed			17	33	7	6⅞	6⅞	− ⅛
9⅝	6⅜	MovieL		..	..	3	7⅛	7	7⅛	.....
3⅞	1	Murpln		..	..	1	1⅝	1⅝	1⅝	− ⅛
		− N−N−N −								
17	3½	NRM n	.80	17.	..	109	4¾	4⅝	4⅝	− ⅛
20⅜	10⅞	NRM	pf2.60	19.	..	35	13¾	13⅛	13¾	+ ⅝
12⅞	7¼	Nantck		..	16	69	12½	12⅛	12½	+ ⅜
14¾	9¼	NtGsO	.40b	4.1	12	1	9⅞	9⅞	9⅞	+ ⅛
26½	12⅞	NtPatnt	.10	.5	..	328	22	21⅛	21⅞	− ⅛
23⅞	15⅞	NMxAr		..	34	10	21⅝	21⅝	21⅝	− ⅛
13	10	NPlnR s	.74	5.9	16	66	12½	12½	12½	− ⅛
29¾	17	NProc	1.38e	5.1	13	83	27⅛	26⅞	27⅛	+ ⅛
19¼	5	NWldP s		..	41	423	18⅞	16¼	18⅜	+2⅜
66½	37¾	NYTimes	.60	1.0	21	833	62½	61	61¼	−1
6⅛	3⅜	NewbE	.25r	5.7	11	3	4⅜	4¼	4⅜	.....
14⅝	9⅛	Newcor	.32	2.6	..	18	12⅛	11⅝	12⅛	+ ½

The Wall Street Journal, *April 14, 1986*

to the information on the NYSE, as you can see from the April 11, 1986, listing, published in the April 14, 1986, *Journal,* which is reprinted on page 205.

Over-the-counter (OTC) stocks, issued by even smaller or newer companies, are not traded on an exchange. Instead, dealers make a market for them with a computer network referred to as *NASDAQ,* which is an acronym for the National Association of Securities Dealers Automated Quotation system. As of April 11, 1986, most of these stocks were quoted in NASDAQ's **National Market Issues** in a fashion similar to the listings of the New York and American Exchanges. Take a look at the reprint, using *Crown Books* as an example.

NASDAQ OVER-THE-COUNTER MARKETS

NATIONAL MARKET ISSUES

4:00 p.m. Eastern Time Prices

Friday, April 11, 1986

Crown Books →

365-Day High	365-Day Low	Stock	Sales (hds)	High	Low	Last	Net Chg.
6⅛	3¼	ConsmrFin .30	5	4⅜	4⅜	4⅜	− ½
36¼	25	ConsumW 1.60	91	35½	35	35¼	...
64¾	31½	CntlBcrp 2.04g	91	64½	64	64	− ¾
26¾	9½	ContlGnIns .30	85	25	23⅞	25	+ ¾
16⅝	8¼	ContlHlth Affil	38	8⅞	8½	8½	− ¼
8⅞	3¼	Contl Hlthcare	131	8¾	8¾	8¾	...
31½	9	Continuum .08	84	10	9½	9⅞	+ ⅛
11¼	4	Control Laser	80	8¾	8⅝	8¾	...
13¼	5¾	ContrlResin s	220	12¼	11¼	11¾	− ½
15¾	6½	ConvFood Mrt	48	13¼	12¾	13	− ¼
14	4⅞	Convergnt Tec	1252	10	9¾	9⅞	+ ¼
18	11¾	Converse Inc	35	16	15¾	15⅞	− ⅛
4	15-16	Cooper Biomd	3122	2⅛	1 15-16	2 1-16	+ ⅛
6⅛	2⅝	Cooper Laser	617	4 15-16	4¾	4¾	...
25¾	17	Co-opBnk .15f	58	25	24¾	25	+ ⅜
27⅞	14¾	CoorsCo B .50	938	26⅛	25⅞	25⅞	− ⅛
20	5½	Copytele Inc	611	7⅞	7⅛	7⅞	+ ⅜
8½	6	Corcom Inc	257	7¾	7¼	7¾	+ ½
12½	8⅛	Cordis Corprn	630	11⅛	10¾	11	+ ¼
44⅛	19⅝	CoreStFin 1.24	1232	41¾	41⅜	41⅜	− ⅜
3⅛	1¼	Corvus Systm	3977	2⅝	2 3-16	2 7-16	− 1-16
5⅞	2¾	Cosmo Comm	220	2⅞	2¾	2⅞	+ ⅛
17⅝	11⅜	Costco Whol	269	13⅞	13⅝	13⅞	+ ⅛
19⅝	5⅝	CottonSLf .24	3	(z)	(z)	(z)	...
29	22½	CourierCp .60	103	29	28⅛	28½	+ ¾
6⅝	4	Courier Dspch	7	5	4⅝	4⅝	− ⅜
(H)	19¼	Cousins Pr .40	160	30½	28½	30	+ 1¼
2⅛	7-16	Covingtn Tech	307	1 7-16	1 5-16	1 5-16	− 1-16
8	3⅝	CP Rehab Cp	635	4½	4¼	4⅜	− ⅛
30¾	14¾	CPI Corp .05d	520	28¼	27¾	28¼	+ ¼
7⅛	4¾	C P T Corp	1101	5⅛	4⅞	5	− ⅛
(H)	10¼	CrackerBrl .14	191	20½	19¾	20¼	...
10⅞	8½	Craftmtc Cntr	569	9⅛	9	9⅛	+ ⅛
10⅜	5	Cramer Inc	25	6¼	6¼	6¼	− ⅜
30¼	5⅜	Crazy Eddie	580	29⅛	28½	29	+ ⅜
29⅝	12⅜	Cronus Indust	282	29¼	29	29¼	+ ⅛
24⅜	11¾	CrossLand Sv	2499	24⅛	23½	24	+ ¼
29	20⅞	Cross Trck .80	3145	25	22⅞	23¾	− 1⅛
11	6⅝	Crown Ander	138	9¾	9⅝	9¾	+ ⅛
4½	3¼	Crown Auto	43	4	3¾	3¾	+ ¼
17	9⅛	Crown Books	69	15¾	15	15	− ¼
25¼	8½	Crump Cos .25	141	24¼	24	24¼	...
14⅝	6⅜	C S P Incorp	112	12⅜	11⅞	11⅞	− ½
24⅝	15⅞	Cullen Frst .94	258	17	16¾	17	+ ¼
23½	11⅜	Cullum .50	679	23½	23¼	23¼	...
11¾	6⅛	Culp Inc .08	513	11	10½	11	...
8⅞	4¾	Cybertek Cmp	285	8⅝	8⅜	8⅝	+ ¼
27¼	19	Cycare Systm	23	26½	25¾	25¾	− ¾
24¼	11	Cyprus Minrl	280	22¼	22	22¼	+ ¼
3½	1	Cyprss Svg wt	50	2⅝	2⅝	2⅝	...
(H)	60	Fst of A pfD	12	84½	83¼	84½	+ 3
13½	7⅝	FABk&T A.40	423	11	10¾	11	+ ¼
22½	6⅜	FstAmFdSL s	51	19¼	18	18	− 1
56	25½	FstAmFnc .80	128	55½	54¾	54¾	− 1¼
30½	17	Fst A Tenn .94	574	28	27⅝	27⅞	+ ¼
47	24¾	FstBOh 1.50	25	47	45½	47	+ 1½
(H)	26	FstCapitl 1.50	9	53¼	52	53¼	+ 1¼
25¼	8¾	FsColnBsA .50	53	24¾	24½	24½	+ ⅛
30	13	FstColum Fcl	21	26½	25	25	...
6¾	4½	FstComrc Bcp	41	6¼	6⅛	6¼	− ½
29¼	18⅛	FstComrc 1.20	222	21¼	20½	20¾	+ ⅛
24¼	17½	FstComrcl .72	11	24	23¾	23¾	− ¼
8¾	5	FstContRE 1b	26	5⅞	5¾	5⅞	+ ⅛
55¾	31	Fst Eastn 1.50	1	52½	52½	52½	...
91	44¼	FstEmpir 1.40	7	85	85	85	− 1
(H)	11	Fst Executive	2258	26⅛	25½	26	+ ¼
28¼	24	FstExec pfF	21	28⅛	27⅞	28⅛	...
20	16	Fst Family	51	18¼	17¾	17¾	...
24½	12¾	FstFBkNH .40	46	23⅞	23⅞	23⅞	+ ⅜
15	6⅝	FFSBMon s.32	61	15	14½	15	+ ½
19	7⅞	FFSL Ch s.10f	213	18	17¼	17½	+ ¼
27¾	10⅛	FFSL FM s.40	282	27	26¼	27	+ 1
22⅛	7⅞	FFSL Kal .06d	35	20⅞	20⅝	20¾	− ⅛
28¼	13½	FFedSv Mad	41	26¾	26¼	26¼	− ½
16⅝	6⅛	FFedSLSC 10l	166	16	15½	16	+ ¼
27⅛	9⅜	Fst Fed Mich	4244	26⅜	25¾	26⅜	+ ½
30¾	7¼	FstFdSvB Cal	166	30½	30	30¼	− ¼
16¼	7⅛	FFSL Brk .16	7	16	15¼	16	...
21½	9	FstFinclCp .40	22	20¼	19¾	19¾	− ½
27¾	16¼	FstFncl Mngt	7	25¼	25¼	25¼	− ½
34¾	22	FstFlaBks .44	42	32¼	32	32¼	+ ⅛
42½	28½	FstHawai 1.60	48	41¼	40¼	41¼	+ ¼
19½	5¼	FstIllinois s.60	89	18½	18¼	18½	...
25¾	12¼	FstInd FSB s	106	25¼	24¾	24¾	− ½
18¾	10½	FstICAlsk 10k	21	11¾	11¼	11¼	− ½
3¾	2 1-16	F Intst Iowa	471	2 15-16	2¾	2⅞	+ ⅛
36¼	21¼	FstIntWis 1.08	26	36	34¾	35¾	+ ¼
47¾	29¾	FstJersNt 1.80	104	46¾	46⅜	46⅝	+ ⅛
41½	26¾	FstKyNt 1.14	11	41¼	40½	40½	− ¼
23	9⅜	Fst Liberty F	22	23	22½	22½	− ½
33	15½	1stMdBc s.88	30	30⅜	30⅜	30⅜	+ ¼
22⅛	10⅝	FMichBk .60g	29	20¾	20¼	20⅝	...
32	16⅞	FMdwstB 1.20	7	30	30	30	...
5½	2	FMidwst .60t	2	2¼	2¼	2¼	+ ¼
34½	24½	FstMutl Savg	213	31¼	28¾	31¼	+ 2¾
8⅝	5⅛	FstMutl SvB	12	7¼	7	7	− ¼
40½	26	FstBcGa .64	12	40	40	40	+ ⅜
44½	27½	FstNtlCin 1.48	9	44¼	43¾	44¼	+ [illegible]
1⅞	1¼	FstNatl Ohio	4	1⅜	1⅜	1⅜	...
31¼	14	FstNHBk .60g	16	28½	28¼	28½	[illegible]

The Wall Street Journal, *April 14, 1986*

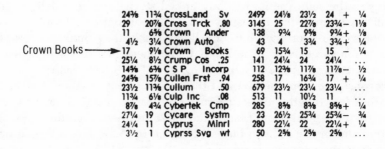

	24⅜	11¾	CrossLand Sv	2499	24⅛	23½	24	+ ¼
	29	20⅞	Cross Trck .80	3145	25	22⅞	23¾	− 1⅛
	11	6⅝	Crown Ander	138	9¾	9⅝	9¾	+ ⅛
	4½	3¼	Crown Auto	43	4	3¾	3¾	+ ¼
Crown Books ——►	17	9⅛	Crown Books	69	15¾	15	15	− ¼
	25¼	8½	Crump Cos .25	141	24¼	24	24¼	...
	14⅝	6⅜	C S P Incorp	112	12⅜	11⅞	11⅞	− ½
	24⅝	15⅞	Cullen Frst .94	258	17	16¾	17	+ ¼
	23½	11⅜	Cullum .50	679	23½	23¼	23¼	...
	11¾	6⅛	Culp Inc .08	513	11	10½	11	...
	8⅞	4¾	Cybertek Cmp	285	8⅝	8⅜	8⅝	+ ¼
	27¼	19	Cycare Systm	23	26½	25¾	25¾	− ¾
	24¼	11	Cyprus Minrl	280	22¼	22	22¼	+ ¼
	3½	1	Cyprss Svg wt	50	2⅝	2⅝	2⅝	...

365 High	365 Low		Sales (hds)	High	Low	Last	Net Chg.
17	9⅛	Crown Books	69	15¾	15	15	−¼

The first two columns give the high and low prices (offered by buyers) for the past year. The column after the company name lists sales in hundreds, informing you that 6,900 shares of Crown Books were traded on April 11, 1986.

The next three columns provide the high (15¾), low (15), and last (15) prices of the day, and the final column tells you that Crown Books' stock closed 25 cents lower than its price at the previous close.

The remainder of the over-the-counter stocks are quoted currently with bid and asked prices (although all OTC stocks will eventually be quoted with closing prices).

With this information, you can track the performance of any share of stock traded on the New York or American exchanges or the OTC market. If you are confident a stock will increase in value, you may purchase it and realize your gain if your prediction proves true. Yet there are a number of ways you can "leverage" your purchase in order to increase your gain. That is, you can capture the increase on a larger number of shares of stock than you can currently afford to purchase. Your *leverage* is the ratio between the value of shares you control and the amount of capital (money) you have invested. The smaller your investment, and the larger the value of the shares you control, the greater your leverage.

For instance, under current regulations set by the Fed you may borrow from your broker up to half the initial value of the shares of stock you purchase, which provides leverage of two to one. It's called *buying on margin.* If you buy $200 worth of stock from your broker, with a margin of $100 and a $100 loan from the broker, and the stock doubles in value (from $200 to $400), you have made $200 on a $100 investment (less interest cost) instead of $100 on a $100 investment. That's leverage.

Options provide another opportunity to leverage your investment. They give you the right (option) to buy or sell stock for future delivery at a small premium (what it costs you to buy the option). People do this for the same reason they buy or sell any stock: they think it's going up or down in value. Only in this case, they believe the stock will be higher or lower than the price at which they agreed to buy or sell it.

For instance, suppose you had the option to buy a share of stock for $25 in a few months' time that currently trades at 23½, and you were convinced the stock would be trading at 28 by then. Wouldn't you offer a premium for the right to buy a $28 stock for $25? That's a good deal, as long as the premium is smaller than the spread between $25 and the $28 price at which you think the stock will trade.

Conversely, if you were convinced that a stock, currently trading at 23½, would fall to $18, wouldn't you pay a fee (premium) for the right to sell it at $20, knowing you could obtain it at $18?

Look at the daily **Listed Options Quotations** from the April 14 *Journal* on pages 209 and 210 in order to see how it works. (Use front-page index to find this listing.) This excerpt uses MCI as an example.

Column 1 informs you that MCI closed at $11.25 (11⅛) on April 11, 1986.

Column 2 lists the prices ($10, $12.50, and $15) at which you have the option of buying or selling the stock in the future. Note that some prices are higher and some are lower than the current price (11⅛). Think of the *strike price* as the price at which you strike a deal.

Columns 3, 4, and 5 list the premium you must pay per share to buy the option to *call* (buy) MCI stock at the applicable strike price by the third Friday of the months listed (April, July, October). Take April as an example. On April 11, 1986, you had to pay a premium of 6¼ cents (¹⁄₁₆ of a dollar) for the right (option) to buy a share of MCI stock at $12.50 (12½) by the close of trading on April 18, 1986 (third Friday of April). Once the deal was struck, the seller (writer) of the option would be bound to deliver the stock to you at that price at any time before April 18, *at your option*.

Why would you buy such a contract? Only because you were convinced that MCI would trade at more than $12.5625 (strike price of $12.50 plus premium of $0.0625) at any time before the third Friday in April. Then you would have an option to buy it at $12.50 (the strike price) from the option writer and sell it at the higher market price. When a call exceeds the strike price, it is said to be *in the money*.

Trading is done in round lots of 100 shares. Suppose your forecast is correct, and MCI trades at $14 by April 18. You paid a $6.25 premium (100 × $0.0625) to buy the option to call 100 shares at $12.50 a share. You now exercise your option and acquire 100 shares for $1,250 (100 × $12.50). Those shares are worth $1,400 (100 × $14) on the market. Thus, you've obtained $1,400 of securities for $1,250, less your premium of $6.25, for a net gain of $143.75 on your $6.25 investment. That's leverage.

You've probably noticed that the $10 strike price is already "in the money"—that is, below the market price. You might think you should buy those options now and make a killing today. Why not exercise the option to buy the stock below market value and sell it immediately at

LISTED OPTIONS QUOTATIONS

Friday, April 11, 1986

Closing prices of all options. Sales unit usually is 100 shares. Security description includes exercise price. Stock close is New York or American exchange final price.

MCI

Option & NY Close	Strike Price	Calls Last Apr	Jul	Oct	Puts Last Apr	Jul	Oct
M C I	.. 10	1 3-16	1 9-16	2¼	r	r	½
11⅛	. 12½	1-16	⅝	1 3-16	1⅜	1⅝	r
11⅛	... 15	r	3-16	9-16	r	r	3⅞
Merck	..115	52½	r	s	r	r	s
166⅛	. 120	47½	r	s	r	r	s
166⅛	. 130	37	r	r	r	r	r
166⅛	. 140	26¾	r	r	r	r	r
166⅛	. 145	22	r	r	r	r	r
166⅛	. 150	16¾	22	26	r	3	r
166⅛	. 155	r	r	r	¼	4½	7
166⅛	. 160	7⅞	15	r	¾	6	r
166⅛	. 165	3⅞	11¾	r	1½	r	r
166⅛	. 170	1¼	9½	15	5¼	10¾	r
166⅛	. 175	9-16	8¼	r	r	r	r
166⅛	. 180	r	6¼	10¾	r	r	r
Midcon	49⅞	8¼	r	s	r	r	s
..	..... 54⅞	3¾	r	s	½	r	s
..	..... 69⅞	r	r	s	12¼	r	s
Monsan	.. 50	12¼	r	r	r	r	¾
62⅜	... 55	7	r	r	1-16	r	r
62⅜	... 60	2¼	4⅞	7	⅜	3¼	3
62⅜	... 65	⅜	2½	r	r	r	r
62⅜	... 70	⅛	r	r	r	r	r
N W A	.. 45	7	r	9½	1-16	r	r
51¾	... 50	2¼	4⅝	5¾	¼	r	r
51¾	... 55	¼	2⅜	r	r	5	r
51¾	... 60	r	1⅛	s	r	r	s
PaineW	.. 30	7¾	r	r	r	r	r
37¾	... 35	3⅜	5	6	1-16	1¼	1⅜
37¾	... 40	¼	2½	3⅞	2¼	3½	r
37¾	... 45	1-16	1⅛	2½	6¼	r	r
Pennz	... 40	r	r	s	r	¾	s
50¾	... 45	10	11½	13¾	⅜	1 9-16	2¼
50¾	... 50	5	6¼	7	1½	4	3¼
50¾	... 55	½	4	4¾	1½	5½	5¾
50¾	... 60	¼	2¼	5⅜	9¾	8	r
50¾	... 65	3-16	1½	3	10⅛	r	r
50¾	... 70	1-16	⅞	2½	15⅝	19⅛	r
50¾	... 75	1-16	⅞	r	24	r	22
50¾	... 80	1-16	½	s	r	r	s
50¾	... 85	r	½	s	r	r	s
Pnnz o	... 60	9⅛	s	s	r	s	s
Squibb	... 85	12	r	r	r	r	r
96¾	... 90	7	r	r	r	2½	r
96¾	... 95	2½	7	r	⅝	4¾	6½
96¾	.. 100	9-16	4½	6½	r	r	r
96¾	.. 105	s	2⅞	5	s	10	r
Tandem	25	r	r	r	r	2⅜	r
Uplohn	105	55	s	s	r	s	s
160½	. 115	44½	r	s	r	r	s
160½	. 125	r	38½	r	r	r	r
160½	. 130	r	r	r	r	1	r
160½	. 135	r	r	r	r	1 1-16	r
160½	. 140	19¾	25½	r	r	1½	r
160½	. 145	15¼	21½	r	¼	r	r
160½	. 150	10	17	22½	¼	r	6½
160½	. 155	6½	r	r	¾	r	r
160½	. 160	2½	12	17	2	8¾	10
160½	. 165	1½	r	r	r	r	r
160½	. 170	⅜	7¼	r	r	15	r
160½	. 175	r	6½	r	r	r	r
Weyerh	.. 30	7½	r	r	r	⅛	r
37½	... 35	2⅞	3¾	4¾	1-16	r	r
37½	... 40	1-16	1¾	2¼	r	r	r

Option & NY Close	Strike Price	Calls - Last May	Aug	Nov	Puts - Last May	Aug	Nov
46	 40	6⅛	7⅞	8¼	5-16	1	1½
46	 45	2⅝	4⅛	5⅜	1 15-16	3⅛	3¾
Rockwl	.. 35	11¾	r	r	r	r	r
46⅝	... 40	7⅛	7½	8½	⅛	r	r
46⅝	... 45	2⅞	4½	5¾	1¼	2⅜	3¼
46⅝	... 50	1	2½	r	4½	r	r
Safewy	.. 35	2⅞	3⅜	r	⅜	1	r
36⅞	... 40	½	1 5-16	1¾	r	r	r
Slumb	.. 25	r	r	8	1-16	r	r
31½	... 30	2⅛	3⅜	4½	⅜	1 3-16	1 7-16
31½	.. 35	¼	1	1 13-16	3¾	r	4
31½	... 40	⅛	r	s	r	r	s
Skylin	.. 15	3¼	r	r	r	r	r
18½	. 17½	2	2⅝	r	r	r	r
18½	... 20	½	1¼	r	r	r	r
Southn	.. 20	r	r	r	r	⅛	r
23¾	. 22½	1¼	1½	r	r	r	r
23¾	... 25	3-16	7-16	¾	r	r	r
Tidewt	17½	r	1-16	s	r	r	s
U A L	... 45	r	r	s	r	9-16	s
56⅛	... 50	7	r	r	r	r	r
56⅛	... 55	3½	5¼	r	2 1-16	3¾	r
56⅛	... 60	1¼	3½	5	r	6	r
56⅛	... 65	⅜	1¾	r	r	r	r
U Tech	.. 45	r	8½	s	3-16	r	s
51¾	... 50	3¼	5⅜	r	⅞	r	r
51¾	... 55	13-16	2 11-16	r	r	4⅞	r
51¾	... 60	5-16	1¼	r	r	r	r
J Walt	.. 40	18	r	r	1-16	r	r
56½	... 45	r	13¼	r	r	r	r
56½	... 50	8	r	r	r	r	2
56½	... 55	3⅝	6¼	r	r	r	r
56½	... 60	1¾	r	r	r	r	r
WarnCm	30	12	r	s	r	r	s
42	 35	7¼	r	r	3-16	r	r
42	 40	3	5	6	11-16	1¾	r
42	 45	15-16	2¾	3½	r	r	r
Willms	.. 20	r	r	r	r	½	r
23⅝	. 22½	r	r	3½	r	1¼	r
23⅝	... 25	½	1¼	r	r	2¼	r
23⅝	... 30	r	¼	s	r	r	s
		Jun	Sep	Dec	Jun	Sep	Dec
AlldSt	... 30	r	s	s	1-16	s	s
38½	. 37½	2¾	r	r	r	r	r
38½	... 40	1 7-16	2½	r	2⅞	r	r
Apache	.. 10	r	⅝	r	r	r	r
BrisMy	.. 60	15¼	r	s	1-16	r	s
74½	... 65	11¼	12¾	r	5-16	r	r
74½	... 70	6⅝	8¼	10¼	1 1-16	2	r
74½	... 75	3⅝	6	7⅞	3	r	r
74½	... 80	2	4	5¼	5¾	r	r
Bruns	... 25	r	r	8¼	r	r	⅞
31¼	. 27½	4⅝	r	s	⅜	r	s
31¼	... 30	3	4⅝	5⅝	1	r	r
31¼	... 35	1 1-16	2½	2½	r	r	r
Celan	... 130	78	s	s	r	s	s
207	... 140	r	69	s	r	r	s
207	... 155	55	r	s	r	r	s
207	... 160	r	r	s	¼	r	s
207	... 170	r	r	s	¾	r	s
207	... 175	r	r	s	1	r	s
207	.. 180	31½	35⅞	s	r	r	s

The Wall Street Journal, *April 14, 1986*

r	Option &	Strike						
r	NY Close	Price	Calls Last			Puts Last		
r			Apr	Jul	Oct	Apr	Jul	Oct
1½	M C I	.. 10	1 3-16	1 9-16	2¼	r	r	½
r	11⅛	. 12½	1-16	⅝	1 3-16	1⅜	1⅝	r
r	11⅛	... 15	r	3-16	9-16	r	r	3⅞

MCI

(1)	(2)	(3)	(4)	(5)	(6)	(7)	(8)
Option & NY Close	Strike Price	Calls	Last		Puts		Last
		April	July	Oct	April	July	Oct
MCI	10	1$\frac{3}{16}$	1$\frac{9}{16}$	2¼	r	r	½
11⅛	12½	$\frac{1}{16}$	⅝	1$\frac{3}{16}$	1⅜	1⅝	r
11⅛	15	r	$\frac{3}{16}$	$\frac{9}{16}$	r	r	3⅞

the market price? Because the premium for all months exceeds the spread ($1.125) between the strike price ($10) and the current market price ($11.125). For instance, the April option to buy a call at $10 carries a premium of $1.1875 (1$\frac{3}{16}$), which when added to the strike price ($10 + $1.1875 = $11.1875) exceeds the current market price of $11.125. Clearly, no option writer (the person selling you the option to buy) would want to risk a loss by selling you the option to buy a stock at less than market value unless he or she can make up the difference in the premium you must pay for the option.

Thus, if you buy a call, you're speculating that the stock's price will rise sufficiently to earn you a return (spread) over and above the premium you must pay to buy the option. But suppose it doesn't? Suppose the stock rises only a little, or even falls in value, so that you have an option to buy a stock at a price greater than market value? For instance, you may have purchased the April option to call MCI at $12.50, and its market price may never rise over $12. What then? Would you have to buy the stock from the option writer at above market value? No, because you have only purchased an *option* to buy. There's no requirement to do so. You can let the option expire without exercising it, and you have only lost your premium of $6.25.

A rising market motivates investors to buy calls. They hope the price of *their* stock will shoot up and they will be able to exercise their option and recover their premium and then some. This does not necessarily mean that option writers (people who sell the option) are counting on the market to stay flat or even fall. The call writer may have decided to sell a stock if it reaches a certain target level—that is, take his or her gain after the stock rises a certain number of points. If it does rise, the call writer will receive the increment and the premium; and even if it doesn't, he or she will still receive the premium. Thus, income is the primary motive for writing the option. Instead of waiting for the stock to move up to the target level, the seller writes a call. If it doesn't move up to that price, he or she will still have earned the premium. If it does, he or she will get premium plus capital gain.

Returning to the option buyer, if you believed that MCI stock would fall to a value below the current price of 11⅛, you could purchase a *put* contract, and the option writer would have to buy the put at the strike price, regardless of current market value. Your option to sell at the strike price would give you an opportunity to buy at the lower market value (assuming your forecast was correct) and profit on the difference.

Columns 6, 7, and 8 provide the put contract premiums for April, July, and October. A strike price of 12½ is already in the money, so you could buy MCI at the current market price of 11⅛ and put (sell) it to the option writer for 12½ before the option expiration date. You would make $1.375 on each share of stock (12½ − 11⅛ = 1⅜ = $1.375). However, your premium (1⅜) would equal the spread, and when added to transactions cost (brokerage fee) would remove any incentive to buy the put.

But it would be a different story if MCI fell to 10 before the April expiration date and you held an April put. With an April put at 1⅜, your premium would be $137.50 (100 × $1.375). If MCI fell to $10, you could buy 100 shares at $1,000 (100 × $10) and sell them to the option writer for $1,250 (100 × $12.50) for a gain of $250, less the premium of $137.50. As long as the market price fell below its April 11 closing of 11⅛ you would stand to make a gain if you exercised your option to sell the put, because the difference between the strike price (12½) and the market price (11⅛) would exceed the premium cost (1⅜).

If the market rose, so that the market price exceeded the strike price, you wouldn't want to exercise your option to sell at a price below market. Instead, you would permit your option to expire without exercising it. Your loss would be only the premium you paid.

Why would someone write a put? Because he or she is prepared to buy a stock if it should drop to a particular price. As was the case with a call, the primary motive is income. The writer earns the premium whether or not the option is exercised. If the writer believes the stock will rise in price, then he has little concern that an option holder will put it to him at less than the market price. And he has collected the premium. But if the market does fall, and falls sufficiently that the contract comes in the money, he'll have to buy the stock at the contract price, which will be above market. That's not necessarily bad, since he had

INDEX OPTIONS

Friday, April 11, 1986

Chicago Board

S&P 100 INDEX

Strike Price	Calls–Last Apr	May	Jun	Puts–Last Apr	May	Jun
190	34⅝	....	....	....	1/16	....
195	29⅞	32	....	1/16	1/16	....
200	24¾	26	26⅝	1/16	¼	13/16
205	19½	20¼	22	1/16	9/16	1 7/16
210	14⅝	16	18¼	1/16	1	2 7/16
215	9⅝	11⅝	14¼	3/16	2⅛	3¾
220	5⅛	8½	10¾	13/16	3⅞	5⅞
225	1 15/16	5⅝	8⅛	2¾	6⅛	7⅞
230	9/16	3½	6	6½	9	10¾
235	⅛	2	4⅛	10¾	12¾	13½
240	1/16	1⅛	2⅞	15⅛	....	17

Total call volume 264,479 Total call open int. 828,451
Total put volume 183,850 Total put open int. 693,898
The index: High 227.15; Low 223.83; Close 224.58, −0.69

S&P 500 INDEX

Strike Price	Calls–Last Apr	May	Jun	Puts–Last Apr	May	Jun
230	....	....	13	....	....	....

Total call volume 2 Total call open int. 104
Total put volume 0 Total put open int. 98
The index: High 237.85; Low 235.13; Close 235.97, −0.47

S&P 500 INDEX (New)

Strike Price	Calls–Last Apr	May	Jun	Puts–Last Apr	May	Jun
230	7⅞	....	....	11/16	....	4⅝
235	2⅞	6⅜	8⅞	1¾	....	....
240	⅝	5	....	....	....	....
245	5/16	2 15/16	4⅝	....	....	....

Total call volume 1,357 Total call open int. 19,962
Total put volume 450 Total put open int. 662
The index: High 237.85; Low 235.13; Close 235.97, −0.47

S&P OTC 250 INDEX

Strike Price	Calls–Last Apr	May		Puts–Last Apr	May	
215	7¾	....	....	....	....	...

Total call volume 55 Total call open int. 30
Total put volume 0 Total put open int. 7
The index: High 223.34; Low 221.87; Close 223.11, +1.24

American Exchange

MAJOR MARKET INDEX

Strike Price	Calls–Last Apr	May	Jun	Puts–Last Apr	May	Jun
290	39½	....	....	....	....	....
295	....	....	....	....	7/16	....
300	30½	....	....	1/16	15/16	....
305	25¾	....	....	1/16	1½	2½
310	20	23	28½	⅛	2⅛	4½
315	16¼	21½	25½	5/16	2⅜	6⅜
320	11¼	15⅞	....	⅝	4½	7¼
325	7¼	12⅝	....	1 15/16	6½	9¼
330	4⅛	9¾	....	3⅞	9⅛	....
335	2⅛	7⅜	12	6⅝	11¾	....
340	⅞	5⅝	9⅞	10½	15	
345	7/16	4	8	15	..	
350	3/16	2¾	6½	....		Jun
355	1/16	2 1/16	6⅛		¾	....
360	1/16	1 5/16	4		....	....
				2½	....	....

Total call volume 45.… Total call open int. 964
Total put volum… Total put open int. 736
The index… …h 118.61; Low 116.84; Close 117.16, −0.04

OIL INDEX

Strike Price	Calls–Last Apr	May	Jun	Puts–Last Apr	May	Jun
115	....	....	....	....	¼	....
120	....	....	....	⅛	....	....
125	3½	5⅜	7½	½	....	....
130	1⅜	3⅜	....	2½	....	....
135	....	1⅝	....	....	....	....

Total call volume 101 Total call open int. 1,867
Total put volume 296 Total put open int. 3,190
The index: High 129.49; Low 128.26; Close 129.26, +0.89

AIRLINE INDEX

Strike Price	Calls–Last Apr	May	Jun	Puts–Last Apr	May	Jun
105	15	....	....	....	....	....
115	5⅝	....	....	....	....	....
120	....	2	....	....	....	....
125	....	1½	....	....	....	...

Total call volume 15 Total call open int. 116
Total put volume 0 Total put open int. 205
The index: High 121.31; Low 119.00; Close 120.94, +1.94

Philadelphia Exchange

GOLD/SILVER INDEX

Strike Price	Calls–Last Apr	May	Jun	Puts–Last Apr	May	Jun
65	....	....	....	....	11/16	1¾
70	....	....	6⅞	½	2	3¼
75	1¼	3⅛	....	2	4¾	5⅝
80	3/16	1½	2⅝	6⅞	7¼	8¾
85	1/16	7/16	1½	....	....	....
90	....	¼	....	....	....	....
95	1/16	....	....	....	....	....

Total call volume 586 Total call open int. 3,779
Total put volume 370 Total put open int. 2,785
The index: High 74.19; Low 72.24; Close 74.19, +1.95

VALUE LINE INDEX OPTIONS

Strike Price	Calls–Last Apr	May	Jun	Puts–Last Apr	May	Jun
200	....	....	35⅛	....	....	....
205	....	....	....	....	....	⅛
215	....	25	....	....	⅛	....
220	....	....	....	....	½	1¼
225	16½	....	17¾	1/16	1	....
230	9½	....	15	3/16	2	....
235	5¼	7⅞	....	1⅛	4⅛	....
240	1 9/16	5¼	8½	3¼	6⅜	....
245	⅜	3⅛	6¼	6	....	....
250	1/16	1¾	....	....	....	....
255	....	1	3⅛	....	....	....

Total call volume 3,058 Total call open int. 27,118
Total put volume 1,305 Total put open int. 23,385
The index: High 240.27; Low 238.62; Close 239.31, +0.04

NATIONAL O-T-C INDEX

Strike Price	Calls–Last Apr	May	Jun	Puts–Last Apr	May	Jun
205	22⅝	....	....	....	....	....
215	....	....	17⅝	....	....	....
225	4½	....	....	....	....	....
230	1⅞	....	....	3¾	....	....

Total call volume 9 Total call open int. 940
Total put volume 5 Total put open int. 1,120
The index: High 228.12; Low 226.23; Close 227.19, +0.96

N.Y. Stock Exchange

NYSE OPTIONS INDEX

Strike Price	Calls–Last Apr	May	Jun	Puts–Last Apr	May	Jun
125	11⅞	11⅝	....	....	⅜	....
130	6 5/16	7	8⅞	1/16		....
135	2	3⅞	5⅝	7′	3½	....
140	3/16	1⅞	3	..o	....	....
145	....	13/16	1 ¹′	4⅝	....	....
150	....	5/¹′	....	7	....	....
Total call v…		…¼	....	....	....	....
Total …		....	....	....	....	....
T…	1/16	....	....	....	....	....
…	....	11/16	....	....	....	....

Total call volume 976. Total call open int. 21,858.
Total put volume 1,623. Total put open int. 9,893.
The index: High 274.32; Low 271.56; Close 272.44, −0.42

Pacific Exchange

TECHNOLOGY INDEX

Strike Price	Calls–Last Apr	May	Jun	Puts–Last Apr	May	Jun
110	8⅝	....	....	....	....	....
115	4¼	5⅞	....	½	....	....
120	1¼	3¼	....	2⅛	....	4⅝
125	⅛	1⅝	....	....	....	....

Total call volume 208 Total call open int. 1,323
Total put volume 44 Total put open int. 560
The index: High 119.15; Low 117.54; Close 118.35, +0.81

NASD

NASDAQ 100 INDEX

Strike Price	Calls–Last Apr	May		Puts–Last Apr	May	
275	32½	....	....	....	....	....
285	21	....	....	....	....	....
290	15½	19¾	....	....	....	....
295	11½	....	....	½	....	....
300	7	13¼	....	1	3¼	....
305	3¾	9⅞	....	3	....	....

Total call volume 611. Total call open int. 923.
Total put volume 277. Total put open int. 687.
The index: High 307.10; Low 303.48; Close 305.33, +1.?3

The Wall Street Journal, *April 14, 1986*

already planned to buy the stock if it fell to the strike price, and he has collected a premium, too.

One last point. Put and call premiums will rise and fall with the market value of the stock. Therefore, even if your option comes in the money, you need not exercise it, because you will be able to sell it on the market and make a gain without buying or selling the underlying stock.

Finally, buying *index options* is another way to invest (or speculate) in the entire market. Instead of buying all the stocks in one of the stock market averages, you can buy a put or call on an index option (such as the *S & P* 100), just as you can invest in options on individual stocks.

The excerpt from the April 14, 1986 *Journal* presents a summary of options trading on April 11, 1986 (see page 212). This report appears daily and you can find it listed in the front-page index.

Many of these possibilities sound intriguing, easy, and potentially profitable. However, in the first place, there are substantial commission costs. Furthermore, as in any leveraged situation, the potential for considerable losses exists. Options are not for greenhorns, and even buying on margin exposes you to up to twice the risk of simply buying a stock with your own money. With leverage you can move a big rock with a small stick, but the stick can also break off in your hands.

If you don't like the risk of index options, you can diversify your portfolio of investments by buying shares in a mutual fund, which will pool the capital of many investors and purchase stocks, bonds or other investments. In a way, you are combining your funds with other people's and retaining the services of professionals to manage your money.

The number of mutual funds has grown rapidly, and you can choose funds with a variety of investment objectives. As you can see from the April 14, 1986, daily *Journal* **Mutual Funds** listing (see front-page index), some companies offer many funds, each with its own special objective (see page 214).

Excerpt from page 214 ⟶

Lehman	Group:	....
Captl	19.38	N.L.+ .23
Invst	19.87	N.L.+ .28
Opprt	27.34	N.L.+ .23
Leverage	8.68	N.L.+ .05

Take an example from the **Lehman Group:**

	NAV	Offer Price	NAV Chg.
Lehman Group:			
Captl	19.38	N.L.	+.23

MUTUAL FUNDS

Friday, April 11, 1986

Price ranges for investment companies, as quoted by the National Association of Securities Dealers. NAV stands for net asset value per share; the offering includes net asset value plus maximum sales charge, if any.

(Column headings for each listing: NAV | Offer Price | NAV Chg.)

Fund	NAV	Offer Price	Chg.
AARP Invest Program:			
Cap Grw	22.30	N.L.+	.01
Gen Bnd	16.17	N.L.-	.03
Ginnie M	16.16	N.L.	...
Gro Inc	21.54	N.L.-	.01
TxFr Bd	16.26	N.L.+	.04
TxF Shrt	15.49	N.L.-	.01
ABT Midwest Funds:			
Emrg Gr	18.50	20.22+	.02
Growth I	13.40	14.64-	.02
Int Govt	10.82	N.L.	...
LG Govt	10.90	11.35-	.02
Sec Inc	11.02	12.04+	.01
Util Inc	15.14	16.55-	.01
Acorn Fnd	40.38	N.L.+	.04
Adtek Fd	12.10	N.L.	
Advest Advantage:			
Govt	10.12	N.L.+	.01
Growth	10.67	N.L.+	.01
Income	10.42	N.L.	
Specl	10.29	N.L.-	.05
Afuture Fd	15.02	N.L.+	.10
AIM Funds:			
Conv Yld	13.40	14.33+	.07
Grnway	10.53	11.26	
HiYld Sc	10.09	10.79+	.01
Summit	7.15	(z) +	.03
Alliance Capital:			
Alli Gov	9.43	9.98-	.01
Alli HIY	10.40	11.01+	.02
Alli Intl	20.92	22.86+	.14
Alli Mtge	9.86	10.43	
Alli Tech	23.46	25.64+	.22
Chem Fd	9.18	10.03+	.01
Surveyr	16.59	18.13+	.18
Alpha Fd	23.16	25.31+	.13
American Capital Group:			
Comstk	15.89	17.37+	.05
Corp Bd	7.60	8.31+	.01
Enterpr	14.71	16.08	
Exch Fd	56.40	(z) +	.05
Fd Amer	12.21	13.34-	.05
Govt Sec	11.96	12.83	
Growth	25.93	(z) +	.14
Harbor	14.85	16.23+	.04
High Yld	10.87	11.66+	.02
Muni Bd	21.56	22.64-	.07
O T C	11.90	13.01+	.01
Pace Fd	24.05	26.28-	.04
Prov Inc	5.06	5.46-	.02
TxE HY	12.42	13.04-	.04
Venture	16.41	17.93+	.24
American Funds Group:			
Am Bal	11.60	12.68-	.03
Amcap F	9.91	10.83+	.02
Am Mutl	18.43	20.14-	.06
Bnd FdA	14.90	16.28-	.01
Eupac	22.83	24.95+	.21
Fund Inv	14.75	16.12-	.01
Govt	15.00	15.75-	.01
Gth FdA	16.58	18.12+	.07
Inc FdA	12.54	13.70-	.02
I C A	13.66	14.93	
Nw Econ	20.52	22.43+	.09
Nw Prsp	10.27	11.22+	.08
Tax Ex	11.19	11.75-	.04
Wash Mt	12.48	13.64-	.02
Am Grwth	9.34	10.21	
Am Heritg	2.42	N.L.+	.01
Am Invest	8.28	N.L.-	.01

Fund	NAV	Offer Price	Chg.
Coutry Cap	19.75	21.35+	.02
Criterion Funds:			
Cm IncS	11.18	12.22-	.02
Inv Qual	11.22	11.75-	.04
Lowry M	10.63	11.62	
Pilot Fd	10.75	11.75+	.01
Qlty TF	11.30	11.83-	.01
Sunblt G	18.36	20.07-	.01
US Govt	10.31	11.06+	.01
Dean Witter:			
Cal TxFr	11.94	N.L.-	.01
Convrt	11.65	N.L.+	.03
DevlGr r	9.77	N.L.+	.02
Div Grw	17.95	N.L.	
High Yld	14.41	15.25+	.01
Ind Val r	14.13	N.L.+	.01
Nat Resr	7.31	N.L.	
NY TxFr	11.12	N.L.-	.01
Option In	10.12	N.L.-	.04
Sears Tx	11.86	N.L.-	.04
Tax Adv	10.60	N.L.+	.01
Tax Ex	11.27	11.74-	.02
US Govt	10.46	N.L.	
WW InTr	15.02	N.L.+	.16
Delaware Group:			
Decatr	17.87	19.53-	.03
Delchs F	8.14	8.90+	.01
DTR Inv	10.12	N.L.	
GF Gin	9.45	9.92-	.02
GF Govt	9.41	9.88-	.01
TxFr Pa	7.81	8.20-	.03
TFr USA	11.49	12.06-	.03
Delw Fd	24.03	26.26+	.02
Delta Td	16.05	17.54+	.13
Destiny	15.55	(z) -	.01
D.I.T.			
Cap Gr	15.44	N.L.-	.03
Agg Gr	26.38	N.L.+	.10
Cur In	10.53	N.L.+	.02
DFA Fxin	102.10	N.L.+	.07
DFA Small	199.23	N.L.+	.32
D G DvSrs	25.63	N.L.-	.03
DodgC Bal	33.37	N.L.-	.03
DodgC Stk	37.98	N.L.+	.01
Double Ex	11.62	12.10+	.02
Drexel Burnham:			
DB Fund	22.44	23.25-	.07
DSTGv r	10.71	N.L.	
DSTOp r	(z)	(z)	
DST Cv r	10.27	N.L.+	.02
DST Gr r	12.31	N.L.-	.02
DST E r	15.56	N.L.+	.12
FenInt r	10.80	N.L.+	.01
TxFr Ltd	10.59	N.L.	
Dreyfus Group:			
A Bonds	15.21	N.L.-	.02
CalT Ex	15.06	N.L.-	.04
Dreyf Fd	13.28	14.51-	.01
Dreyf Lv	20.59	22.50+	.02
GNMA	15.82	N.L.-	.02
Growth	11.60	N.L.	
Insr TF	18.12	N.L.-	.02
Intrmd	13.70	N.L.-	.01
Mass Tx	16.46	N.L.-	.01
New Ldr	22.32	N.L.+	.11
NYT Ex	15.46	N.L.-	.02
Spl Incm	9.11	N.L.+	.02
Tax ExB	12.57	N.L.-	.02
Third Cn	8.14	N.L.+	.04
Eagle Gth	8.03	8.78	
Eaton Vance Funds:			
Cal Mun	10.41	N.L.-	.01

Fund	NAV	Offer Price	Chg.
44 WS Eqt	5.76	5.82-	.04
Founders Group Funds:			
Growth	9.74	N.L.	
Income	15.35	N.L.-	.04
Mutual	11.10	N.L.-	.02
Special	32.25	N.L.+	.13
FPA Funds:			
Capital	13.34	14.50+	.06
New Inc	9.62	10.13	
Paramt	13.93	15.22+	.03
Perenni	18.81	20.56-	.02
Franklin Group:			
AGE Fd	3.81	3.97+	.02
Cal TxFr	6.99	7.28	
Corp Csh	9.38	N.L.	
D N T C	11.47	12.37+	.03
Equity	6.75	7.28-	.01
Fed TxF	11.63	12.11-	.04
Gold Fnd	8.06	8.69+	.18
Growth	15.15	16.33-	.04
Income	2.27	2.45+	.01
Ins TxFr	11.63	12.11-	.04
MN Ins	11.67	12.16-	.03
N Y Tax	11.53	12.01-	.01
OHIn TF	11.35	11.82-	.03
Optn Fd	6.28	6.77	
Mich TF	11.32	11.79-	.02
US GvSc	7.51	7.82	
Utilities	7.89	8.51-	.01
Freed Gold	16.38	17.24-	.01
Freed Reg	12.61	13.41+	.02
FundTrust:			
Aggr f	13.82	N.L.+	.11
Grow	13.26	N.L.+	.09
GroInc	13.08	N.L.+	.07
GT Pacific	21.44	N.L.+	.32
Gatewy Op	15.02	N.L.+	.06
Geico ARP	25.94	N.L.-	.02
GenAgg G	21.31	N.L.+	.09
Genl Elec Invest:			
Elf TxE	11.41	N.L.-	.02
Elfn Inc	12.13	N.L.+	.01
Elfn Tr	29.82	N.L.-	.06
S&S LT	12.56	N.L.	
S&S Pro	40.79	N.L.+	.10
Genl Secur	13.89	N.L.+	.01
Genl TxEx	14.40	N.L.-	.03
Gintel Group:			
Cap App	11.32	N.L.-	.02
Erisa	41.75	N.L.-	.19
Gintl Fd	91.96	N.L.-	.32
Grad Emr	13.31	N.L.-	.03
Grad EstG	15.58	N.L.-	.08
GIT Incm	10.00	N.L.+	.01
GIT TxFr	11.71	N.L.-	.02
Grth IndSh	10.92	N.L.+	.02
GrF Wash	11.83	12.45	
Guardian Funds:			
Bond	12.20	N.L.-	.02
Park Av	22.80	24.92	
Stock	17.36	N.L.	
Hamltn Fd	7.88	8.61	
Hartwll Gt	11.53	N.L.+	.05

Fund	NAV	Offer Price	Chg.
Lehman Group:			
Captl	19.38	N.L.+	.23
Invst	19.87	N.L.+	.28
Opprt	27.34	N.L.+	.23
Leverage	8.68	N.L.+	.05
Lexington Group:			
CpLdr fr	14.98	16.05+	.09
Gold Fd	3.76	N.L.+	.08
Gnma	8.10	N.L.-	.01
Growth	11.28	N.L.-	.02
Resrch	18.90	N.L.-	.01
Liberty Family Fds:			
Fed	13.56	N.L.-	.02
Tax Free	10.41	N.L.-	.06
US Gvt S	8.82	N.L.+	.01
Ltd Term	12.76	13.12+	.01
Lndner Dv	24.53	N.L.	
Lindner Fd	20.69	N.L.+	.07
LMH Fund	28.17	N.L.-	.01
Loomis Sayles Funds:			
Cap Dev	24.09	N.L.-	.05
Mutual	23.46	N.L.-	.15
Lord Abbett:			
Affilatd	(z)	(z)	
Bnd Deb	x10.67	11.66-	.29
Devl Gro	8.80	9.62+	.03
Govt S	3.35	3.59-	.01
TxF Natl	10.74	11.28-	.08
TxFr NY	10.88	11.42-	.11
Value Ap	12.79	13.98+	.06
Lutheran Brotherhood:			
Broth Fd	17.23	18.14-	.02
Bro Inc	x9.00	9.47-	.07
Bro MBd	8.17	8.60-	.03
Mass Financial Services:			
MIT	13.75	14.82-	.05
MFD	14.10	15.20	
MIG	12.84	13.84+	.02
MCD	13.41	14.46	
MSF	9.83	10.60+	.01
MEG	19.67	21.21+	.13
MFG	10.39	10.91	
MFI B	12.23	13.19-	.05
MGH	9.98	10.48	
MST Md	10.48	11.00	
MFB	15.00	16.17-	.03
MFH	7.22	7.78-	.01
MMB	10.60	11.13-	.01
MMH	10.31	10.82-	.01
MST NC	11.17	11.73	
MST VA	10.73	11.27-	.01
MST Ma	10.63	11.16	
MTR	10.99	11.85-	.03
Mathers	18.79	N.L.-	.06
Meeschr C	28.50	N.L.+	.03
Merrill Lynch:			
Basc Val	17.54	18.76	
Cal TxE	11.42	N.L.-	.01
Captl Fd	25.87	27.67-	.05
Corp Dv	10.85	11.07	
EquiBd 1	14.18	14.77-	.03
Fed Sec	10.27	10.95-	.0?
FdF Tm	15.31	N.L.	

} **Lehman Group**

In the first column, *NAV* stands for net asset value (per share). It is calculated by totaling the market value of all securities owned by the fund and subtracting the liabilities (if any), then dividing by the number of fund shares outstanding. In short, NAV equals the dollar value of the pool per mutual fund share. At the close of business on April 11, 1986, Lehman Capital's net asset value per share was $19.38.

The last column informs you that this was a 23 cent gain over the previous day. Your objective is to choose a fund that invests successfully, so that the pool's value grows as does the net asset value of each share.

The middle column tells you that this is a *no-load (N.L.)* fund, which means there's no sales commission, although with such funds you do pay a management fee.

You should also be aware of dividends, an important source of income for many stockholders, even though most investors buy stock because they expect its price to increase. You can check the stock pages for the current annual dividend, and you can also use the *Journal's* daily **Corporate Dividend News,** listed in the front-page index, to be informed of future dividend payments.

The April 22, 1986, report provides dividend news for April 21 (see pages 216 and 217). The companies listed under the heading **Regular** will pay regular cash dividends on the payable date to all those who were stockholders on the record date.

For instance, the April 22, 1986, article reported that *Yellow Freight System* announced a quarterly dividend of 13½ cents per share payable on May 23, 1986, to all stockholders of record on May 12, 1986.

Some companies prefer to pay dividends in extra stock rather than cash. Returning to pages 216 and 217, you can see that *Citizens First Bancorporation* announced a two-for-one stock split effective June 9, 1986, for all holders of record on May 14, 1986. This was not a stock dividend, but you will see stock dividends listed in this section of the report.

Rather than hoping for a price increase, some investors (and speculators) borrow stock from their broker and sell it in the hope of a price *decrease.* If the stock falls, they'll pay back the stock and pocket the difference between the high price when they borrowed and sold the stock and the low price when they bought and returned the stock. This is called *selling short.*

For instance, if you borrow a $2 stock from your broker and sell it, you have $2. If it falls to $1, you can buy it on the market and return the stock to the broker and you keep the other dollar. Brokers lend stocks because you have to leave the cash from your sale of the stock with them as collateral for the borrowed stock, and they can then lend the cash at interest.

Around the 20th of each month the *Journal* publishes an article on short interest and a table (see page 219) entitled **Big Board and AMEX Short Interest** (check the front-page index). *Short interest* is the number of borrowed shares that have not been returned to the lender. A great deal of short interest in a stock indicates widespread speculation that a stock will fall. Remember, however, that those shares must be repaid, and that those who owe stock must buy it in order to repay it. Their stock purchases could bid the stock up.

The April 22, 1986, *Journal* article reports (see pages 218 and 220) that short interest was more than double the average daily trading volume

CORPORATE DIVIDEND NEWS

ConVest Energy Reduces Its Quarterly to 10 Cents

HOUSTON—ConVest Energy Partners, citing tumbling oil prices, said it reduced its quarterly distribution to 10 cents a unit from 45 cents.

In addition, the master limited partnership said its principal lending bank, Texas Commerce Bank, Houston, a unit of Texas Commerce Bancshares Inc., has agreed to reduce its $14.2 million debt outstanding by $1,375,000 by June 30. After June 30, ConVest will pay $425,000 a month to the bank through December 1986.

ConVest said the amount of future quarterly distributions will depend on how much cash it has available after its bank payments.

* * *

Walker Energy Suspends First Quarter Distribution

HOUSTON – Walker Energy Partners said it suspended its first quarter distribution.

The partnership, which became public last November, has been paying quarterly distributions of 32 cents a unit.

Walker said it suspended the distribution because of, among other things, declining oil prices and a requirement in its loan agreement to pay 65% of its $15 million of debt over the next 18 months.

John Walker, chairman and chief financial officer, said: "I am hopeful of resuming cash distributions for the second calendar quarter."

* * *

Dividends Reported April 21

Company	Period	Amt.	Payable date	Record date
REGULAR				
Calif Water Service	Q	.70	5–15–86	5– 1
Cross & Trecker Corp	Q	.20	5–31–86	5– 9
Dana Corp	Q	.32	6–13–86	5–28
First Federal SavingsCT	Q	.16	5–16–86	4–30
Goodrich (BF) Co	Q	.39	6–30–86	6– 6
Goodrich (BF) Co pfA	Q	1.96¼	6–30–86	6– 6
Goodrich (BF) Co pfB	Q	.24⅜	6–30–86	6– 6
Jorgensen (Earl) Co	Q	.25	5–14–86	4–30
Knape & Vogt Mfg	Q	.35	6– 6–86	5–23
Lamaur Inc	Q	.06	6–18–86	6– 4
Legg Mason Inc	Q	.05	7–14–86	6–26
Lilly (Eli) & Co	Q	.45	6–10–86	5–15
Mfgrs Hanvr adjpfB	Q	1.11⅞	5–15–86	5– 1
Mellon Bank Corp	Q	.69	5–15–86	5– 5
Mellon Bank Corp pfA	Q	.70	5–15–86	5– 5
Merchants Bancorp	Q	.25	5–15–86	4–30
Noble Affiliates	Q	.03	5–19–86	5– 5
Nocen Energy Resour	Q	b.12½	6– 1–86	5– 8
Old National Bancorp	Q	.40	6–16–86	6– 2
Science Management	Q	.02½	5–27–85	5– 5
Sea Containers Ltd	Q	.10½	5–22–86	5– 5
South Carolina Natl	Q	.24	7– 1–86	6–10
Southern Co	Q	.51	6– 6–86	5– 5
Southwstrn El Svc	Q	.47	6–25–86	6–11
Sunair Electronics Inc	S	.12	7– 8–86	6–16
Twin Disc Inc	Q	.22½	6– 2–86	5– 9
Visual Graphics Corp	Q	.07½	7– 2–86	6– 2
Yellow Freight System	Q	.13½	5–23–86	5–12 ← Yellow Freight System
IRREGULAR				
Centerbanc Savings Assc		.10	5–20–86	5– 5
Farm & Home Sav Assc		.12½	6–30–86	5–30
Warner Communications		.12½	5–15–86	4–28
FUNDS–REITS–INVESTMENT COS				
Centennial REIT		nn.26	5–15–86	5– 6
nn-Initial dividend.				
Cenvill Investors	Q	.50	7– 3–86	6– 2
Circle Income Shares	M	.11	6– 6–86	5–23
Circle Income Shares	M	.11	7– 3–86	6–20
Convest Energy Partners	Q	.10	5–23–86	5– 9
Dreyfus Fund	Q	h.07	4–25–86	4–21
Mesa Royalty Trust	M	h.118211	7–31–86	4–30
Pilgrim Reg'l Bnk Shrs		v.07	5– 5–86	4–28
v-Initial dividend.				
VMS Mortgage Investors		.09	8–15–86	5– 1
Walker Energy Partners		w	..– –	..–
w-Omitted distribution.				
EXTRA				
First Federal SavingsCT		.01	5–16–86	4–30
STOCK				
Citizens First Bancorp		y	6– 9–86	5–14 ← Citizens First Bancorporation
y-Two-for-one stock split.				
First Federal SavingsCT		n	5–16–86	4–30
n-Two-for-one stock split.				

INCREASED

Company	Period	Amounts New	Amounts Old	Payable date	Record date
Iowa Southern Utl	Q	.96	.94	6– 1–86	5–14
Natl SecurityIns	S	.27	.25	6– 2–86	5–15
Union Bancorp	Q	.16	.14	6–13–86	5–16

REDUCED

Company	Period	Amounts New	Amounts Old	Payable date	Record date
InterFirst Corp	Q	.02½	.15	6–30–86	6–12

Company	Period	Amt.	Payable date	Record date
FOREIGN				
Heineken N.V. ADR	F	p	6–12–86	5– 2
p-Approximately $.637 per Depositary Share.				
INITIAL				
CitizensFirstBancorp new	Q	t.15	8– 1–86	7–18
t-An effective increase following a two-for-one stock split.				
Zero Corp new	Q	.072	6– 2–86	5–16
SPECIAL				
Genuine Parts Co		.55	7– 1–86	6– 9

A-Annual; Ac-Accumulation; b-Payable in Canadian funds; F-Final; G-Interim; h-From income; k-From capital gains; M-Monthly; Q-Quarterly; S-Semi-annual.

* * *

Stocks Ex-Dividend April 23

Company	Amount
Banco Central SA ADR (k)	
(k)-approx. $.329 per Depositary Share.	
GeothermlRes.Int'l $1pf	.25
Parker Drilling	.02
Security Pacific	.37
Sony Corp Amer Shs	(n)
(n)-approx. $.102 per Depositary Share.	
TexAmerEnrgy $2.575pf	.64⅜

The Wall Street Journal, *April 22, 1986*

Southwstrn El Svc .... Q	.47	6–25–86	6–11
Sunair Electronics Inc ...... S	.12	7– 8–86	6–16
Twin Disc Inc .... Q	.22½	6– 2–86	5– 9
Visual Graphics Corp .... Q	.07½	7– 2–86	6– 2
Yellow Freight System ..... Q	.13½	5–23–86	5–12 ◄────

Yellow Freight System

STOCK

Citizens First Bancorp	v	6– 9–86	5–14 ◄
y-Two-for-one stock split.			
First Federal SavingsCT .	n	5–16–86	4–30
n-Two-for-one stock split.			

Citizens First Bancorporation

for the month ending April 15, 1986. This indicates strong sentiment on the part of the short-sellers that the market will fall. Once again, however, short interest represents stock that must be repaid and hence purchased, bringing upward strength to the market.

Finally, you can buy shares of stock on **Other Markets** (some Canadian and some U.S.) and on **Foreign Markets.** The *Journal* provides daily listings, and you can find them in the front-page index. A representative sample is included from the April 22, 1986, edition (see pages 221, 222, and 223). Remember that when you invest in foreign markets you must be concerned with the fluctuation of foreign currency values as well as the value of the shares you purchase.

Let's return to the Dow Jones Industrial Average. You know that the price of a share of stock reflects the ability of the corporation to earn profits. This relationship is expressed as the *price-earnings* (P-E, or price divided by per share earnings) *ratio* between the price of the stock and the profits per share of stock earned by the corporation (profits divided by number of shares outstanding). The price-earnings ratio answers this question: "What is the price an investor must pay to capture a dollar of earnings?" For instance, a P-E ratio of 10 might mean that a company earned $10 per share per annum and that a share sold for $100, or it might mean that a company earned $7 per share per annum and that a share sold for $70, and so on.

Keep in mind that the investor seeks the highest yield consistent with safety. The earnings yield is annual profit expressed as a percentage of market price. If you earn $100 a year on an investment of $1,000 the yield is 10 percent. A P-E ratio of 10 (10/1) represents a 10 percent yield because earnings are $\frac{1}{10}$ (10 percent) of the price per share. Similarly,

Short Interest Fell Slightly on Big Board, Rose to Record on Amex in Latest Month

By a WALL STREET JOURNAL Staff Reporter

NEW YORK—Short interest fell slightly on the New York Stock Exchange, while American Stock Exchange short interest reached a record level for the month ended April 15.

Big Board short interest fell one-tenth of a percentage point, or 325,088 shares, to 318,299,016 shares from the record 318.6 million shares a month earlier.

In the previous month, Big Board short interest had risen 8.4%. Short interest was 223.5 million shares a year earlier.

On the Amex, short interest rose 4,498,-324 shares, or 18%, to a record 29,436,624 shares from the adjusted 24,938,300 shares a month earlier. Amex short interest was 17.6 million shares a year earlier. Amex short interest had fallen 2.1% in the previous month.

A short sale is the sale of borrowed stock. An increase in short interest is considered bullish by some investors because the borrowed shares eventually must be bought back.

The seller in a short sale expects a price decline that would enable the purchase of an equal number of shares later at a lower price for return to the lender. The short interest is the number of shares that haven't been purchased for return to lenders.

Fluctuation in short interest of certain stocks also may be caused partly by arbitraging.

In a major method of securities arbitrage, a profit can be made when a company's stock is to be exchanged for that of another, or for a new issue, in a proposed merger. The profit opportunity arises when

The Wall Street Journal, April 22, 1986

the stocks sell at disparate prices.

An arbitrager may make a small per-share profit by buying stock of one company involved in the prospective merger and selling short the stock of the other.

Big Board short interest fell to 2.02 times the average daily trading volume from 2.05 the previous month. 〉 Short Interest Ratio to Trading Volume

Philip Erlanger, chief technical analyst for Advest Inc. of Hartford, Conn., calculates a version of the short interest ratio that excludes stocks involved in arbitrage for what he considers a more accurate indicator.

His so-called at-risk short interest ratio was unchanged in the period, remaining at 1.15. The drop in short interest on the Big Board doesn't indicate a trend, according to Mr. Erlanger. Both the standard and Mr. Erlanger's indicators don't reflect very high ratios, "meaning the market has over the last 18 months been using up the very high short interest we saw, and the shorts are being squeezed."

Some big drops in short interest for the latest month came in the auto sector. Short interest in Ford Motor Co. fell sharply to 743,602 shares in the latest period from 1.9 million shares the prior month. Short interest dropped in General Motors Corp. to 530,-361 shares this month from 1.2 million shares last month. Other big declines showed up in particular drug, airline, hospital and banking stocks.

Some increases in short interest came in the tobacco, chemical, retail, oil and telecommunications industries. Short interest rose strongly in Navistar International, to 7.9 million in the latest period from 4.6 million in the prior period.

---

a P-E ratio of 5 (5/1) is the equivalent of a 20 percent yield because earnings per share are one fifth (20 percent) of invested capital. A P-E ratio of 20 (20/1) represents a 5 percent earnings yield. And so on.

Chart 13–3 (page 224) shows the Dow's P-E ratio fell from the end of World War II until the beginning of the Korean War, because earnings grew while share prices languished. Following the uncertainties of the 1930s and World War II, investors were still tentative about the market.

Then the great *bull market* (a bull attacks by thrusting upward, hence this term for a rising market; a bear fights by slapping downward, hence

Big Board and Amex Short Interest

	4/15/86	3/14/86	Avg. Daily Volume
†E Systems	229,431	241,450	106,142
†Eastern Airlines	1,476,788	1,493,063	490,085
Eastern Air Wts 83Sr	44,400	69,400	20,819
†Eastern Airlines Wts	126,124	86,421	30,828
†Eastern Gas & Fuel	200,422	151,096	90,342
†Eastman Kodak	1,058,529	1,046,709	1,038,614
Eckerd (Jack) Corp	80,202	73,700	224,747
Edwards(AG)&Sons	46,355	49,383	49,228
EG&G	46,799	65,145	54,800
Elscint	30,500	1,561	16,614
†Emerson El	277,351	328,667	127,809
†Emerson Radio	210,382	422,452	136,295
†Emery Air Freight	130,715	462,760	69,404
†Enserch	115,980	117,458	173,342
EQK Realty I	1,100	93,100	35,652
Equimark	48,403	59,177	92,742
†Equitec Financial	103,040	137,106	13,400
†Exxon	2,715,906	2,540,937	861,838
Family Dollar Stor	223,105	234,355	85,019
†Fed Express	629,432	843,799	448,357
Fed Hm Loan Prt Pr	100,000	1,034	10,000
†Fed National Mtge	523,202	875,536	580,371
Fed Paper Board	31,058	57,876	92,604
Federal Co	44,148	60,481	25,252
†Fedl Realty Inv T	159,200	157,000	10,000
†Federated Dept	162,057	96,350	140,938
Fieldcrest Mills	2,300	34,423	28,833
Fin Cp Santa Barbra	62,400	43,400	35,576
†Financ'l Corp Am	802,139	1,243,466	345,042
†Firestone Tire	310,010	514,958	127,042
†First Boston	194,364	471,108	162,528
†First Chicago	239,725	215,048	182,038
†First City Bancorp	508,748	548,550	119,076
First Fidelity	786,459	539,274	14,623
First Intst Bancorp	44,558	268,582	79,742
†First Pennsylvania	455,924	284,760	58,714
†First Wachovia	263,850	341,554	68,766
†Fleet Financial	209,467	556,561	46,119
†Fleetwood Enter	268,302	284,440	172,514
Flightsafety Intl	360,750	362,274	51,680
Florida Progress	103,167	280,036	73,738
Flowers Ind	70,000	56,612	29,890
†Fluor	134,371	149,108	249,561
†FMC	155,928	6,919	186,109
†Ford Motor	743,602	1,903,851	679,957
Fort Howard Paper	41,034	18,800	92,833
Foster Wheeler	97,892	76,310	55,047
FreeptMcMoRanO&G	24,500	400	18,747
Freeport-McMoRan	54,406	31,105	166,009
Frigitronics	73,500	118,225	11,561
†Fruehauf	166,619	159,607	259,700
†GAF	213,509	198,956	80,690
†GCA	198,749	189,849	75,790
Gannett	98,565	132,372	117,500
Gap	72,739	47,796	67,295
Gencorp	13,342	52,714	98,585
†General Dev	338,500	142,600	58,747
†General Dynamics	146,063	107,224	158,947
†General El	220,832	385,834	689,333
General Homes	34,900		36,976
†Genrral Instrument	555,556	623,402	93,500
†General Mills	259,136	255,688	149,261
†General Motors	530,361	1,218,206	1,026,461
General Nutrition	41,300	48,408	31,185
General Signal	481,681	463,935	43,938
Genesco	92,712	84,100	83,323
†Genl Mtrs Cl E Com	229,098	218,107	134,519
Genstar	43,675	315	901,161
Genuine Parts	93,831	123,516	80,604
Georgia Pwr PrD	2,000	64,430	7,238
Georgia Pwr Pfd I	100	47,660	57
†Georgia-Pacific	735,150	616,841	365,038
Gerber Products	90,162	43,774	175,823
Gerber Scientific	17,375	67,475	96,423
†Giant Group	138,538	127,050	9,480
†Gibraltar Financial	1,336,800	1,182,600	88,204
†Gillette	100,351	85,941	94,314
Glenfed	207,776	270,300	159,119
†Global Marine	2,128,733	2,110,587	73,071
†Global Marine $3.50	110,070	109,884	5,223
GM Class H	19,275	219,107	109,600
Golden Nugget	74,760	77,941	87,995
Golden West Fincorp	118,700	26,050	155,838
†Goodyear Tire & R	430,539	368,767	379,023

	4/15/86	3/14/86	Avg. Daily Volume
Measurex	8,543	29,679	44,923
Medtronic	80,421	62,273	63,276
Mellon Bank	82,456	73,408	94,480
Mellon Bnk PrA	40,500	40,500	976
†Merck	416,192	436,496	242,495
†Merrill Lynch	1,969,620	1,949,322	710,180
†Mesa Partner	124,800	25,332	435,176
†Mesa Petroleum	104,409	21,000	154,504
†Mfrs Hanover	703,087	938,165	298,852
†MGM Grand Hotels	123,500	162,588	9,319
MidCon	2,830	253,189	110,500
Middle South Util	38,917	88,249	818,919
†Minn Mng & Manu	341,559	404,552	287,385
Minnesota Pwr & Lt	9,403	46,600	32,080
†Mitel	170,303	171,003	79,604
†Mobil	681,821	633,585	974,314
†Monsanto	683,680	628,024	244,071
Moore	1,836	43,549	22,019
†Morgan (JP)	252,158	599,398	363,180
Morgan Stanley	426,414	Not Listed	359,517
Morton-Thiokol	125,437	94,876	340,585
†Motorola	799,631	982,098	496,133
Murphy Oil	482,640	457,709	62,380
NL Ind	66,105	257,200	212,233
NVF	60,409	70,617	38,609
Nat'l Dist PrC	80,800	34,200	1,871
†National Distill	219,692	211,086	57,338
National Gypsum	217,962	154,525	287,023
†Natl Intergroup	197,552	229,823	62,742
†Natl Medical	1,381,184	1,207,831	309,871
†Natl Seimconductor	963,720	780,610	421,257
†Navistar Int'l	7,931,195	4,632,719	771,642
Navistar Warrants A	76,300	76,913	120,795
†NBI	145,900	130,900	25,347
NCNB	87,450	52,100	57,819
†NCR	342,233	485,700	487,819
Nevada Pwr	97,155	101,386	13,366
New Eng El System	126,719	136,407	60,728
New York State E&G	45,252	34,605	82,819
†Newell	136,935	45,543	42,900
Newhall Land&Farm	97,050	101,400	32,780
Niagara Mohawk Pw	73,466	154,901	249,166
Niagara Share	482,200	482,200	11,833
Norfolk Southern	22,662	62,129	100,566
†Nortek	831,888	384,058	105,938
Northeast Util	30,427	101,764	194,709
†Northrop	192,590	278,016	222,095
†Norwest	104,917	96,187	110,942
†Novo	348,949	294,491	100,700
†NRN Indiana Pub	345,405	339,300	165,966
NRN Sts Pwr	33,440	59,812	101,780
†NRN Telecom	674,472	525,450	154,266
Nucor	38,282	15,400	45,271
†NWA	173,058	260,332	167,642
†Nynex	213,206	242,862	173,514
†Occidental Pet	7,172,170	6,708,097	778,942
†Ocean Drill & Exp	102,500	84,100	66,609
Ohio Ed Cl A Ser B	25,200	302	142
†Ohio Ed	331,531	1,403,401	196,352
Ohio Ed PrH	51,400	None	256
Ohio Ed PrH	187,020	None	7,633
Ohio Pwr PrG	38,652	1,360	36,647
Oneok	29,869	6,734	40,352
Orion Capital	513,392	615,902	76,423
†Orion Pictures	102,756	68,565	73,128
†Owens Illinois	294,562	249,448	171,419
†Owens-Corn Fiber	644,920	603,249	543,911
Pacific Gas & El	34,329	66,188	61,538
Pacific Lighting	115,914	122,114	24,352
†Pacific Resources	277,627	314,246	149,300
†Pacific Telesis	58,280	580	86,104
Pacificorp	286,664	352,555	134,266
†PaineWebber	2,216,080	2,972,550	573,695
†Pan Am	75,381	71,600	20,995
Pandick	233,044	141,872	134,609
†Panhandle Eastern	43,448	18,415	29,452
Pansophic Sys	96,580	145,058	334,240
Pantry Pride	45,583	18,583	66,775
Paradyne	925	47,725	6,676
Park Electro Chem	369,500	370,000	38,828
Parker Drilling	340,200	8,734	233,204
Payless Cashways	51,340	354,000	13,642
†Pengo	130,701	15,491	74,719
Penn Pwr & Lt		183,542	181,533
†Penney (JC)			

The Wall Street Journal, *April 22, 1986*

Short Interest ⌈   **Big Board short interest fell to 2.02**
Ratio to ⌉   **times the average daily trading volume**
Trading Volume ⌊   **from 2.05 the previous month.**

that term for a falling market) of the 1950s began, and the P-E ratio
rose. Investors were at last convinced of a "return to normalcy" and
were willing to stake their future in shares of stock. The market was
clearly "undervalued" (a P-E ratio of seven was roughly a 15 percent
earnings yield), so it is not surprising that stock prices climbed rapidly.
Stocks were a good buy because their price was very low compared to
their earnings per share and their potential for even higher earnings. As
investors rushed into the market, stock prices soared. Enthusiasm was
so great and share prices advanced so rapidly that the P-E ratio rose
despite stronger earnings per share.

The P-E ratio had climbed to 20 (a 5 percent yield) by the early 60s,
so the market was no longer "undervalued." The ratio plateaued or fell
slightly to the end of the 60s because share prices were no longer increasing
faster than corporate earnings. The great bull market had ended.

During the 70s, investors became frightened of the impact of inflation
and severe cyclical fluctuation on corporate earnings, since earnings fell
sharply with each recession. At the first hint of declining profits brought
on by the tail end of the cycle, investors unloaded their shares and stock
prices plunged. As a result, the Dow remained in a range for a decade,
fluctuating between the high 500s and 1,000. Investors had been so badly
burned by the market's decline in 1969 and 1974 that they refused to
be swayed by the strong recovery of profits after each recession.

Yet profits rose over the decade, and thus the P-E ratio fell, so that
by the early 1980s it was almost as low as it had been at the outset of
the Korean War. The market had not kept pace with profits, and stocks
were undervalued once again.

To some, this indicated that we were on the verge of another bull
market, such as that of the 1950s. The situation seemed similar to that
of the late 1940s, with investors hesitant after years of bad news, yet
willing to take the plunge when it became clear that the fundamentals
had changed. One indication was that stock prices fell little in the recessions of 1980 and 1981–82 when compared with those of 1970 and 1974.
It was as if investors were positioning themselves for the bull market
that was just around the corner.

There were two very auspicious signs. First, the breaking of the boom-
and-bust inflationary spiral with the back-to-back recessions of 1980 and

OTHER MARKETS

Selected Stocks; Dually Listed Issues Excluded

Monday, April 21, 1986

Toronto Exchange
Quotations in Canadian funos
Quotations in cents unless marked $

Sales	Stock	High	Low	Close	Chg.
54030	Abtl Prce	$25¾	25⅛	25⅝	+ ⅛
45208	Acklands	$20¾	20⅝	20¾	+ ⅜
13220	Agnico E	$24⅝	24⅜	24⅜	− ⅛
3835	Agra Ind A	$17¾	17½	17½	− ⅛
14610	Alt Energy	$12½	12⅜	12⅜	− ⅛
14975	Alta Nat	$12¾	12	12	− ¼
12894	Algoma St	$18¾	18½	18½	
11130	A Barick o	$12	11⅝	11⅝	− ⅜
15313	Atco I f	$9	8¾	9	+ ¼
50438	BCED	495	485	495	+ 5
1109	BP Canada	$27¼	27	27¼	
48210	Bank BC	360	350	350	− 10
55273	Bank N S	$14¾	14½	14¾	
3250	Baton	$24¾	24½	24¾	+ ¼
5230	Bonanza R	215	215	215	
2550	Bralorne	151	150	151	+ 1
56069	Bramalea	$19⅛	18⅝	18⅝	− ⅛
300	Brenda M	$8¾	8¾	8¾	
145813	BCFP	$14½	14¼	[illegible]	[illegible]
85505	BC Res	138	[illegible]	[illegible]	− 1
38700	BC Phone	[illegible]	[illegible]	16⅜	+ ½
5600	Brunswk	[illegible]	31¾	32	
1465	Bud[illegible]	$19½	19½	19½	
1199[illegible]	[illegible] Co	$33	32⅜	32⅞	+ ⅝
[illegible]	[illegible]masco	$39⅛	38¼	38¾	− ½
6300	Indal	$28¼	27½	28¼	+ ⅝
400	Inglis	$23	23	23	− 1
2340	Inland Gas	$11½	11⅜	11½	
11205	I Corona o	$22⅜	22¼	22¼	− ⅛
53025	Intl Thom	$11⅛	11	11	− ⅛
8884	Intpr Pipe	$44	43⅝	43⅞	− ⅛
75015	Ipsco	$10½	10¼	10½	+ ¼
17633	Jannock	$28¾	28¼	28¾	+ ½
1200	Kelsey H	$29	28¾	28¾	− ¼
310	Kerr Add	$16	16	16	
4792	Labatt	$44¼	43⅝	43⅞	− ⅜
12500	Lacana	$8¼	8¼	8¼	− ⅛
13650	LOnt Cem	$27¾	27¼	27½	− ¼
8500	Loblaw Co	$27¼	27	27¼	+ ⅛
4400	Lumonics	$17¾	17½	17¾	+ ¼
21480	Magna A f	$31½	30⅞	31⅜	+ ⅞
2500	MDS H A	$18¼	18	18	− ⅛
25362	MICC	450	410	440	+ 30
31153	Mclan H X	$20	19⅞	20	
1547	Maritime f	$15⅛	14⅞	15	+ ⅛
2475	Merland E	224	220	220	− 5
200665	Molson A f	$27¾	26½	27¾	+ 1⅛
1900	Murphy	$20	20	20	
2325	Nabisco L	$41¼	40½	41¼	+ 1¼
100073	Noranda	$17¾	17⅛	17¾	+ ½
10164	Norcen	$12⅛	11¾	11¾	− ⅜
276790	Nva AltA f	480	470	475	− 15
3500	Nowsco W	$10	9¾	10	+ ¼
70820	NuWst sp A	33½	33½	33½	
528	Oakwood	415	415	415	
31325	Omnibus o	400	390	390	
6885	Oshawa A f	$40¾	40⅛	40⅜	− ⅜
23075	Pac W Airln	$14⅝	13¾	14⅝	+ 1
15000	Pamour	$11¼	11¼	11¼	− ¼
34830	PanCan P	$24	23½	23½	− ¾
200	Pembina	$15¼	15¼	15¼	− ¼
1125	Pine Point	$9¼	9¼	9¼	
72600	Placer	$21⅝	21⅛	21⅝	+ ⅜
100	Que Sturg o	370	370	370	
100	Rayrock f	$6¾	6¾	6¾	
4175	Redpath	$26	25⅝	26	+ ½
9173	ReedSt 1 Sp	$52¼	52¼	52¼	+ ¼
5260	Rogers A	$20⅝	20½	20⅝	− ⅛
1000	Roman	$9⅝	9½	9½	− ¼
15825	Rothman	$40⅜	40	40¼	+ ½
1390	Sceptre	255	250	250	
14900	Scotts f	$40	38½	40	+ 2⅛
49760	Sears Can	$16¼	16	16⅛	
4961	Selkirk A f	$25¼	25	25	
11640	Shell Can	$24⅝	23⅝	23⅝	− 1
5912	Sherritt	$7	6¾	6⅞	
700	Slater B f	$13	12¾	13	+ ⅛
5621[illegible]	Southam	$25¾	24⅜	24⅜	− 1
15675	Spar Aero f	$30½	30¼	30¼	
14760	Stelco A	$27½	27¼	27⅜	+ ⅛

Sales	Stock	High	Low	Close	Chg.
13275	Sulptro	70	70	70	
200	Steep R	275	275	275	
3000	Teck Cor A	$21⅝	21	21	+ ¼
14644	Teck B f	$22¾	22⅜	22⅝	− ⅛
20300	Tex Can	$27¾	27⅝	27⅝	− ¼
26130	Thom N A	$30⅛	30	30⅛	
31544	Tor Dm Bk	$25⅞	25⅝	25¾	
8736	Torstar B f	$58½	58	58⅛	+ ⅛
152	Traders A f	$38¼	38¼	38¼	+ ¼
650	Trns Mt	$11⅞	11¾	11¾	
18900	Trinity Res	55	55	55	
100719	TrnAlta UA	$28⅝	28¼	28⅝	+ [illegible]
118247	TrCan PL	$19¾	19⅜	[illegible]	[illegible]16
2900	Trimac	240	[illegible]	[illegible]	+ ⅛
31851	Trilon A	[illegible]	15¾	15¾	+ ⅛
1826	Trizec A	[illegible]	32¼	32¼	+ ½
471632	Turbo	21¼	21	21	− ½
46280	[illegible]ac	2½	2½	2½	1-16
[illegible]	AmPace s	10	10	10	− ¼
500	Amfac pf	20¼	20	20	− ½
200	Buttes	⅝	⅝	⅝	....
4500	CanSoPt g	2 11-16	2½	2 9-16	− ¼
1300	ChiefCnMin	5⅝	5½	5½	− ⅛
100	ClaryCp	1 1-16	1 1-16	1 1-16	+ 1-16
5900	CliniTh	5	4¾	4¾	− ⅛
5800	ComTel	15-16	⅞	15-16	
300	vjCwthO	3-16	3-16	3-16	....
2100	Datamet	3⅝	3½	3⅝	− ⅛
5000	DivrIn wt	⅛	⅛	⅛	....
1000	vjEvanP	2¼	2⅛	2¼	....
15500	GenExp	13-16	13-16	13-16	....
5500	GldStd	9-16	½	9-16	....
1800	Imreg	9¼	9⅛	9⅛	− ⅜
19900	KaiS pfA	4⅛	3⅝	3¾	− ¼
536800	KaiS pfB	4⅞	3¾	4⅜	1⅜
28100	Kenai	⅛	⅛	⅛	
6100	MagelPt	2 9-16	2 7-16	2 7-16	....
500	MiniCptr	1 9-16	1 9-16	1 9-16	+ 1-16
20700	MisnIns	4	3⅞	4	+ ¼
55200	Mitral	1¼	1 1-16	1⅛	− 1-16
1200	NeOhio	10¾	10½	10½	....
8700	OKC LP un	7½	7⅜	7½	− ⅛
38600	OcciSLC wt	21	19⅞	20⅝	+ ½
200	OceanE	1¼	1¼	1¼	− 1-16
1300	PopeRs	18½	18¼	18½	+ ½
52200	PSNH wt	6⅞	6⅞	6⅞	....
600	RckwdN	3 13-16	3¾	3¾	....
200	SCGspfA	17	17	17	....
400	TxAir pfE	20⅝	20⅜	20⅝	+ ¼
1800	TucsnEP pf	29⅛	28¾	28¾	....
500	WAir pf	29⅜	29⅛	29⅛	− ½
37500	WldAr wt	1	15-16	1	....
3000	Yuba A	3¾	3 11-16	3 11-16	− 1-16
3200	Z Sevn	27¼	25¾	27¼	+ 1⅞

BONDS

Sales	Bond	High	Low	Close	Chg.
30000	AFinl 10s99	88½	88⅛	88⅛	− ⅞
1000	AFinl 12s99A	100	100	100	− 2
5000	Bastn 12s97	75½	75½	75½	+ ⅝
10000	DataDes 12¼00	110	110	110	....
2000	McGreg 15½94	102	102	102	+ 4
93000	Paprcft 15s00	53¼	52⅜	53¼	....
4000	RapAm 10s06	77⅝	77⅝	77⅝	− ⅜
1000	Tiger 11½95	75½	75½	75½	+ 1½

Total sales .... 7,787,000 shares

Philadelphia Exchange

Sales	Stock	High	Low	Close	Chg.
1500	Cent Jersln	23	22½	22½	− ¼
3600	HlthCpAm	2⅛	1⅝	2⅛	+ 3-16
14900	TimberR	11¼	11	11	....
2100	Wash Co	4¼	4⅛	4⅛	− ⅛

BONDS

Sales	Bond	High	Low	Close	Chg.
61000	RelGpHld 17s	113	113	113	+ 3
15000	RelGp 9⅞98	85¾	85¾	85¾	− ¾

Total sales 3,369,000 shares.

Boston Exchange

Sales	Stock	High	Low	Close	Chg.
4000	Cstl Carib	1½	1 7-16	1½	+ 1-16
500	FstNE Bksh	28	28	28	+ ⅞
2600	Hodgson	5¾	5	5¾	+ ⅝
125800	Lo[illegible]ack	6 3-16	5¼	5 9-16	− 5-16
100	Pant[illegible]pec	⅞	⅞	[illegible]	+ 9-16

Total sales 2,000,000 shares.

The Wall Street Journal, *April 22, 1986*

FOREIGN MARKETS

Monday, April 21, 1986

LONDON (in pence)

	Close	Prev. Close
Allied Lyons	313	298
Babcock	192	193
Barclays Bk	534	534
B A T Indust	423	425
Bass Ltd	810	808
BOC Group	353	371
British GE	196	198
BTR PLC	476	478
Cable&Wi	725	738
Cadbury Sch	185	190
Charter Con	256	258
Coats Patons	310	312
Consol Gold	464	464
Dalgety	303	300
Distillers Co	668	688
Glaxo	1,032	1,070
Grand Metro	406	408
Guest Keen	354	361
HansonTrust	165	168
Johnson Mat	168	170
Legal Gen	749	749
Lonrho	271	277
Lucas Indust	625	626
MIM Hold	116	114
Nat'l WestBk	895	895
Nrthrn Food	270	270
Racal Elect	202	206
Redland	444	448
Reed Int'l	904	904
Rio Tinto	709	722
STC	154	156
Tate&Lyle	640	635
TaylrWoodrw	631	633
Thorn EMI	499	501
Trust House	185	189
T I Group	565	567
Ultramar	178	183
Utd Biscuit	257	261
Vickers	503	508

BRUSSELS (in Belgian francs)

	Close	Prev. Close
ARBED	3,210	3,200
Gevaert	6,400	6,600
GB-Inno-Bm	7,310	7,300
GrpBrLambrt	3,215	3,200
Metal Hobokn	7,650	7,800
Petrofina	7,500	7,500
SocGenerale	3,190	3,195
Solvay	8,500	8,410

MILAN (in Lire)

	Close	Prev. Close
Buitoni	9,020	9,120
Ciga	6,710	6,599
Fiat	12,875	12,660
Generali	139,900	139,975
La Rinas	1,295	1,295
Mont Ed	4,529	4,379
Olivetti	18,850	18,800
Pirelli	6,139	6,090
Snia Visc	7,340	7,249

South African Mines (in U.S. currency)

	Close	Prev. Close
Bracken	1.60	1.60
Deelkraal	2.30	2.30
Doornfontein	9.63	9.75
DurbanDeep	7.00	6.88
East Rand	4.62	4.62
Elandsrand	5.75	5.75
Elsburg	2.35	2.35
Ergo	5.06	5.05
General Mng	c8.63	c8.75
Grootvlei	3.70	3.62
Harmony	10.25	10.25
Hartebeest	3.85	3.85
Johannesb C	c76.00	c78.00
Kinross	13.12	13.50
Leslie	1.45	1.45
Libanon	13.75	13.75
Loraine	3.65	3.65
Randfontein	8.00	7.90
Rustnbg Plat	10.40	10.37
Southvaal	32.00	31.50
Stilfontein	6.37	6.37
Unisel	6.50	6.50
West Areas	3.45	3.50
Winkelhaak	16.00	16.00

c-In British pounds.

FRANKFURT (in marks)

	Close	Prev. Close
AEG-Tele	340.70	340.70
Allianz Vers	2,830	2,785
BASF	327.30	331.80
Bayer AG	337.50	342.50
BMW	600	615
Cont'l Gummi	251	251
Commerzbnk	367	369
Daimler-Benz	1,507	1,530
Degussa	524.50	527
Deutsche Bk	893	893.50
Dresdner Bk	490	495.50
Hoechst AG	317.20	320.30
Lufthansa	265	263
Nixdorf AG	635.20	638
Porsche AG	1,219.50	1,230
RWE	274	270
Schering AG	610	612
Siemens	712	716.50
Thyssen-Hut	186	189.50
Veba	345	344.50
Volkswagen	661	661

STOCKHOLM (in Swedish krona)

	Close	Prev. Close
AGA	215	212
Alfa Laval b	368	371
Electrolux b	293	304
Svenska Cel b	224	233

TOKYO (in yen)

	Close	Prev. Close
Ajinomoto	1,650	1,650
Asahi Chem	858	873
Bk of Tokyo	780	790
BridgestnTire	615	614
C. Itoh	457	455
Daiwa House	1,350	1,370
Daiwa Secur	1,390	1,380
Eisai	1,650	1,640
Fuji Bank	1,520	1,510
Fujitsu	1,080	1,060
Isuzu Mot Ltd	355	350
Kalima Corp	739	740
Kansai Elec	2,640	2,580
Komatsu Ltd	491	475
MaruiDeptStr	2,480	2,490
Marubeni	333	335
Mazda	409	401
MitsubishiEst	1,880	1,870
MitsubishiInd	388	392
Mitsui & Co	478	465
MitsuiRealE	1,690	1,690
Nikko Secur	994	990
NipponKogaku	1,140	1,150
NipponGakki	1,490	1,500
NipponSteel	167	167
NomuraSecur	1,940	1,910
Ricoh	951	964
Sekisui House	1,170	1,180
Sharp El	965	955
SumitomoBk	1,880	1,890
SumitomoCh	331	326
Taisei Const	433	431
Takeda Chem	1,510	1,540
Teijin	515	515
Tokyo Elec	4,110	3,990
Toshiba	428	430
YamaichiSec	968	971
Yasuda F&M	649	650

PARIS (in French francs)

	Close	Prev. Close
AirLiq	790	780
Aquitaine	340	319.90
BSNGrD	3,820	3,780
Club Med	555	554
Imetal	95.80	94.90
L'Oreal	3,769	3,690
Hachette	2,650	2,570
LafargeCoppee	1,490	1,470
Machines Bull	82.70	78.75
Michelin	3,245	3,095
MoetHen	2,420	2,415
PeugtCtn	1,058	1,025
Source Perrier	710	688
Total CFP	376	363

SWITZERLAND (Closed) Basel

	Close	Prev. Close
vHoffmn-LaR	12,250	12,300
Pirelli Intl	481	479

v-1/10 share.

AMSTERDAM (in guilders)

	Close	Prev. Close
AKZO	180.10	179.30
Ahold	78.70	78
Algemene Bk	582.50	580
Amst-Rot Bk	104.50	103.80
Elsevier-NDU	185	189
Fokker	95	96.20
Heineken's	218.50	219
Holec	345	355.80
Hoogovens	116.40	118
Nation Neder	84.50	83.50
Nedlloyd	175	180.50
Robeco	92.60	93.10
Rolinco	85.20	85.40
Rorento	50.40	50.50
Wessanen	283.50	284.50

a-Ex-dividend.

HONG KONG (in Hong Kong dollars)

	Close	Prev. Close
Bk of East Asia	19.30	19.20
Cheung Kong	20.80	21
Hang Seng Bk	37	37.50
Hong Kong El	8.90	8.85
Hong Kong Lnd	6.30	6.30
HongkongShBk	6.65	6.60
Hutchsn Whmp	30.75	30.50
Jardine Mathsn	13.30	13.30
SunHungKaiP	12.10	12.20
Swire Pacific	14.20	14.20
World Intl	2.45	2.50

z-Not quoted.

SYDNEY (in Australian dollars)

	Close	Prev. Close
ANZ Bk Grp	6.30	6.16
Central Norse	8.40	8.80
Coles GJ	6.10	6.08
CRA	6.66	6.36
CSR	3.26	3.30
LeightonHld	0.82	0.83
Natl Aust Bk	6.60	6.58
News Corp	18.90	19
RensnGoldFlds	5.34	5.30
Repco	1.96	1.90
Santos	3.75	3.80
SouthrnPacPet	0.16	0.16
Westrn Mining	3.25	3.30
Westpac	6.24	6.78
Woodside Pete	1	1.03
Woolworth Ltr	3.45	3.50

The Wall Street Journal, *April 22, 1986*

1981–82 was a key signal that henceforth corporations could produce growing and stable earnings. Second, the low P-E ratio meant that stocks were undervalued. Growing earnings would generate rising share prices, and when sufficient numbers of investors realized that the earnings improvement was permanent, the P-E ratio would rise to higher levels as buying pressure drove stock prices up.

The bull market of the 80s began in the summer of 1982, when it became clear that the Fed had loosened its monetary vise. The decline in interest rates mattered to investors because the rate of interest is an alternative return to earnings per share (P-E ratio). As interest rates fell, investors moved out of interest-earning instruments and into stocks.

FOREIGN SECURITIES

Unless noted, all issues are American Depositary Receipts, or ADRs, representing ownership of securities physically deposited abroad. Quotes are in U.S. dollars. n-Not ADR. Explanatory notes on Over-the-Counter page.

Monday, April 21, 1986

stock & div		sales 100s	bid	asked	net chg.
GREAT	**BRITAIN**				
Beecham G	.05d	726	6 7-16	6 15-32	– 1-16
Burmah Oil	.06d	2	5 7-16	5½	...
Rank	Organ	47	8½	8 9-16	...
JAPAN					
Fuji Photo	.05d	3947	28¼	28⅜	+ 1¾
NissanMotr	.09b	111	6 9-16	6⅝	+ 5-16
TokioMarine	F	17	338½	340	– 9
ToyotaMotr	.07d	2074	17⅝	17¾	+ 1⅛
MEXICO					
TeleDeMex	.01e	12000	3-32	⅛	...
SOUTH	**AFRICA**				
AngloAGld	.32d	104	7⅜	7 7-16	+ 1-16
AngAm SAf	.47b	54	13¾	13⅞	– ⅛
BlyvoorGld	.29d	496	5 3-16	5¼	...
BuffelstnG	3.27b	262	21	21¼	– ¼
DeBeersMn	.16d	1636	7 19-32	7⅝	– 1-32
Driefontn	1.21b	381	16½	16⅝	– ¼
FreeStCon	Gold	1627	11¼	11⅜	– ⅛
Gold Fields	.20d	135	11½	11¾	– ⅛
Kloof Gold	.20d	266	7 3-16	7¼	+ 1-32
Lydenbrg	Plat	39	9⅜	9 9-16	– 3-32
Orange	FreeSt	242	27	27¼	...
StHelenGd	1.04d	138	11½	11¾	...
Sasol	Limitd	104	2 7-32	2 9-32	– 1-32
VaalReefs	.44d	831	6 13-16	6⅞	– 1-16
Welkom	Gold	191	7	7⅛	...
WstDeepL	1.73d	93	35	35⅛	– ⅛

The Wall Street Journal, *April 22, 1986*

P.E. Ratios →

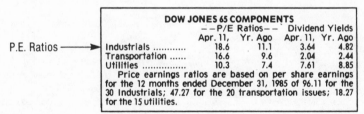

DOW JONES 65 COMPONENTS

	--P/E Ratios--		Dividend Yields	
	Apr. 11,	Yr. Ago	Apr. 11,	Yr. Ago
Industrials	18.6	11.1	3.64	4.82
Transportation	16.6	9.6	2.04	2.44
Utilities	10.3	7.4	7.61	8.85

Price earnings ratios are based on per share earnings for the 12 months ended December 31, 1985 of 96.11 for the 30 Industrials; 47.27 for the 20 transportation issues; 18.27 for the 15 utilities.

The Wall Street Journal, *April 14, 1986*

The shift into stocks continued because investors now recognized the growing potential for increased corporate profits (nominal earnings). This drove the Dow's P-E ratio up from barely over 10 to almost 20. You can see in the excerpt above from the April 14, 1986, *Journal* that the P-E ratio had climbed to 18.6 on per share earnings of $96.11. Investors had bought stocks to position themselves for a great improvement in earnings; the Dow was no longer undervalued.

Chart 13–3
Dow Jones Industrial Average (price), Earnings per Share, and Price-Earnings Ratio

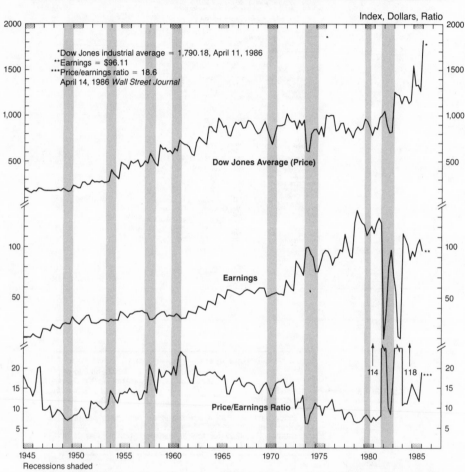

Index, Dollars, Ratio

*Dow Jones industrial average = 1,790.18, April 11, 1986
**Earnings = $96.11
***Price/earnings ratio = 18.6
April 14, 1986 *Wall Street Journal*

Dow Jones Average (Price)

Earnings

Price/Earnings Ratio

114   118

Recessions shaded

Source: Phyllis S. Pierce, ed., *The Dow Jones Investors Handbook* (Homewood, Ill.: Dow Jones-Irwin, 1986), and *Barron's*.

Investors sensed the potential for higher *nominal* earnings because of the sharp improvement in the quality of *real* earnings, shown in Chart 13–4 on page 225. Once real earnings cracked the plateau of the 1965–80 period, nominal earnings could not be far behind, and investors correctly predicted that the Dow, too, would respond by breaking out of its 1965–80 range.

Now the intimate correlation between real earnings and the Dow should be clear to you. In the mid-80s, as in the 50s, investors bid up the Dow

Chart 13–4
Dow Jones Industrial Average and Real Earnings (corporate profits in 1982 dollars with inventory valuation and capital consumption adjustment)

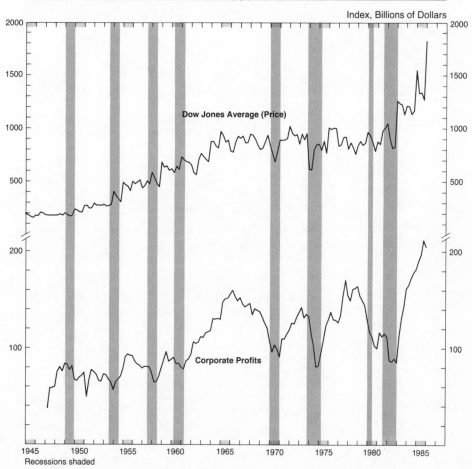

Source: Phyllis S. Pierce, ed., *The Dow Jones Investors Handbook* (Homewood, Ill.: Dow Jones-Irwin, 1986); *Barron's;* and U.S. Department of Commerce, *Business Conditions Digest* and *Handbook of Cyclical Indicators,* series 80.

to a high P-E ratio in anticipation of the nominal earnings heralded by the improvement in real earnings. In the near future, as nominal earnings rise to justify the lofty multiple of the P-E ratio, you can expect a slow, continuous improvement of the Dow.

14

U.S. International Transactions

*F*oreign exchange rates, IMF, balance of trade, balance of payments— and the other terms used to discuss America's international economic relations—can be defined and described in the context of current events. But to understand them thoroughly, you must think back to World War II. Most of our modern international economic institutions were formed at the end of the war and immediately afterward, when the American dollar assumed the central role it still occupies today. Let's take the time to review developments since then before plunging into the data and terminology by means of which current international transactions are discussed.

In the summer of 1944, in the resort town of Bretton Woods, New Hampshire, well before World War II came to a close, the Allies were so certain of victory that the United States hosted a conference to plan international monetary affairs for the postwar years. The United States knew that the war was taking a drastic toll on the rest of the world's economies, while the U.S. economy was growing stronger. Both victor and vanquished would need food, fuel, raw materials, and equipment, but only the United States could furnish these requirements. How were other nations to pay for these imports? They had very little that Americans wanted. If they sold their money for dollars in order to buy goods from us, the strong selling pressure on their currencies and their strong demand for dollars would drive their currencies down in value and the dollar up. Soon the dollar would be so expensive, in terms of foreign currency, that the rest of the world could not afford to buy the American goods necessary to rebuild.

It would have been very easy to say that this was everyone else's problem, not ours, but America's statesmen knew that it was our problem as well. This lesson had been learned after World War I, when similar difficulties had faced the world economy. Following that war, the United States had washed its hands of international responsibilities; consequently, the world economy had suffered through a dollar shortage. Many nations had been forced into currency devaluations, and the United States had ended up with most of the world's supply of gold, as other nations had used gold in desperation to settle their accounts with the United States. Moreover, each nation had sought shelter in shortsighted protectionist devices, shattering the world economy. Economic nationalism had spilled into the diplomatic arena and had been partly responsible for World War II.

Determined to avoid these mistakes the second time around, the United States convened the Bretton Woods Conference to deal with such problems before they arose. The conference's principal task was to prevent runaway depreciation of other currencies after the war. It therefore created the *International Monetary Fund* (IMF), a pool of currencies to which all nations (but mostly the United States) contributed and from which any nation could borrow in order to shore up the value of its own currency. If a nation's currency was under selling pressure, and weak and falling in value compared to other currencies, buying pressure designed to drive its price upward could be implemented with strong currencies borrowed from the IMF. For instance, Britain could borrow dollars from the IMF to buy pounds, thus supporting the price of the pound.

The dollar was pegged to gold at $35 an ounce, and all other currencies were pegged to the dollar, so that a dollar was worth a fixed number of francs, pounds, and so forth. At the time, the United States had most of the world's gold and other nations had hardly any, so the entire system was tied to gold through the U.S. dollar. This system of fixed exchange rates was constructed to provide stability in international economic relationships. Traders and investors knew exactly what a contract for future delivery of goods or future return on investment was worth in terms of the foreign exchange in which the contract was written. There was no need to speculate on shifting exchange rates, which could wipe out profit margins or generate large losses.

To draw an analogy, consider a shipment of oranges from California to New York and investments made by Californians on the New York Stock Exchange. Californians must be concerned about the price of oranges in New York and the price of a share of stock on the exchange, but they need not be concerned about fluctuations in the value of New York currency versus California currency, since both states use dollars.

Now think how much more difficult selling and investing in New York would be for Californians if the exchange rate between their currencies fluctuated. The diplomats wished to avoid precisely that problem after World War II, and that's why the Bretton Woods Conference established the IMF and a system of fixed exchange rates.

Unfortunately, after the war the U.S. *balance-of-trade surplus* (the amount by which the revenue of all exports exceeds the cost of all imports) created a greater dollar shortage than the conference had anticipated. Other nations were continually selling their currencies in order to buy American dollars with which to buy American goods. Selling pressure forced down the price of other currencies despite the IMF, which was not large enough to bail them out, and many of these currencies faced runaway depreciation against the dollar.

The United States responded to this crisis with the Marshall Plan. George C. Marshall, a career soldier, had been chairman of the Joint Chiefs of Staff during the war. At the war's end, President Truman appointed him secretary of state. Marshall understood that Europe's recovery was hobbled by a shortage of food, fuel, raw materials, and machinery and equipment, and that the United States was the only nation that could supply Europe's needs in sufficient quantities. He further understood that the dollar shortage prevented Europe from importing what it needed from the United States. He proposed, and President Truman and Congress approved, a plan whereby the European nations drew up a list of their needs and the United States provided them with the dollars they required to satisfy those needs. In that way, the European nations' balances of payments were not strained and their currencies were freed from the pressure of devaluation. American exports, of course, benefited as our dollars bounced right back to us for purchases of American goods.

By the time of the Korean War, everyone was talking about the "economic miracle of Europe." The Marshall Plan had been extended to victor and vanquished, probably history's greatest example of benevolence as enlightened self-interest. The United States had learned from its mistakes following World War I. Isolationism was myopic; the United States had to play an active role in world affairs. And our generosity would be repaid many times over as foreign markets for our goods recovered rapidly.

The Marshall Plan became a cornerstone of American foreign policy. Yet the United States also provided the rest of the world with desperately needed dollars in a number of other ways, not all of them on purpose. For example, the United States began to maintain a substantial military presence overseas, and our foreign bases provided their host countries with dollars when native civilians employed at the bases and American personnel spent their paychecks. In addition, American business firms resumed overseas investing, especially in Europe, providing dollars to countries where subsidiaries were purchased and facilities built. Finally, Americans started to travel abroad in great numbers, seeding Europe with funds. All of these activities meant that dollars were sold for foreign exchange (foreign currency) and offset the constant sale by other nations of their currency in order to buy American goods.

Furthermore, whenever foreign banks, businesses, or individuals received more dollars than were immediately required, they were delighted to deposit those dollars in either American or foreign banks in order to hold them for a rainy day. Since dollars were in vigorous demand because of the continuing need to buy American exports, those dollars could always be sold in the future, and meanwhile they were a handy private reserve should an occasion arise to spend them later.

To summarize, there were four principal outflows of dollars from the United States: foreign aid (such as the Marshall Plan), foreign investment, military presence overseas, and tourism. These outflows were offset by the two principal influxes of foreign exchange: foreign purchase of American exports, which greatly exceeded our purchases of imports, and foreigners' willingness to hold dollars as a liquid investment. The four outflows of dollars (roughly) equaled the two influxes of foreign exchange.

By the late 1950s and early 60s, however, some foreign banks, businesses, and individuals found that they had more dollars than they could use. They did not wish to buy American goods, and they had found making other investments more attractive than holding dollars, so they decided to sell them.

The United States did not have to rely on the IMF to support the dollar and maintain a fixed exchange rate between the dollar and other currencies. Rather, the U.S. Treasury stood ready to redeem dollars with gold whenever selling pressure on the dollar became heavy. That is, the United States propped up the price of the dollar relative to other currencies by buying the dollar for gold. Since a foreign holder of dollars could buy gold at $35 per ounce and sell that gold for foreign exchange anywhere in the world, there was no need to sell dollars below the fixed rate of exchange. Whenever the dollar fell a little, foreigners would buy gold with their dollars and cash that gold in for other currencies at full value, which kept the dollar up. And the U.S. price of $35 per ounce of gold set the world price for gold, simply because the United States had most of the world's supply. As a result, gold started to leave the United States in a stream as dollars were redeemed for it. American holdings of gold were cut almost in half by the time increasing alarm was voiced in the early 60s.

An alternative solution had to be found, or else the U.S. supply of gold would disappear. The foreign central banks stepped in and agreed to support the price of the dollar as part of their obligation to maintain fixed exchange rates under the Bretton Woods agreement. They had potentially limitless supplies of their own currencies. If a bank, business, or individual in another nation wanted to sell dollars, and this selling pressure tended to force the price of the dollar down in terms of that nation's currency, the foreign central bank would buy the dollars for its currency and thus support the price of the dollar. This could not be accomplished by the U.S. Treasury or the Federal Reserve System because neither had limitless supplies of foreign currency. As long as the foreign central banks were willing to buy and accumulate dollars, private citizens, banks, and businesses in other countries were satisfied. In this way, the system of fixed exchange rates survived.

However, by the late 60s and early 70s the situation had become ominous. The United States no longer had a favorable balance of trade. Other nations were selling more to, and buying less from, the United States. America's favorable balance of trade had been the single big plus in its balance of payments, offsetting the outflows of dollars mentioned earlier: foreign aid (the Marshall Plan), American tourism, foreign investment, and the American military presence overseas. Now the dollar holdings of foreign central banks began to swell ever more rapidly as their citizens liquidated dollar holdings. These central banks realized that they were acquiring an asset that ultimately would be of little value to them. Having been put in a position of continually buying dollars they would never be able to sell, they insisted that the United States do something to remedy the situation.

The French suggested that the dollar be officially devalued as a first step, because it had had a very high value in terms of other currencies ever since World War II. They reasoned that if the dollar were worth less in terms of other currencies, American exports would be cheaper for the rest of the world, imports would be more expensive in the United States, and thus the U.S. balance of trade would shift from negative to positive as the United States exported more and imported less. In addition, if foreign currencies were more expensive, Americans would be less likely to travel and invest overseas. This would partially stem the dollar hemorrhage. Others suggested that the foreign central banks stop supporting (buying) the dollar and that the dollar be allowed to float downward to a more reasonable level as foreigners sold off their holdings.

For many years, the United States resisted both devaluation and flotation, until, in a series of developments between 1971 and 1973, we ceased redeeming the dollar for gold and permitted it to float. It promptly fell, relative to other currencies, because foreign central banks no longer felt obliged to purchase it in order to support its price.

At the same time, the price of gold increased because the United States would no longer redeem dollars with gold. The willingness of the United

States to sell gold virtually without limit at $35 per ounce had kept its value from rising, but now the price of gold could increase according to the forces of private supply and demand. It fluctuated with all other commodity prices, rising rapidly during the general inflation at the end of the 1970s and then falling with commodity prices after 1980.

The dollar fell until the summer of 1973, and then it fluctuated in value until the end of the decade. Foreign central banks no longer felt obliged to buy the dollar in order to support its price, though they occasionally did so to keep it from plummeting too far or too rapidly. They took this action in their own interest at the suggestion of exporters, who knew that a low value for the dollar and a high value for their own currencies made it difficult to export to the United States.

The dollar broke out of the range in which it fluctuated during the 1970s, and its value today is greater than it was in those years. A discussion of the reasons for this should be put in the context of an introduction to the balance of payments, the balance of trade, and foreign exchange rates, all of which are published regularly in *The Wall Street Journal.*

Few statistical series generate as much confusion as those portraying America's international transactions; you will see that they are really not difficult to understand or follow on a regular basis.

BALANCE OF PAYMENTS AND BALANCE OF TRADE

In order to understand the *balance-of-payments* accounts, think of yourself as representing the United States in all dealings with the rest of the world. If you wish to do business with the rest of the world, you must buy its currencies (called *foreign exchange*). Likewise, in order to do business in the United States, the rest of the world must buy dollars.

U.S. Balance of Payments

Money going out (−)	Money coming in (+)
Uses by United States for all foreign exchange purchased with U.S. dollars	Uses by rest of world for all U.S. dollars purchased with foreign exchange

Now set up an accounting statement. The left side will include all the uses you had for all the foreign exchange you purchased. The right side of the account will include all the uses for the dollars that the rest of the world purchased. The two sides must balance, because for every dollar's worth of foreign exchange that you buy with a dollar, the rest of the world must use a dollar's worth of foreign exchange to buy that dollar. You have just constructed a balance-of-payments statement.

Once the accounting statement has been set up, you may add other details. Each side of the statement will have a *current account* and a *capital account.* The current account will be subdivided into merchandise trade, services, and foreign aid; the capital account will be subdivided into private investment and central bank transactions.

U.S. Balance of Payments

U.S. purchase of foreign money (debit) (−)	Foreign purchase of U.S. money (credit) (+)
Current account payments by United States to rest of world	Current account payments to United States by rest of world
Goods and services imports by United States	Goods and services exports by United States
Merchandise trade imports	Merchandise trade exports
Services for which United States pays rest of world	Services United States sells to rest of world
Foreign aid payments by United States to rest of world	Foreign aid payments by the rest of world to United States
Capital account outflows of funds from United States	Capital account inflows of funds to United States
Private investment by United States in rest of world	Private investment by rest of world in United States
Central bank transactions such as Fed buys foreign currencies	Central bank transactions such as foreign central banks buy dollars

To summarize: the left side of this account *(debit)* shows what you, representing the United States, are doing with the foreign exchange you purchased with American dollars. The right side of the account *(credit)* shows what the rest of the world is doing with the dollars it purchased with its money. Remember, the two sides must be equal; a transaction can take place only if things of equal worth are exchanged.

Now, nothing has yet been said about the price you must pay to buy foreign exchange or the price the rest of the world must pay to buy dollars. The rate of exchange between dollars and foreign currency will fluctuate with the forces of supply and demand. That is, if your demand for foreign money is relatively stronger than the demand of the rest of the world for dollars, your selling pressure on the dollar in order to buy foreign currency is going to force the dollar down in relative value. You will have to give up more dollars in order to get a unit of foreign exchange, or to put it the other way around, you will get less foreign exchange for your dollars. If, on the other hand, the demand of the rest of the world for your dollars exceeds your demand for its currency, the reverse will be true and the dollar will increase in value compared to foreign currencies as the rest of the world must use more and more of its currency to buy a dollar.

Return to the balance-of-payments account. Although the total for each side is equal, the individual categories are not equal, so that you can balance one category against another in order to arrive at a merchandise trade balance, goods and services balance, and so on. Each category in the balance of payments will be examined in turn.

Balance on Current Account

Balance on Goods and Services.
Merchandise Trade.   You can use the foreign exchange you have purchased to buy foreign goods, and the rest of the world can use dollars to buy American goods. Thus, if you import goods into the United States, you have incurred a debit (−) because you have sold dollars to buy foreign currency in order to make the transaction; in other words, money has left the United States. On the other hand, if the rest of the world buys American goods, you have earned a credit (+). It is customary to talk about the *balance on merchandise trade* by netting imports against exports to determine whether we have an export (+) surplus or an import (−) deficit.
Services.   If you use your dollars to buy foreign currency in order to travel in a foreign country, or use a foreign air carrier, or pay interest on a foreign debt, all this would be classified as an outflow of funds or debit (−). On the other hand, if the rest of the world used the dollars it bought to travel in the United States, or fly with an American air carrier, or pay interest on a debt to the United States, that flow of money to the United States would be a credit (+).

If the net credit (+) or debit (−) balance on this account is added to the credit (+) or debit (−) balance of the merchandise trade account, this subtotal is referred to as the *balance on goods and services.*

Foreign Aid.   If you use the foreign money you have purchased to make a gift to the rest of the world, that's a debit (−); and if the rest of the world uses the dollars it has purchased to make a gift to the United States, that's a credit (+) (and a miracle).

When the foreign aid transaction is combined with the balance on goods and services, it completes the *balance on current account,* which will be a debit (−) balance or a credit (+) balance, depending on whether more funds flowed out of or into the United States.

The Capital Accounts

As a private investor, you may wish to sell U.S. dollars and buy foreign exchange in order to make an investment in the rest of the world. This could be a direct investment in the form of plant and equipment expenditures or the purchase of a foreign company, or it could be a financial asset, either long term or short term. (Stocks and bonds, for instance, are long-term financial investments, while a foreign bank account or a holding in foreign currency is a short-term investment.) Any of these transactions will be a debit (−) in the American account because dollars have left the United States. Conversely, when a private investor in the rest of the world sells foreign exchange in order to use U.S. dollars to make a direct or financial investment in the United States, whether long term or short term, this is classified as a credit (+).

If, as a representative of the Federal Reserve System, you sell dollars in order to buy foreign currency, this too is a debit (−), and when foreign central banks buy dollars, it is a credit (+). These central bank transactions conclude the discussion of balance-of-payments components.

A further point must be made before you plow into the data. References are constantly being made to deficits or surpluses in the balances on trade, goods and services, and current account. Now and then you may encounter a comment about a deficit or surplus in the balance of payments despite this chapter's assertion that it always balances.

Trade, goods and services, and current account are easy. You already know that there can be a surplus (+) or a deficit (−) in these separate accounts. But how could anyone speak of a *deficit* in the total balance of payments when it must always *balance?* Because that is the shorthand way of saying that the nation's currency is under selling pressure and that the value of the currency will fall unless some remedial action is taken.

For instance, at the time the foreign central banks were supporting the value of the dollar, their purchases of dollars constituted a "plus" (+) in the American balance of payments because they sopped up the excess dollars that their own economies didn't need. (Had they not done so, the dollar would have fallen in value.) Obviously, if you remove a plus from an accounting system that is in balance, what remains has a negative bottom line. Since the plus that made the account balance was a remedial action and since without it the account would have been negative, reference was made to a deficit in the balance of payments.

When the United States still made sales of gold internationally, in order to redeem the dollar, these sales were "plus" (+) entries in our balance of payments. If you wonder why the loss of gold is a plus, remember that anything sold by the United States is a plus because the rest of the world must pay us for it. Now, if you remove gold sales from the balance of payments, the remaining items must net out to a negative balance. Therefore, people often referred to the size of the U.S. gold loss as its deficit in its balance of payments.

And now for one final tip before you look at the data: keep your eyes on the money. That's the best way to determine whether something is a "plus" (+) or "minus" (−) in the balance of payments. If *we* pay for it, that's a minus, because money is going out. If *they* pay for it, that's a plus.

The Wall Street Journal regularly publishes two Commerce Department reports dealing with the balance of payments and the balance of trade that will be useful to you.

1. *Balance-of-payments* figures for the previous *quarter* appear between the 18th and the 20th day of the last month of each quarter.
2. *Monthly balance-of-trade* figures for the previous month are published between the 25th and the 28th of each month.

Look for the following in the typical (March 19, 1986) balance-of-payments article: *current account balance, merchandise trade balance, services,* and *foreign aid.* Very few of the items in the capital account are reported, so the article will not present a complete record of the balance of payments. (See page 237).

The March 19, 1986, *Journal* article presents the information you need. According to the first paragraph, the current account deficit was $36.56 billion in the last quarter of 1985. This was generated by the merchandise trade deficit of $39.48 billion (seventh paragraph) and foreign aid payments of $4.19 billion (sixth paragraph from end), and occurred despite net service income of $7.11 billion (eighth paragraph).

Put these figures in the accounting format used earlier (as shown below and on the top of page 237).

The March 19 article devoted most of its attention to the annual (1985) data. See if you can put those annual figures into the accounting framework used for the quarterly data. The current account balance (−$117.66 billion) is in paragraph 1, the merchandise trade balance (−$124.29 billion) in the seventh paragraph, and service income (+$21.41 billion) and foreign aid (−$14.78 billion) in the eighth paragraph and the sixth from the end, respectively.

U.S. Balance of Payments
Fourth Quarter 1985

U.S. purchase of foreign exchange (−)		Foreign purchase of dollars (+)	
Merchandise trade deficit	$39.48 billion	Service income	$7.11 billion
Foreign aid	$ 4.19 billion		
Current account deficit	$36.56 billion		
(trade deficit and			
foreign aid less			
service income)			

Merchandise trade (deficit)	−$39.48 billion
Service income (surplus)	+ 7.11 billion
Foreign aid (deficit)	− 4.19 billion
Balance on current account (deficit)	−$36.56 billion

Trade Gap Set Mark in Quarter And Full Year

By ROSE GUTFELD

Staff Reporter of THE WALL STREET JOURNAL

WASHINGTON—The broadest measure of the nation's trade deficit widened to a record $36.56 billion in the fourth quarter and $117.66 billion in all 1985, the Commerce Department said.

The balance of payments deficits on the current account followed a revised deficit of $29.30 billion in the third quarter and a $107.36 billion gap in 1984. The third-quarter figure was originally reported as $30.45 billion.

The swelling of the deficit is the latest illustration of the battering that domestic producers have taken from imports. Many economists contend it will be midyear before the trade picture starts to improve, in response to the dollar's sharp decline in foreign-exchange trading. The dollar has fallen nearly 30% in the past year against major currencies, and a lower dollar makes U.S. exports more competitive and imports more expensive.

"It's still too early to see much effect from the fall of the dollar," said Bluford Putnam, vice president and senior economist at Morgan Stanley & Co. Mr. Putnam doesn't expect substantial improvement until the second half of the year.

"It takes a long time for a decline in the value of the dollar to really have an impact," said David Berson, senior economist at Wharton Econometric Forecasting Associates in Philadelphia. The first effect of a decline in the dollar is an increase in prices of imports. But because it takes awhile for consumers to change their buying habits, people initially keep buying more expensive imports. This makes the deficit swell until people reduce purchases of imports.

Mr. Berson said he expects the trade picture to improve in coming months, in part because the value of oil imports is dropping, reflecting the steep drop in oil prices.

The Wall Street Journal, *March 19, 1986*

The nation's merchandise trade deficit widened in the fourth quarter to $39.48 billion from $32.96 billion in the third quarter. For the year it widened to $124.29 billion from $114.11 billion in 1984.

The U.S. continued to run a surplus in the so-called services trade, however. This surplus dropped to $7.11 billion in the fourth quarter from $7.65 billion in the third. For the year it grew to $21.41 billion from $18.16 billion in 1984.

Services trade includes earnings brought back to the U.S. by companies with subsidiaries overseas. In the fourth quarter earnings from direct investment abroad fell to $10.98 billion from $11.04 billion in the third quarter. For the year, this figure grew to $35.29 billion from $23.08 billion in 1984.

Overall exports of goods and services rose to $91.25 billion in the fourth quarter from $90.77 billion in the third. Imports rose to $123.62 billion from $116.07 billion. For 1985, exports fell to $359.7 billion from $362.02 billion in 1984. Imports rose to $462.58 billion from $457.97 billion.

The current account figures also include nonmilitary grants, pensions and other government payments abroad, which rose to $4.19 billion in the fourth quarter from $4 billion in the third. For the year, this category totaled $14.78 billion, compared with $11.41 billion.

A measure of the net flow of capital into the U.S. rose to $48.54 billion in the fourth quarter from $34.55 billion in the third period. This reflected an increase in private foreign investment. Foreign official assets in the U.S. declined $1.6 billion.

For the year, this flow of capital into the U.S. increased to $123.11 billion from $97.32 billion the year before.

A measure of U.S. investment abroad rose in the quarter to $22.42 billion from $12.75 billion. For the year, it increased to $38.18 billion from $20.45 billion in 1984.

U.S. official reserve assets in the quarter increased to $3.15 billion from $121 million in the previous quarter. This largely reflected U.S. purchases of foreign currencies as part of the five-country effort that the U.S. engineered in September to bring down the value of the dollar, the Commerce Department said.

For the year, reserve assets rose to $3.86 billion from $3.13 billion the year before.

Current Account Balance—First Paragraph.

WASHINGTON—The broadest measure
of the nation's trade deficit widened to a
record $36.56 billion in the fourth quarter
and $117.66 billion in all 1985, the Com-
merce Department said.

Merchandise Trade Balance—Seventh Paragraph.

The nation's merchandise trade deficit
widened in the fourth quarter to $39.48 bil-
lion from $32.96 billion in the third quarter.
For the year it widened to $124.29 billion
from $114.11 billion in 1984.

Services—Eighth Paragraph.

The U.S. continued to run a surplus in
the so-called services trade, however. This
surplus dropped to $7.11 billion in the
fourth quarter from $7.65 billion in the
third. For the year it grew to $21.41 billion
from $18.16 billion in 1984.

Foreign Aid—Sixth Paragraph from End of Article.

The current account figures also include
nonmilitary grants, pensions and other
government payments abroad, which rose
to $4.19 billion in the fourth quarter from
$4 billion in the third. For the year, this
category totaled $14.78 billion, compared
with $11.41 billion.

Chart 14–1

Balance of Payments (quarterly data): Current Account Balance, Goods and Services Balance, and Merchandise Trade Balance

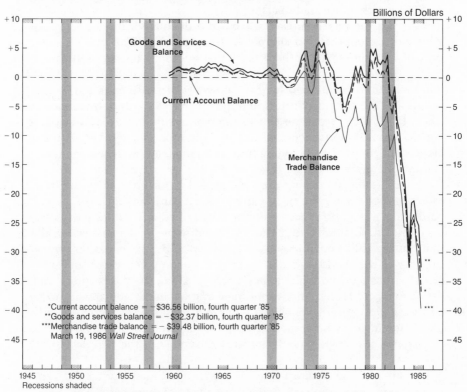

Billions of Dollars

*Current account balance = – $36.56 billion, fourth quarter '85
**Goods and services balance = – $32.37 billion, fourth quarter '85
***Merchandise trade balance = – $39.48 billion, fourth quarter '85
March 19, 1986 *Wall Street Journal*

Recessions shaded

Source: U.S. Department of Commerce, *Business Conditions Digest* and *Handbook of Cyclical Indicators,* series 622 and 667; U.S. Department of Commerce, *Business Statistics;* and *Federal Reserve Bulletin.*

The quarterly and annual figures tell the same story. The outflow due to the trade deficit and foreign aid swamped service income—hence, the current account deficit.

Use Chart 14–1 on page 239 to analyze these developments. You can make two observations. First, the merchandise trade balance and the balance on current account are virtually congruent and dropped like a stone in the early 80s. Second, the balance on current account remained positive until lately, after a brief dip in 1977 and 1978, even though the merchandise trade balance became sharply negative as early as the mid-70s.

The gap between the current account and merchandise trade balances is composed of service income, such as the net earnings that the United

States receives from foreign investments, the sale of banking, transport, and insurance services, and foreign tourism in the United States. In other words, until just recently, U.S. service earnings grew so rapidly that the balance on current account remained positive (+) despite an acutely negative (−) merchandise trade balance.

Why did the merchandise trade balance fluctuate in the late 70s, and why did it deteriorate so sharply in the early 80s? The business cycle provides an answer to both parts of this question. Imports fell sharply in 1975 because the recession reduced demand, including demand for imports. Exports continued to grow, however, because recession had not yet gripped our trading partners, and thus 1975 was a year of trade surplus. Then, in 1976–77, recession spread internationally and exports began to lag just as our imports increased sharply with economic recovery at home. Hence, our trade balance swung into, and remained in, deficit as imports and exports grew at similar rates, with a steady gap between them.

Imports fell again during the 1980 recession, while exports continued to grow. As a result, the trade gap narrowed substantially. And imports hardly had a chance to recover before they fell off again during the 1981–82 recession. Consequently, the merchandise trade deficit was smaller than during the economic expansion of 1978. But as recession gripped the rest of the world and the American economy recovered and grew, our exports stagnated while imports rose, pushing the merchandise trade deficit to record levels. And it continued to grow in the mid-80s as Europe recovered slowly from its slump while our economy expanded. Swiftly improving incomes here have boosted our demand for imports, whereas our exports to Europe have languished in sync with the European economy.

In addition, high interest rates in the United States during the 1981–82 recession, and a more favorable investment climate here than abroad, attracted foreign funds to the United States and discouraged American funds from leaving. The net drop in demand for foreign currencies (increased demand for dollars) pushed up the value of the dollar, making American goods more expensive, making foreign goods less expensive, and discouraging exports while encouraging imports.

You can use the *Journal* to follow the Commerce Department's monthly *merchandise trade* report. The March 28, 1986, article provides data for February. Focus your attention on *imports, exports,* and the *balance* between the two. (See page 241.)

According to the *first, last, and next-to-last paragraphs,* the United States ran a $12.49 billion trade deficit in February 1986 as exports rose and imports fell. And elsewhere, the article tells you that many expect the merchandise trade deficit to be only slightly larger in 1986 than it was in 1985. That's consistent with steady improvement in the European economies and a decline in the dollar's value since late 1985.

U.S. Merchandise Trade Deficit Shrinks, Reflecting Oil Prices and Falling Dollar

By PAUL BLUSTEIN
Staff Reporter of THE WALL STREET JOURNAL

Merchandise Trade Deficit {

WASHINGTON—The nation's merchandise trade deficit narrowed in February to $12.49 billion, the Commerce Department said, reflecting lower oil prices, seasonal factors and a modest contribution from the falling dollar.

January's deficit figure was revised to $14.42 billion. Commerce Department statisticians caution against comparing revised figures with preliminary figures, however, and they say a more valid comparison is with the original January figure of $16.46 billion, a record for any month. The revision left December's $14.91 billion as the record. The deficit in February 1985 was $8.49 billion.

The White House described the report as "welcome news." Presidential spokesman Larry Speakes said the February figure "should signal the start of a fairly steady decline in the trade deficit."

But many economists said that the February data overstate the improvement in the trade picture, and that continued progress will come slowly.

"We're still going to have huge trade deficits," said Bluford Putnam, vice president and senior economist at Morgan Stanley & Co., although he added that the "worst" of the monthly trade gaps seen in recent months have probably passed.

David Hale, chief economist at Kemper Financial Services Inc., said the February figures indicate that the trade deficit in the current quarter is stabilizing instead of growing, as some analysts had feared when the January numbers were released. But for the year, the 1986 trade deficit should exceed 1985's record $144.59 billion by a "modest" amount, Mr. Hale said.

Part of the improvement in February arose from the decline in world oil prices, a factor that should continue to help the trade balance in months to come, Commerce Secretary Malcolm Baldrige said. The average price of imported oil was $24.85 a barrel in February, down from $27.14 a barrel in January but still several dollars above the level at which many analysts expect the price to settle.

And an improved trade balance with Europe shows that the decline in the dollar is beginning to influence the trade figures, Mr. Hale said.

But many months remain before the full beneficial effect of the lower dollar shows up in the trade figures, analysts said. That's because as import prices rise, consumers and businesses in the U.S. switch to domestic goods slowly; thus, the nation's overall import bill tends to swell a bit at first before it declines. Many economists expect the dollar's fall to have a big impact on the trade deficit in the second half of 1986 at the earliest.

There are other reasons to doubt that the improvement in the February trade data will be sustained in the next several months. For one thing, the Commerce Department figures aren't seasonally adjusted for such factors as February's fewer days.

What's more, the Commerce Department has had severe problems in calculating trade data on a timely basis. The department said that in the February figures, 32.5% of imports and 11.4% of exports actually occurred in prior months but that the data were received late and included in the latest month.

The department is working with the Customs Service to speed up the computation of trade figures, and in the meantime it has been adjusting for reporting delays one month after the data are initially released.

The department said imports totaled $30.22 billion in February, down from an initially reported $33.46 billion in January and a revised $31.46 billion for that month. In February 1985, imports totaled $26.48 billion. } **Imports**

Exports totaled $17.73 billion in February, the department said. That's up from the $17.01 billion initially reported for January and the revised January figure of $17.04 billion. In February 1985, exports totaled $17.98 billion. } **Exports**

The Wall Street Journal, *March 28, 1986*

Merchandise Trade Balance—First Paragraph.

WASHINGTON—The nation's merchandise trade deficit narrowed in February to $12.49 billion, the Commerce Department said, reflecting lower oil prices, seasonal factors and a modest contribution from the falling dollar.

Exports—Last Paragraph.

Exports totaled $17.73 billion in February, the department said. That's up from the $17.01 billion initially reported for January and the revised January figure of $17.04 billion. In February 1985, exports totaled $17.98 billion.

Imports—Next-to-Last Paragraph.

The department said imports totaled $30.22 billion in February, down from an initially reported $33.46 billion in January and a revised $31.46 billion for that month. In February 1985, imports totaled $26.48 billion.

FOREIGN EXCHANGE RATES

Each day *The Wall Street Journal* publishes a report on foreign exchange trading activity. You can see the April 24, 1986, article on page 243. The *Journal* also publishes daily a table of *Foreign Exchange* quotations. The April 24, 1986, table is reproduced on pages 244 and 245.

You can use the *Journal*'s daily **Foreign Exchange** report (check the front-page index) to keep abreast of the dollar's value. For instance (see excerpt on page 245), on Wednesday, April 23, 1986, the British pound was worth approximately $1.53, the French franc, approximately $0.14, the Japanese yen, more than half a cent, the Swiss franc, approximately $0.54, and the German mark, approximately $0.45. Most foreign exchange trading is conducted by banks on behalf of their customers. Banks will also provide future delivery of foreign exchange for customers who want a guaranteed price in order to plan their operations and limit risk due to exchange rate fluctuation. The price for future delivery is known as the *forward rate,* and you can see forward quotes for the major currencies immediately beneath the current rate. Future contracts for foreign currencies are also available on a number of exchanges.

Recall the brief outline of the dollar's postwar history.

You can see from Chart 14–2 on page 247 that, with the exception of the Japanese yen, the value of foreign currencies in terms of dollars

U.S. Currency Eases as Traders Remain Bearish

But Dollar Rebounds a Bit In New York From Level Reached in Asia, Europe

By CHARLES W. STEVENS
Staff Reporter of THE WALL STREET JOURNAL

The U.S. dollar eased in relatively quiet foreign-exchange trading yesterday but rebounded slightly in New York from levels reached earlier in Asia and Europe.

Traders remained bearish toward the currency, but they were cautious about

In other major international news, Union Carbide closes door on last month's tentative settlement of claims stemming from Bhopal gas disaster. Please see page 8.

driving the dollar sharply lower in the face of rising U.S. interest rates and s~ _w tion that Japan may lobby th~ ۱۱ 167.98 major industrial natio~ ۱۰ late in New intervention to ۲' scent. . auing in Tokyo Thursday, the ۲ .ell against the Japanese currency ۱۰ 166.70 yen from 167.98 in New York yesterday afternoon.

In other late New York dealings, the dollar eased to 2.1810 West German marks from 2.1828 on Tuesday, and to 1.8255 Swiss francs from 1.8338. The dollar edged up to 6.9678 French francs from 6.9675.

Benefiting from the dollar's general weakness and firmer oil prices, the British pound climbed to $1.5368 from $1.5183. In addition, the pound gained against other European currencies, rising to 3.35 marks from 3.31, for example.

Stronger oil prices help the pound as Britain is a major oil exporter. Because British North Sea crude is priced in sterling, higher oil prices increase the incentive for Britain's oil customers to hold the currency to cover their petroleum purchases.

The Wall Street Journal, *April 24, 1986*

chases.

The dollar remained the focus of attention in foreign-exchange trading, which

CURRENCY RATES

	New York Wed	Home Mkt. Wed	New York Tues
(in U.S. dollars)			
British pound	1.5368	1.5258	1.5183
Canadian dollar	0.7186	0.7190	0.7190
(in foreign units to U.S. dollar)			
French franc	6.9678	6.9545	6.9675
Japanese yen	167.98	167.85	168.58
Swiss franc	1.8255	1.8320	1.8338
West German mark	2.1810	2.1819	2.1828

Based on average of late buying and selling rates. Home markets: London, Toronto, Paris, Tokyo, Zurich and Frankfurt.

GOLD PRICES
(in U.S. dollars per troy ounce)

Comex Wed	London PM Wed	London AM Wed	Comex Tues
346.00	346.20	347.25	346.80

Comex based on settlement price for gold for delivery in the nearest month on Commodity Exchange in New York.
London based on morning and afternoon price fixings of five major dealers.

was light because dealers, who are inclined to sell the dollar, were nervous over rising bond yields and reports in Tokyo that Japan's central bank has asked the U.S. Federal Reserve to join it in intervening to support the dollar.

"People are a little scared," said Fr~ coise Soares-Kemp, vice presi~' chief corporate trader a⁺ ۲ ۱۰ 15 pfennigs New York. .ці mark and 11 yen

Dealers ۰ ۲۰ ۱۱۱ese unit since April 15, of .Ja~ .ers believe the U.S. currency is .sed for a correction before moving downward again. They note that the dollar's latest dive has been the steepest since last September, when the five-nation effort to push the currency lower was launched.

Axel Coym, vice president and chief trader at European American Bank, New York, said a correction of the dollar back up to the "low-2.20s" against the West German currency was "warranted," echoing a view held by other traders.

Traders said they remain very bearish toward the dollar, mainly because they believe the Reagan administration still wants the dollar lower to cool protectionist fires. A weaker currency increases the cost competitiveness of exports while making imports more expensive.

On the Commodity Exchange in New York, gold fell 80 cents an ounce, to $346, in light trading on volume of 1.7 million ounces.

Gold was quoted at $346.10 an ounce during early trading in Hong Kong Thursday.

FOREIGN EXCHANGE

Wednesday, April 23, 1986
The New York foreign exchange selling rates below apply to trading among banks in amounts of $1 million and more, as quoted at 3 p.m. Eastern time by Bankers Trust Co. Retail transactions provide fewer units of foreign currency per dollar.

Country	U.S. $ equiv. Wed.	U.S. $ equiv. Tues.	Currency per U.S. $ Wed.	Currency per U.S. $ Tues.
Argentina (Austra)	1.2034	1.2034	.831	.831
Australia (Dollar)	.7303	.7305	1.3693	1.3689
Austria (Schilling)	.06515	.06481	15.35	15.43
Belgium (Franc)				
Commercial rate	.02241	.02224	44.62	44.97
Financial rate	.02219	.02205	45.06	45.35
Brazil (Cruzado)	.07262	.07262	13.77	13.77
British Pound → Britain (Pound)	1.5330	1.5160	.6523	.6596
30-Day Forward	1.5280	1.5108	.6545	.6619
90-Day Forward	1.5208	1.5036	.6575	.6651
180-Day Forward	1.5109	1.4937	.6619	.6695
Canada (Dollar)	.7174	.7193	1.3939	1.3902
30-Day Forward	.7157	.7176	1.3972	1.3936
90-Day Forward	.7127	.7146	1.4031	1.3994
180-Day Forward	.7089	.7109	1.4107	1.4067
Chile (Official rate) ...	.005345	.005345	187.10	187.10
China (Yuan)	.3138	.3138	3.1871	3.1871
Colombia (Peso)	.005429	.005429	184.20	184.20
Denmark (Krone)	.1238	.1230	8.0800	8.1275
Ecuador (Sucre)				
Official rate	.009174	.009174	109.00	109.00
Floating rate	.006897	.006897	145.00	145.00
Finland (Markka)	.2010	.2012	4.9750	4.9700
French Franc → France (Franc)	.1434	.1433	6.9750	6.9975
30-Day Forward	.1433	.1432	6.9785	6.9820
90-Day Forward	.1432	.1431	6.9855	6.9880
180-Day Forward	.1429	.1429	6.9960	6.9975
Greece (Drachma)	.007299	.007273	137.00	137.50
Hong Kong (Dollar) ...	.1286	.1286	7.7780	7.7790
India (Rupee)	.08123	.08097	12.31	12.35
Indonesia (Rupiah)	.0008881	.0008881	1126.00	1126.00
Ireland (Punt)	1.3855	1.3855	.7218	.7218
Israel (Shekel)	.6761	.6761	1.479	1.479
Italy (Lira)	.0006667	.0006658	1500.00	1502.00
Japanese Yen → Japan (Yen)	.005936	.005926	168.45	168.75
30-Day Forward	.005950	.005939	168.08	168.39
90-Day Forward	.005969	.005958	167.52	167.85
180-Day Forward	.006003	.005989	166.58	166.97
Jordan (Dinar)	2.9499	2.9499	.339	.339
Kuwait (Dinar)	3.4542	3.4542	.2895	.2895
Lebanon (Pound)	.04386	.04386	22.80	22.80
Malaysia (Ringgit)	.3927	.3918	2.5465	2.5520
Malta (Lira)	2.4661	2.4661	.4055	.4055
Netherland(Guilder) .	.4049	.4027	2.4700	2.4830
New Zealand (Dollar) .	.5780	.5715	1.7301	1.7498
Norway (Krone)	.1432	.1429	6.9850	7.0000
Pakistan (Rupee)	.06150	.06150	16.26	16.26
Peru (Intl)	.07168	.07168	13.95	13.95
Philippines (Peso)	.04878	.04878	20.50	20.50
Portugal (Escudo)	.006849	.006826	146.00	146.50
Saudi Arabia (Riyal) ..	.2740	.2740	3.6500	3.6495
Singapore (Dollar)	.4602	.4585	2.1730	2.1810
South Africa (Rand)				
Commercial rate	.4970	.5005	2.0121	1.9980
Financial rate	.3225	.3375	3.1007	2.9629
South Korea (Won) ...	.001128	.001128	886.50	886.50
Spain (Peseta)	.007176	.007161	139.35	139.65
Sweden (Krona)	.1415	.1410	7.0650	7.0900
Swiss Franc → Switzerland (Franc) ..	.5469	.5459	1.8285	1.8320
30-Day Forward	.5483	.5472	1.8238	1.8274
90-Day Forward	.5506	.5494	1.8162	1.8202
180-Day Forward	.5548	.5532	1.8025	1.8078
Taiwan (Dollar)	.02590	.02590	38.61	38.61
Thailand (Baht)	.03774	.03774	26.50	26.50
Turkey (Lira)	.001467	.001467	681.63	681.63
United Arab(Dirham)	.2723	.2723	3.673	3.673
Uruguay (New Peso)				
Financial	.007200	.007200	138.88	138.88
Venezuela (Bolivar)				
Official rate	.1333	.1333	7.50	7.50
Floating rate	.05221	.05221	19.15	19.15
German Mark → W. Germany (Mark) ...	.4574	.4571	2.1865	2.1875
30-Day Forward	.4584	.4581	2.1817	2.1831
90-Day Forward	.4600	.4597	2.1737	2.1753
180-Day Forward	.4630	.4624	2.1600	2.1628
SDR	1.17583	1.17279	0.850464	0.852668
ECU	0.982366	0.981059		

Special Drawing Rights are based on exchange rates for the U.S., West German, British, French and Japanese currencies. Source: International Monetary Fund.
ECU is based on a basket of community currencies. Source: European Community Commission.
z-Not quoted.

Britain (Pound)	1.5330	1.5160	.6523	.6596
30-Day Forward	1.5280	1.5108	.6545	.6619
90-Day Forward	1.5208	1.5036	.6575	.6651
180-Day Forward	1.5109	1.4937	.6619	.6695
France (Franc)	.1434	.1433	6.9750	6.9975
30-Day Forward	.1433	.1432	6.9785	6.9820
90-Day Forward	.1432	.1431	6.9855	6.9880
180-Day Forward	.1429	.1429	6.9960	6.9975
Japan (Yen)	.005936	.005926	168.45	168.75
30-Day Forward	.005950	.005939	168.08	168.39
90-Day Forward	.005969	.005958	167.52	167.85
180-Day Forward	.006003	.005989	166.58	166.97
Switzerland (Franc) ..	.5469	.5459	1.8285	1.8320
30-Day Forward	.5483	.5472	1.8238	1.8274
90-Day Forward	.5506	.5494	1.8162	1.8202
180-Day Forward	.5548	.5532	1.8025	1.8078
W. Germany (Mark) ..	.4574	.4571	2.1865	2.1875
30-Day Forward	.4584	.4581	2.1817	2.1831
90-Day Forward	.4600	.4597	2.1737	2.1753
180-Day Forward	.4630	.4624	2.1600	2.1628

Excerpts from page 244

has declined dramatically (that is, the dollar has risen in value) since the late 70s, despite the recent partial recovery. The French franc has fallen from $0.25 to less than $0.15; the British pound, from $2.50 to $1.53; the Swiss franc, from over $0.60 to $0.55; and the German mark from $0.55 almost to $0.45. The balance-of-payments discussion will aid your understanding of the dollar's rise.

The dollar fell to its post–World War II low against most currencies in the late 70s because of severe inflation here at home. (You can observe the increase in value of the key currencies in Chart 14–2 on page 247.) The merchandise trade balance sank dramatically, as rising prices impeded our ability to sell and whetted our appetite for imports. (Chart 14–1 on page 239). Since people in the rest of the world needed fewer dollars (because they weren't buying as many of our goods) and we needed more foreign exchange (because we were buying more of their goods), the dollar's value plunged.

The dollar's rally in the early 80s was a two-phase process. The first phase in 1981–82 had four causes.

First, high interest rates strengthened the dollar. When interest rates in the United States are higher than interest rates elsewhere, foreign exchange is sold for dollars and the capital accounts will show a net flow of private investment into the United States. The Fed's tight money policy pushed interest rates in the United States higher than those in Europe and Japan, prompting heavy dollar purchases by foreign investors who wished to enjoy the high interest rates available here.

Second, the U.S. balance on current account improved dramatically until late 1982 because of rapidly growing service income and despite a sharply negative balance of trade. This positive element in the American balance of payments not only generated a flow of dollars into the United States but also encouraged private businesses and individuals in the rest of the world to invest in dollars because they believed that the dollar would remain strong in the future. And the dollar has indeed remained strong despite the recent deterioration in the current account balance.

Third, through the actions of the Fed, the United States had come to grips with inflation, driving the rate of price increase from double-digit figures to a negligible level in just a few years. Moreover, the Fed made it clear that it would not permit a resurgence of inflation. The Fed's actions gave investors throughout the world confidence in the dollar's strength because the price stability of American products would maintain America's competitiveness in world markets. This assistance to America's trading position encouraged investors to keep their dollars here, thus boosting the dollar's price.

Fourth, the decline in America's oil imports and the weakening of OPEC's price grip meant a reduced value for American imports. This helped the U.S. trade and payments balances and encouraged investors to keep their dollars here.

The second phase in 1983–84 is somewhat more complex. Since mid-82 the interest rate differential between the United States and the rest of the world narrowed (see the first cause listed above), while the balance on current account deteriorated rapidly (see the second cause listed above) due to the plunge in our merchandise trade balance (see Chart 14–1 on page 239). Under these circumstances, the dollar's value should have fallen.

Nevertheless, it improved, because of the flow of investment dollars into the United States and the reduced flow of our investment dollars to the rest of the world. The rest of the world believes America is the safest, most profitable home for its funds. To foreigners—and, indeed, to many Americans—President Reagan symbolized America's protection

Chart 14–2
Foreign Exchange Rates

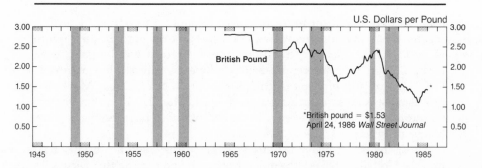

U.S. Dollars per Pound

British Pound

*British pound = $1.53
April 24, 1986 *Wall Street Journal*

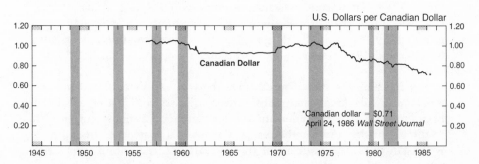

U.S. Dollars per Canadian Dollar

Canadian Dollar

*Canadian dollar = $0.71
April 24, 1986 *Wall Street Journal*

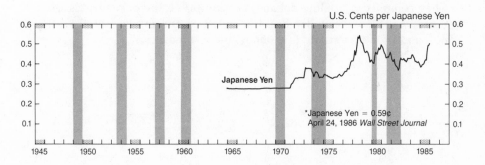

U.S. Cents per Japanese Yen

Japanese Yen

*Japanese Yen = 0.59¢
April 24, 1986 *Wall Street Journal*

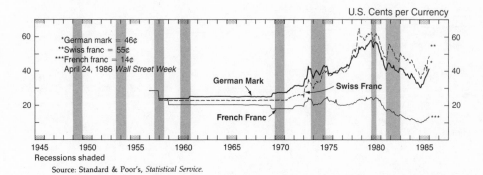

U.S. Cents per Currency

*German mark = 46¢
**Swiss franc = 55¢
***French franc = 14¢
April 24, 1986 *Wall Street Week*

German Mark

Swiss Franc

French Franc

Recessions shaded

Source: Standard & Poor's, *Statistical Service.*

of, and concern for, business interests. Certainly, the United States is a secure haven: investments will not be expropriated, nor will their return be subject to confiscatory taxation. And the return will be good; even if the interest rate differential between here and abroad has narrowed, U.S. rates are still higher than those in most other countries. Moveover, profits have been strong, and the stock market has reflected this. Foreign investors who have a stake in American business have been rewarded handsomely.

Thus, the dollar remained strong because the huge net capital flow into the United States bid the dollar's price up and forced other currencies down. The rise in the dollar's value, together with the more rapid economic expansion here than abroad, depressed our exports and stimulated our imports. Consequently, the deterioration in our merchandise trade balance in 1983 and 1984 was *a result* of the dollar's appreciation, not a *cause* of it.

But by 1985 the merchandise trade balance had deteriorated to such an extent, while American interest rates continued to slide, that the dollar began to weaken. Foreign demand for our currency was not strong enough to offset our demand for the rest of the world's currencies. In addition, we began to pressure our major trading partners, requesting their assistance in reducing our trade deficit by driving the dollar's value down. They complied by selling dollars, contributing to the dollar's slide. As a result, by 1986 the dollar had lost much of the increase of the early 80s, and its future strength is impossible to predict.

15

Leading Economic Indicators

*N*ow that you have examined the business cycle in detail, and learned to use *The Wall Street Journal's* statistical series, you may be looking for a device to make analysis somewhat easier. Perhaps, while wading through the stream of data, you felt the need for a single indicator that could predict changes in the business cycle. You wanted something akin to the meteorologist's barometer, to inform you of rain or shine without a detailed examination of cloud formations.

Unfortunately, economists have never agreed on a single economic indicator to predict the future. Some indicators are better than others, but none is consistently accurate; all give a false signal on occasion. To deal with this, economists have devised a composite or combination of statistical series drawn from a broad spectrum of economic activity, each of which tends to move up or down ahead of the general trend of the business cycle. These series are referred to as leading indicators because of their predictive quality, and a dozen have been combined into the *composite index of 12 leading indicators.*

The components of the index of 12 leading indicators are:

1. Average workweek, production workers, manufacturing.
2. Average weekly initial claims, state unemployment insurance.

3. Manufacturers' new orders for consumer goods and materials in 1982 dollars.
4. Vendor performance, percent of companies receiving slower deliveries.
5. Net business formation.
6. Contracts and orders for plant and equipment in 1982 dollars.
7. New building permits, private housing units.
8. Net change in inventories on hand and on order in 1982 dollars.
9. Change in sensitive materials prices.
10. Change in credit outstanding—business and consumer borrowing.
11. Stock prices, 500 common stocks.
12. Money supply—M2—in 1982 dollars.

There are three general criteria for inclusion in the index. First, each series must accurately lead and reflect the business cycle. Second, the various series should provide comprehensive coverage of the economy by representing a wide and diverse range of economic activity. And, third, each series must be available monthly, with only a brief lag until publication, and must be free from large subsequent revisions.

The 12 leading indicators meet these criteria, and weaving these series into a composite provides a statistic that is more reliable and less erratic than any of the individual components.

Finally, some of the indicators measure activity in physical units, others in current dollars, still others in constant dollars, and some use an index form. This variety of measurements is reduced to an index with 1967 assigned a base value of 100 percent. All other months and years are expressed as a percentage of the base year.

The February 1986 index, published in the March 31, 1986, issue of *The Wall Street Journal,* is representative. The series usually appears around the first of the month. The chart accompanying the article, and the fifth paragraph from the end of the article, inform you that the index stood at 175.4 in February 1986. (See pages 251 and 252.)

Chart 15–1 on page 253 confirms that this was an all-time high, and you can see that the index has historically turned prior to the cycle. In February 1986 there was no recession in sight.

Remember, however, that this series is only a composite of unrelated series, woven together because they provide an omen of future events. You need all the statistical reports appearing in the *Journal* in order to build an understanding of the timing, direction, and strength of the business cycle. After all, a meteorologist needs more than a barometer, and most Americans who make decisions in the business community, or wish to be fully informed of current economic events, need far more than a crude, general directional signal to guide their long-range planning.

Leading Index Increased 0.7% For February

Last Month's Gain Suggests Economy Will Pick Up, But Timing Is Uncertain

By PAUL BLUSTEIN
Staff Reporter of THE WALL STREET JOURNAL

WASHINGTON—The February rise in the government's main index of future economic activity bolsters predictions of solid growth ahead, though it isn't clear how soon the economy will pick up speed.

The Commerce Department reported that the index of leading economic indicators increased 0.7% in February. In addition, the department revised the figure for January to show the index unchanged from December, following an original report that the measure had dropped 0.6%. In December, the index rose 1.5%.

With the January revision, the index has "gone through 10 months without a setback," noted Commerce Secretary Malcolm Baldrige, who said the "recent trend in the overall index is signaling a near-term pickup in growth."

Pattern of Sluggish Growth

But one of Mr. Baldrige's ...omist dinates said that m~ ... ~u that much before the e~- __ ~. in the index has patter~ ...iancial components, such . prices and the money supply. ...ese indicators tend to have a long and uncertain lead time to general movements in the economy.

Still, Mr. Dederick and a number of other analysts agreed that the report suggests the economy will begin to gather momentum later this year. "It certainly looks basically favorable," said Geoffrey Moore, director of the Center for International Business Cycle Research at Columbia University.

Largest Contribution

The component making the largest contribution to the February increase was a rise in contracts and orders for plant and

The Wall Street Journal, *March 31, 1986*

Leading Indicators

In percent (1967 = 100).

COMPOSITE of key indicators of future economic activity rose in February to 175.4% of the 1967 average from a revised 174.1% in January, the Commerce Department reports.

equipment, an indicator that has been bouncing around lately. A drop in that indicator had been the chief negative factor in the January index.

An increase in four other indicators contributed to the February rise in the index. They were stock prices, the money supply, net business formations, and companies receiving slower deliveries from vendors.

Six indicators had negative effects: ** average workweek, building per~ ... sumer and business borr~~ __port.) turers' new orders f- __ ~otained up-materials, s~' __ ~ ~light upward revi-new ~' __ ~~ and orders for plant and __ ..., net business formations and ...isumer and business borrowing.

The February increase brought the index to 175.4% of its 1967 average from 174.1% in January (see chart on page one).

The department's index of coincident indicators, which tends to rise and fall with current economic activity, increased 0.4% in February to 163.3% of its 1967 average after decreasing a revised 0.1% in January to 162.6%.

The index of lagging indicators, which trails economic trends, rose 0.1% in February to 133% of its 1967 average after increasing a revised 1.2% in January to 132.9%.

The ratio of coincident to lagging indicators, which some analysts believe signals turning points in advance of the leading indicators, inched upward slightly in February to 1.227 from 1.223 in January.

The index figures are adjusted for seasonal variations.

Leading Indicators

In percent (1967=100).

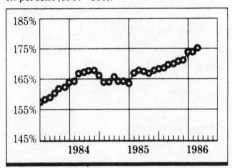

COMPOSITE of key indicators of future economic activity rose in February to 175.4% of the 1967 average from a revised 174.1% in January, the Commerce Department reports.

The Wall Street Journal, *March 31, 1986*

Leading Indicators—Paragraphs Two and Fifth from the End

The Commerce Department reported that the index of leading economic indicators increased 0.7% in February. In addition, the department revised the figure for January to show the index unchanged from December, following an original report that the measure had dropped 0.6%. In December, the index rose 1.5%.

The February increase brought the index to 175.4% of its 1967 average from 174.1% in January (see chart on page one).

Chart 15–1
Composite Index of 12 Leading Indicators

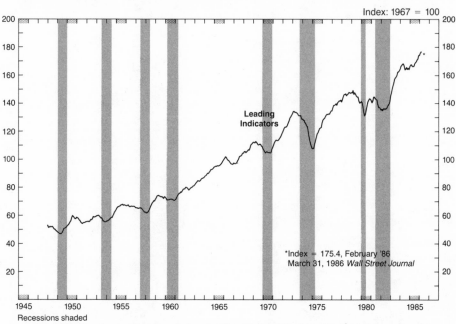

Index: 1967 = 100

Leading Indicators

*Index = 175.4, February '86
March 31, 1986 *Wall Street Journal*

Recessions shaded

Source: U.S. Department of Commerce, *Business Conditions Digest* and *Handbook of Cyclical Indicators,* series 910.

16

Federal Fiscal Policy

F iscal policy refers to the federal government's taxing and spending programs and their impact on the economy.

In order to sort out the continuing debate surrounding this topic, you must go back to the 19th and early 20th centuries. Economics then was governed by an axiom known as *Say's Law:* "Supply creates its own demand." This meant that economic recession and depression and their accompanying unemployment were temporary and self-correcting phenomena. After all, capitalists produce goods for market, and workers offer their labor for hire *so that they in turn can demand goods in the marketplace.* If the goods cannot be sold or the labor is not hired, then a lower price or wage will be asked, until price and wage cutting permit all of the goods or labor to be sold. No goods will remain chronically unsold and no labor will remain chronically unemployed as long as prices and wages remain flexible.

Using this line of reasoning, economists argued that recession and its concomitant unemployment were transitory phenomena and should generate neither a great deal of concern nor any corrective policy prescription by the government. Society and government ought to let well enough alone (that is, follow the policy of laissez-faire) and let market forces prevail. The operation of the market would eventually restore full employment.

With Say's Law as their guide, no wonder economists could not understand the Great Depression, which began in 1929 and hit bottom in 1933.

Nor could they understand why the economy's performance remained anemic for so long after 1933. After all, they reasoned, the economy should naturally return to conditions of full production and full employment as business cut prices in order to sell its products and workers cut their wages in order to find employment. If the economy continued in a slump, that was the fault not of the economists and their theories, but of employers and employees who refused to cut prices and wages.

The economists' logic did not help the businesses that were failing or the workers who were out of a job. Prices and wages had fallen, yet conditions remained dismal; something was dreadfully wrong, and somebody had to do something about it. President Roosevelt was elected, and his response was massive public-works programs. These were funded by deficits, despite the economists' insistence that the federal government's efforts would merely deny resources to the private sector, and thus provide no net benefit. F.D.R. was a practical man with a practical solution: if people were out of work, then the government would be the employer of last resort and put them to work building roads, parks, bridges, dams, and so forth.

In 1936 an Englishman named John Maynard Keynes (rhymes with *brains*) gave intellectual credentials to F.D.R.'s practical policies by proposing that the problem was the economists' theories, not the economy. Keynes tackled Say's Law (and the economics establishment) at the knees by declaring that demand *could* be chronically insufficient and the economy *could* be chronically plagued with substantial excess capacity and unemployment. Keynes scolded his fellow economists for arguing that their theories were right but that the practical world of business and work was not living up to theoretical expectations. Science—even "the dismal science" of economics—dictates that a theory that does not conform to the facts must be discarded.

Keynes declared that it was ridiculous to expect price and wage cuts to solve the economy's problem. A totally new approach had to be devised. He believed the only answer was to boost demand by the use of some exogenous (outside) force. Workers could not be expected to buy more under conditions of actual and threatened unemployment nor business to spend more on plant and equipment when excess capacity and weak profits were the rule. But if consumers and business would not spend, how could the economy pull out of its slump? Through government spending, Keynes argued, even if the government had to borrow funds because tax revenues were inadequate. Once government began to spend on roads, dams, bridges, and other public works, the people who were employed on these projects would spend their earnings on privately produced goods and services. In a multiplier effect, the total level of demand would be lifted and full employment restored. When the pump-priming operation was over and the private economy was back on its feet, the government could gradually withdraw from the economic scene. Pump priming by government intervention became known as *Keynesian* economics.

Keynesian (pronounced "brainsian") theory came to dominate economics, rendering Say's Law archaic. The next generation of economists pushed Keynesian theory a bit further, reasoning that a tax cut could be as effective in priming the pump as an increase in government expenditures. Reducing taxes would increase consumers' disposable income and their consumption expenditures. The new generation believed this would be as effective as an increase in government expenditures for restoring demand to a level sufficient to ensure full employment.

Economists now argued that it didn't matter how the pump was primed—whether through expenditure increases or tax cuts. Putting more into the expenditure stream than was removed from the income stream (in the form of taxes) would always create a net boost in total demand. If government expenditures increased while tax revenues remained the same, the increase in public expenditures would boost demand. If government expenditures remained the same while taxes were cut, the increase in private consumption expenditures would boost demand. In either case, or in both together, a net addition to total demand was made possible by the increased government deficit and the borrowing needed to fund that deficit.

Now, it might seem that government borrowing from the public would have the same effect as taxing the public and would thus neutralize the spending increase. After all, if the public refrains from spending to buy government bonds, isn't the public's expenditure reduced in much the same way? The answer is yes, if the bonds are purchased by private citizens; however, this is generally not the case. The largest share of bonds is sold to the banking system, which purchases them by creating a demand deposit for the government. This is known as "monetizing" the debt, as mentioned in Chapter 5. As the debt is monetized, demand grows because borrowing from the banks permits an increase in government spending without a decrease in private spending.

The federal government's attempts to influence economic activity through its power to tax and spend came to be known as *fiscal policy*. Although this chapter discusses fiscal policy in the context of stimulating demand in order to deal with recession, it should be clear that fiscal policy could also be employed to deal with inflation. For example, increasing taxes or reducing expenditures, which would create a surplus, removes more from the income stream than from the expenditure stream, reducing total demand and, consequently, cooling inflation.

Fiscal policy should not be confused with *monetary policy* as discussed in Chapters 4, 5, and 6. Monetary policy refers to the actions of the Federal Reserve System; fiscal policy refers to the actions of the federal government. Monetary policy works through its influence on the banking system, the money supply, bank lending, and interest rates; whereas fiscal policy works through its direct impact on aggregate demand.

Also keep in mind that fiscal policy is the province solely of the federal government, not of state or local government. Only the federal government has the flexibility to run the necessary budget deficits (and surpluses). Most state and local governments are limited, either de facto or de jure, to operating with a balanced budget.

Keynesian economics may have won the hearts and minds of academic economists by the early 1960s, but not everyone else was convinced. When President Kennedy assumed office in 1961 and proposed a tax cut to stimulate the level of economic activity, Republicans and conservative Democrats in Congress attacked it as fiscally irresponsible. They demanded a balanced budget and argued that tax cuts would generate unacceptable deficits. President Kennedy's Keynesian reply was that the deficits would disappear as soon as the tax cut stimulated the level of demand, output, and income, providing even greater tax revenues despite the decline in the tax rate. These arguments did not persuade Congress, and the tax cut did not pass until the spring of 1964, following President Kennedy's assassination.

The nation enjoyed full employment and a balanced budget in 1965, and Keynesian fiscal policy became an accepted method of "fine-tuning" the economy to achieve the objectives of full employment without inflation. Indeed, this policy became so legitimate that it was employed by the next two Republican presidents. President Nixon cut taxes to deal with the 1970 recession, and President Ford cut taxes to deal with the 1974–75 recession. In each case, the Federal Reserve also pursued an easy money policy in order to stimulate demand. Conservatives joined liberals, and Republicans agreed with Democrats that tax cuts were necessary to get the economy moving.

By the late 1970s, however, severe inflation had prompted a growing group of economists to conclude that attempts to stimulate demand with easy money and easy fiscal policies, in order to guarantee full employment, had not achieved their objectives. Escalating inflation, which reduced real income, had drawn more and more people into the labor force. The new entrants to the labor force, usually the secondary or tertiary wage earners in the family, had fewer skills and thus were more difficult to employ. Unemployment and inflation grew hand in hand. Thus, this group of economists and politicians argued that "full-employment policy" (the Keynesian prescription of stimulating demand through easy monetary and easy fiscal policies) had been a failure.

Moreover, they continued, increased inflation had discouraged savings and investment. Rising prices penalized savers for their thriftiness, because the value of real savings fell. This encouraged personal indebtedness rather than saving, and inasmuch as saving is the ultimate source of all funds for investment, the level of investment was bound to shrink over time. These critics charged that the lack of savings, and the resulting lack of investment, were reflected by the low levels of business investment in new machinery and technology and by declining productivity.

Finally, they attacked the progressive income tax, which propelled people into higher tax brackets despite a drop in real income. Higher marginal tax rates, they said, removed the incentive to work more and work harder. Why should businesses invest in new ideas and new products and more efficient ways of doing things if higher taxes confiscated the profits? Why should workers put in more hours on the job if higher taxes reduced the additional pay to a meaningless figure?

The views of these economists and politicians came to be called *supply-side* economics, which they developed in contrast to *demand-side,* or Keynesian, economics. The supply-siders argued that it was more important to support policies that bolstered the economy's ability to supply or produce more goods than to enhance demand. Therefore, the supply-side economists advocated drastic federal income tax reductions over a three-year period, with deficits to be avoided by a parallel reduction in federal spending. Federal expenditure programs, in their view, tended to overregulate private activity and to waste tax dollars in needless boondoggles and unnecessary transfer payments.

A massive, across-the-board tax cut would accomplish two major objectives. First, it would provide incentives for increased work, thus boosting output. A greater supply, or output, of goods and services would dampen inflation. Second, increased disposable income would lead to increased savings, providing a pool of funds to finance investment. Once again, the supply of goods and services would be stimulated, and increased output would reduce inflation.

Supply-side economics was a total contradiction of the Keynesian revolution, which had prevailed for almost half a century, and it was widely and correctly viewed as a device to restrict and contract the federal government. As the supply-siders began to make their voices heard, their demands caused President Carter difficulty. He had pledged to balance the federal budget by the end of his first term in office. Rapid economic expansion and inflation had pushed revenues upward more rapidly than expenditures; consequently, his goal was in sight by late 1979. But a tax cut without a spending cut would have postponed that goal, and as a Democrat, President Carter could not endorse the large reductions in federal expenditures that the supply-siders demanded.

The 1980 recession created an even sharper dilemma for him. He might have advocated a tax cut (the traditional Keynesian prescription for recession), but this would have played into the hands of the supply-siders, who by now had a presidential candidate, Ronald Reagan, as their principal spokesman. In addition, the supply-side tax cut favored upper-income groups, rather than the lower-income groups traditionally favored for tax cuts by the Democrats. Thus, circumstances precluded President Carter from trying to deal with the 1980 recession by means of tax reductions.

After his inauguration in 1981, as the economy slid into the 1981–82 recession, President Reagan pushed for and obtained the supply-side tax cuts. What a strange historical reversal: 20 years after President Kennedy battled conservatives and Republicans for his tax cut, President Reagan now had to battle liberals and Democrats for his. Whereas Democrats had once advocated tax cuts to stimulate the economy and the Republicans had opposed those cuts, it was now the Republicans who were advocating tax cuts over the opposition of the Democrats. Both parties had done a complete about-face.

The shift of the mantle of fiscal conservatism from Republicans to Democrats is one of the most important political changes since World War II. President Reagan's (supply-side) tax cut of 1981–83 accompanied the recession of 1981–82. It generated a chaotic reduction in federal revenue, because a smaller proportion of a declining level of income was collected. Meanwhile, total expenditures continued to grow despite reductions in the budget left by President Carter. Democrats criticized the resulting deficit and demanded that the tax cuts be rescinded. Republicans insisted on no tax increase, despite the deficits.

The debate occurred in the midst of recession and recovery. The Republicans contended that any tax increase would jeopardize the (supply-side) expansion. The Democrats countered that continued deficits and the accompanying government borrowing drove up interest rates and jeopardized the expansion. But, practical considerations aside, both sides had ideological positions to defend. The Democrats realized that continued deficits put relentless pressures on domestic expenditures. Only a tax increase could generate the revenue that made the expenditure programs affordable. The Republicans were also aware that the only way to deliver a knockout punch to these programs was to hold taxes down and let the clamor to end the deficits force legislators to curtail government expenditures. So the real battle was over expenditure programs, not taxes, the deficit, or even supply-side economics.

In the end, no compromise was attained. The Democrats held on to the domestic programs, the Republicans held on to the military programs, and President Reagan made it clear that he would veto any tax increase. The deficit remained. Finally, in desperation, the Gramm-Rudman balanced budget act was passed in late 1985, mandating gradual elimination of deficits over a five-year period. The Democrats hoped that military expenditures would be cut and taxes raised, the Republicans and the president hoped that domestic expenditures would be cut, and they all hoped that this procrustean bed would dismember someone else.

Meanwhile, the argument over supply-side economics has been lost in the shuffle. The Democrats insisted that the increased federal borrowing due to the tax cut would crowd out private borrowing (and hence capital expenditures). Ironically, Republicans criticized President Carter's deficits in the late 1970s on precisely the same grounds. Yet you have seen that private borrowing exploded in those years.

Indeed, this fear about "crowding out" is misplaced, for it is the Federal Reserve that will largely determine whether private borrowing at reasonable rates will be possible. If it pursues a tight money policy, private borrowers will have to compete with the government for funds; if it pursues a sufficiently easy policy, there will be room for both private and public borrowing. The point is that difficulty or ease of credit conditions will be determined largely by the Fed rather than by any crowding out. Keep in mind, too, that the Fed's objective *should* be to restrain the expansion rather than stimulate it, so perhaps a little crowding out, if it helps prevent credit conditions from becoming too easy, would not be unhealthy. Tight money will restrict consumer borrowing more than business borrowing, allocating funds (and resources) away from consumption expenditures toward investment expenditures in new plant and equipment. And as expansion develops, private borrowing will grow while federal borrowing shrinks.

To relate this discussion to the business cycle, you need to know how *not* to relate it. That is, please realize that the huge federal deficits were responsible for neither the 1981–82 recession nor the recent recovery and expansion. The Federal Reserve's tight money policy generated the recession; the recession choked off inflation; and the stifling of inflation, along with the release of the Fed's grip, is what produced recovery and expansion.

Thus, President Reagan's administration should neither be blamed for the recession nor lauded for the recovery and expansion. Those phenomena were produced by monetary policy, not fiscal policy.

You can see from Chart 16–1 on page 262 that the federal deficit has grown enormously with each recession—for two chief reasons. First, recession reduced receipts because of higher unemployment (the unemployed pay no income tax) and lower revenues from the profits tax. Second, tax cuts accompanied the recessions of 1970, 1974–75, and 1981–82. In addition, note that federal expenditures have continued to grow during each recession despite revenue's setback. This generated the budget gap. Since the deficit grew with each successive recession, closing this deficit gap became more difficult and took longer every time.

In order to close the gap, receipts must grow more rapidly than expendi-

Chart 16–1
Federal Government Expenditures and Receipts

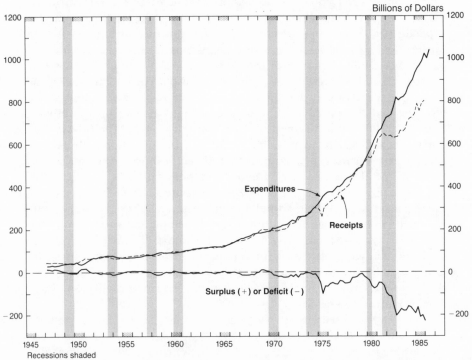

Billions of Dollars

Recessions shaded

Source: U.S. Department of Commerce, *Business Conditions Digest* and *Handbook of Cyclical Indicators,* series 500, 501, and 502.

tures. It took four years after the 1970 recession and five years after the 1974–75 recession. How long will it take this time? That's hard to say, but if the gap is not substantially narrowed before the next recession, many will wonder whether it can ever be eliminated.

But why worry about the deficit if its impact on the business cycle and on crowding out is so negligible? There are two good reasons for concern. First, as the federal government's debt mounts, interest payments become an increasing share of federal expenditures. There are historical examples of nations borrowing to the point that debt service composed the majority of their budget, crowding out other expenditures and compelling increased borrowing to meet the interest payments on old debt. Second, the day could come when the creditworthiness of the federal government became suspect as the financial markets saw little chance of the federal government's meeting its debts.

Despite these concerns for the government's fiscal health, some say that Gramm-Rudman and the other attempts to balance the budget are inappropriate now because the reduction in spending (or the increase in taxes) will have a depressing impact on the economy. But that would be helpful in an economy like ours that has a chronic bias toward inflation. All signs indicate that private demand will grow rapidly in the second half of the 80s. A restrictive fiscal policy would offset that damaging tendency.

Therefore, the soundness of both government finance and the economy would be strengthened by deficit reduction and a balanced budget.

Summary and Prospect

*T*he business cycle is inevitable in an unfettered capitalist economy, and its fluctuations and vicissitudes are the price that must be paid for economic progress. It's a cruel system because the price is not paid by all, just as the system's benefits are not shared by all. The load is borne mostly by the workers who suffer cyclical unemployment. Their misfortune is due to the commodity they produce for market; it is not due to any fault of their own.

But, you may ask, wasn't the cycle unusually severe in the 1970s? And wasn't there some period in our recent past when the cycle was kinder to us than in the 70s, with less severe bouts of inflation and recession? Maybe, if we can't return to those good old days, we can at least use them as a model so that the smooth sailing since the 1981–82 recession can be maintained.

The first half of the 1960s provides hope. This half decade followed the Eisenhower years, which were severely criticized by President Kennedy and his advisers for sluggish economic performance and too many recessions. Both the fiscal policy of President Eisenhower's administration and the monetary policy of the Federal Reserve at the time were excoriated for excessive concern with inflation and complacency about economic growth and unemployment. The critics charged that because of the attempt to restrain demand in order to combat "creeping inflation," the economy's growth rate had fallen and recovery from frequent recessions had been weak.

All the arguments over creeping inflation seem laughable in the light of the experience of the 70s; inflation really did creep along at only about 2 percent a year in the early 60s. What's more, the Fed switched to a policy of relative ease in the early 60s. The low level of inflation and the Fed's easy money policy were the most important ingredients in the healthy economic expansion of those years.

Modest increases in the CPI permitted strong growth in consumer real income. As a result, consumer sentiment improved steadily. This, together with the ready availability of loans, prompted consumers to resort to record levels of mortgage borrowing and consumer credit. Home construction and automobile production set new highs. Business responded by investing heavily in new plant and equipment, so that general boom conditions prevailed by the middle of the decade.

The tax cut proposed by President Kennedy has received most of the credit for this prosperity. Inconveniently, however, it was not enacted until 1964, after his death, and it is difficult to understand how an expansion begun in 1962 can be attributed to a tax cut enacted two years later.

The relaxed and easy progress of the expansion was its most important feature. There was no overheating. Housing starts, auto sales, consumer credit, and retail sales gradually broke through to new ground. By 1965 there had been three solid years of expansion, reflected in a strong improvement in labor productivity and a solid advance in real compensation.

Will the second half of the 80s be like the early 60s? Will the economy expand slowly and gradually, bringing prosperity without severe fluctuation?

Certain features of the mid-80s were similar to those of the early 60s. The rate of inflation had been reduced, although violently this time rather than gradually, as was the case 25 years before. There was substantial slack in the economy, both in terms of low capacity utilization and high unemployment. Productivity had risen and unit labor costs were down. All of this augured well for continued expansion.

But there was an important difference between the mid-80s and the early 60s. The Fed followed a very expansionary policy in the first half of the 60s, providing the banking system with ample free reserves. Interest rates were far higher in the mid-80s because the Fed pursued a deliberate policy of restraint in the early 80s. What difference will this make?

Paradoxically, those tight conditions may help sustain the expansion, because overheating is the chief threat now. Twenty years ago, the consumer had to be cajoled into mortgaging the future; today, people are far more willing to borrow and spend. An easy money policy enabled the boom of the early 60s. Monetary restraint will permit the expansion of the early 80s to continue because today the chief concern is preventing a rapid increase in demand from driving production up too quickly, bringing about a decline in productivity and rapid cost and price increases. Only continued restraint by the Fed can prevent that.

And therein lies the problem. Interest rates fell sharply in late 1985 and early 1986, capping off the gradual decline following 1984's minislowdown. If the Fed does not exercise restraint, easy credit conditions could catapult us back into the inflationary cycle of the 70s. It would be tragic if the errors that have taken a generation to discover, and half a decade to correct, were to be repeated by those who should have understood them best.

Alphabetical Listing of Statistical Series Published in The Wall Street Journal

Chapter Number	Series Description	The Wall Street Journal Publication Schedule
13	Advance/decline (stocks)	Daily
13	American Stock Exchange	Daily
8	Auto sales	Monthly
14	Balance of payments	Quarterly
14	Balance of trade	Monthly
6	Banxquote (deposit interest rates)	Weekly
6	Bond markets	Daily
6	Bond yields (chart)	Weekly
12	Building awards	Monthly
6	Buying and borrowing (interest rates)	Weekly
7	Capacity utilization	Monthly
7	Commodity futures and prices	Daily
8	Consumer credit	Monthly
8	Consumer price index	Monthly
6	Consumer savings rates	Weekly

Chapter Number	Series Description	The Wall Street Journal Publication Schedule
13	Corporate profits (Commerce Department)	Quarterly
13	Corporate profits (*The Wall Street Journal* survey)	Quarterly
6	Credit ratings	Daily
13	Dividend news	Daily
13	Dow Jones Averages (six-month charts)	Daily
7	Dow Jones commodity indexes (chart)	Weekly
12	Durable goods orders	Monthly
13	Earnings reports	Daily
8	Employment	Monthly
4, 5	Federal Reserve data	Weekly
14	Foreign exchange rates	Daily
13	Foreign stock markets	Daily
7	GNP	Quarterly
13	Highs/lows (stocks)	Daily
8	Housing starts	Monthly
7	Industrial production	Monthly
11	Inventories	Monthly
6	Key interest rates	Weekly
15	Leading indicators	Monthly
12	Machine tool orders	Monthly
12	Manufacturers' orders	Monthly
13	Markets and money (two-year Dow chart)	Daily
6	Money fund assets	Weekly
6	Money market mutual funds	Weekly
6	Money rates	Daily
5	Money supply (chart)	Weekly
6	Mortgage rates	Monthly
6	Municipal bond index	Weekly
13	Mutual funds (stock)	Daily
6	New York Exchange Bonds	Daily
13	New York Stock Exchange composite transactions	Daily
13	Odd-lot trading	Daily
13	Options	Daily
13	Over-the-counter stock market (NASDAQ)	Daily
8	Personal income	Monthly
6	Prices of recent issues (bonds)	Weekly
7	Producer price index	Monthly
7	Productivity	Quarterly
8	Retail sales	Monthly
6	Securities offering calendar (bonds and stocks)	Weekly
13	Short interest (stocks)	Daily
6	Short-term interest rates (chart)	Weekly
13	Stock market data bank	Daily
13	Stock markets	Daily
6	Tax exempt bonds	Daily
6	Treasury bill auction	Weekly
6	Treasury bill rates	Daily

Appendix

Statistical Series Published in The Wall Street Journal *in Chapter Order*

Chapter Number	Series Description	The Wall Street Journal Publication Schedule
4, 5	Federal Reserve data	Weekly
5	Money supply (chart)	Weekly
6	Banxquote (deposit interest rates)	Weekly
6	Bond markets	Daily
6	Bond yields (chart)	Weekly
6	Buying and borrowing (interest rates)	Weekly
6	Consumer savings rates	Weekly
6	Credit ratings	Daily
6	Key interest rates	Weekly
6	Money fund assets	Weekly
6	Money market mutual funds	Weekly
6	Money rates	Daily
6	Money supply (chart)	Weekly
6	Mortgage rates	Monthly
6	Municipal bond index	Weekly
6	New York Exchange bonds	Daily

Chapter Number	Series Description	*The Wall Street Journal* Publication Schedule
6	Prices of recent issues (bonds)	Weekly
6	Securities offering calendar (bonds and stocks)	Weekly
6	Short-term interest rates (chart)	Weekly
6	Tax exempt bonds	Daily
6	Treasury bill auction	Weekly
6	Treasury bill rates	Daily
7	Capacity utilization	Monthly
7	Commodity futures and prices	Daily
7	Dow Jones commodity indexes (chart)	Weekly
7	GNP	Quarterly
7	Industrial production	Monthly
7	Producer price index	Monthly
7	Productivity	Quarterly
8	Auto sales	Monthly
8	Consumer credit	Monthly
8	Consumer price index	Monthly
8	Employment	Monthly
8	Housing starts	Monthly
8	Personal income	Monthly
8	Retail sales	Monthly
11	Inventories	Monthly
12	Building awards	Monthly
12	Durable goods orders	Monthly
12	Machine tool orders	Monthly
12	Manufacturers' orders	Monthly
13	Advance/decline (stocks)	Daily
13	American Stock Exchange	Daily
13	Corporate profits (Commerce Department)	Quarterly
13	Corporate profits (*The Wall Street Journal* survey)	Quarterly
13	Dividend news	Daily
13	Dow Jones Averages (six-month charts)	Daily
13	Earnings reports	Daily
13	Foreign stock markets	Daily
13	Highs/lows (stocks)	Daily
13	Markets and money (two-year Dow chart)	Daily
13	Mutual funds (stock)	Daily
13	New York Stock Exchange composite transactions	Daily
13	Odd-lot trading	Daily
13	Options	Daily
13	Over-the-counter stock market (NASDAQ)	Daily
13	Short interest (stocks)	Daily
13	Stock market data bank	Daily
13	Stock markets	Daily
14	Balance of payments	Quarterly
14	Balance of trade	Monthly
14	Foreign exchange rates	Daily
15	Leading indicators	Monthly

Listing of Statistical Series According to The Wall Street Journal *Publication Schedule*

Quarterly

Day of Month Usually Published in *The Wall Street Journal*	Series Description	Chapter in Which Series Introduced
1st	Corporate profits (*The Wall Street Journal* survey)	13
18th to 20th	Balance of payments	14
20th	GNP	7
	Corporate profits (Commerce Department)	13
Last day of month	Productivity	7

Monthly

Day of Month Usually Published in *The Wall Street Journal*	Series Description	Chapter in Which Series Introduced
1st	Building awards	12
1st	Leading indicators	15

Monthly (continued)

Day of Month Usually Published in *The Wall Street Journal*	Series Description	Chapter in Which Series Introduced
1st week	Manufacturers' orders	12
1st week	Mortgage rates	6
5th	Auto sales	8
Monday of 2nd week	Employment	8
2nd week	Consumer credit	8
Middle of 2nd week	Retail sales	8
Midmonth	Inventories	11
Midmonth	Industrial production	7
3rd Monday	Producer price index	7
3rd week	Capacity utilization	7
17th to 20th	Housing starts	8
3rd week	Personal income	8
Thursday or Friday of next-to-last week	Durable goods orders	12
25th to 28th	Balance of trade	14
Last Monday	Machine tool orders	12
4th week	Consumer price index	8

Weekly

Day of Week Usually Published in *The Wall Street Journal*	Series Description	Chapter in Which Series Introduced
Thursday or Friday	Banxquote (deposit interest rates)	6
Monday	Bond yields (chart)	6
Monday	Buying and borrowing (interest rates)	6
Thursday	Consumer savings rates	6
Monday	Dow Jones commodity indexes (chart)	7
Friday	Federal Reserve data	4
Tuesday	Key interest rates	6
Friday	Money fund assets	6
Thursday or Friday	Money market mutual funds	6
Friday	Money supply (chart)	5
Friday	Municipal bond index	6
Monday	Securities offering calendar (bonds and stocks)	6
Thursday	Short-term interest rates (chart)	6
Tuesday	Treasury bill auction	6

Daily

Series Description	Chapter in Which Series Introduced
Advance/decline (stocks)	13
American Stock Exchange	13
Bond markets	6
Commodity futures and prices	7
Credit ratings	6

Daily

Series Description	Chapter in Which Series Introduced
Dividend news	13
Dow Jones Averages (six-month charts)	13
Earnings reports	13
Foreign exchange rates	14
Foreign stock markets	13
Highs/lows (stocks)	13
Markets and money (two-year Dow chart)	13
Money rates	6
Mutual funds (stock)	13
New York Exchange bonds	6
New York Stock Exchange composite transactions	13
Odd-lot trading	13
Options	13
Over-the-counter stock market (NASDAQ)	13
Prices of recent issues (bonds)	6
Short interest (stocks)	13
Stock market data bank	13
Stock markets	13
Tax exempt bonds	6
Treasury bill rates	6

Index

A

Agriculture and the business cycle, 7
American Stock Exchange (AMEX), 195,
    204–5, 218
    short interest, 218–19
Anheuser Busch Company, 203
Auto sales, 129–34
    recession, 154–55, 157
    seasonally adjusted data, 131
Averages, stock market, 191–94

B

Balance of payments and trade, 232–40
    business cycle, 240
    capital account, 233, 234–35
    current account, 232–34, 239, 246
    deficits and surpluses, 235–36
    explained, 232–34
    foreign aid, 234, 236
    foreign exchange rates, 227, 233, 242–48
    interest rate, 240
    merchandise trade balance, 231, 234, 238–
        42
    recession affecting, 240
    reports on, 236–40
    services balance, 234, 238–39
Bank of America, 17
Bank of England, 17

Bank of France, 17
Bank notes, 29
Bank reserves, 18, 30–31
Banxquote Deposit Index, 48, 50
Bear market, 218, 220
Bonds, 60
    corporate, 63–64
    credit ratings, 64, 66
    municipal, 65, 68
    tax-exempt, 65, 67
    utility, 61
Bretton Woods conference, 227, 228
Budget deficit, 260–63
    business cycle, 262
    interest on, 263
    recession and recovery, 261
Bull market, 218, 220, 222
Bureau of Labor Statistics (BLS), 111, 114
Business capital expenditures; see Capital
        expenditures
Business cycle
    agriculture, 7
    balance of payments and trade, 240
    bank lending, 18
    budget deficit, 262
    capital expenditures, 169, 179
    contraction, 9–10, 73–74
    credit, 9
    expansion to peak, 145–51

Business cycle—*Cont.*
  Federal Reserve System, 12–15
  government fiscal policy, 261–62
  inevitability of, 265
  interest rates, 40
  inventories, 161–62, 166–67
  peak, 75
  peak to contraction, 153–60
  profits, 183–88
  railroads, 7–8
  recession, 73, 75
  recovery to expansion, 109–44
  stocks, 182
  supply and demand, 9
  trough to recovery, 73–107
  westward movement, 5–8

C

Call (buy), 208, 210, 213
Capacity utilization, 75, 85–91, 107
  capital expenditures, 109, 179
  definition, 87
  effect on productivity, 88–91
  expansion, 145, 148
  GNP, 95, 96
Capital expenditures, 169–79
  business cycle, 168, 176
  capacity utilization, 169, 179
  equipment replacement, 169–70, 175
  interest rates, 170
  profit expectations, 170
Carter, Jimmy, 25, 147, 149, 189, 259, 260,
  261
Central banks, 17
Certificates of deposit (CDs), 47–48
Checking accounts, 29, 30
Chicago Mercantile Exchange, 100–101
Coins, 29
Commerce Department reports
  balance of payments and trade, 236
  GNP quarterly release, 76
  installment debt, 134
  personal income, 125
  profits quarterly survey, 183
  retail sales, 136–37
Commercial paper, 47
Commodity prices, 79–107
  Dow Jones Index, 102, 106
  futures, 100–5
Constant dollar (real) GNP, 79–80
Consumer credit, 134–36, 143
  cyclical sensitivity, 135–36
  economic contraction, 155, 159

Consumer credit—*Cont.*
  installment debt, 134
  interest rates, 136
Consumer demand, 129–44
  auto sales, 129–34
  housing, 138, 140–43
  installment debt, 134
  mortgage debt, 143
  retail sales, 136–38, 139
Consumer price index (CPI), 81, 111–16, 266
  measurement of inflation impact, 154
Consumer real income; *see* Personal income
Consumer sentiment, 17–21, 266
  marginal employment adjustments, 121,
  124
Continental Illinois Bank (Chicago), 17
Contractionary monetary policy, 23
Contraction stage of business cycle, 9–10,
  73–74
Corporate bonds, 63–64
Credit rationing, 69, 71
Creeping inflation, 265–66
Crowding out of private borrowing, 261
Currency
  devaluation, 229, 231
  money supply, 29
Current dollar (nominal) GNP, 80, 81

D

Deflator, 80–81
Demand deposits, 29, 30
Demand side economics, 259
Discount rate, 20, 46
Disintermediation, 55
Dividends, 182, 203, 215–16
Dodge (F. W.) report on building awards,
  170, 175
Dollar, U.S.
  floated, 231–32
  outflow from U.S., 230
  pegged to gold, 228, 230
  rise and fall against other currencies, 242,
  245–48
Donoghue's Money Fund Report, 54
Dow Jones commodity index, 102, 106
Dow Jones Industrial Average, 3, 181, 191–
  94
  correlation with real earnings, 224
  divisors, 191
  price-earnings ratio, 217–18, 220, 222–25
Drew, Daniel, 7
Durable goods, 170

E

Earnings Digest, 189
Easy money policy of Federal Reserve, 39–40
Economic contraction, 9–10, 153–60
Economic expansion, 9–10, 145
  1975–78, 146–51
Economic indicators, 249
  business cycle, 249
  composite of, 250
  index of leading indicators, 249–53
Economic nationalism, 228
Eisenhower, Dwight, 12
Employment
  full employment policy, 13, 255, 258
  Labor Department report, 121
  marginal adjustment, 121, 124
Excess reserves, 20
Expansionary monetary policy, 23
Expansion stage of business cycle, 9–10, 73–74
Exports, 240, 242

F

Factory operating rate, 85
Factory orders, 170, 171, 172
Farmers, 5–6
  productivity, 92
Federal funds, 46
Federal funds rate, 46
Federal Reserve Data, 20, 23, 31, 32
Federal Reserve system, 12–15
  bank reserves, 18–19
  Board of Governors, 19, 28
  business cycle, 12–15
  contractionary policy, 34
  expansionary policy, 34
  history, 17–19
  inflation curb, 1981–82, 37, 73, 120–22, 246
  interest rates, 39
  monetary policy, 36–37, 257
  money supply, 30, 36–37
  open-market operations, 19–20
Fine-tuning, 55, 75, 258
Fiscal policy, 255–63
  business cycle, 261–62
  crowding out of private borrowing, 261
  deficit, 260–63
  economic theories on taxation
    Keynesian, 257
    Say's Law, 255
    supply-side, 259–60

Fiscal policy—Cont.
  fine-tuning of economy, 258
  inflation, 257, 263
  influence on economic activity, 257
  monetary policy compared, 257–58
  pump-priming, 256–57
  Reagan tax cuts, 260
  recession, 257–58
  unemployment, 256–58
Fisk, James, 7
Fixed exchange rates, 228
Ford, Gerald, 258
Ford, Henry, 131
Foreign aid, 234, 238
Foreign exchange, 232
  used for goods and services, 234
Foreign exchange rates, 227, 233, 242–48
Foreign securities, 223
Foreign stock markets, 217, 222
Free reserves, 20–25
  negative, 23
  positive, 24
Full-employment policy, 13, 255, 258
Futures prices, 100–5

G

General Motors, 131
German central bank, 17
Gould, Jay, 7
Gramm-Rudman balanced budget act, 260, 263
Great Depression, 11–13, 255–56
Gross national product (GNP), 75, 77–82, 95–96
  capacity utilization, 75, 85–91
  constant dollar (real) GNP, 79–80
  current dollar (nominal) GNP, 80, 81
  deflator, 80–81
  growth in, 186
  industrial production, 75, 83–85
  seasonally adjusted annual rate, 79
GTE Corporation, 189–91

H

Hamilton, Alexander, 17
High Yield Jumbos, 48, 50
High yield savings, 48, 50
Hill, James J., 7
Housing starts, 138, 140–43
  cyclical sensitivity, 142

I

IBM bonds, 63–64
Implicit price deflator, 81

Imports, 240, 242
Indexes
    Banxquote Deposit, 48–50
    consumer price; *see* Consumer price index
    consumer sentiment, 117, 120–21, 154, 156
    Dow Jones commodity, 102, 106
    industrial production, 85, 86
    leading economic indicators, 249–53
    major stock markets, 194
    producer price, 81, 95, 97–101
    Standard & Poor stocks, 182
    wholesale price, 95
Index options, 212–13
Industrial production, 75, 83–85
    GNP, 87, 90, 95–96
    index of, 85, 86
Inflation
    breaking the spiral, 1981–82, 37, 75, 120–
        22, 246
    consumer price index, 154
    creeping, 265–66
    definition, 109
    expansion phase of business cycle, 146–
        51
    Federal Reserve, 13, 246
    fiscal policy, 257
    implicit price deflator as measure of, 81
    mortgage borrowing, 142–43
    postwar period, 14
    wartime related, 109–10
Installment debt, 134; *see also* Consumer
    credit
Institute for Social Research (University of
    Michigan), 117
Interest rates
    balance of payments and trade, 240
    bonds, 60
    budget deficit, 263
    business cycle, 40
    capital expenditures, 170
    definition, 39
    deregulation, 58–59
    discount rate, 46
    federal funds rate, 46
    Federal Reserve system, 39
    key rates, 49
    long-term rates, 60–72
    mortgage notes, 65
    prime rates, 58
    secondary market in treasury bills, 44
International Monetary Fund (IMF), 228
International transactions, 227–48
    history since World War II, 227–32

Inventories
    business cycle, 161–62, 166–67
    inflation, 163–64
    involuntary accumulation, 162–63, 165
    involuntary depletion, 162–63
    speculation, 163
    unemployment, 166
Inventory-sales ratio, 163–68

J–K

Jones & Laughlin Industries, 64
Kennedy, John F., 12, 13, 258, 260, 266
Keynes, John Maynard, 256
Keynesian economic theories, 256–57
    fine-tuning method, 258

L

Labor productivity, 91–96, 107, 147–48
Leading economic indicators; *see* Economic
    indicators
Leverage, 207
    buying on margin, 207
    options, 208–9

M

Machine tools, 171, 174–76
Margin buying, 207
Markets and Money charts, 194, 196
Marshall, George C., 229
Marshall Plan, 229–30
MCI, 208
M1, 32–35
Merchandise trade balance, 231, 234, 236,
        238–42
    business cycle, 240
Monetarist school of economics, 35–37
Monetary policy, 257–58; *see also* Federal
        Reserve System; Interest rates *and*
        Money supply
    expansionary, 23
    contractionary, 23
    fiscal policy compared, 257–58
    responsibility for recession and recovery,
        261
Monetizing the debt, 30, 31, 257
Money market discounts, 59
Money market mutual funds; *see* Mutual
    funds
Money supply, 29
    Federal Reserve System, 30, 36–37
    growth of, 30–31
    M1, 32–35
    seasonally adjusted, 34

Moody's bond rating service, 66
Morgan, J. P., 17
Mortgage funds market, 65
Mortgage loans
  growth of borrowing, 142–43
  passed through, 67
  rates, 65, 70
Municipal bonds, 65, 68
Mutual funds, 49, 51, 53–54, 213–15
  no-load, 215

N

National Association of Security Dealers
  Automated Quotation (NASDAQ), 195,
  206
National Machine Tool Builders Associa-
  tion, 170, 171
Net asset value (NAV), 214
Net borrowed reserve, 23, 24, 25–26
New York Exchange Bonds, 62–63
New York Stock Exchange (NYSE), 152, 195
  Composite Transactions, 203–5
  highs/lows, 200–1, 203
  short interest, 219
Nixon, Richard M., 147, 149, 189, 258
No-load (N.L.) fund, 215
Nominal earnings, 223–25
Nominal (current dollar) GNP, 80, 81
Nondefense capital goods, 170, 171, 173
Nonresidential building, 175, 177

O

Odd-lot trading, 200–3
Over-the-counter (OTC) market, 195, 207
Options, 208–13

P

Pacific Stock Exchange, 203
Personal income, 125–29
  business cycle, 144
  Commerce Department report, 125
  definition, 128
  historical data, 128
Planned obsolescence, 132
Price-earnings (P-E) ratio, 203, 217–18, 220,
  222–23
Producer price index, 81, 95, 97–107
Product inflation, 131–32, 134, 143
Productivity; see also Industrial production
  capacity utilization, 88–91
  farm, 92
  GNP, 95–96

Productivity—*Cont.*
  labor, 91–95, 107
  output per hour, 94
Profit rate (profit per unit of output), 185
Profits
  business cycle, 183–88
  capital expenditures, 170
  dividends, 182
  measure of corporation's success, 182–83,
    189
  stock value, 182, 230
  surveys of, 183–88
Profit squeeze, 185
Public utilities, 61
Pump priming, 257
Put contract, 211, 213

R

Railroads and business cycle, 7–8
Reagan, Ronald, 246, 259, 260
Real earnings, 224–25
Real (constant dollar) GNP, 79–80
Recession, 73, 75, 153
  balance of payments and trade, 246
  business cycle, 73, 75
  deficit, 261
  economic theories, 255
  Great Depression; *see* Great Depression
  Keynes' theories, 256–57
  monetary policy, 261
  1980, 154–57, 259–60
  1981–82, 157, 260
  root cause, 154
  unemployment, 255
Retail sales, 136–38, 160
Roosevelt, Franklin D., 256
Round-lots, 201

S

Savings and loan associations, 57–59
Say's Law, 255
Selling short, 215
Short interest, 215, 218–19
Specie, 29, 31
Standard & Poor's bond rating services, 64
  bond rating services, 64
  stock index, 182
Stanford, Leland, 7
Statistical Series, *Wall Street Journal*, 269–75
Stock, 182
  dividends, 203
  price-earnings ratio, 203

Stock Market Data Bank, 194
  breakdown of trading in NYSE stocks,
      194, 198, 200
  diaries, 195–96
  major indexes, 194–95
  most active issues, 198–99
  percentage gainers and losers, 194, 196,
      200
Stock markets, 191
  American Stock Exchange; see American
      Stock Exchange
  business cycle, 182
  Data Bank, 194–200
  Dow Jones averages, 191–94
  foreign markets, 217, 222
  leverage, 207
  Markets and Money Charts, 194
  New York Stock Exchange; see New York
      Stock Exchange
  options, 208–13
  other markets, 217, 221
  over-the-counter market, 95
  undervalued, 220
Strike price, 208–10
Supply and demand, law of, 9
  business cycle, 9
  interest rates, 39
Supply-side economics, 259, 261
Supply-side shocks, 150

T

Taxation
  Keynesian theory, 257
  progressive income tax, 259
  Reagan tax cuts, 260
  supply-side theory, 259–60

Tax-exempt bonds, 65, 67
T-bill accounts, 58
Tight money policy of Federal Reserve, 40
Treasury bills (T-bills), 40–45
  auction, 40, 42–43
  secondary market, 44

U

Unemployment, 122–24
  cyclical, 265
  economic theory, 255–58
  fiscal policy, 256–58
  Great Depression, 12, 255–56
  inflation control affecting, 37
  inventories, 166
  Keynes' solutions, 256–57
  recession, 157, 255
Unit labor cost, 93–95, 101, 107, 147–49
U.S. Treasury
  bond issues, 30
  money supply, 29–30
  Treasury bills; see Treasury bills

V–W

Value Line Cash Management funds, 81
Vanderbilt family, 7
Volcker, Paul, 36, 37
Wage and price controls, 147, 149–50, 189
Wall Street Journal, 2
  Earnings Digest, 189–90
  Federal Reserve data, 20, 32
  statistical series, 269
Westward migration and business cycle,
      5–8
Wholesale price index, 95